# A Spiritual
# HOME

# A Spiritual
# HOME

*Life in British and American Reformed
Congregations, 1830–1915*

*Charles D. Cashdollar*

The Pennsylvania State University Press
University Park, Pennsylvania

Library of Congress Cataloging-in-Publication Data

Cashdollar, Charles D., 1943—
A spiritual home: life in British and American Reformed congregations,
1830–1915
Charles D. Cashdollar.
p.      cm.
Includes bibliographical references (p. ) and index.
ISBN 0–271–02014–8 (cloth : alk. paper)
ISBN 0–271–02015–6 (pbk. : alk. paper)
1. Reformed Church—United States—History—19th century.
2. United States—Church history—19th century.
3. Reformed Church—Great Britain—History—19th century.
4. Great Britain—Church history—19th century. I. Title.

BX9495 .C37 2000
285'.0941'09034—dc21        99–042595

✠

*For the members and ministers of*

Old Union United Presbyterian Church
*Mars, Pennsylvania*

First Presbyterian Church
*Philadelphia, Pennsylvania*

Calvary Presbyterian Church
*Indiana, Pennsylvania*

# Contents

# Preface

This is a time of pronounced interest in the history of religious congregations, those omnipresent yet understudied mainstays of spiritual activity. Once abandoned to church anniversary committees, the story of local church life has recently been pursued with new energy by both historians and practical theologians.

For historians, a study of local religious institutions extends naturally from the emphasis on social history since the 1960s. However, historians more often have used local church records to pursue other stories—marriage and family, immigration and ethnicity, class and gender—than to understand the intrinsic nature of congregations. Historians of the 1970s saw congregations as institutions through which local elites exercised power; seating arrangements, church discipline, temperance sermons, Sunday Schools, and city missions were all instruments of "social control."

More recently, however, those looking at history "from the bottom up" have recognized that nonelite groups were far from passive participants. Workers, minorities, women—and for religious historians, the laity in general—used local institutions creatively to construct their own meanings and at least a measure of self-control in their own lives. Black churches were dynamic, liberating forces in African American life. Women, though they were excluded from ordained leadership, could also find—as Elizabeth Fox-Genovese has observed—that churches "offered them a preeminent way of endowing their lives with positive meaning."[1]

My own turn toward the history of congregations was urged along by the persistent questioning of students in my university classes. I had written an intellectual history of late-nineteenth-century religion, *The Transformation of Theology: Positivism and Protestant Thought in Britain and America, 1830–1890* (Princeton, 1989). Its characters were philosophers and theologians who thought deeply about the epistemological and ethical implications of Comte, Mill and Spencer, of Darwin, Kant and Hegel. My students politely asked what "ordinary people" thought—that is, those folk who never put their noses inside the covers of the *Bibliotheca Sacra* or the *Edinburgh Review*.

I could not answer that question except to say that most "ordinary people" were not much involved, at least not at any level of sophistication. An occasional pastor introduced such issues in a sermon, but most confined their preaching to biblical and pastoral topics. Of course, such an answer only begged the question of what *did* constitute the religious experience of the unexceptional churchgoer.

Martin Marty's *A Nation of Behavers* (1976) had long before taught me that there were alternate ways of mapping the past.[2] As I thought back to the brief histories that I had written of two western Pennsylvania congregations, I realized again that only a small portion of local behavior fit easily into any standard national plot line. Moreover, my own observations as a church member seemed to confirm the same point: there was another story waiting to be told. And so I returned to the nineteenth century, this time from the perspective of the pew.

As I proceeded, I discovered that practical theologians—those who teach liturgics, homiletics, pastoral care, church administration, Christian education, and mission—were also taking a new, deeper interest in how local churches functioned. This is not the place to explain the emergence of this "congregational studies" movement in any detail.[3] Suffice it to say that practical theologians were impelled partly by liberation theology's emphasis on base communities, partly by the critical work of theorists such as Clifford Geertz and Hans-Georg Gadamer, and mostly by practical concerns about the very survival of mainline congregations. In Barbara Wheeler's words, the pastoral question was "What, if anything, can we do about this?"[4]

While early efforts in congregational studies were dominated by sociologists and church consultants, there has been since the publication of James Hopewell's important *Congregation: Stories and Structures* (1987) an increasing appreciation for what historical studies can contribute. Thus the concerns of historians and practical theologians converged, most notably in the Congregational History Project which was based from 1987 to 1990 at the University of Chicago Divinity School; its meetings resulted in *American Congregations* (1994), two volumes of theoretical essays and congregational histories compiled by the project's directors, James P. Wind and James W. Lewis.

Hopewell argued that congregations do not merely react to external forces; they have their own identities, which are created and sustained through the stories they tell, the narrative history they share. If so, E. Brooks Holifield is correct when he urges historians to seek a new plot outline that describes the larger history of congregational practice on its own terms, with its own turning points and themes.[5] As the introduction will explain, this book attempts one such composite portrait of congregational life—from the inside and as much as possible from the perspective of the laity.

A few methodological clarifications are in order before we begin. Because my emphasis is on life inside the congregation, what follows is different from the numerous local studies that probe the churches' success, or more usually lack of success, in attracting attenders. Such a demographic focus has often occupied the attention of social historians, particularly those studying nineteenth-century Britain. One reason for this emphasis in British history is the ready availability of the well-known 1851 census of church attendance, which recorded the number of persons present at worship services on 30 March of that year. Assuming the accuracy of the count (which historians have contested), this total, when compared with the whole population, easily produces the percentage of residents who participated in worship; generally speaking, about half were in worship that Sunday, although the aggregate percentage obscures considerable geographical and denominational variation. More to the point for modern social historians, however, the 1851 data revealed a striking socioeconomic pattern: the middle class came to church on census Sunday in far greater numbers than did the working class. Thus, analysis of the 1851 census (and of several other regional and local censuses taken during the century) has fed directly into ongoing historical debates about the extent and means of middle-class efforts to extend social control over the working class. Because the churches did not draw in the masses, both contemporaries in 1851 and many historians since have criticized them sharply.

There is no need here to discuss these studies in detail because, focused as they are on the extent to which church participation appealed to the whole population, they ask a different question.[6] Here, I am interested primarily in the experiences and behaviors of those who *were* attracted to the church, and whether these individuals made up a larger or smaller portion of the general population has tangential interest, but no more. Whether these individuals represented a single social stratum or came from a variety of economic stations is more important, but still not my primary focus.

Parenthetically, I might suggest that a research model comparing Sunday attendance to the size of the whole population implicitly presumes the parish model adopted by the Church of England or the Church of Scotland. This model was not one, however, that nonestablished Reformed congregations would have accepted. On the contrary, they believed that a congregation was naturally, and rightly, a "gathered" portion of the nation rather than the whole of it. Such a perspective suggests different bases for historical judgment and makes the degree to which the church appealed to the general population less central, although of course not irrelevant.

There is a second methodological consideration, and it relates to the meaning of "local." Research at the local level demands some principle of limitation, else a scholar quickly would be overwhelmed with sources. Historians who are more interested in the relationship of the church to its specific environment use tight geographical boundaries as a control. The usual practice is to choose a town or section of a city and study how its churches affected and were affected by local situations. Here, however, I am interested primarily in those internal elements of local church life that transcended locality, that were common to the Reformed church experience whether in Chicago or London, Iowa City or Aberdeen, Pittsburgh or Manchester. Thus, the better procedure is to survey a widely scattered selection of congregations, albeit at the expense of depth in any specific locality.

Lastly, it needs to be said that I do not intend this to be a study in practical theology. As psychologist Don S. Browning has aptly noted, historians tend to leave the implications of their work "inexplicit," and properly so, else they would be writing ethics or theology.[7] And yet, it can be hoped that the descriptive passages presented here will nonetheless be useful to those with other agendas.

# Acknowledgments

At a crucial stage in the preparation of this book, the American Council of Learned Societies provided a generous year-long fellowship that together with a sabbatical leave from Indiana University of Pennsylvania provided uninterrupted time for research and writing. Grants from the American Philosophical Society and the Pennsylvania State System of Higher Education funded travel to collections in Britain and America. Librarians and archivists at New College Library and the Scottish Record Office in Edinburgh; the Strathclyde Regional Archives in Glasgow; the Congregational Library, Dr. Williams's Library and the United Reformed Church History Society in London; the Presbyterian Historical Society in Philadelphia; and the Congregational Library in Boston were uniformly generous with their time and expertise, and their permission to use and quote from their collections; permission was granted by the Director of Dr. Williams's Library on behalf of the Trustees to quote from the records of the Lyndhurst Road and King's Weigh House churches. The interlibrary loan office at IUP's Stapleton Library found copies of obscure titles when I needed them. The Charles Barbour Library at Pittsburgh Theological Seminary was as indispensable for this project as it was for my earlier ones; once more it is difficult to imagine ever having completed this book without the ability to roam freely through its rich stacks and to borrow its books.

Intellectual exchanges with students and colleagues helped give the book its current shape. Students in the Robert E. Cook Honors College at Indiana University of Pennsylvania read and discussed earlier versions of Chapter 9, as did those enrolled in "Thought and Culture in Modern America"; Eric Cook shared insights on nineteenth-century church music based on his senior honors thesis. Harold Scott shared wisdom based on his many years of ministry, teaching, and church administration. Editor James Moorhead of the *Journal of Presbyterian History* provided an opportunity to write a review essay that encouraged me to relate my work to that of pastoral theologians. Neil Lehman, Larry Miller, Anne Rose, Louise Stevenson, and John W. Stewart read drafts and made valuable suggestions. History department secretary Florence Prato manipulated computer files with her customary expertise and good humor. Peter Potter and the staff at The Pennsylvania State University Press expertly steered the book through to publication.

I am especially grateful for the support and encouragement of my wife, Donna Evans Cashdollar, who has once more helped in more ways than can be set down here. Every historical work has an autobiographical component whether acknowledged or not, and thus this book is dedicated to the congregations that have been for me spiritual homes.

# PART I

The Context for
Worship and Work

# one

## Introduction
### From the Perspective of the Pew

Participation in the worship and life of a local congregation was not the only form of nineteenth-century religious expression, but it was by far the most common. Belonging to a church located belief in time and place, gave it form, and bound it up in community. An English Presbyterian described her congregation as "a spiritual home."[1] When Mr. and Mrs. David Whyte left Britain for Wisconsin in the 1850s, they connected with a Congregational Church in Watertown. Whyte recalled that, shortly after their arrival, "in the Evening service there was sung There is a land of pure delight I says to Magt you see we are not so fare from home."[2]

This book seeks to understand life inside local congregations—specifically British and American Reformed congregations—from about 1830 to the eve of the First World War. The "Reformed" tradition refers to those Protestants who traced their heritage back to the leader of the Geneva Reformation, John Calvin; for the moment, let us say in general terms that here this means the established and free churches in Scotland plus American and English Presbyterians and Congregationalists.

Our initial purpose is to learn how these Reformed congregations functioned. When people went to church, what did they experience and do? What were their expectations for worship and common life? How did they interact with each other? How did they organize themselves to manage their own affairs and to affect the larger society?

A second goal is to comprehend how local religious life changed during an age of industrial and urban growth. How successful were these religious institutions in maintaining their integrity and at the same time adapting to the powerful surge of change? If someone from the early Victorian period were magically transported to the first decade of the twentieth century, what differences would have been apparent?

The English Congregationalists, one of the several denominations within the scope of this study, were a loosely connected body with roots in the Independency movement of the late sixteenth century and in the Puritan Revolution and Commonwealth of the seventeenth. Jealous of their local independence, they had only just formed the most minimal association, the Congregational Union, in 1831. Still, connections among local churches remained primarily voluntary and informal. The denomination's size increased substantially during the Victorian years as it gained members from the expanding middle class. It also benefited from the removal by 1880 of the remaining disabilities that had been imposed on dissenters—marriage registration, church rates, university exclusion, and burial restrictions.[3]

The equivalent American group dated to the early Puritan settlements in New England in the 1620s and 1630s. Although in the 1820s, American Congregationalism suffered significant losses by the departure of the Unitarians, it remained the region's largest and most powerful denomination. During the nineteenth century, Congregationalism expanded westward across New York, along the shores of Lake Erie and into the Midwest. Although local ministerial associations and ad hoc national meetings emerged earlier, it was not until 1871 that the National Council of Congregational Churches was formed to provide a permanent, if loosely woven, denominational structure.[4]

Connectional arrangements came more naturally to Presbyterians. In nineteenth-century Scotland, there were three major church bodies.[5] The most venerable was the Church of Scotland, which in one guise or another had carried the authority and duties of being the country's established kirk since the days of John Knox. The church's parishes traditionally fulfilled civic as well as religious roles, and although responsibility for poor relief and education were removed in 1845 and 1872, respectively, the church's life was still much entwined with that of official Scotland.

Schisms had produced two other Scottish churches. The more recent was the Free Church of Scotland, whose birth was occasioned by the Disruption of 1843. The ascent of an Evangelical party within the Scottish church had created tensions over the legal relationship of the kirk to the state. The issue at the separation was patronage, the right of a patron to choose a congregation's minister. The Evangelical party objected to this practice, and, led by Thomas Chalmers, it established a competing Free Church. Just under 40 percent of the ministers withdrew, even though doing so cost them their manses and stipends. The Free Church made its greatest gains among the middle class and throughout the century remained a formidable competitor to the established church. Although patronage was abolished in 1874, the Disruption was not healed until a reunion of the two sides in 1929.

The United Presbyterians, Scotland's third denomination, traced their roots to two eighteenth-century schisms over patronage. In 1733 a group of Seceders left the established church when a patron refused to appoint the popular favorite, Thomas Erskine. Additional opponents of patronage broke away in 1761 and established the Relief Church. A merger of the Relief and United Secession churches in 1847 created the United Presbyterian Church, a small denomination with significant appeal to the lower middle class. A union of this denomination and the Free Church in 1900 created the United Free Church of Scotland.

As Scots migrated to England, they carried Presbyterianism with them and united with those few, scattered assemblies of an earlier seventeenth-century English Presbyterianism that had not become Unitarian. In London and the northern cities especially, there was a market for a Scottish-style church, and from those congregations an English synod was formed in 1836. An English synod of United Presbyterians was created in 1867, and a merger between the two created the Presbyterian Church of England in 1876.[6]

Presbyterians arrived in the American colonies and organized their first presbytery in 1706. After the Revolution, the largest body of Presbyterians organized itself nationally in 1788 as the Presbyterian Church in the United States of America. As Congregationalists were strongest in New England, Presbyterians were most plentiful in the middle states, where large numbers of Scottish and Scots-Irish immigrants made their homes. For a little more than thirty years, from 1837 to 1869, the church was divided into two factions, an Old School and a New School. The Old School was, as the name implied, the more conservative of the two parties, while the New School gave a more cordial welcome to the modifications of Calvinism emanating from Nathaniel Taylor's New Haven theology and also to reform movements such as antislavery and temperance. The outbreak of the Civil War in 1861 created another division when Southern congregations separated and remained apart for over a century, until 1983.[7]

The various Scottish schisms cast their shadows on New World Presbyterianism also. Descendants of the Covenanters, the most militant Scots who had refused to accede to the Restoration settlement of the 1660s, organized in America as Reformed Presbyterians in 1774. Some years earlier, in 1753, Scottish Seceders had constituted themselves as the Associate Presbyterians. In 1858, these two Scottish streams combined to form the United Presbyterian Church of North America. More tradition-minded than the mainstream Presbyterians, this Pittsburgh-based denomination found its greatest strength in western Pennsylvania.[8]

These eight groups—English Congregationalists, American Congregationalists, the Church of Scotland, the Free Church of Scotland, the Scottish United

Presbyterians, the Presbyterian Church of England, the Presbyterian Church in the United States of America, and the United Presbyterian Church of North America—are the basis for this study of congregational life. We have already hinted at certain divergences in theological position and openness to change, and these will become more evident as we move along, although quite frankly, subtle shadings of theology carried significantly less weight for those in the pews than they did for professional theologians.

Chapter 2 will examine the manner in which these local churches governed themselves. Here at the outset, it is enough merely to mention the basic differences in church polity that distinguished *congregationalism* from *presbyterianism*. Governance in Congregational churches was centered in the congregation, which functioned quite independently, and connections above the local level were minimal. Presbyterian congregations belonged to a district *presbytery*, a representative body of clergy and laity to which local judgments could be appealed and whose approval was needed for important congregational decisions such as calling a minister.

As we are thinking about differences among these Reformed denominations, there was an important one that set the Church of Scotland apart. The Scottish kirk was "established," that is, officially the nation's church by government edict; none of the other groups had this position (although the last vestiges of Congregational establishment survived in Connecticut until 1817 and in Massachusetts until 1833). Indeed, it was *opposition* to the state's religion that more nearly provided self-definition to the remainder of the Reformed churches.

In its national capacity, the Scottish kirk functioned with a different understanding of the nature of the local congregation, too. It had organized the country into a system of geographical parishes, each of which was understood to be responsible for the religious life of persons living within its bounds. The other denominations understood the local church as individuals who had voluntarily gathered together and were united not by geography but by the decision to join. The distinction between the "parish" model of Scotland's national church and "gathered church" model accepted by the other Reformed groups will also come up from time to time throughout the book.

However real the ecclesiastical distinctions between congregationalism and presbyterianism, between local church as place and local church as gathered people, these Reformed denominations were enough alike, particularly from the perspective of the pew, to allow the story of their changing religious life to be told together. They were part of the common transatlantic culture that historian Frank Thistlethwaite described some years ago as "the Anglo-American Connection" and that David

Hall more recently referred to as "the Victorian Connection." Indeed, the historical profession's adoption of the phrase "Victorian America" simply testifies to the hybrid nature of the two nation's cultures.[9]

Within the general Victorian climate, the Reformed groups felt an especially close bond. They held a common understanding of sacrament and worship and a common Calvinist theology, and they engaged each other in conversation about how this heritage should be modernized. Although professional theologians argued the points, by the mid-nineteenth century divine love was emphasized over divine justice in the popular mind, and personal responsibility took precedence over God's election.

There was a shared history as well. During the British Reformation, their ancestors had battled episcopal polity and disdained the Anglican *Book of Common Prayer*. In the 1640s, Scottish divines had joined English Puritans at Westminster to create documents that still carried immense symbolic and practical importance for these churches—the Westminster Confession, the Longer and Shorter Westminster Catechisms, and the Westminster Directory of Worship. In 1801, America's Congregationalists and Presbyterians joined together in the Plan of Union, which enabled local congregations to affiliate with both denominations and to draw ministers from either pool of candidates. If by the middle years of the century both sides became more concerned with denominational purity than with cooperation, the "Presbygational" system had worked well in its time, especially at the western fringes of settlement. By the end of the nineteenth century, there were other official opportunities for transatlantic cooperation. Delegates from both sides of the ocean assembled in "The Alliance of the Reformed Churches throughout the World holding the Presbyterian System," which met first in Edinburgh in 1877, or in the International Congregational Council, which gathered initially in London in 1891.[10]

More than these formal ecumenical assemblies, however, it was the pervasive informal connections that had a greater impact on congregational life and bound the Reformed community together. Presbyterians and Congregationalists were prominent participants in the myriad voluntary societies that sprang up to carry on benevolent work and foment reform. Much of the effort was national, but interest reached across the Atlantic, too.[11] For instance, funds were raised in support of American antislavery in St. George's Free Church in Edinburgh, and the same congregation heard a speech from Mr. Jackson, "a fugitive slave" whose abilities had been recommended by American Congregationalist Harriet Beecher Stowe.[12]

The movement of people, both clergy and laity, from one denomination to another and from one nation to another also gave the Reformed community a sense of oneness. Whyte's remark at the beginning of this chapter reveals how an

English Congregationalist could migrate to Wisconsin and feel at home. Letters of transfer from congregations in Scotland and Ireland were carried across the Atlantic to American Presbyterian churches. Populations were mobile within nations as well—indeed, so mobile that one of the great challenges for local churches was simply the maintenance of an accurate list of members and addresses. Wherever people moved, they carried with them ideas and expectations, thereby linking the practice of their former church homes to their new.

Clergy travelled, too, and this was another way in which practical ideas spread throughout the Reformed community. Historian Richard Carwardine has documented the transatlantic nature of revivalism during the first half of the nineteenth century,[13] and the pattern continued afterward. The two most famous American revivalists, Charles Finney and Dwight L. Moody, each made circuits through the British Isles. Lesser-known evangelists also travelled across the ocean, and not always eastward; London Congregationalist Campbell Morgan arrived in Rochester, New York, in 1899 to conduct "a series of meetings" at Central Presbyterian Church.[14] Similar interrelationships among those engaged in reform work have allowed historian Paul Phillips to write of an "Anglo-American Social Christianity" by the end of the nineteenth century.[15]

Pastors who gained renown for their pulpit oratory were also highly sought after. City Temple, a mammoth Congregational church in London, was filled to capacity for the guest appearances of the two Brooklyn powerhouses, Henry Ward Beecher and T. DeWitt Talmadge, and it did not matter to the listeners that one was a Congregationalist, one a Presbyterian.[16] At the top levels, where congregations had adequate financial means to conduct an international search, there was a common pool from which ministers were selected. When Beecher died in November 1887, the pulpit of Plymouth Church was offered first to Charles Berry of Wolverhampton, England. Although in that instance, the transatlantic offer was declined, there were numerous other cases when a British pastor readily accepted a call to America. Scotland, it seemed, was the most abundant "exporter" of preachers, as it supplied talent to the English Presbyterians and Congregationalists as well as to America. While it was more common for churches to seek a minister from a part of the Reformed community that followed the same form of government, this was not always the case; English Congregationalist J. H. Jowett, for instance, was called from Carr's Lane in Birmingham to New York City's Fifth Avenue Presbyterian Church in 1911.[17]

Seminaries and colleges, as well as congregations, drew talent from across denominational and national lines. Early in the nineteenth century, New England Congregationalist Lyman Beecher had served as president of Lane Seminary, a Presbyterian institution in Cincinnati. Finney, ordained a Presbyterian, became president of Congregationalist Oberlin. James McCosh, a transplanted Scot, was made president of the College of New Jersey in 1868. Hugh Black, another Scot, left St. George's Free Church, Edinburgh, in 1906 for Union Seminary, a New York City institution that throughout its history had played an important role in continuing a close, cordial relationship between Presbyterianism and New England Congregationalism.[18]

Books, periodicals, and local congregational publications moved, if anything, more easily than people and were another means of exchanging practical ideas for congregational life. The religious press, both monthly and weekly, covered news in other parts of the Reformed community, and often listed innovative activities in local congregations. Scholarly quarterlies reached a more limited, but influential, audience and carried articles giving practical suggestions on everything from administration and architecture to the work and worship of the congregation.

Books found a market in both British and American editions. As we shall see, collections of prayers, children's sermons, and other liturgical resources crossed both the Atlantic and denominational boundaries. Psalters and hymnals included an overlapping repertory of tunes and texts, and Whyte was not the only lay person for whom the familiarity of music made a new church seem like home. Local churches also put forth a large number of church manuals, directories, handbooks, hymnals, service books, and centenary memoirs which were proudly exchanged with other congregations. Even a cursory perusal of such local publications suggests that there was a great deal of influence, indeed copying, from one church to another. Carr's Lane acknowledged in a small note that the "Questions for Self-Examination" in its 1835 members' handbook were reprinted from an American manual,[19] but usually the imitation went without remark. Good words, like good ideas, were meant to be shared.

The behavior of a newly founded church on the American frontier makes an interesting measure of the speed with which eastern (actually international) urban patterns were replicated. A Congregational church was organized in Huron, South Dakota, in June 1884. Within a week, it had organized a Sunday School for its children. By September, there was a complete set of church officers—deacons, deaconesses, and trustees. Soon there was a Women's Missionary Society, a Young People's Society, a Ladies' Aid group, and a Children's Missionary Band. When the congregation laid the cornerstone for its sanctuary the following April, the popular Gothic style was chosen. There was much about the Huron congregation's early history that suggested instability; there were, for instance, ten different ministers in the first fourteen years. Yet worship occurred on Sunday and prayer meeting on Wednesday, the Lord's Supper was administered bimonthly, and committees on membership and visitation were established. In 1888, the church reorganized its youth group along the lines of the international Christian Endeavor Society; in doing so it was no more than a year or so behind most east coast churches, and ahead of many. A new family arriving in Huron would have found a pattern of church life that made them feel quite at home.[20]

As much as possible, this study takes its perspective from the level of the pew, not from the desks of denominational officials or academic theologians. It is based heavily upon local church records—minutes of governing boards, committees, and organizations; financial records; annual reports and yearbooks; membership directories; manuals or handbooks provided to members; locally written congregational histories; and a miscellaneous assortment of handbills, posters, Sunday morning bulletins, blank forms, pew cards, photographs, newsletters, clippings and other miscellaneous items that have survived.

Some 150 congregations are represented by such local material, together with another score or so for which information is drawn from modern secondary sources. Admittedly, these churches do not comprise a perfect sample in any meaningful statistical sense. Some churches were sought out because of their prominence or reputation for innovation, but simple availability played a strong role for the remainder. Large churches whose members displayed a higher than average level of affluence and education naturally left more of a written trail. Because the plan called for looking at churches within a context of industrialization, urban growth, an expanding middle class, and an emerging consumer culture, churches from rural areas, the American South, and the Scottish Highlands are significantly underrepresented, although not excluded.

When congregational life is examined through the eyes of local records, it is striking how small a role is given to the famous theological disputes over Darwin, the higher criticism, positivism, German idealism, or fundamentalism. This is partly because local congregations were self-selected communities, and thus more homogeneous than national denominations. One church might draw a revivalistic clientele while another of the town's churches catered to those of a high-church inclination, or one might be more liberal and another more conservative without those differences entering very much into the internal discussions of either congregation. Nor was theological disputation very welcome inside the local church. As one London Congregationalist put it, the purpose of a sermon was "to make of the church a religious home, not a theological battlefield."[21]

Local discussions tended to center on very practical matters such as how to meet the budget, whether to have an afternoon or evening service, or how to recruit volunteers. As we shall see, liturgical changes such as whether to stand or sit or kneel for prayer could cause local division, but even in these instances local decisions were reached more on practical than theoretical grounds. What local churches—like families—could not shortchange and survive were internal peace and financial stability.

As we proceed, several ongoing themes will emerge. It is always dangerous in books with multiple themes to single out one as more important, but if this were done here, the change in emphasis from piety to fellowship would be a prime candidate. A simple change in the meaning of the word "social" is indicative. In 1830, it was an adjective applied to the congregation's mid-week prayer meeting; by 1900, a church social implied tea and sandwiches, strawberries and ice cream. A congregation in 1830 engaged in little except worship, pastoral care, and mission; by 1900, a fully functioning church included sports teams, literary clubs, and organized groups of every sort. In 1830, the primary qualification for membership was piety; by 1900, affability, sociability, and willingness to participate were at least as important.[22]

At the same time, religious life was becoming more private, less public. This focus will be seen in several areas, such as the shift from pew rents to donations sealed in envelopes or from public discipline to pastoral counseling. A third theme will be the increased importance of efficiency and standardization, together with the incorporation of modern business methods into church administration. Fourth, congregations experienced, along with the rest of society, a growing tendency toward professionalization. Early in the period, even large congregations were typically staffed by a single minister aided by a host of volunteer workers and paraprofessionals. By the end of the period, more tasks were given over to professional clergy and social workers.

Professionalization had significant implications for gender roles within the congregation, a topic that in its own right is a fifth consideration. These congregations, as we shall see, had about a two-thirds majority of female members. In the course of their work, congregations provided many outlets for the leadership and managerial talents of women as volunteers and paraprofessionals—this despite the severe limitations on women's access to elected church offices. Ironically, professionalization minimized many of women's most productive opportunities for volunteer leadership and church employment at the very time that women's formal rights within congregations were expanding.

A sixth aspect is a growing demand for luxury and elegance that accorded with the emerging middle-class definition of "respectability." In 1830, Reformed tastes in worship, music, and architecture were plain, even austere. As middle-class standards rose, congregations demanded sophistication that could equal what they displayed in their homes and experienced in secular concert halls. A seventh, and closely related, theme was the insistence upon a level of comfort and convenience equal to that advertised by the consumer culture of the age.

Finally, we shall see the church interacting with the emerging diversions of leisure and entertainment. Churches reacted by trying to make their worship services and activities more entertaining—"Pleasant Sunday Afternoons," as meetings were popularly called in Britain. Churches also went into direct competition by organizing their own athletic teams, soirees, excursions, clubs, coffee houses, concerts, limelight shows, and bazaars. This, of course, brings us full circle to the transformation of church life from piety to fellowship. It anticipates much of what is to come, and it will be part of the story of the transformation of congregational life as it unfolds.

# two

## Leadership, Power, Governance

In April 1850, William Darrach, a ruling elder in the Second Presbyterian Church of Philadelphia, sent a letter to his fellow officers. He was feeling discouraged, frustrated, and more than a little self-righteous. For years, he said, he had been part of a slim majority, "a majority of one," that had held back the tide of change. So far, his faction had prevented the secular values of business efficiency and coordination from creeping in as new standards for church administration; it had blocked the introduction of choral anthems, any enlargement of mission Sunday Schools' sphere of activity, and the commercialization threatened by church "fairs" and socials.[1]

But by 1850, the winds were shifting, and Darrach now found himself in the minority on the congregation's governing board, and so he had decided to resign. The Presbyterian eldership (as the Congregational diaconate) was then a life-time position, and resignations were unusual. Men sometimes retired from the active eldership because the infirmities of age made further service impossible, but resignations of conscience were rare indeed.

Darrach's departure from the church session was as intriguing as it was unusual. He had always served, he said, "to sustain the purity, unity, and peace of the church." The battle for purity, at least according to his definition, had apparently been lost. But surprisingly, he did not make the defeat itself central to his resignation, and he indicated no intention to leave the congregation in search of a more congenial church home. His concern in quitting the session was less "purity" than "unity and peace." Perhaps he knew his own temperament too well, but he could see nothing but "useless and injurious strife" if he stayed on the board, and so, thinking it "unpresbyterian to continue acting a moment longer," he stood aside.

This preference for harmony over conviction strongly characterized the local governance of British and American Presbyterians and Congregationalists.

Nationally and regionally these denominations were disrupted by frequent and bitter theological rivalries, occasional heresy trials, and even schism. But locally, where people lived in constant and close proximity and more often than not knew each other also as business associates and neighbors, as kin and friends, there were strong reasons to avoid conflict. To be sure, individuals at times became angry and left their congregations; local churches sometimes feuded and even broke apart. But when they did, they were neither ideal nor typical.

Inside the local congregation, persuasion was valued over the ballot. Consensus was sought, and when a vote resulted in a narrow margin, the majority might postpone action rather than risk alienating the losing side. The more significant the issue and the more closely it touched upon deeply held convictions, the less likely it was to be settled by a tally of votes.

The two most expected and admired characteristics of lay leaders were certainly spiritual depth and faithfulness to the office, but an irenic spirit was not far behind. The stern, forbidding, austere, aloof elder or deacon exists more in myth than in local reality. It was customary in the nineteenth century for a memorial tribute to be entered into the church's official minutes whenever an elder or deacon died, and when viewed together these obituaries provide an interesting composite of leadership qualities. The writers regularly described their subjects as "amiable," "warm," and "genial," or "gentle," "humble," and "meek." Ideal leaders were "self-forgetting," "forbearing," and "self-sacrificing." Words such as "rugged" or "self-made" might be used to describe a male in the congregation, but not a deacon or elder. These were men of "quiet" disposition and "sweet" temperament who gave "cheerful acquiescence" when in the minority, and who were neither "ostentatious" nor "assertive of self" when on the winning side.[2]

The undoubtedly idealized and somewhat sentimental characterizations found in memorial minutes do not mean that power was nonexistent or unexercised. But they do suggest that the formal authority defined by civil or ecclesiastical law or even by local by-laws frequently gave way before custom or personality or more subtle political actualities.

On the formal, constitutional level, local governance among British and American Congregationalists and Presbyterians consisted of two parallel orders—one that can be termed spiritual or ecclesiastical, and the other, temporal or financial. The congregation was organized as the *church* to deal with ecclesiastical affairs and as a *society* or *corporation* to manage its financial concerns. Each dimension of the congregation's life had its own officers, procedures, and eligibility for voting. Unfortunately for the outside observer, there were also variations in vocabulary. Presbyterians and Congregationalists (and sometimes Britons and Americans) used different titles for the same or analogous church official or applied the same label to a quite different office; the word *deacon,* as we shall find, meant something quite different in Congregational, American Presbyterian, and the Scottish Free churches.

The ecclesiastical or spiritual side of the congregation's life was placed by Presbyterians into the hands of elected officials called *elders,* who when assembled together with the minister formed the church *session.* Among Congregationalists, lay leaders called *deacons* provided the spiritual direction. The roles of these elders or deacons—all males during the entire period of this study[3]—had much in common despite basic differences between the two forms of polity. In the Presbyterian system of representative government, the elders, once elected, had considerable scope for independent action, but in the Congregational system of direct government, primary decision-making power remained with the full membership, which assembled frequently in church meetings to take action. Congregational deacons thus had less direct power than Presbyterian elders.

In actuality, Congregationalists found the entire membership too large to undertake the real work of the church, and they set up standing committees—referred to as Prudential Committees or more simply as the Church Committee—to manage the church's spiritual life. Typically the committee consisted of the pastor, the deacons and an equal number of at-large members; some committees were augmented by ex officio members such as the Sunday School superintendent or the clerk who kept the church roll and minutes.[4]

For those in the pews, the work of the elders or deacons was most evident when they assisted the minister in the administration of the Lord's Supper. The elders or deacons handed out the tokens or cards that admitted members to the Lord's Supper, and on the day of the service itself they prepared the bread and wine and participated in their distribution.

The duties of the officers extended beyond their sacramental function. Presbyterian elders had full jurisdiction over disciplinary cases and admission to the congregation; Congregational deacons, augmented by the other members of the Church Committee, acted as preliminary examiners of potential members although final decisions were made by the entire membership. As members of the session or church committee, they managed the poor fund, visited members in their homes, promoted the congregation's spiritual growth, oversaw worship and singing, and collected benevolence funds (that is, money transmitted to denominational or independent charitable or mission societies). They also oversaw the congregation's local work and activities—mission projects, Sunday Schools and, as the century went on, an increasing array of organizations and social activities.

The number of elders or deacons increased according to the size of the congregation and the complexity and magnitude of their responsibilities; especially where significant house-to-house visitation was expected, the official board had to be expanded in proportion to the congregation's growth. There were, however, no set rules about numbers, and congregations followed their own judgment and habit. In general, Presbyterian elders were more numerous than Congregational deacons, in part because the deacons were augmented by at-large members on the church committee, and in part because the primary decision-making power was retained by the whole church. Britain's tradition of geographical parishes or church districts to which elders or deacons were assigned for house-to-house visitation meant greater numbers were needed there. Consequently, some large Scottish and English Presbyterian congregations operated with nearly fifty elders, while equally large American Congregational churches worked with as few as three or four deacons. Among the various churches surveyed for this study the average number of elders in Scotland was twenty-two, and in America, ten; English Congregationalists averaged seven deacons, and American Congregationalists, six.[5]

The traditional practice of electing elders and deacons for life meant that in many cases, these boards were functionally smaller than their totals indicate. Occasionally, officers did resign when age began to impede their work, but this was not expected. Old South Church in Boston found itself in a situation in 1866 where two of its four deacons were unable to function. One, so the church minutes explained, "is far advanced in life & hardly expects ever to visit the city again," and a second "by the Providence of God is permanently laid aside from all participation in the duties of this church or the community." The congregation's response was to choose one additional deacon, increasing the board's size to five.[6]

As this suggests, elections were unscheduled and typically occurred when death or infirmity had diminished the roster of officers to an intolerably low count. Election procedures were informal enough that it was not always possible to predict how many would be elected. When Old South Church members met in March 1851 with the intent of electing two deacons, they could manage to get only one. On the first ballot, all but one vote went to a Mr. Plumer, who was declared elected. But on a second and then a third ballot, votes were scattered among five individuals, with none gaining a majority. Following a five-minute recess, they decided to proceed no further, and after singing a hymn and offering a prayer, they adjourned; one new deacon would have to suffice.[7]

In the United States during the nineteenth century, elders or deacons were elected by church members, but British church boards were still self-perpetuating in the 1830s. Until the 1874 revision of the Patronage Act, the kirk session in each parish of the established Church of Scotland controlled its own size and membership; the parish had the right only to raise an objection after an "appointment" was made public. If no valid complaint about the proposed elder's character or behavior emerged after the congregation had been "thrice called," the appointment stood.[8]

After 1874, everyone on the Scottish parish's communion roll gained the power to make nominations, and communicants were asked to submit "slips" naming those deemed worthy of the office. Just how those "nominations" were handled, however, varied considerably, as a glance at three Edinburgh parishes reveals. The Greenside kirk session, after it tallied the slips, worked its way down the list in order of votes received until it got the desired number of acceptances. The elders of Greyfriars parish, however, considered the congregational slips to be no more than suggestions and did not think they were bound to honor the order of the tallies. St. George's session, at least in the case of previously ordained elders moving into St. George's from another parish, continued to appoint without waiting for nominations.[9] One could easily imagine that a system giving this much control to incumbents might tend toward small kirk sessions because current elders would resist sharing power with newcomers. But in Scotland this did not happen; elders added steadily to their numbers because otherwise they would have been overwhelmed by the work of parish visitation.

The Free Church, from the time of the Disruption, placed the election of elders in the hands of church members. In St. George's Free Church in Edinburgh, when the first election was held in November 1843, members were instructed to hand to the current elders "signed lists" of up to eight choices; the men whose names appeared on a majority of the lists were elected and an edict announcing the choices was issued from the pulpit. When this system was first tried, the incumbent elders, having experienced nothing but the self-perpetuating kirk sessions of the established church, were more than a little uncertain whether it would work. They announced coyly to the congregation that they would "have in their possession a list of several persons who appear to the Session to be suited" should anyone wish to consult it before marking a ballot. Whether anyone took them up on the offer is not recorded, but the elders soon learned to trust the members and stopped going about with a list in their pockets at election time. In fact, the system proved so satisfactory that the congregation was still using it on the eve of World War I.[10]

English Congregationalists in the 1830s also had self-perpetuating boards of deacons. By the mid-1840s, however, they began to adopt the system of signed lists used in the Scottish Free Church. In 1846, King's Weigh House in London started "leaving the business in the hands of the Church." Every member was to write up to four names on a paper, sign and seal it, and submit it on the following Sunday; two members of the congregation were selected to help the deacons count the ballots.[11]

A difficulty with these early procedures, of course, was the uncertainty of the yield. Congregations entered elections with a target figure in mind, and they tried to ensure this by telling members how many names to write on the slip—up to four, or up to eight, or whatever seemed likely to produce the desired number of winners. But there were no guarantees. On the one hand, votes could be so scattered that no one was elected; on the other, an unanticipated consensus could produce more new officers than expected. A further complication was that, because the potential officers had not been consulted beforehand, some declined, often after several weeks of prayerful consideration, forcing the procedure to be repeated.

By the 1860s, with a rising demand for business-like regularity in church affairs, congregations tried to be more systematic about their elections. King's Weigh House, for instance, decided in 1860 to place the question of additional deacons on the church agenda at regular five-year intervals.[12] A more common approach, copied no doubt from the world of secular politics, was to insist on nominations prior to the election. King's Weigh House adopted a two-stage process in 1860. The names of all male members were printed out on a ballot, and each member (including women) marked all they thought qualified—"three, six, or eight, or ten, less or more." The names of the thirteen highest vote-getters were placed on a second ballot, and members voted for six, the number of new deacons being sought. Congregations more typically solicited nominations during a meeting of members. Cowcaddens Free Church in Glasgow, for example, took nominations from the floor, with any name put forward and seconded going on the ballot. In an 1867 election, Cowcaddens then printed a ballot listing the nominees and asked that it be marked, sealed, and placed in the collection plate on a subsequent Sunday. Later in the century, large congregations commonly turned the preparation of a slate of candidates over to a committee; Boston's Old South Church, for instance, was relying on a three-person nominating committee by the mid-1870s.[13]

The desire for a more efficiently administered church encouraged some congregations to dispense with the traditional life-time eldership or diaconate and elect officers for set terms, either three, four, five, or six years; incumbents could be reelected. The principle attraction of a term system was the ability to replace aging or incapacitated officers with younger, and what were assumed to be more vigorous, forward-looking men. Opponents argued that finite terms diminished the stature of the office and forced incumbents to seek popularity rather than faithfulness.[14]

Presbyterian congregations, lacking local option in such matters, were unable to place term limits on elders until the denomination permitted the change in 1875.[15] Central Presbyterian Church in Rochester was one congregation that took up the "rotary" option immediately by organizing its twelve-elder session so that one-third of the terms expired each year.[16] Congregationalists were free to change according to the desires of the local congregation, and began to do so in the 1870s. The non-deacon members of the Church Committee had always been elected to terms either of a year's duration and, if longer, arranged so that a proportion rotated off every year.[17]

Once elected, new elders or deacons were "set apart" to their offices by ordination during Sunday morning worship, or perhaps during the day's second service of worship in the afternoon or evening. First, they verbally affirmed their faith and commitment to the office by answering a series of questions; then a "solemn prayer to the Almighty God" marked them for their new responsibilities. After the ordination prayer, the new elders or deacons were offered the "right hand of fellowship" by the minister and their fellow officers. The minister then addressed the newly installed officers on their duties, their names were entered on the official roll, and in some localities, they were asked to sign the congregation's covenant.[18]

Individuals selected as deacons or elders had typically achieved a respectable position in the world, although the definition of worldly success varied according to the social level of the congregation. In St. George's parish church, located in the prosperous New Town section of Edinburgh, thirteen of the sixteen elders in 1868 were entitled to write "Esquire" after their names. Meanwhile, on the other side of the city, Bristo United Presbyterian Church catered to a more modest clientele, and its session was populated mainly by shopkeepers (bookseller, wine merchant, tobacconist, grocer, flesher, baker, or druggist) and craftsmen (tanner, upholsterer, venetian blind maker, or wright).[19]

But a well-ordered business and family life, however universally present they were, did not in themselves mark a man as a potential elder or deacon; an exemplary Christian character and a record of active church work did that. When the session clerk of the North Church of Perth, Scotland, prepared brief "personal notes" on each of the current elders for the parish's 150th anniversary booklet in 1897, he did not mention occupation or family for any of his twenty-two subjects. Rather, his biographies emphasized each elder's long, faithful record of service, and as his accounts unfolded, the years upon years of Sunday School teaching, youth work, choir singing, parish financial management, benevolent and missionary society leadership, and local mission work mounted up impressively.[20]

In addition to devotion to the church and its work, elders or deacons were chosen for their character. It was not so much piety that set them apart, although they were typically described as prayerful and as faithful attenders at worship.

What mattered was that they were reliable: they were men of constancy and consistency. They had proved themselves thoughtful, practical and useful, and they possessed an even temperament and a warm heart. They could be trusted with the spiritual life of the congregation.[21]

All of these denominations, in one way or another, kept the management of the congregation's worldly concerns—money and property—separate from its spiritual governance. The manner in which they did this depended more on civil law and custom than on theology. In the United States, the most common practice was to place secular responsibility in the hands of a second group of officers called *trustees,* a name which matched the legal incorporation that American congregations increasingly found advantageous.[22] Even where state laws of incorporation did not mandate a board of trustees separate from the elders or deacons, the preference for division of responsibility was strong. At minimum, there was a separate committee charged with handling finances and property.[23]

The reasons for dividing ecclesiastical and temporal affairs reflected both tradition and contemporary inclination. The roots of the separation go back to the established or state church patterns of Britain and colonial America. In the New England colonies where Congregationalism enjoyed the status of an established church, the church received tax monies; by the late seventeenth century, non-member taxpayers insisted on having some say in parish affairs, and colonial governments responded. Ecclesiastical matters remained in the hands of church members (the *church*) while financial control was shared with the parish taxpayers (the *society*).[24] By the time state support ended, the habit of separating church and society business was deeply ingrained among Congregationalists. American Presbyterians brought similar habits with them from their experience with established religion in Britain. By the mid-eighteenth century, it was customary for them to have property held by trustees and, where possible, to seek a charter from the state.[25]

The tradition continued in the nineteenth century because it matched contemporary inclinations. The churches were suspicious of worldly concerns and wished to hold them at arm's length. They feared that if the two spheres were merged, financial business would dominate church discussions and drive out spiritual concerns. Two boards and two meetings would insure that each got its due. The separation of function also allowed congregations to elect different types of individuals to the two boards. Although trustees had to be suitably religious, they were chosen primarily for their business skill, and many of them proved quite entrepreneurial in their management of church investments and building projects. The two boards also represented different stakeholders, even in the nineteenth century. As we shall see in more detail later on, members and financial contributors were overlapping but not identical cohorts. Church members elected elders or deacons and voted in church meetings, but financial subscribers or pewholders joined in the election of trustees and participated in corporate or society meetings.[26]

Because the Church of Scotland was still established, it makes a case of its own in this regard. Scotland's ancient parishes were all-purpose geographical units serving both civil and religious purposes—that is, *Quoad Omnia*. Parish kirks had responsibility until 1845 for poor relief and until 1872 for basic education.[27] Spiritual matters rested with the kirk session, but the parish's property and revenues were controlled by a patron or, in cities, by the town councilors who paid the clergy and maintained the building. By the 1860s, large cities delegated to Ecclesiastical Commissions the temporal roles once held directly by the councils.

The official parish kirks were the most common, but not the only, congregations in the Church of Scotland. As large urban parishes became too populous, they were subdivided for religious, though not for civil, purposes—that is, *Quoad Sacra* only, not *Quoad Omnia*. Once a new subdivision raised an adequate endowment to ensure its stability, it became independent as a *Quoad Sacra* parish with its own minister and elders. Following the precedent that was now well established, the new parish's temporal affairs were kept separate from its spiritual life. Ownership of the property was vested in trustees, and a group of managers was appointed to tend the secular business of the parish.[28]

It was the *Quoad Sacra* model that Scottish dissenters adopted. In the United Presbyterian churches, *trustees* held title to the church property, and a board of *managers* supervised ordinary business affairs. When the Free Church split away in 1843, it followed the same practice, except its managers were called *deacons*.

Although the system of dual governance generally worked well, there were times when it led to gridlock or to disappointment, even to bitterness. Kirk sessions in Scotland not infrequently complained about the unwillingness of the town council or Ecclesiastical Commission to maintain the church building or to make improvements for the comfort of the congregation. Responsibility for certain expenses was admittedly vague, and there are examples of disagreements about adequate fire insurance or heating fuel, or about the payment of overhead expenses incurred in collecting contributions. Once, when Edinburgh's Ecclesiastical Commission chided the Greenside session for ordering unauthorized coal, the elders fired back a sharp reply asking just "how the Ecclst. Com[n] intend to fulfil [sic] their obligations to heat the Churches &c."[29] Parishes were especially irritated when they believed they could demonstrate, as was the case in Dumfries, that the town was making a profit because the parish income exceeded the outlays for the minister's stipend and building maintenance.[30] But it was more often the case that the Ecclesiastical Commissions' funds fell short of what was truly needed, especially when significant structural repairs to ancient churches were required, and the trend was to shift responsibility increasingly to the parish.[31]

In the nonestablished churches, the separation of religious from temporal governance led, on occasion, to jurisdictional disputes between the ecclesiastical and temporal boards. Given that the two groups of leaders had different constituencies, priorities, and personalities, perhaps the surprise is that disputes were not more frequent. Church music is an example of one area that was prone to disagreement because the elders or deacons appointed and oversaw the work of musicians while the financial board set and paid the salaries. In Philadelphia's Second Presbyterian Church the elders and trustees had a particularly tempestuous relationship that extended over more than a decade, with the elders searching the church records back into the 1780s for precedents that would buttress their side of the argument. In that congregation, quarrels about music spread to arguments about the Sunday School and even to something seemingly so minor as the right to call the congregation together to vote on a new minister. Second Church's disputes stayed within the congregation, but those a few blocks away at Walnut Street Presbyterian Church ended up in the city court before the elders secured their right to appoint the church organist in 1869.[32]

Congregations did not relish contention between their ecclesiastical and temporal boards, and they sought ways to avoid it. A plea for "union & harmony" was sometimes enough,[33] but usually not. Congregational churches, especially, tried to write clear jurisdictional boundaries into their local by-laws.[34] The Scottish Free Church kept disputes to a minimum by having their spiritual and temporal officers—elders and deacons—meet together monthly in a Deacons' Court for the transaction of ordinary business.[35] By the 1860s when "efficient" and "systematic" became the favored adjectives of congregational practice, there was a movement in the United States to do away with the dual structure entirely. Congregationalist H. M. Storrs was one who made the case for a single-board government. "We want simplicity," he wrote. "No merchant would keep two sets of books when one would do."[36] Some congregations, particularly small ones with limitations to the number of office-holders they could find, did use single boards.[37] But the tradition and the hesitancy to mix sacred and secular were stronger than the want of efficiency, and the dual system continued to characterize most local church governments well into the twentieth century.

The selection of clergy—who during this period were exclusively male, with the exception of a very few Congregationalists[38]—was another time when the two dimensions of government had to work in tandem. The established Church of Scotland again presents a special case, at least until the end of patronage in 1874. The patron's right to appoint a parish minister had been removed and restored more than once since the Reformation, and in its current form dated from 1712.[39] The exclusion of the congregation from the selection of its own minister was long a source of fierce argument and schism; both the Secession of 1733 and the Disruption of 1843 turned on this point. The 1712 Patronage Act was weakened in 1844 when congregations gained the right to register objections to an appointment, and the presbytery the right to judge whether the objections were sufficient to nullify the call. In 1874, patronage was ended, and the election of a minister devolved to the communicants.[40]

After 1874, then, laity in all these denominations held the right to elect their minister. The responsibility belonged, in the first instance, to the members of the church, but the temporal side of the church's government, representing the congregation's financial supporters, became involved, too. Some American Presbyterian congregations, following Scottish custom, permitted baptized pewholders to add their ballots to those of the members.[41] Congregational churches spelled out in their by-laws exactly what the jurisdiction of each was: the Church vote came first, after which the Society acted, "confirming or rejecting the nomination" and setting the salary.[42]

When a pastoral vacancy occurred, a nominating committee did the preliminary work of sifting through possible candidates. Among Congregationalists, committees included both church and society representatives; among Presbyterians, they were typically comprised of church officers from each of the two governing boards plus at-large representatives from the congregation. The size of the committees varied considerably. For an 1882 search at Old South Congregational Church in Boston, there was a committee of five—four from the Church and one from the Society. Second Presbyterian Church, Philadelphia, selected an 1895 committee of five—two elders, two trustees, and one congregational representative; a few years later, Central Presbyterian Church, Rochester, New York, used three elders, three trustees, and one at-large member. Not every congregation was so sensible; when Glasgow's Cowcaddens Free Church in 1895 added non-office-holders from the congregation to its entire session and board of deacons, it ended up with an unwieldy committee of about a hundred.[43]

In the years before midcentury, the meetings in which church members elected their ministers were preceded by prayer and fasting. As the congregation of Second Presbyterian Church in Philadelphia embarked on a pastoral search in

1833, the session appointed a day to be "set apart for . . . fasting, humiliation and prayer, that God in his mercy would send a man after His own heart, who shall prove a blessing to our own souls and the souls of our children." Two months later, as the day of voting approached, there were again "special meetings for prayer, to invoke the Divine direction and guidance."[44] Even though the habit of fasting and humiliation waned later in the century, the meetings were still framed with special prayers and singing.

When forty members of Old South Church in Boston met in January 1834 to consider a call to the Rev. Samuel Stearns, they had already heard him preach "for several Sabbaths." Typical of the openness in Congregational meetings, people "expressed their minds freely and fully." The discussion "touched . . . upon the early history and education of M^r Stearns, his intellectual qualification,—social habits—colloquial powers—health—age—religious character—discourses— manner of delivery—prayers, &c, &c." When the talking ended, all forty stood and, one by one, voted aye. A copy of the action was then transmitted to the Standing Committee of the Society which called a meeting of pewholders for their concurrence. As the church meeting drew to a close, they offered a "prayer of gratitude & thankfulness to God,—craving for the future, a continuance of the care and blessing which has hitherto been extended to us as a church." Then, before leaving, they sang together the "Christian Doxology in Long Metre."[45]

Votes on the election of ministers tended to be unanimous or nearly so; internal harmony was simply essential at the beginning of a pastorate. If doubt emerged, delay was the most common consequence. In 1856, when electing an associate pastor, Old South members found themselves divided about the Rev. J. M. Manning. They decided to listen to him preach again and reconvene. When they did, they engaged in a remarkable exercise in consensus building. First, they took an informal vote, allowing each person to make remarks of explanation. The tally was twenty-eight yes, five no, and three abstentions from individuals who had heard him preach only once. With that known to all, they took the "official" vote and wrote in their minutes that it was "nearly unanimous." Manning was asked to come.[46]

That Manning spent the next three weeks making his own inquiries and seeking God's will indicates that these congregational votes did not presume a prior commitment from the minister to accept even a unanimous call. Particularly in the competition among important city pulpits for star preachers, it was not uncommon for a congregation to be turned down. Usually, congregations accepted this and looked elsewhere, but in other instances they were persistent. King's Weigh House, for instance, tried to convince William Pulsford to come from Glasgow to London in 1870; when he declined, the congregation successfully pursued William Braden of Huddersfield. But they had not forgotten Pulsford entirely. After Braden's unexpected death from a heart attack at age thirty-eight in 1878, they tried Pulsford a second time, again without success. Even the most prominent churches could be turned down. The members of St. George's Free Church in Edinburgh—that denomination's most prestigious pulpit—tried twice to convince James Hood Wilson to join them. Plymouth Church's effort to bring Berry from Wolverhampton to Brooklyn as Beecher's successor was no more successful. Money seemed not to have an effect. King's Weigh House had made a particular point of guaranteeing a generous stipend to Pulsford, but could not entice him to leave Scotland. Berry's reply was equally simple; he preferred "to stay with his own people."[47]

For congregations certain that they had found a extraordinary talent and willing to wait, patience could pay off. St. George's Free sought to bring Black to Edinburgh in 1892, but he declined, saying he could not interrupt work underway at his current charge in Paisley. The church held the offer open, and three years later in 1895, he accepted their call. A similar situation occurred in Boston when Old South invited George Gordon in 1882; he replied that he was unable to leave his Greenwich, Connecticut, people "in the Red Sea." Old South wrote back to say that he was nevertheless wanted in Boston, and he was to come "at the earliest practical time." The members of Old South waited one year to hear him say yes, and yet another three months before he arrived.[48]

Clergy had certain powers by virtue of their office. Their ordination declared them specially marked for preaching, teaching, and administration of the sacraments. They performed marriages, attended funerals, and cared for their flock with comfort and counsel. They chaired the presbyterian sessions or congregationalist church meetings and standing committees, and their inclinations affected the format and procedures used, as well as the range of issues likely to come before the group. Additionally, pastors were the ones left to implement policy in the end.[49]

Much of a minister's power, then, derived from persuasion, example, or expertise rather than stipulated authority. The force of personality counted for much in attracting the flood of new members hoped for upon one's arrival, or deciding a potentially difficult issue such as installing an organ in a church that previously had only unaccompanied singing. One woman in Glasgow's Maxwell parish, thinking of the sway held by the ambitious young pastor Archibald Scott, recalled, "there was great feeling against an organ in Maxwell, but Mr. Scott was so strong, he consulted nobody, and all acquiesced." Even more easily, a strong minister could prevent or delay action. In deference to Thomas Binney's preferences, King's Weigh House had no organ until his long tenure ended; then it had one almost instantly. The coming of a new pastor could, therefore, provide opportunity for change, and undoubtedly many selections were made with that in mind, as when impatient Presbyterians at St. John's, Kensington, had an organ "within a few months" of Charles Moinet's arrival in 1882.[50]

Despite the ministers' considerable power to shape congregational life, their professional roles were less discretely defined in practice than in theory. By the World War I era, several decades of aggressive professionalization had narrowed lay responsibility, but during much of the nineteenth century, many nominally pastoral roles were routinely assumed by strong laity.

This blurring of clerical and lay roles arose in response to urgent needs. Few congregations employed assistant or colleague ministers, and the burgeoning size of urban churches left no alternative to a heavy reliance on volunteers and paraprofessionals. Beecher had no assistant minister until 1870 in a church that by then had two thousand members and had counted more than one thousand for twelve years. As one member recalled, "For a long time, Mr. Beecher and Plymouth Church followed the prevailing custom, relying upon volunteer service for such extra visitation as was beyond the pastor's power."[51]

The church officers provided one level of volunteer labor. Trustees and managers carried the burden of routine church administration. Elders and deacons became de facto counselors to troubled souls as they made their own rounds of members' homes and weighed the disciplinary cases that came before them. In addition, elders and deacons relieved busy pastors by taking charge of mid-week prayer meetings, leading worship at mission chapels, teaching Bible classes, preaching at outdoor evangelistic services, or becoming all-purpose deputies during the minister's vacation or during a pastoral vacancy.[52] Short of administering the sacraments and performing marriages, there were few pastoral duties that elders or deacons did not assume.

Pastoral chores also fell to committees known as "pastor's helpers" or sometimes the "Pastor's Aid Society," that carried out routine parish visitation, prayed with the sick, contacted prospective members, or assisted the needy; the amount of unofficial pastoral counseling that occurred during the visiting is unrecorded, but it likely was significant. Because women's daily schedules more readily accommodated volunteer work, the typical volunteer was a "lady visitor," thereby placing women at least partially in the pastoral role from which they were otherwise excluded.[53]

A minority of congregations formalized this lay ministry to the congregation's sick and aged by instituting, or rather recovering, the servant offices of *deacon* and *deaconess*. Deacons, in this sense, were not found in the Scottish Free Church where the word was already employed in temporal government, but a growing number of American Presbyterian congregations elected deacons beginning as early as the 1850s. By the early 1880s a few American Presbyterian congregations were appointing deaconesses as well, although denominational sanction for the inclusion of women did not come until 1892.[54] At the instigation of the Rev. Archibald Charteris, the Church of Scotland in 1887 established an order of deaconesses with expanded medical training and responsibilities for women who wanted to make a professional commitment to the work.[55]

Congregationalists, of course, were already using the word deacon to identify their lay ecclesiastical officers, but they were quick to see the potential of deaconesses. Beecher, often an innovator, began to use deaconesses in his Brooklyn church in 1868 "to visit the sick and poor among the women and children of the church and congregation."[56] Boylston Church in Boston was choosing deaconesses annually by 1879 to visit the sick, bring cases of need to attention, and invite new families to the church.[57] Among Congregationalists, the presence of deaconesses could mean, though it more often did not, that women gained representation on church committees, and thereby access to the centers of power.[58]

In addition to their visibility as deaconesses, women were also prominently represented among the nineteenth-century paraprofessionals. Variously referred to as catechists, parish missionaries or Bible women, these workers comforted the sick, ran mission houses, extended social and educational services to the poor, read and interpreted the Bible and led prayers in homes, and taught the faith to the young. Some congregations teamed up a committee of lady visitors with a paraprofessional worker in an effort to get the most out of each contribution. Eventually, the trend toward a sharper definition of the clergy's professional role diminished the reliance on paraprofessionals; pastors (and congregations, too) began to insist on a seminary-educated, ordained assistant minister rather than a lay catechist, parish missionary, or Bible woman.[59]

Church officers, ministers, and paraprofessional workers were, of course, only a fraction of the congregation's body politic. Discounting visitors, two constituencies, each with its own rights and powers, could be found assembled at Sunday worship: *members* and *pewholders*. Members (or *communicants* in the Church of Scotland) had made the fullest individual commitments to the church's spiritual life; they submitted to its discipline and were entitled to receive its sacraments. Pewholders contributed financially to the church by purchasing or renting seating for themselves and their families; in the minority of congregations with free seating, those who subscribed financial support were equivalent. As already intimated, members and pewholders were overlapping, but not identical, groups. For instance, a woman might be a member, yet sit in a family pew held in her husband's name, or in her father's name if she were unmarried. Conversely, not everyone who paid for seating made the deeper, personal commitment to membership.

Members and pewholders had both formal and informal means of influencing the direction of the congregation. The most obvious was the right to vote. Opportunities to exercise the right of suffrage varied considerably over the course of the nineteenth century, with the overall trend being toward expanded opportunity. In the parish kirks of the Church of Scotland, voting scarcely mattered before the Church Patronage Act of 1874; kirk sessions were self-perpetuating, and temporal matters and the selection of pastors were in the hands of the patron or town council. In *Quoad Sacra* churches, however, the right to elect a pastor was given to adult males who were both communicants and pewholders. Among the other Scots and the American Presbyterians, congregations had power to elect their officers and ministers, but no more. The presbyterian approach was representative, not direct, democracy.

In theory, at least, Congregationalists practiced direct democracy, with nearly all decisions made by the whole body. In practice, however, direct democracy was cumbersome, and on most matters the Standing Committee or Church Committee functioned as powerfully as a presbyterian session. Moreover, quorums for church or society meetings were low, and fortunately so, because attendance was seldom high, and it would thus be easy to say that the democratic aspects of Congregationalism were much exaggerated but for one exception: a controversial issue could mobilize the members instantly. During the 1890s, meetings at Old South Church in Boston seldom produced more than twenty or thirty votes, yet in 1896, 170 ballots were cast on a question about common versus individual communion cups, and in 1899 a revision of the congregation's statement of faith brought out 280 voters.[60]

There were some important restrictions on voter eligibility, however. Not surprisingly, members had to be in good standing, that is, not under church censure for any misdeed or negligence; in some places continued local residence was required, and those who had joined within the last year or six months were commonly excluded by Congregational by-laws. Likewise, in temporal elections, pew renters had to be current with their payments, and new renters were generally ineligible.[61]

Age and sex were two other common limitations. Nearly all Congregational by-laws had clauses restricting voting to "adults" or "those of lawful age," which was usually eighteen or twenty-one, but occasionally nineteen or as low as fifteen.[62] In the United States, Presbyterians worked by the principle that anyone mature enough to accept the responsibilities of membership was old enough to vote.

State laws of incorporation determined eligibility to vote for trustees and to conduct corporate business, and these commonly stipulated age, citizenship, and sometimes sex.[63]

Restrictions on women's ability to vote in ecclesiastical elections decreased over the century and did so at a pace well ahead of the general movement for women's suffrage in politics. The variations were considerable, even within the same denomination or nation. One faction of Scottish Seceders had permitted women to vote in 1747, and with each successive merger, other portions of what became the United Presbyterian Church gave voting rights to women. The Scottish Free Church permitted women to vote from its origin in 1843. The following year, members of the Church of Scotland gained the right to object to a patron's ministerial nomination, and women were included in the process, though some historians have suggested by inadvertence rather than intent. By the 1840s, then, women throughout Scotland participated in ecclesiastical elections.[64]

Among American Presbyterians, women's participation in ecclesiastical meetings was accepted as a matter of course. Although women were restricted from preaching or leading prayer in public worship, there were no legal barriers to their speaking and voting in ecclesiastical meetings.[65]

Congregational churches had the power of local option on women's suffrage as well as other questions, and thus policies varied. Sixteenth and seventeenth-century Congregationalists uniformly restricted voting to the "brethren," and this practice remained almost universally in place at the beginning of the nineteenth century. The Rev. George Punchard, writing in 1840, cautioned that "the female members of a church should be present at the transaction of all ordinary business, for their satisfaction and instruction; but, it is utterly inconsistent with established usage for females to take any part in business transactions. Their views are to be expressed privately to their pastor or their brethren. We suffer not a woman to speak in the church, agreeably to apostolic injunctions."[66] Despite such admonitions, the trend by the last half of the nineteenth century was toward the inclusion of women. Still, as late as 1880, one author estimated that more congregations held to the traditional practice than allowed women to vote.[67] Historian Michael Watts found that "most" British Congregationalists continued to disallow women's participation in church meetings "well into the nineteenth century," too.[68]

Both in America and Britain, therefore, Congregationalist women found that it could matter very greatly which local church they had joined. Even when permission to vote came, it was not always accompanied by a genuine welcome. When women were permitted to vote in Ridgefield, Connecticut, the church's 1843 manual added the cunning remark that it was "the special duty of all male members of the Church" to be certain they attended meetings.[69] Apparently, males found it harder to concede suffrage in the direct democracy of Congregationalism than in the representative-style presbyterian polity where the eldership was firmly in their hands.

Generally, restrictions on women's suffrage lingered longest in long-established congregations while newly organized ones accepted change more readily. For example, Boston's Old South, despite its liberalism in theology, continued the tradition of male-only voting until the very last years of the nineteenth century, twenty or more years after women in some of the city's other Congregational churches voted.[70] In the new congregations on the southern extremities of Boston—Jamaica Plain (1853) and Hyde Park (1868)—women had the vote from the start. Across the Atlantic, the new suburban church developments to the north of London, such as Lyndhurst Road (1880) in Hampstead Heath, also began with women voting.[71]

The formal political process—office holding, meetings, and elections—was, however, only one way in which ordinary congregants accessed power. Both women and men had informal methods of influence and pressure. Simply by withholding their money, congregations could effectively veto a costly venture planned by the officers or pastor. In Fourth United Presbyterian Church in Pittsburgh, pewholders held back payments to drive out an unpopular minister, and if the point was not obvious at the time, it was amply manifest when the church's income surged by nearly 90 percent the moment a new pastor was settled—"a handsome addition," the trustees noted with satisfaction.[72]

Members could also register dissatisfaction by withholding attendance or volunteer labor. Presence at the morning service on Sunday was considered an obligation for members, and avoiding it would not have been an acceptable, or very effective, form of protest. But church boards understood low attendance at Sunday afternoon or evening services, or mid-week services, as an expression of dissatisfaction with the hour or style of those services. By the same token, a good turnout for a program or Bible class or mission activity was seen as an endorsement. Because churches relied so heavily on volunteer labor, the choice of supplying it or not was a powerful lever for the congregation. Women, in particular, played indispensable roles in fund-raising, teaching, visiting, mission work, and church socials, and they used this indispensability as a wedge to redress their exclusion from office holding. In fact, as a result of their success at independent fund-raising, women frequently controlled a significant proportion of the congregation's discretionary money, while the funds of the church boards were obligated to fixed costs such as salaries or heat and light. A chronicler of Pilrig Free Church in

Edinburgh noted, "From the first to last [lady members] have been in the van of every movement for its material prosperity."[73]

Understandably, the male power structure listened carefully for signs of discontent among women members. When the "brethren" of Old South Church met in 1834 to elect a pastor, the clerk recorded, "It was also stated that the Sisters of the Church were to a considerable known extent in favor of M^r Stearns."[74] Women were quite skilled at making their voices heard through political tactics such as lobbying, persuasion, and pressure. A young woman, reflecting on her situation in 1912, showed both a hint of impatience for a more equal future and an ability to function quite well in the present. "Though as yet debarred from attendance at meetings of Session and from membership of the Young Men's Committee," she wrote, "there is not much to which [we young women] are not privy, sooner or later, and generally sooner!"[75]

Males outside the circle of officeholders also availed themselves of informal channels of power. Men, or men and women together, could circulate a petition and submit it to the officers. In Edinburgh's Greyfriars Church, parishioners formed a delegation and called on the kirk session to seek a repositioning of the church organ.[76] Sessions, standing committees, and trustees took such expressions, or even rumors of discontent, seriously. When a report of a disgruntled member reached the session at Fourth United Presbyterian Church in Pittsburgh in 1857, they quickly sent one of their number to "see Mr. F. Young and learn the cause of his reported dissatisfaction."[77]

Church officers grew hesitant when they did not think they had a good sense of the congregation's will. Rather than move forward blindly on a potentially divisive issue, they sought ways to discern the congregation's mind. The deacons at King's Weigh House, in 1863, organized a series of social meetings where they hoped to sound out members about a plan to shift from quarterly to weekly offerings. The Lyndhurst Road deacons took a nonbinding straw vote asking their suburban London membership about a new hour for Sunday evening worship, and they carefully noted not only which time each member preferred, but also whether either time would foreclose the possibility of attending.[78]

The price of miscalculating on a potentially explosive issue was high, and the officers mostly understood that. On those occasions when they did not, or pressed ahead with their own agenda, the pain of mass defection, schism, or simply anger followed by bitterness was a powerful reminder that peace and unity were to be prized above purity. Inside the congregation, the exercise of power had to be tempered by the demands of community.

# PART II
Worship Together

# three

## The Lord's Day

The reputation of celebrated preacher T. DeWitt Talmadge had already spread
from Brooklyn to London, from his regular audience of American Presbyterians
to the English Congregationalists who were eagerly anticipating his visit. On the
day of his sermon at London's City Temple in 1892, "some 10,000 people tried
to get in, many of them arriving more than an hour before the service began."
City Temple's organist Ebenezer Minshall remembered that when the doors were
finally opened, "The rush to get in . . . was terrific, clothes were torn and people
were much crushed."[1] This was an extreme example, perhaps, of the zeal with
which nineteenth-century churchgoers sought out fine preaching, but the point
is sound: eloquent preachers could pack the pews. Some years earlier, when the
famous Glasgow preacher John Caird was scheduled for a guest appearance at
Edinburgh's Greenside Church, the hosts had the good sense, at least, to issue
advance tickets as a way of managing the crowd.[2]

   It was a century for stars, both in Britain and America. Joseph Parker
held forth regularly at the spacious City Temple, and in Brooklyn, Beecher
did the same from his Plymouth Church pulpit. Every city and town had
its greater or lesser lights. Audiences craved sermons, the daily press provided
rapid reportage, and enthusiastic readers awaited the release of the latest printed
collections.

   From a perspective outside the local congregation, the pulpit stars often
seem to be the main story of Victorian worship, and with some reason. They
were uniquely visible and centrally placed. Together with the sparkling talents of
the stage, recital and lecture halls, they were testimony to the age's devotion to
virtuosity. Their oratory readily pulled individual listeners into its grasp. One of
the ushers at Plymouth Church studied the young men around him, and while
Beecher preached, they sat poised and receptive, "all sense of surroundings . . .
lost, and bending forward, with eye fixed on the speaker, and even the mouth

open, as if in fear of closing any possible avenue by which the thought might enter mind and heart."[3]

Viewed from inside the congregation, however, the perspective is less one-dimensional. Preaching was important, but it was linked to the congregation's ongoing life and work, and set in a context of worship. Clergy who did not have the status of celebrities successfully nurtured congregations, even if they did not draw curiosity seekers and tourists. Indeed, preaching itself changed over the century, both in terms of its style and its prominence during worship. Sermons became shorter by a third, dense theological argument gave way to practical illustration, and dramatic rhetoric yielded to everyday language.

The worshipper encountered preaching within a whole that included music, liturgy and sacrament. One frequent visitor to Parker's services at City Temple confessed, "I can listen to the sermon without a tear, but I cannot do so to one of the prayers."[4] Similarly, a keen observer of the experience at Plymouth Church concluded that newcomers, even skeptical ones, seldom got "little farther than the prayer or the second hymn before there was a very perceptible unbending. Somehow few could withstand the power of Plymouth Church singing, and Mr. Beecher's prayers had a wonderfully moving influence." The weekly sermon may have been what, in the end, "captured all," but the process began earlier. Yet even this was not the ultimate Plymouth Church experience, the same witness thought; Beecher was not seen at his best until the bimonthly communion service, "distinctively a family gathering in which the host was not Mr. Beecher, or Plymouth Church, but the Saviour."[5]

Music will receive its own chapter; here the attention is on word and sacrament, and there are four overlapping and interacting themes that emerge. First, nineteenth-century Reformed congregations reevaluated, and shifted, the balance between the devotional and the didactic aspects of worship. The richness of the liturgy and the frequency of sacramental celebration increased until they achieved a new, more equal relationship with the proclamation of the word. The heart became important as well as the head, and the eyes as well as the ears. The festive took a place alongside the conventional in the yearly schedule of worship events. Second, worship like all aspects of church life was affected by the midcentury desire for system, order, and efficiency; services became not only shorter, but more standardized. Worshippers grew to appreciate the regularity offered by denominational service books, set prayers, and repeated responses. These innovations not only standardized expression, but controlled length better than the older extempore custom. As the Sunday schedule grew more crowded with Bible classes, youth meetings, fellowship gatherings, and mission work, worship had to fit efficiently within its allotted time. Thus, there were shorter sermons, shorter prayers, and more expeditious ways of distributing the bread and wine at communion services. Third, worship was forced to compete with the rising number of leisure activities; it now had to please rather than merely edify its audience. Fourth, partly as a result of this competition with secular entertainments and partly as a result of the evangelical party's insistence that worship lead to conversion, the basis for evaluating worship shifted; the old measure, Biblical authenticity, became less important than the impact a service had upon the participants.[6]

On Sunday morning, the congregation gathered for public worship. It was not the only time for worship during the week nor even the only occasion on Sunday, but it was the most important. Members were expected to be there, and attendance was normally high, slackening during summer heat when those who could fled the cities.[7] By the last third of the century, worshippers might have attended a Sunday School or Bible class or a young men's or young ladies' prayer meeting prior to the service; in earlier times, they would more likely have come directly from the breakfast table and a brief period of family devotions at home.

Eleven o'clock was the preferred hour for morning worship in Britain and ten-thirty the most common in America.[8] Punctuality was valued, although the abundance of complaints and dire warnings suggest that urban dwellers did not easily learn to govern their lives by the clock. The editor of the *Presbyterian* in 1856 chided his readers for the "well-known grievance" of tardiness; he was sure each congregation had "certain persons—church members, too—whom their pastors have never seen present at the opening invocation, a single Sabbath morning in their lives."[9] Worshippers at Carr's Lane Church were reminded in their members' handbook that lateness was "disrespectful to the minister, . . . irreverent towards God, . . . disturbing to the devout worshipper, . . . [and] detrimental to the unpunctual themselves."[10]

The difficulty with tardiness was that it revealed a lack of serious intent, and worship in early nineteenth-century Reformed congregations was, if nothing else, meant to be a solemn undertaking. The proper approach to worship, so the Carr's Lane faithful were told, was to be a few minutes early, allowing time for "silent meditation" and "mental prayer" so that the "mind is thus composed for worship, and prepared for spiritual profit." A similar solemnity was expected at the end of the service when worshippers were to "silently and devotionally retire." In short, "the house of God is not the place for chit-chat, nor the exchange of compliments, nor the communication of domestic intelligence, much less for making engagements; but for divine worship, and the business of our souls."[11]

New York Presbyterian Samuel Miller advised his fellow ministers to leave the service "gravely, silently, and alone."[12]

These Reformed groups had emerged from the Calvinist Reformation and come under the influence of the Puritan movement. It was their forebears who had drafted the Westminster Directory of Worship in 1644, and even after two hundred years, its spirit was strong. The Directory was just that—a directory, not a service book. It gave broad guidelines about content, order, and style, but it did not prescribe a liturgy or furnish written prayers. Its authors, Scottish Presbyterians and English Puritans together, viewed the Anglican *Book of Common Prayer* as their foe, and a suspicion of any imposed pattern of worship was part of the heritage these Reformed groups brought into the nineteenth century.

Thus, Reformed worship during the first third of the century remained plain, even austere. The Directory's insistence that each component be put to a scriptural test remained the measure; if no explicit Biblical warrant could be found, the action was rejected. Practices of "human invention" were banned from divine worship. Prayers were extempore and spoken by the minister alone, not by the congregation in unison. The Lord's Prayer, clearly Biblical, was sanctioned, but its use by the minister was not universal; there were many who recognized its value as a model but viewed its repetition as an uninstructive ritual.

The demand that each element must prove edifying to the congregation had in the past raised questions even about the reading of scripture unless it was immediately accompanied by an explanation. Such scruples were no longer common by the early nineteenth century, but where suspicions about "dumb reading" did linger, explication still accompanied the lesson. One Scot, recalling his United Presbyterian youth in a Highland village, figured that he got two sermons—the interpretation or "lecture" attached to the reading, and then the "discourse" or sermon itself.[13]

Although the *Directory's* minimalism encouraged local variation, a certain uniformity had settled in by the early Victorian era. A typical order of service among Reformed congregations included

*Singing*
*Opening Prayer or Invocation*
*Scripture Reading*
*Singing*
*Long Prayer*
*Sermon*
*Singing*
*Blessing*[14]

In some congregations, the service commenced with the first prayer rather than with singing; elsewhere, a brief prayer might be inserted after the sermon. People customarily stood during public prayer, and the "long" prayer, which included adoration, confession, thanksgiving, supplication, and intercession, was indeed long. The American Presbyterian directory of 1787 recommended twenty minutes, and thirty minute prayers could apparently be heard among English Congregationalists. By the 1840s, there was already a movement toward briefer prayers; an American pastor's handbook recommended ten to fifteen minutes as more reasonable.[15]

Though some were also calling for shorter sermons, the standard discourse early in the century could still last an hour or, by some reports, as much as two.[16] Traditional preaching styles emphasized exegesis and doctrine, assembled ideas and arguments, and drew illustrations primarily from Biblical sources. Rhetoric was formal; later generations would consider it stilted. The customary practice was to read the sermon from a prepared manuscript, although some recited their words from memory.

But even at the beginning of the Victorian era, a new kind of sermon, reflecting the influence of evangelical preaching, was beginning to be heard. In content, the new style moved away from pure doctrine and toward more personal, practical applications; the sermon aimed to persuade, to sway, to convince rather than to expound doctrine. In length, forty minutes became the new norm. Language became more accessible and informal. Binney, a leader in reshaping English Congregational preaching, "abandoned the rhetorical, rather theatrical style of the previous generation, and adopted a quiet, colloquial manner; [he] used everyday speech for his sermons, and drew his illustrations from everyday life."[17] As time went on, Parker forswore detailed exposition of long Scriptural texts and "selected only a few suggestive words and treated them discursively, seeking to enforce and illustrate their central thought, and their application to every-day life."[18] In America, Finney referred to his discourses as "talking sermons," a term that conveyed their more conversational style. Beecher's illustrations were as apt to come from daily life or nature as from Scripture, and he prided himself in choosing words that were "home-bred."[19]

Pastors were also encouraged, and in some cases required, to abandon their manuscripts as well as their formal eighteenth-century rhetoric. Congregationalists had never looked favorably on sermons that were read rather than preached, although R. D. Dale and others certainly continued to prepare manuscripts. American Presbyterian and Scottish Free Church congregations preferred ministers who spoke without a manuscript. Even in the Church of Scotland, the lackluster reading of sermons could provoke controversy. Scottish United Presbyterians simply forbade their preachers to read sermons.[20]

The new sermon was popular with the laity. Its brevity appealed, certainly, and its informality was more pleasing to the ear. Because it touched daily life more closely, its usefulness was more apparent. In time, the new style made its effect known among nonevangelicals as well, and even when not fully adopted produced a sort of hybrid of the old and new. By the end of the century, the liturgical revival which embraced written rather than extempore prayers made the reading of carefully prepared sermons more acceptable again, although the emphasis continued to be practical and the language informal. Prominent Church of Scotland minister Archibald Charteris prepared sermons that "dealt with doctrinal truth yet led to very practical issues, and, [were] expressed in language abounding in unforgettable phrases, lit up with happy illustrations."[21]

Preaching was not the only change that worshippers noticed. By the end of the century, Reformed congregations routinely included once-forbidden practices, reallocated time within the service, and availed themselves of printed worship aids. Some of the most striking changes were in music and architecture, and even if we set those aside for later chapters, we can see evidence that the sights and sounds of worship were recast dramatically.

Visually, worship became more colorful. Many British and American clergy were still wearing the traditional Geneva gown and bands at the beginning of the nineteenth century, but their use soon waned except in certain large urban churches, particularly those in the Church of Scotland, where preaching robes were worn throughout the period. By 1900, however, the Geneva gown made a comeback; its use was by no means universal, but it was much more widespread, even among those of more evangelical spirit. Parker, for instance, wore a gown when he was at City Temple during the last quarter of the century. In America, too, where revival movements and a democratic egalitarianism had discouraged vestments, more clergy appeared in gowns. By the 1880s, some Scottish pastors had added a colorful academic hood to their costumes. While a minority of laity undoubtedly objected, wherever members sought respectability and social prominence, they took pride in the more elegant appearance of their pastors. When John S. MacIntosh, just arrived in Philadelphia from Scotland in 1881, told the elders of Second Presbyterian Church that he was used to wearing the Geneva gown and hoped to continue the practice, they said without hesitation that "the custom would be most acceptable to our people."[22]

Flowers added another touch of color when they began to be placed routinely in the front of the church on Sundays. The story is told that one morning in 1852, someone gave Beecher a "small bouquet in a vase." Ever an admirer of God's presence in nature, Beecher "took it to church with him, placed it on the little table at his side, and there it remained during the service." As one of his members recalled nearly a half century later,

> It is difficult in these days to understand what a commotion it occasioned. Such a thing as bringing flowers into a church on the Sabbath day had never been heard of, and was not at all in accord with traditional New England ideas. Everyone in the congregation of course noticed it, and the bouquet of flowers became during the week the talk of all Brooklyn. [Some] . . . declared that Henry Ward Beecher had desecrated the House of God by taking flowers into the pulpit during religious worship! This, however, affected neither Mr. Beecher nor the church. Flowers on the pulpit had come to stay, and stay they did.[23]

By the early twentieth century, flowers were a common adornment at worship. Volunteers organized to manage the weekly arrangements; they were usually a committee of ladies, but in Rochester's Central Presbyterian Church, the task fell to the Young People's Society. In Hyde Park, Massachusetts, a Flower Committee arranged the blooms before the service and then took the flowers to the sick afterward. Where the flowers could not be gathered from a local garden, either a new line item appeared in the budget or special donations were solicited. Laity were most often the ones who first suggested having floral displays, perhaps because they knew of the practice elsewhere or simply found the beauty appealing. In Glasgow's Lansdowne United Presbyterian Church, it was "the pleasing effect of flowers on the Church table at the Harvest Thanksgiving Service in October [1906, that] suggested the ideas of continuing the custom throughout the year."[24]

The changes did not stop with the visual but moved on to the form of the service itself. One group of modifications increased the direct participation by the laity. By the 1870s and 1880s, congregations began to pray the Lord's Prayer in unison with the pastor or take their part in a responsive reading of scripture, alternating verses with the minister; by 1900 such practices were no longer remarkable.[25] The Lord's Prayer and responsive readings were the two most common additions because they were unarguably "biblical," but research into sixteenth-century Reformed worship practice suggested other possibilities such as the Apostles' Creed or the Ten Commandments, both of which had a place in Calvin's services. In a few places, such as Clinton Congregational Church in Brooklyn or Bristo United Presbyterian Church in Edinburgh, worshippers knelt for prayer.[26] Still other additions reflected contemporary congregational life. During the last third of the century, new fund-raising approaches made the Morning Offering a standard part of the service, and the proliferation of church meetings and organizations demanded a time set aside for notices or intimations.

As Reformed congregations began to recover elements lost to Puritan austerity, they revived the liturgical year. Only the barest rudiments of a liturgical calendar could be found in any of these groups during the first half of the century. It is true that a number of congregations listed their yearly schedule of communion dates from December through November, suggesting they considered Advent, not the secular New Year's Day, to be the beginning of the church calendar.[27] But if so, the logic of the Christian year was hidden deep in tradition and gave no evidence of surfacing in any meaningful way. Charles Hodge, preaching in the environs of Philadelphia in the 1820s, left no reference whatsoever to either Christmas or Easter in his diary of sermon texts.[28] The *American Presbyterian,* a weekly religious newspaper, featured the crucifixion during the last week of December 1869, perhaps in defiance rather than ignorance of proper liturgical sequence.[29]

Celebrations of Christmas and Easter entered the churches first in the relative safety of the children's Sunday School or church socials; only slowly did they make their way into worship. Some pastors wanted strong church celebrations to confront the growing commercialization of Christmas and Easter, but for most laity the logic went the other way around. Once the holidays, with all their overtly religious elements, were well established as family and commercial celebrations, there seemed no good reason to ban them from church. When Philadelphia Presbyterian William Mactier's minister preached a Christmas Sunday sermon on death and resurrection in 1859, Mactier found it "inappropriate, and not in unison with the feelings and flow of thought of most of his hearers."[30] Pressed by members, congregations began in the 1870s to hold special Christmas worship, and in the 1880s, Easter and Holy Week services began to appear in scattered locations. By the late 1890s or the first years of the new century, such celebrations were common.[31]

The liturgical revolution was a true grass roots movement, with changes bubbling up from the most daring local churches and pastors. In not a few cases, the changes reflected not only the congregation's tastes, but its competition with neighboring churches. For instance, King's Weigh House, surrounded by London's many Anglican parishes, moved to the forefront of liturgical reform among English Congregationalists under Binney's leadership. Binney was a keen observer of the influence John Henry Newman and the Tractarians were having on Anglican worship, and like them, he turned to the past for inspiration. Looking back beyond the Puritans to the Reformation itself, he found a richer, more elegant liturgical tradition. In 1856, he edited and enlarged for English Congregational audiences a version of *Eutaxia, or the Presbyterian Liturgies: Historical Sketches,* a collection of Reformed liturgies published the preceding year by American Charles Baird. Grounded by that precedent, Binney soon enriched worship in his own church by "responsive reading of psalms, vocal confession of sins, and recitation of the Apostles' Creed and the Lord's Prayer."[32] In Brooklyn, New York, a quite different competitive situation led to similar results. Clinton Avenue Congregational Church, unable to compete with Beecher's pulpit wizardry at nearby Plymouth Church, marked out a niche for itself in fine liturgy and music. During the early 1870s, it attracted worshippers with unison prayers, doxologies, the Gloria Patri, responsive readings, chanted psalms, and kneeling for prayer.[33]

In Rochester, New York, where the revival spirit had swept over every Presbyterian church in town, lay leader Levi Ward wanted an alternative, and he built St. Peter's Presbyterian Church in 1852–53. Ward craved more lay participation; he thought worshippers deserved a chance to "*express* themselves," and so he put a service book in every member's hands. Under his strong direction, St. Peter's became a veritable "liturgical laboratory" for high-church Presbyterianism over the next seventeen years.[34]

In Philadelphia, during the 1850s and 1860s, Second Presbyterian Church was losing younger members to the Episcopal Church. New members were rare, Sunday attendance was down, mid-week services were shaky at best, and there was talk of consolidating with another congregation. Minister Charles Shields delivered excellent, carefully prepared sermons, but he was unable to ignite the congregation with words alone. In this circumstance, Shields's interest in liturgics (he had prepared a worship manual for use by Civil War soldiers) served him well. He created special services for communion, baptism and marriage incorporating the Apostles' Creed and Gloria in Excelsis.[35] In the early 1870s, after Shields left for a teaching position in Princeton, the congregation built a splendid Gothic structure which strengthened its ability to compete. In this light, it was not surprising that MacIntosh found his pulpit robes welcomed when he arrived; the congregation's preference for elegant music and worship was already established, and MacIntosh's arrival from Scotland, together with some of the energy generated by liturgical reform there, only reinforced the church's consciously cultivated reputation.[36]

Liturgical renewal promised the Church of Scotland a way to recover its momentum and forge a discrete identity after being sorely wounded by the departure of the Free Church in 1843. In January 1865, a group of clergy founded the Church Service Society, dedicated to discovering and restoring the liturgical richness of the ancient church. The Society expanded to include lay men, and eventually lay women. Whatever their background, as one participant put it, members wanted to be rid of the "curse of Cromwell."[37] The Society had a tremendous impact both in Britain and America. It published worship manuals and collections of prayers for the home and the church. It recovered and republished historic liturgical texts. Its agenda was sweeping: unison prayers, recitation of ancient creeds, shorter sermons (by the early twentieth century, the recommendation was twenty minutes), more frequent communion, children's talks, clerical vestments, and observance of the Christian year. Since the Society's proposals carried no force of law, parishes were free to accept or reject them. Congregations took what they wanted; St. Stephen's in Edinburgh was among the first to mark Holy Week with special services, yet it resisted a unison Lord's Prayer until the mid-1920s.[38]

Because acceptance of liturgical change was a local decision throughout the Reformed community, congregations exhibited much less uniformity by the last years of the century. Obviously, forceful clergy or impatient laity could vault one congregation well ahead of its neighbor. Leadership mattered, but so did education, social aspirations, and resources, and it is no surprise that affluent urban congregations led the way. Laity there had more exposure to the aesthetic models provided by elite secular culture and a greater need to belong to a church that mirrored their own social status. The changes carried a price tag, too. Building renovations and highly paid professional musicians were expensive. Responsive readings meant the purchase of psalters. As services grew complicated and included more elaborate congregational responses, the cost of printed programs had to be added to the budget.

Laity were by no means passive participants in the movement. They spoke out more confidently on architecture or decoration or music, questions that seemed to them as much aesthetic as theological. In some instances, they brought their memories of revival meetings or their knowledge of worship in the town's more socially prominent churches; they always brought their own experiences from family worship, where the use of worship handbooks and collections of prayers, kneeling, and reading verses of scripture by turns were everyday occurrences long before they made their way into public worship.[39] A small number of exceptional lay leaders made enough of a study of liturgics to become true experts and publish worship manuals; Ward was one, and another was Benjamin Comegys, Philadelphia banker and Presbyterian elder.[40] Generally, however, laity were better at evaluating or modifying an existing practice or borrowing from another congregation than in liturgical research or innovation.

Significant departures needed to be interpreted to the worshipping body. The elders or deacons might direct the minister to provide an explanation from the pulpit, or a printed explanation could be distributed in the pews or mailed to homes. When Govan parish initiated the first daily Holy Week services in Glasgow in 1884, the church distributed a four-page rationale written by minister John Macleod. Carefully avoiding the words Lent and Holy Week, worshippers were asked to attend an "annual commemoration of the Resurrection and the other great events of our Redemption." Services were nightly at eight o'clock, and at noon on Friday. Macleod acknowledged that attendance at every service would be difficult, especially at the mid-day service on Friday when attendance was "most needful." Nevertheless, Macleod wrote, "God will help you in any effort that you make. Much may be done by pre-arrangement and self-denial."[41]

Later in the Spring, Macleod sent letters introducing his parishioners to Ascension Day and Pentecost; the next winter, there was a Christmas letter. Macleod was concerned that if the church did not make something of festival days like Easter and Christmas, the commercial culture would. It was important that Christmas be observed in the right way, that the weeks before it be "devoted to meditation," and that time on Christmas Eve and Christmas Day be preserved for worship.[42] There were a few members who grumbled about Macleod's "alleged innovations," but both the kirk session and the presbytery brushed the complaints aside.[43] The majority expressed itself more convincingly by furnishing large attendances at Govan's holiday services, and by requesting more, rather than less, opportunities for worship. Christmas Eve carol services and festive Easter celebrations were overwhelmingly popular, and the daily services during Holy Week were expanded so that, by the early 1890s, worshippers could choose from among three daily services—at ten, three, and eight o'clock—giving them every chance to fit one into their weekday schedules.[44]

Among Macleod's plans for the Christian year was a more frequent celebration of the Lord's Supper. There was communion on Easter Day that first year 1884 (Macleod's letter had been careful to explain that it was a practice sanctioned by John Knox). Macleod gradually increased the number of communion services from four to seventeen per year. That number was unusual, but it no more than put Govan at the extreme end of widespread Scottish trend toward a more frequent celebration of the sacrament.

Sacramental frequency varied among the denominations. In Scotland, the established church at first limited itself to two "communion seasons" per year, April and October. The number of celebrations increased incrementally with the addition of a winter, and then a summer communion; by the 1870s, quarterly communion was the most common pattern. A decade or so later, a few exceptional urban parishes such as Govan refashioned themselves along the lines of English cathedrals and offered more numerous opportunities.[45] The Free Church practiced quarterly communion from its organization in 1843. By the 1870s, United Presbyterians in Edinburgh and Glasgow observed six communions per year.[46] Quarterly communion became the habit of English Presbyterians, from either the 1840s or 1870s depending on whether they took their cues from the Free or established Scots. English Congregationalists celebrated the Lord's Supper monthly, while American Congregationalists did so every other month. American Presbyterians were almost all on a quarterly schedule, although the Congregationalist norm of six per year could be found in upstate New York and the Midwest, areas affected by the 1801 Plan of Union; by the last third of the century important downtown Presbyterian churches in New York, Philadelphia, Pittsburgh, and Chicago had increased to every other month, too.[47]

Over the course of the nineteenth century, Reformed celebration of the Lord's Supper underwent a remarkable transformation in nature as well as frequency. While liturgical experts may have evaluated various proposals on theological grounds, the criteria at the congregational level were quite practical and personal. Laity were looking for three things—convenience, efficiency, and dignity. They wanted the sacrament to be accessible, offered at convenient times of the day and at frequent enough intervals that one brief illness did not foreclose participation for too long. They also wanted to find more efficient ways of distributing the elements to large numbers of people; in short, they did not want the service to go on all day. The demands for convenience and efficiency were connected: if the sacrament became available more regularly, it could not be such a marathon production. The laity's third criterion set a direction, and indeed a limit, for whatever changes were made: the essential dignity of the service had to be maintained or, when possible, enhanced.

It was in Scotland that the greatest modifications occurred. At the beginning, sacramental seasons came only infrequently and were highly protracted events when they did. The twice-yearly communion season began on Thursday with a Fast Day. This "day of Solemn fasting and prayer,"[48] did not entail abstention from food, but rather from normal commerce and recreation, much like on Sunday. Businesses remained closed, and members were served two "diets" of preparatory worship, morning and afternoon. Because only members in good standing were permitted to receive the sacrament, they were given small metal "tokens" that admitted them to the table on Sunday. Visitors could also have a token if they produced a certificate from their home congregations. Another worship service on Saturday afternoon concluded the work of preparation.

Then, at last, the morning of the Lord's Supper arrived. Worshippers arrived to find long tables laid with white linen; if the center aisle was not wide enough, a portion of regular seating was removed to accommodate them. The service proceeded as usual with its psalms and prayers until the end of the sermon, then members moved to the tables where they turned in their tokens and received the sacrament. In all but the tiniest congregations, the tables could not seat all at once, and members approached in shifts. Because each table group was conducted as if it were a full, independent service, it could easily be four or five o'clock in the afternoon before all members had partaken of the bread and wine. At St. Andrew's, Greenock, in 1835, each of four tables heard the words of institution (I Corinthians 11:23–36), a prayer of thanksgiving, and the minister's "table address" before the elements were distributed by the elders. Then came another "address" by the minister and the singing of Psalm 89 or 103 before it was the turn of the next group to repeat the process. In Greenock, as elsewhere, communicants reassembled on Monday to conclude the communion season with a service of thanksgiving.[49]

It should surprise no one that this lavish expenditure of time and disruption of customary week-day business did not survive the transition to an industrial economy. The communion season had always been more of a rural convention; it made sense for widely scattered country folk to assemble once in the early spring before planting, once in the fall after harvest, for what was part spiritual nourishment and part local festival—a "holy fair," as it came to be known. There is testimony to the deep piety expressed in these rural gatherings. One description of a Free Church communion in the Highlands shortly after the Disruption, reported that it "lasted for five or six hours, but the audience showed no signs of being wearied; for the Holy Spirit rested upon them."[50] However, other people remembered communion seasons as anything but pious occasions. Six hours was a long time to go without food, actually longer than could be expected, and those awaiting their turn at the table wandered out in search of refreshment. In the parish of Urr, "some frugal people brought baskets of provision with them; some resorted to the ale-houses which were generally placed in convenient proximity . . . ; not infrequently, the sacrament degenerated into a merrymaking, if not a debauch."[51]

Whatever the truth or exaggeration of such conflicting memories, the communion season never fit well with the rhythm of urban life, and nineteenth-century city dwellers found it increasingly inconvenient, inefficient, and lacking in dignity. One complaint related to the twice-yearly schedule. Having only two chances for communion each year took little account of the possibility for temporary illness or unavoidable conflict. If a person missed just one occasion, the interval between communions stretched to a full year. Perhaps in scattered rural areas, that was the best the church could do, but it made no sense in cities where parishioners were close at hand and clergy were plentiful. Would it not be more convenient, laity asked, to increase the opportunities? Park Church in Glasgow added a winter communion in 1867, justifying it as a convenience to those who missed the half-yearly communion due to sickness.[52] Since the Free Church already offered its members quarterly sacramental services, it would have been difficult for the established church parishes to resist indefinitely. St. George's parish in Edinburgh was already offering four communions by the beginning of the 1860s; by the end of the 1870s, quarterly communion was available nearly everywhere.[53]

Doubling the number of communions certainly made the sacrament more accessible, but it also drew attention to difficulties surrounding the fast days. Civil authorities were unwilling to increase the number of legal holidays by declaring two more fast days. It was possible, of course, to continue with fast days before two communions but not before the third and fourth. Free Church congregations had done just that since 1843. Twice a year, they fell in step with the official fast days and held forenoon and afternoon worship; for winter and summer communion, they substituted a Thursday evening service since members were not available during the day. It was not very consistent, but then the Free Church did not expect or want support from the government. The established church found it more difficult to beg the question. Why was a fast day necessary in April and October if it was not needed in January and July? There was no good answer to be given either to communicants or to town officials. For United Presbyterian congregations celebrating six communions a year the inconsistency must have been even more apparent.

To make the matter worse, no one had any confidence that the fast days were being well used. Far from being the days of solemn fasting and prayer they once were, they had become by the 1880s occasions for railway excursions or popular amusements.[54] Some parishes broke ranks and discarded the tradition; Greyfriars in Edinburgh decided to hold "no Fast day services in the Church" in October 1885.[55] The year before, Glasgow's Govan Church, which had been celebrating monthly communion for two years, emphatically resolved that "in this Parish the Fast Day be abolished as unnecessary owing to the more frequent Celebration of Holy Communion."[56] When churches in Edinburgh were polled in 1886 about abolishing the fast days entirely, the elders at St. George's Free Church were equally decisive: the fast days, once a valuable "means of grace," should go. Most people, they admitted, now "turn them statedly to secular purposes, a source of mischief and demoralization." Elimination was simply an acknowledgement of "the altered condition of things, especially in our cities and towns." Other kirk sessions in Edinburgh sent similar replies, and the Fall 1886 Fast Day was the city's last.[57]

The end of government ordained fast days forced a shortening of the communion season; Thursday evening, not Thursday morning, was the earliest practical starting time. But quite apart from any discussion of the fast day, congregations were finding ways to condense the exhausting communion season. Every congregation had a mid-week prayer meeting, and it presented a possibility for consolidation. Instead of a separate Thursday evening preparatory service, a congregation could convert its usual Wednesday or Friday evening prayer meeting into a precommunion service. Or, the Saturday service could be consolidated with a regular Friday evening prayer meeting. Elsewhere the regular Sunday evening worship became the closing Thanksgiving service, thereby eliminating the need for a Monday service. Another tactic was to redefine the Thursday service or the Monday service (or both) as special youth services, reducing the obligations of most members. One way or another, the Scots found ways to abbreviate the communion season and make it more convenient.[58]

Of course, not only the protracted communion season came under attack; so did the day-long Sunday event itself. Efficiency-loving Scots turned their minds to finding more expeditious ways of dispensing communion. The traditional mode of several shifts taking turns around tables had little to recommend it if efficiency were the ideal. More time was spent waiting than communing. The setting up and taking down of tables was labor intensive, especially if the regular seating had to be removed. Leaving the area in front of the pulpit open year round carried its own form of inefficiency—the waste of prime seat locations for all the other Sundays.

The sequential table communion could seem undignified as well as slow. St. George's Free Church received complaints in 1862 about communicants on one side of the tables having to sit with their backs to the minister, and the deacons puzzled over whether some rearrangement might remedy the difficulty.[59] There was also the awkwardness that those returning for later tables never knew quite when to reappear and could end up waiting outside for the preceding group to vacate the tables; in urban settings, this meant waiting not in a pleasant country church yard but on a city street corner.

Not surprisingly, lay leaders looked for more expeditious ways of dispensing communion. The Seceders, before they joined with the Relief Church to become United Presbyterians, took the earliest and most forthright approach; they stopped using tables and served communion to people in their pews. Broughton Place Church in Edinburgh (founded in 1821 as a Secession Church) was the first to adopt "simultaneous communion," as the new system was called. One memoir describes eight hundred being served at once in Broughton Place: "The minister in the midst of his supporting body of elders looks grave, and weighted by a sense of responsibility. . . . All the communicants are still and attentive, many being engaged in deep devotion and silent contemplation of the meaning and mystery of Christ's sacrifice; while children look down from the galleries with wondering interest on their faces."[60] The practice, with its obvious practical advantages, spread not only to other Secession churches, but into the established church, too. Thomas Chalmers began to use "simultaneous communion" at St. John's parish church in Glasgow in 1819, and other parishes—Tron and St. George's—followed his lead. Glasgow presbytery was able to stop the system from spreading, but the precedent had been set.[61]

Given time, the awkward tables went. In Edinburgh, St. Andrew's had the empty area in front of the pulpit fitted out with fixed pews in 1878, "as the old 'Tables' for Communion were now disused." With some ingenuity, congregations found they could still keep the semblance of tables even if they were in pews. Pews could be designed with a ledge that could approximate a "table" if covered with white cloth.[62] Members still left their family pews and took places in the designated seating, but "table" was becoming more a figure of speech than an actuality.

The use of pews, even if those in the galleries and far corners of the area were not employed, markedly increased the number of communicants that could be served at one time, and consequently the number of shifts could be reduced from four or five down to three, even two. St. George's Free Church found itself in this situation in the mid-1880s. By using all the main floor pews, the elders proposed to accommodate everyone in two services, one in the morning and one in the afternoon, with an interval between. The separation between the services provided another benefit. The starting time for the second service would be fixed, and its attenders could enter the empty sanctuary at their convenience. There would be no more waiting on street corners; if parents needed to attend different services so that one could remain on home duty, they could do so "without any hurrying or uncertainty about the time." By purchasing two more cups to speed the distribution, the elders noted with satisfaction that neither forenoon nor afternoon should take much more time than "the ordinary Sabbath services."[63]

By the end of the century, either one simultaneous communion or two (morning and afternoon) communion services had become customary; the simultaneous system had perhaps an edge in efficiency, the other in convenience since members could opt for whichever hour fit their needs. The parish of St. George's, Edinburgh, had its communion tokens stamped "First Service" or "Second Service" to guarantee a smoothly running operation. In the parish of Urr, the minister proudly reported that the daylong custom of four sequential tables had been reduced to one—the "whole service kept within two hours."[64]

Although other denominations did not face such severe challenges, they also tried for greater efficiency, convenience, and dignity. Among American Presbyterians the protracted Scottish communion season was a staple of colonial practice, but it was virtually gone by the second quarter of the nineteenth century.[65] The custom of sitting around tables lingered longer among the more tradition-oriented United Presbyterians; Pittsburgh's Fourth United Presbyterian Church did not give up its tables until 1893.[66] Outside Scotland, there was only a single preparatory service, usually on Friday evening, though it was sometimes placed on Wednesday or Thursday to coincide with the regular mid-week prayer meeting; American Presbyterians and Congregationalists in both nations, followed this pattern.

Some of these congregations planned communion as a separate afternoon service, but most chose to place it "at the close of the morning service." In the interest of time, the ordinary morning service could be abbreviated; in Philadelphia, a congregation omitted one hymn, the reading of the Ten Commandments, and one Scripture lesson on communion Sundays.[67] As the century went along, more Americans tended to have the communion take the place of the ordinary Sunday morning service rather than follow it. English Congregationalists stayed with the end-of-service practice, but added flexibility by holding at least some of the monthly communions after the evening service for those who had difficulty attending in the morning.[68] Members at Lyndhurst Road Congregational Church in London petitioned the deacons for a week-day morning option, arguing also for convenience.[69]

A special case of convenience applied to those confined to their homes by illness—"disabled by sickness," as one session clerk put it.[70] The Puritans had banned home communion, arguing that the sacrament had validity only within the full community. American Presbyterians reauthorized home communion during the 1860s, but congregations were sparing in its use.[71] It seems to have been taken out only in exceptional situations, and session clerks recorded each recipient's name and circumstances—Miss Irving "who was sick at City Hospitle" or Miss Nevins, "an Invalid for several years [who] had expressed a very strong desire to have the Sacrament of the Lord's Supper administered to her today."[72] In Scotland, the Free Church likewise administered "private communion" only in exceptional situations—Miss Mackenzie, "one of our oldest members and who was in weak health" or Miss Brittain "who is very ill."[73] In time, the exceptions became an expected routine. Scotland's established church carried communion routinely to shut-in members by the first decade of the twentieth century, with clerks simply noting that communion had gone out to the "aged and infirm" following quarterly communion.[74]

Before ending this discussion of sacramental practice, we need to examine three other traditional customs—communion tokens, fermented wine, and the common cup—that came into conflict with important nineteenth-century movements. The tokens fell into disuse because they did not meet the age's desire for efficiency and order. Church leaders wanted a system that would accomplish two things: keep non-members from the table and reveal which members were present and which were not. These small coins were distributed prior to communion Sunday and then were collected at the table as the individual's token of admission—no token, no communion. So far, so good; the tokens appeared to have satisfied one of their purposes. After the service was over, the elders or deacons counted the tokens and did a little simple arithmetic. If they had distributed, say, 300 and got 295 back, they knew five were absent. The problem was, which five? In theory, any one who received a token and was unable to use it was supposed to return it with an explanation. But this did not always happen, which was a problem for those trying to keep an attendance roll. It also meant that there were in circulation tokens that could not be accounted for. The occasional discovery of a token from another congregation simply emphasized that the system was not foolproof.

The solution, so efficiency-minded leaders pointed out, was to use cards on which members' names could be written. King's Weigh House adopted a card system in 1834, which Binney saw would help in "ascertaining the attendance of the Members." A book of twelve "tickets," a year's supply, was delivered to homes by the deacons.[75] A card system became standard practice among English Congregationalists and improved the accuracy of their attendance rolls. The only difficulty, which surfaced virtually everywhere, was people's forgetting their cards; the common remedy, written into local by-laws, was that "the member's name should be written on a slip of paper and placed in the box."[76] The obvious advantages of the card system made it popular in Scotland and America, too. In 1846, St. George's Free Church gave cards a first trial, and "the accuracy and general efficiency of the plan were approved by the Session."[77] This congregation, like others in Scotland, continued to pass out the sentimental tokens as well, although in time the redundancy of cards and tokens was ended.[78]

Some of the obstacles to a smoothly functioning card system disappeared as congregations became less concerned about keeping the unworthy from the table. Beecher's Plymouth Church in Brooklyn had open communion from an early date; one member recalled that the congregation welcomed to the table "all who loved the Saviour, whatever their formal creed or church connection, or even if they were without any creed or connection."[79] If the only function of the card was to record members' attendance, not to fence the table, then supplies of cards could simply be made available in the pews, which was the practice in Second

Presbyterian Church, Philadelphia, in 1881. The was no problem with forgotten cards; members wrote their name on the blank card and left it lying in the pew, from which it was gathered up after the service. The same system was in place in Birmingham's Moseley Road Congregational Church, which announced that "all Christians are cordially welcomed to this Service"; the cards in this case simply provided an reliable attendance record.[80]

A second old custom, the use of fermented wine, came into conflict with one of the century's widespread social reform movements. The temperance movement impacted all Reformed congregations to one extent or another, from lukewarm support to whirlwind activity. Inevitably, they had to confront the question of alcoholic wine in their communion cup, and responses varied. When the session of St. George's Free Church received a notice from the British Women's Temperance Association calling for an elimination of intoxicating wine at the Lord's Supper, the elders quietly "decline[d] to take any action." But other congregations put aside wine for grape juice. In Billerica, Massachusetts, a Congregational church wrote a prohibition of fermented wine into its by-laws. In 1903, the Free church in Airdrie abandoned its "usual port wine."[81]

Palatability seems to have been an important counterweight to temperance sentiments. In 1882, Central Presbyterian Church, Rochester, sent two elders on a tasting expedition before agreeing to change to unfermented wine.[82] The deacons at Lyndhurst Road heard complaints about the quality of what they were serving, and agreed that "the [unfermented] Wine now in use at the Communion Service might well be improved upon, and, on the suggestion of Mr. Horton, it was decided to order some specimen bottles of unfermented Wine as prepared specially by Mr. Frank Wright of High St., Kensington."[83]

The results of the Lyndhurst Road tasting were not recorded, but an episode in Edinburgh showed how divisive the issue could be. In 1873, sixty members of the Newington United Presbyterian Church petitioned the session for a switch to unfermented wine. The elders agreed, "provided that a really suitable wine could be obtained." None met the elders' taste, and the traditional wine stayed. Three years later, the temperance party petitioned again, this time asking for the "introduction of two different cups at Communion." The elders balked, perhaps because two cups was an altogether too obvious symbol of just how divided the congregation had become. Instead, the elders promised "to make use in future of the lightest wine brought into the country." It was not enough. The anti-alcohol faction, including two of the elders, separated to form a new congregation where their temperance principles would not be compromised.[84]

The communion cup—the cup itself in this case, not its contents—was a third communion custom that came under fierce attack at the end of the century. Sharing the same cup with other communicants was a powerful symbol of Christian unity, but it also ran counter to what church-goers now knew about germs and communicable disease. The proposed alternative was passing trays of tiny individual cups made of brass, aluminum, or glass.

Two persons later claimed to have thought of the individual cup idea first. John G. Thomas was a Welsh-born Congregational minister with medical as well as theological training, who was by the 1890s retired and living in Lima, Ohio. He was an advocate of individual cups, and in 1894 he patented a contraption capable of filling twenty-four at once.[85] Also in 1894, Central Presbyterian Church in Rochester, New York, started using individual cups, a practice its elders declared "in every way satisfactory" after a first trial in May.[86] Among upstate New Yorkers it was accepted knowledge that Central's pastor, Henry H. Stebbins, was "the originator of the individual communion cup idea."[87]

Advertisements from the manufacturers of the tiny cups and trays soon appeared in religious periodicals. The Thomas Communion Service Company of Lima, Ohio, touted its system as one which "betokens cleanliness and good manners, and is a safeguard of health"; the company promised that "a complete outfit will be sent any church for trial upon request." The Sanitary Communion Outfit, produced in Rochester, was promoted with the query, "Why do you permit a custom at the communion table which you would not tolerate in your own home?"[88]

Churches were intrigued with the advertisements, but change came slowly. Congregations had a great deal invested, financially as well as emotionally, in their finely crafted communion ware. Many of the tankards, cups, and platters (made of pewter or silver, depending on the church's financial resources) were intrinsically valuable works of art; they were likely to have been donated as family memorials, too. In addition, some congregations had only recently invested in additional silver to speed along the distribution of communion. So there was a strong sense of what was being lost as well as gained. In Philadelphia, the Second Presbyterian Church debated for two years before switching to individual cups in 1902.[89] In Helensburgh, Scotland, a congregational vote in 1906 was almost equally divided: 109 for individual cups, 105 against, and 25 "willing" to change. Such a slim majority was not deemed sufficient, and the church delayed. In the end, however, the concern for health proved irresistible; in 1912 the congregation opted for individual cups and for good measure decided its communion bread should be "cut into cubes" rather than presented as a whole loaf from which people tore pieces.[90]

The decision for individual cups was not made easily in Boston's Old South Church either. The congregation took up the matter quickly enough: it was less than a year after the little cups were first used in Ohio and New York that Old South appointed six men and five women to investigate. The committee's lengthy report, submitted in January 1896, recommended adoption of the new system. The argument was a medical one: "the discoveries and investigations of the last fifteen or twenty years have shown clearly that diseases are communicated by micro-organisms which enter the system in many instances though the mouth." The writers concluded there was a "small" but "real" danger of consumption, sore throat, diphtheria, even syphilis, and this was enough to "warrant a change." In a strict sense, they added, the common cup was already gone; for speed, Old South was using twenty cups, not one, and the new system would be simply a "multiplication."[91]

Ten committee members had signed the report; one man, Henry Hyde, circulated a minority report. Hyde argued that one cup was the Lord's way, that individual cups were a fad perpetrated by companies trying to sell new equipment, and that the danger of contagion was no greater than in a street car. But Hyde's essential point was the value of tradition. He could not bear to give up the church's historic silver chalices which dated as far back as 1730. How could one not be inspired by touching the same cup as the saints of old?[92] When the members voted at the end of November 1896, Hyde's views carried.[93]

But they did not prevail forever. At Old South, as elsewhere, so much of the old communion service had already disappeared that it was difficult to sustain any argument against change. The congregation accepted individual cups in 1915. Looking back, the preamble to the original 1896 report was correct, if a bit premature, in its understanding of what was happening to the church's worship. "The changes in population that have taken place in our large cities and towns during the last two decades," the report contended, "have made necessary many changes in our manner of living with the result that customs which were once venerated and revered on account of their associations have been modified and in many instances become obsolete." This was true in the culture at large, and it was equally true in religion. "In our church life," the majority report continued, "many changes have also been made. Our services, our singing, even our definition of many of the important truths have been restated, so as to conform to a broader apprehension." The change to individual cups was "simply a natural one growing out of the general movement."[94]

No one considered one morning service of worship a sufficient diet for the Lord's Day, even on non-Communion Sundays. Every congregation added an afternoon or evening service, and these, too, were affected by the general movement that the Old South committee had noticed. In earlier days, three services—morning, afternoon, and evening—would not have been unusual, and in a very few places this was still the case in the nineteenth century. But it took a very large or a very committed body of worshippers to sustain three services. The extra service took its toll on the clergy, too, and unless there were two ministers, one service was likely to devolve into an informal prayer meeting led by a deacon or elder.[95]

Two services, however, were expected—one in the morning and another either in the afternoon or evening. Evening services were the more common, with 6:30 o'clock being the typical hour in Britain and 7:30 o'clock the choice in America. Worshippers were more likely to find afternoon worship early in the century before Sunday afternoon was reserved for other activities, either religious ones like Sunday School and mission work or secular ones like family and leisure. By 1900, an evening hour was the overwhelming choice.

In form, the second worship experience was nearly identical to the forenoon service; at Brooklyn's Clinton Congregational Church in 1875 the only differences were the substitution of a choral anthem for the opening prayer of invocation, and the shifting of the doxology from the start of the service to the end of the responsive reading.[96] Where the morning service had taken on high church characteristics, the evening services generally remained less formal; Philadelphia's Second Presbyterian Church, for instance, dispensed with the Doxology, the Commandments, the Lord's Prayer—and also the collection.[97] Some ministers referred to their evening words as a lecture rather than a sermon, implying more freedom to address a missionary subject or another topic of current relevance.

At the beginning of the Victorian period, there was little question that members were expected to be present for the second service. The 1835 handbook for Carr's Lane members said plainly, "No professing christian should allow himself to be satisfied with only one service on the sabbath, unless prevented by age, infirmity, or distance, from attending twice."[98] But by the middle years of the century, it was clear that the obligation was lessening. St Paul's Chapel in Hawley Road, London, told its members that "*if* they also attend in the evening (a helpful and useful custom)," they might invite some of the unchurched to accompany them.[99]

When attendance dropped, church boards puzzled and worried and tried as best they knew to adapt. One common response was to search for a more convenient hour. Those with afternoon services moved them to evening, perhaps first only for the summer, but eventually year round. Church boards tried moving a service a half hour one way or the other to see if that helped.[100] In cities, the second worship service often stopped for the summer months; it was partly a concession to vacation schedules and the heat, but it was also an acknowledgement that members were apt to be otherwise engaged on a warm summer evening. The payoff for juggling worship hours was usually not as great as the church officers had hoped. The Free College Church on Lynedoch Street in Glasgow switched to an evening service and gained no significant increase in attendance; the sole advantage was that those who had always attended now came "more free from physical exhaustion, owing to the longer interval." With considerable truth, the elders concluded, "It is to be feared that the cause [of poor attendance] lies deeper than in any matter connected with the particular hour of worship."[101]

Lay leaders tended to think of the problem as one of marketing. They tried better advertising—posters, circulars left in the pews, or verbal encouragement from the pulpit. A second, and usually helpful, approach was to declare all the rented seats free and open for the evening service. More significantly, church boards worked to make the service more appealing. The Congregationalists in Lyndhurst Road continually struggled to make the service "more real & stimulating." By 1913, they were using a brass band to gather up those returning from Sunday outings on Hampstead Heath, leading them to the church and entertaining them with a lantern slide presentation rather than a sermon.[102]

Although not many went that far, the problem was widespread. In 1885, the elders at Central Presbyterian, Rochester, gave the pastor liberty to alter the order "to increase the interest and power of the Service." For this evangelical congregation, the result was the purchase of Moody-Sankey hymnals to liven up the singing.[103] However, three fashionable East Coast congregations chose an opposite musical direction to reinvigorate their evening services. First Congregational Church in Hartford, Brick Presbyterian Church in New York City, and Second Presbyterian in Philadelphia all moved their evening service to 4:00 or 4:30 P.M., renamed it vespers and loaded it with elegant liturgy and sophisticated music from professional choirs. The Hartford church reported its success succinctly: "Vespers thronged."[104]

Understood one way, the congregations were seeking to redefine themselves in a new environment; some settled on revival hymns, others on Handel. Understood another way, they were trying to find a market niche. The difficulties were no smaller when they began to consider their mid-week prayer meetings and worship services targeted to special audiences, but that is the tale of the next chapter. Already, we have seen worship for the Lord's Day transformed so that the devotional and didactic elements achieved a new balance. Theological tradition was part of that story, but so were demands for dignity, good taste, efficiency, comfort, and convenience.

# fou̇r

## "Without Ceasing"
*Prayer Meetings and Occasional Services*

The principal Sunday services were not the only occasions for public worship. When the Congregationalists in Carr's Lane opened their 1835 members' handbook, they found both an exhortation and a rationale for additional meetings. "The week day services," they were told, "are of considerable importance as aids to religion, tending, as they certainly do, to check the encroachments of the world, and the increase of earthly-mindedness. No professing christian who can spare the time, ought to neglect these opportunities."[1]

The standard mid-week service options were the lecture and the prayer meeting. The *lecture* was a devotional service of prayer, song, and scripture reading that featured a substantial address on a spiritual or mission-related topic by the pastor. The *prayer meeting* was also a devotional gathering including song and brief commentary on a passage of scripture, but its most important activity was the offering of prayers by the leader or by others who felt moved to pray.

A few ambitious congregations held one of each, at least early in the period, but the more common pattern was a combined lecture-prayer meeting, a sort of hybrid of the two. Various names were given to the amalgam. The obvious "Lecture and Prayer Meeting" was the choice of Second Presbyterian Church in Philadelphia, while Edgbaston Congregational Church in Birmingham used the equally straightforward "Prayer Meeting and Address." Brick Presbyterian Church gave its members an indication of what the minister intended to do with the lecture when it advertised "Bible Study, Prayer, and Song"; the tone was clear, if different, at Cowcaddens Free Church, too, when it billed its service as an "Evangelistic Meeting." In Rochester, New Hampshire, the Congregational church wanted to emphasize the opportunity for individual spiritual consultation with the pastor at the end of the service, and so its service was known as the "Prayer and Conference Meeting"; the deacons at Union Park Congregational Church in Chicago, not wanting to omit anything, asked its members to assemble for "Prayer,

Praise, Conference, and Bible Study." Others chose plainer words and called it the "devotional meeting" or the "Midweek Service" or, still more simply, "Worship."[2]

Prayer meetings had their own conventions and rules of etiquette. In the first place, they were understood to be meetings for church members, not the public at large. When members of the Bowdoin Street Church in Boston met on Friday evenings for "devotional exercises and religious conference," visitors could be admitted only by a "special vote" of the membership.[3] Legalism of this sort was unusual and generally unnecessary; prayer meetings were not likely to draw a wide audience anyway, and even where congregations were more flexible and open, these remained primarily in-house events. It was the church community gathered as a family, and it was often referred to as the "social prayer meeting" or "social meeting" in recognition of its interpersonal dimension. In this sense, then, it sat midway between wholly public worship and the private family or individual devotions that took place in the home.

Prayer meetings were believed to carry great value for the individual participants and the church. An 1835 handbook for Carr's Lane members maintained that a "well conducted" prayer meeting had multiple benefits:

> It tends to keep alive the spirit of devotion—demonstrates, by the prayers of so many brethren who engage, the minor varieties, yet prevailing uniformity, of christian experience,—humbles the rich by the holy gifts and graces of the poor—encourages the poor by the sympathies, confessions, and acknowledgements of the rich—cheers the heart of the minister by the kind interest and fervent supplications of his flock—cements the minds of the members,—and may be supposed to bring down the blessings of God upon the church, which is thus united in supplication, and also upon all those varied objects which the church bears before God in believing prayer.[4]

The components of a prayer meeting varied slightly depending on the size of the group and the formality of the occasion. At Second Presbyterian Church in Chicago, the prayers were always preceded by the reading and expounding of scripture by the minister or lay leader, after which "invitation [was] then given to others for remark or exhortation."[5] Psalm singing was another typical accompaniment because the psalms exemplified all the components of prayer— adoration, confession, petition, intercession, and thanksgiving. Extempore prayers were then offered by a number of participants, who may or may not have been appointed ahead of time.

The quality of the prayers no doubt varied. One person, writing about the prayer meetings of his Shropshire boyhood, recalled a man who prayed interminably and another who prayed "so we always knew what was coming. He began with his 'native town,' then wandered abroad to various 'mission fields,' and after mentioning pretty well all the countries in the world would return home and finish by asking a blessing on 'Thy servant our pastor.' "[6] Perhaps because of such dangers, Carr's Lane provided six rules for its members who engaged in prayer. First, "*prayers should be short*," not exceeding ten minutes. No one should try to "embrace all the topics that are usually brought into our devotions"; one or two per person was enough. Prayers should be spoken "*sufficiently loud to be heard by all, but not so loud as to be unpleasant.*" Prayers should avoid "*all poetry*" and flowery language. Fifth, "when the prayer is obviously *coming to a conclusion* it should not *be renewed again* because something else has come into the person's mind." Finally, prayers should be "in the strictest sense *prayers*, and not *preaching.*"[7]

There was an implicit seventh rule—that only male members should voice their prayers; Carr's Lane had, after all, preceded the six recommendations with a reference to "the brethren" who engaged in prayer. The issue of women's participation in prayer meetings was a troublesome one for nineteenth-century congregations. While these groups traditionally had taken to heart St. Paul's admonition that women should be silent in church, the matter was no longer routine. Revivalists during the Second Great Awakening encouraged women's prayers, and women prayed in various circumstances—Sunday Schools, missions, women's organizations, family devotions—which if not technically "in church" were certainly church related. Some made a distinction between public worship and social prayer meetings, arguing that the rules of family devotions were more applicable to the latter and hence women might participate. Others drew a line between single-sex and mixed (or "promiscuous") prayer meetings, and accepted women's participation in the former only.

Congregationalists operated according to local option and thus women's opportunities varied, but women's prayers generally remained unwelcome when men were present.[8] The main American Presbyterian body in 1832 took a firm stand against women's praying in "promiscuous" meetings, but in 1874 softened its position by allowing local churches the option of permitting women to pray during the "social prayer-meeting," but not during formal Sunday worship.[9] Certainly by the end of the century, restrictions on women's participation in prayer meetings had diminished in all these demoninations. What we do not know, however, is how many women felt comfortable enough with their newly won freedom to stand and pray during the church's midweek service even though they typically comprised a substantial majority of those present.

The main congregational prayer meeting was seldom the only one of the week; other meetings were held to accommodate the needs of special groups within the congregation, or to respond to a particular crisis or need. In 1856, Chicago's Second Presbyterian Church had its general prayer meeting on Saturday evening, but there was another held by "the young men of the Church" on Sunday morning prior to regular morning worship, and during the week, there were "one, and sometimes two Female prayer meetings . . . held at private residences." In addition, there was a monthly "concert of prayer" for missions and a second one for the denomination's colleges and seminaries.[10]

Women and youth, two groups apt to feel shut out of equal participation in the general prayer meeting, were the most likely to hold separate prayer meetings, but Redland Park Congregational Church held a special prayer meeting for "working men" of Bristol at 7:30 A.M. Monday as they were on their way to start another week's labor.[11] Youth services were occasionally scheduled for a weekday evening, but toward the end of the century, the hour just before Sunday evening worship became more popular. Women's meetings were typically afternoon assemblies, with Friday being the most common day of choice. Like their counterparts elsewhere, the women of Third Presbyterian Church, Chicago, rotated their meetings among private homes until, later in the century, a church building project provided a "parlor" for their meetings.[12]

Women were not the only ones to hold prayer meetings in homes; in the 1840s, young men at St. George's Free Church in Edinburgh showed a "marked increase of seriousness" and began some spontaneous "private prayer meetings."[13] Where elders or deacons were assigned care of a district, organizing home prayer meetings in their corner of the parish was part of that responsibility. At Cowcaddens Free Church, the elders saw their "kitchen prayer meetings" as part of the congregation's thriving evangelistic work.[14]

When congregations were confronted with a crisis or felt a strong spiritual need, they called extra prayer meetings. Philadelphia's Second Presbyterian Church, as we have already noted, set aside a day of "fasting, humiliation, and prayer" as it embarked on the search for a new minister in 1833.[15] A year later, the illness of a pastor was reason for a "day of fasting, humiliation, & prayer" in Boston.[16] An impending epidemic or natural disaster could lead to a day of prayer. The threat of cholera—"the calamity with which [God] seems about to visit this land"— caused churches in Boston and Glasgow to call for prayer.[17] Fast days, connected to civic crises or to what church leaders perceived to be a "low state of religion among us," were a New England tradition. The day commenced with "individual members of the Church . . . in private devotion in the morning"; later, during the afternoon, there was a prayer meeting and, in the evening, a preaching service.[18]

During the last third of the century, public pleading for special divine intervention faded under the influence of more moderate theology and an increasing preference for privacy in spiritual expression.[19] At the outbreak of World War I, Glasgow's Park Church illustrated the newer tendency when it arranged only to open the sanctuary for private prayer daily from two o'clock until dusk for the duration of the war.[20]

Not every special prayer meeting disappeared; there were a few programs, such as the Monthly Concert of Prayer for Missions that kept or even gained popularity over the course of the century. This habit of a special monthly prayer meeting to solicit prayers for the "conversion of the world" was begun at Park Street Congregational Church, Boston, in 1826, and the concept spread widely until it became a primary forum for the century's powerful missionary impulse. In time, however, the Monthly Concert focused less on prayer and more on "missionary intelligence" and fund raising; in Chicago in 1887, forty minutes of the hour went to reports of missionary activities locally and worldwide.[21]

The special prayer services appointed at the new year, either on Watch Night (New Year's Eve) or the morning of New Year's Day, also maintained their appeal and indeed gained momentum from an increased willingness to acknowledge holidays.[22] The beginning of January was an occasion in some congregations for a weeklong series of prayer meetings. At Lyndhurst Road, the London Missionary Society's "self-denial week" was a January event. In Rochester, congregations began at the end of the American Civil War to mark the first week of each new year with nightly prayer services of an evangelistic nature, and the services continued long enough to celebrate a new century.[23]

There was, of course, an intimate connection between the prayer meeting and the revival, more so earlier than later. The relationship was reciprocal: revivals often emerged from intense prayer meetings, and a multiplication of prayer meetings was an important evidence of revival. When a revival swept through the Scottish fishing village of Buckie in 1860, "churches were thronged, Sabbath attendances were greatly augmented, [and] prayer meetings were numerous and numerously attended."[24] In Chicago, an "unusual descent of the Holy Spirit" was connected with "a daily morning prayer meeting from 8 to 9 o'clock," and after three months of prayer there were twenty-five new members drawn into the church.[25]

Revival techniques transferred back to the regular congregational prayer meetings, too. One easily adapted measure was the opportunity for religious conversation at the close of a service; an "after meeting," as it was called, could be attached to the end of the weekly lecture-prayer meeting or the Sunday evening worship service. One St. Louis congregation announced in its manual that every

Sunday after the evening service, "all serious persons wishing to converse with the Pastor or Elders about the salvation of their souls, have an opportunity of doing so, and are made subjects of special prayer."[26]

By the 1870s, however, both revivals and prayer meetings had changed in ways that altered the bond between them. Whereas revivals might once have sprung spontaneously from prayer meetings, now they started with the arrival of a virtuoso evangelist—Moody, Chapman, or some lesser luminary. In 1894 when two Rochester congregations decided it was time for a revival, their first concern was to "engage an Evangelist to conduct special services in March 1895."[27] By way of contrast, back in 1859 when Canning Street Presbyterian Church in Liverpool heard about revivals in Ireland, it had responded by "joining in supplication for 'the outpouring of the Holy Spirit.' "[28] Prayer meetings were still organized before and after the star's appearance, but they were quite secondary to the main performance.

Under pressure to be more interesting and more attractive to members, prayer meetings themselves were changing. Mission-centered prayer meetings, as we have already noted, adapted by highlighting exotic foreign lands, perhaps enhanced by an illustrated presentation. Prayer meetings that served women and youth evolved gradually into project-oriented associations or purely social activities.

The congregation's general prayer meeting had more difficulty redefining itself. The stated expectation was that all members would attend these meetings, and this was made explicit in congregational by-laws and members' handbooks during the first half of the century. "Every member is expected to be present, unless Providence prevents," said one American manual.[29] An English manual drew a sharp portrait of those who ignored prayer meeting: "such persons may be *church members,* but it is a serious doubt if they are *christians.*"[30]

Actual attendance, however, had never come close to fulfilling the stated expectations. St. George's Free Church, for instance, managed a turnout of only about 20 percent in 1846, and that in an unusually vibrant, committed congregation still flushed with the zeal of Disruption.[31] Congregations recognized this reality by scheduling midweek meetings in the smaller 'lecture room' or chapel rather than in the main sanctuary, and on both sides of the Atlantic church officers and pastors lamented low attendance. A group of Philadelphia elders wondered in 1882 what to do about "unsatisfactory attendance" at their Friday night prayer meetings. Four years later in Manchester, England, a pastor was regretting that his congregation's turnout was "so scanty"; he partly consoled himself by noting that it was a problem "in common with most Churches."[32]

Leaders understood some of the reasons behind the problem, and they did what they could to improve attendance. Although they tried exhortations and sent out reminders, they sensed that simple inattention to duty was not a very significant factor; there were legitimate barriers to attendance. One was certainly what a Boston congregation termed "the world & the business & the cares of the world." Churches in a town cooperated to minimize conflicts with business, civic, and cultural functions by setting a common night for their mid-week services. For instance, Friday was marked off for church activities in Brooklyn and Boston, and Wednesday was church night in Chicago, Birmingham, and Manchester. Churches also experimented to find more convenient meeting hours; two churches, in Philadelphia and Edinburgh, moved evening prayer meetings to five o'clock, hoping to catch people on the way home from work.[33] In New York City, Brick Church served a noontime lunch followed by a twenty minute daily service to attract city workers.[34]

But church leaders also sensed that even the most conflict-free, convenient schedule would not necessarily guarantee large audiences for mid-week prayer meeting; the service itself had ceased to excite. The deacons at Lyndhurst Road were not alone in wondering what they could do "to make it more attractive & useful." Part of the trouble was that prayer meetings often were conducted by lay officers—"led in turn by the brethren" was the way it was explained.[35] Whether lay leadership should have or not, it made prayer meetings seem less important. What members wanted was an address by the pastor—a sterling lecture or sermon, not merely a "short devotional address" by a lay leader and amateur prayers by their peers.[36] Parker's thirty to forty minute sermons could draw a thousand hearers into City Temple for a weekly noon hour service on Thursdays.[37] But mid-week services based on participatory prayer found it hard to compete in a world where public events were dominated by virtuoso performers. With good reason, Brick Church's brief mid-day service featured organ and soloist. In England, the Rev. James Williamson thought perhaps he needed to introduce "a more varied interest" by giving talks about great missionary adventures, with maps for illustration.[38]

Williamson worried, too, about the competition from an increasing variety of educational and cultural events offered in the city. In truth, he admitted, "many of our Congregation are usefully employed both in teaching and in receiving instruction elsewhere during the week evenings, especially of the winter months." However commendable, these activities "*compete* though they do not *conflict*" with the work of the church; the truth, he acknowledged, was that "the services of the Church do not hold the same relative position" that they once did.[39]

What Williamson should have noticed, however, was that the competition came as much, if not more, from inside the church as without. His own congregation had a popular, weekly "literary and discussion association" as well as other activities and groups. In the 1820s and 1830s, the prayer meeting was typically the only church event scheduled for a weekday, or at most it was one of two or three. By the end of the century, however, active congregations scheduled dozens of events every week—clubs, musicales, literary groups, athletics, craft workshops, and volunteer work with the poor. As we shall see in Part 2, turn-of-the-century churches were filled with busy activities, and the central position of the mid-week prayer meeting was lost as much to competing church work as to anything secular.

The midweek service was still part of congregations' weekly schedules in 1914, but the language in members' handbooks reflected its more marginal position. Lyndhurst Road's manual that year carried none of the old, demanding language; it said only, "It is earnestly desired that a larger number should be present to share in the manifest blessings which have been experienced by those who have regularly attended."[40] The expression was more a wish than an expectation.

Children provided still different challenges to those responsible for worship. The nineteenth century marked a turning point in society's understanding of children.[41] An older Calvinist tradition that stressed strong external discipline was giving way to new approaches that emphasized self-control. Small boys and girls were believed to be highly impressionable, and particularly so when it came to religion. Not surprisingly, church leaders increased their attention to children's roles within the congregation.

If the traditional worship service, with its long prayers and longer sermon, proved too arduous for some adults, it was even less suitable for small children. One solution was the insertion of a brief children's sermon into the adult service so that each family member could each find something attractive and beneficial. At the end of the 1860s, one denominational newspaper, imagining the plight of children who sat through one-and-a-half hours of church after an hour or more of Sunday School, recommended "a pause" in the sermon during which the preacher spoke suitably to children before returning to his regular discourse.[42] The practice caught on in a number of places, although in Huddersfield's Congregational Church and most other places, the children's talk was "in addition to" rather than in the middle of the sermon. In Rochester, the five-minute children's sermon came "at the opening of the regular sermon." In Philadelphia, Second Presbyterian Church chose a "children's hymn" to precede the short talk, as did Regent Square Presbyterian Church in London.[43] Writing in 1880, one chronicler of worship changes in Scotland reported that children's sermons were used "in not a few churches . . . [and had] proved highly acceptable, not only to parents, but to the people in general."[44]

A second, more ambitious approach was a separate worship service designed entirely with children in mind. In one variation of this concept, the service ran simultaneously with the congregation's forenoon worship; adults went to their service, children went to "children's church." Since the pastor was busy with the main worship service, lay leadership was required for such an undertaking. For this, the Sunday School could be counted on. Typically, congregations operated one or more mission Sunday Schools in addition to their home Sunday School, and the mission school often included a "Children's Forenoon Service" designed to draw children into the mission hall on Sunday morning. Once the techniques for managing the behavior and holding the attention of a crowd of street children had been mastered, it was not difficult to adapt the program for the home church youngsters.[45]

It was also possible to schedule children's church later in the day so that it could be led by the pastor. Charteris held a children's meeting in the afternoon between his two regular Park Church services; at Lozells Church in Birmingham, an average of 255 children met from six to seven o'clock on Sunday evening. Not every minister was able to manage, or thought it necessary to have, a weekly service. In Glasgow at the Free College Church and in Pittsburgh at Fourth United Presbyterian, children's worship was held once a month. In Edinburgh's Barclay Free Church, children's services occurred only quarterly.[46]

Third Presbyterian Church in Chicago described its children's service as singing, prayer, a responsive reading of Scripture, and "a short discourse." John Macleod, minister of the Govan Church in Glasgow, designed a service that took advantage of the children's recitation abilities. The Beatitudes were a weekly feature, and it is easy to imagine even the smallest child learning to chime in on the second half of each verse after it had been started by others. Children also recited the Lord's Prayer and the Apostles' Creed, thereby learning skills they would need later for adult worship. Macleod's own prayers, written out beforehand, were short, the longest extending to no more than a minute and a half.[47]

Preaching to children did not come naturally to many pastors, and some of the best children's sermons were published as aids for other ministers or lay leaders. Judging by the sales figures, parents bought the volumes, too, and read them aloud to family gatherings; the collections by Wilson of the Barclay Free Church, Edinburgh, sought to maximize home sales by providing a hymn (printed full-staff) and closing prayer to go with each sermon. Other popular authors were James Wells, pastor of Pollokshields Church, Glasgow, and Episcopalian Richard Newton, rector of St. Paul's Church, Philadelphia. English Congregationalist Eustace R. Conder's "Talks with Children" were serialized monthly in the *Congregationalist* during 1879. The sermons were filled with stories and every day examples and were conversational in tone. They were not, however, particularly short; Wilson recommended that parents read only half at one sitting for home devotions. Of course, their original effectiveness would have depended on the manner in which they were delivered, and Wilson lamented that when reproduced in written form, "the principal charm of addresses to the young, viz., liveliness of tone and manner, the throwing in of supplementary remarks on the spur of the moment, and the occasional use of illustrative objects" was lost.[48]

Each sermon carried a practical, moral point. The characters in Wells's *Bible Children* (1885) illustrated how to live, or how not to live. Miriam, for instance, "trusted in God . . . [and] loved her family." Although Wells managed a reassuring ending for his sermons, a substantial part of each was a graphic warning of the consequences of disobedience.[49] Wilson's sermons were much more reaffirming; his goal, he said, was to "make the morning of life bright and joyous, as well as pure and earnestly Christian."[50] His sermon "What Would Jesus Do?" began with a story of Orkney and Shetland seafarers who always carried a mariner's compass. Wilson told the children he wanted to give them "a kind of *spiritual mariner's compass.*" The Bible was too big to fit into their pockets, "so carry with you the question or motto "What would Jesus do?" Wilson added examples, including this one on lying, to illustrate how their compasses might work: "I can hardly fancy that any of those whom I address, can be in the habit of telling downright, open, and deliberate, unblushing lies,—of saying *Yes,* when they know they should say *No*. But sometimes you are tempted to equivocate, to deceive, to pretend to be what you are not. . . . Jesus never dreamt of doing such a thing. . . . You *should* ask, '*What would Jesus do?*' "[51]

Children and holidays went well together, and Victorian celebrations often featured special services for the youngsters. In Bristol, the children of Redland Park Congregational Church assembled on May Day morning at seven o'clock for the annual "Flower Service for the Young."[52] The idea of Children's Day, a festival dedicated entirely to childhood, gained a following in the 1880s; American Presbyterians appointed the second Sunday of June for such a celebration in 1885. In Lansdowne United Presbyterian Church in Glasgow, Children's Day meant that all the youngsters attended the regular worship service (the session clerk noted they were "attentive and orderly"). In many places, the day's activities included the baptism of infants and the presentation of Bibles to seven year olds.[53]

Christmas was a time for children's programs, too. It was "*the* holiday of the year," according to one religious newspaper in 1856; the "little ones" were up at dawn to unwrap the gifts that "Christmas has brought them" and greetings for "a happy Christmas" were exchanged by all. It was also a time to give charity to orphans and the poor. The "Family Circle" story in the Christmas 1856 issue of the *American Presbyterian* portrayed a family that had just gathered round its holiday tree laden with gifts when the young daughter chanced to look out the window and see a lone child huddled against the wind; as the story unfolded, the girl and her siblings volunteered some of their own presents, and the father carried the charity to the street child's home.[54]

While, as we have noted, general congregational Christmas services were not found until the last quarter of the century, children's programs preceded them by a decade or more. In London, the New Broad Street Congregational Church held a Sunday School breakfast on Christmas morning during the mid-1850s. Beginning with the 1862 season, in Glasgow's Bellgrove United Presbyterian Church, "the young people got presents of articles supplied by the congregation and friends, and hung up on a large Christmas Tree"; at the end of devotional exercises on New Year's Day, each child went forward and picked something from the tree. For the first time in 1873, the chapel at Boston's Old South was "decorated for the use of the Sabbath School who are to hold Christmas Services," and there was "no one voting in opposition," the clerk noted.[55]

Bethany Presbyterian Church, where Philadelphia merchant John Wanamaker led the Sunday School, developed children's Christmas programs into extravaganzas. On Christmas Day 1887, the school sponsored a "Children's and Parents' Celebration in the evening" (there was also a "School Donation Party" the following morning "with gifts for the poor, the orphans and the sick"). The program opened with music by the organ and orchestra, and then was carried along by a mix of nine carols, four responsive readings, musical selections from a soloist and the infant school children, five recitations, two dramatic dialogues, the Christmas story rendered by the pastors, the offering and doxology, and the benediction—all before a climatic ending of "Come Hither, Ye Faithful" performed by organ, orchestra, choirs, and congregation to the tune *Adeste Fideles.*[56]

Holidays were not only for children, of course, and congregations observed their midweek occurrence with special services. Harvest Thanksgiving was celebrated in British churches during the late Victorian period, but it paled in comparison to the American Thanksgiving Day, which was a public holiday as well as a church celebration. During the 1850s, the observance spread from New England to the rest of the nation. According to one 1856 report, businesses remained closed, "churches of various denominations were well filled, . . . and the sermons preached were good and acceptable, taking the cheerful, hopeful, and thankful tone."[57] As historian Kenneth Ames has noted, the day linked the Puritan tradition to nineteenth-century family and domestic values, while giving a religious blessing to the Victorian love of dining.[58]

Other occasions called for special commemorative worship. In America, Decoration Day at the end of May was time for memorial services with guest speakers and perhaps the attendance of Civil War veterans from the local Grand Army post.[59] In Britain, congregations might mark the significant anniversaries in Victoria's reign with a "thanksgiving service," or place a flag over the church door and ring the church bell in celebration of Edward VII's coronation in 1911.[60]

Anniversaries and special moments in a congregation's own life called for celebration. The dedication of a building was certainly one of these; congregations invited neighboring churches and former pastors, and themselves turned out in large numbers to solemnize the results of their financial subscriptions and hard work. When Rochester's Plymouth Church opened a new building on 21 August 1856, worship began with a concert of sacred music and, after an invocation, scripture reading, hymn, and sermon, the congregation's Confession of Faith and Covenant were read. Then came the dedicatory service itself—a prayer of dedication, a hymn, the congratulatory "right hand of fellowship," a "charge to the congregation," and a final benediction.[61] Congregations planned festival services to mark anniversaries of their founding; some Congregational churches were apt to do so annually, but more typically the occasion was a jubilee or centennial. Newington United Presbyterian Church celebrated fifty years in Edinburgh with four days of services—a children's gathering on Friday evening, preparatory service on Saturday evening and three services, including Communion, on Sunday; on Monday there was a "reunion" tea followed by a "public meeting" with prayers, hymns, a Handel chorus, various addresses, and the reading of a history of the congregation.[62]

Significant points in the lives of individuals—birth, marriage, death—were also honored liturgically. Baptism was the church's first sacrament, equivalent with the Lord's Supper in its divine institution, and normally administered by sprinkling with water soon after birth; at least one of the parents had to be a member of the church.[63] Adults who had not been baptized as children received the sacrament based on their own commitment at the time they joined the church; in some congregations adult baptisms occurred at the preparatory service, in others just before the individuals were seated for the first time at the communion table.

Despite the implication of the 1644 Directory of Worship that the sacrament ordinarily should not be separated from public worship, infant baptism was frequently administered in the home during the early part of the century.[64] Health considerations dictated as much in days when it would have been foolhardy to carry a newborn to an unheated sanctuary. In addition, when the very precariousness of infancy itself recommended as early a baptism as possible, a home ceremony permitted the participation of the mother, herself likely still confined indoors.

Medical advances, both for infants and mothers, together with more comfortably heated sanctuaries made church baptisms increasingly common in practice as well as theology. A few congregations were doing so early in the Victorian period. Carr's Lane, in 1835, specified baptism "before the whole congregation." The Presbyterian Church in Binghamton, New York, was already promoting the church as the appropriate site for baptisms in 1833. In other places, the change came later. Second Congregational Church, Hartford, made it plain in its 1860 *Manual* that baptism should be a "*public* rite," and would not be given privately "except where sickness or other cause prevents its being administered in a general meeting." In Edinburgh, it was not until about 1867 that St. Stephen's parish began using its baptismal font for infants.[65]

Once baptism at the church was the standard, church boards dutifully recorded the exceptions in their minutes—an infant "too ill to be brought to the church for said service" or "a scholar of our Sunday School, now lying quite low with consumption." Occasionally, the words barely masked an unfolding tragedy, as was the case of "Wm Gray, Infant son of W^m F. Alling [who] was Baptised by the Pastor, over the Coffin of his Mother at the house of W^m Alling, upon the funeral occasion. Nov 24/63."[66]

Originally, infant baptisms were simply scheduled as needed. While such informality continued to work well in small congregations, elsewhere the mid-century Victorian craving for system and order took effect. Particularly as medical advances (and more compassionate theological views about the fate of unbaptized infants) decreased the sense of urgency, baptisms could be efficiently grouped on a few Sundays of the year. The common practice was to link infant baptism to the communion schedule. In some places it was administered on the same day, but mostly communion day services were considered long enough already without extending them for several infant baptisms. The typical solution was to set baptism for the third Sunday of the month if communion was the first, or for the Sunday following a bimonthly or quarterly Lord's Supper.[67]

Another sign that large congregations were having to impose greater systematization was the request that name cards be prepared for each child before they were carried to the font. In Beecher's large Plymouth Church, parents were required to "present, *in writing,* their own names, together with the full name of each child, and the date of its birth."[68] It is not too difficult to comprehend the reason when one thinks of the pastor and clerk in Rochester who, on Children's Day 1879, were confronted with the daunting task of trying to match names to twenty-one babies and afterwards record the vital statistics in the church register.[69]

The service itself was simple. The parents and infants took their places at the font, which was often a silver or pewter basin resting on the communion table.

In places where there were choirs, an appropriate chant or hymn accompanied the arrival of the participants. After a prayer, the parents promised to raise their children in the Christian faith. In one Chicago church, they pledged to "have them taught to read God's Holy Writ; to instruct them in the principles of the Christian religion, of which there is an excellent summary in the Shorter Catechism; to pray *for* and *with* them; to set an example of piety and godliness before them, and by all the means of divine appointment, to bring them up in the nurture and admonition of the Lord."[70] Then the infants were baptized "in the name of the Father, and of the Son, and of the Holy Ghost." A short benediction, and perhaps an additional musical selection from the choir, concluded the sacrament.[71]

The Puritans viewed marriages as civil, not religious, compacts and beyond the duties of church and clergy. In England, where nonconformist clergy did not have legal right to perform marriages until 1836, the separation was reinforced.[72] By the Victorian era, clergy presided at services, but the old heritage kept weddings in homes, not churches. The return of church weddings was part of the general effort to expel lingering Cromwellian influences. Perhaps more to the point for the laity, church weddings became marks of social respectability in part because they were more elaborate—and therefore more costly—than home weddings. Handsworth Congregational Church, Birmingham, had its first church wedding in 1838, but that was by no means typical. In London at New Broad Street Church in 1857, the practice was still viewed only as a possible, and somewhat unconventional, option: "those persons who desire religious services in connection with the marriage ceremony are requested to apply to any of the Deacons, who will make necessary arrangements with the Minister."[73] St. Stephen's parish in Edinburgh did not have a wedding in the church until 1881, but by the early twentieth century marriages were frequent enough in Glasgow and Edinburgh that the duty appeared on the job description of Park Church organist, and St. George's Free Church officers had printed a "scale of charges" associated with the use of the building and payment of the organist and choir.[74] But church weddings were never universal; when Gordon, then minister of Old South Church, Boston, was himself married to the eldest daughter of his late predecessor in June 1890, the service was performed at noon by Episcopalian Phillips Brooks "at the residence of the bride's mother."[75]

Marriage services were among the first departures from the extempore style of worship; pastors and congregations alike accepted set forms for occasional services more quickly than they did for regular Sunday preaching services. Perhaps the very fact that they were exceptional permitted more deviation from traditional practice. There was also the very understandable expectation by participants that there should be no surprises when it came to marriage vows (or baptismal covenants). Wedding ceremonies were among the earliest publications to emerge from the Scottish Church Service Society, and pastors without the benefit of denominational guidance wrote out or borrowed services on their own. Some locally produced liturgies found their way into congregational manuals, and these give an indication of the simple, straightforward rites that were used. In one Brooklyn church, the service opened with a scriptural warrant for marriage, followed by a prayer and then the exchange of vows. In this congregation, the promises were terse and identical: "Do you, ——— , take her (him) whom you now hold by the hand, to be your lawful and wedded wife (husband)?" After the presentation of a ring to the woman, the minister pronounced the couple "lawfully married, husband and wife, in the name of the Father, and of the Son, and of the Holy Ghost. And whom God hath joined together, let not man put asunder!"[76]

The final worship experience that came to every churchgoer was the funeral. Like weddings, burial services had been banished from the church by Puritan fears of Roman ritual, and they were slow to return. But the nineteenth-century liturgical renewal did have some success in encouraging church funerals; at Glasgow's Park Church, funerals joined weddings in the organist's job description.[77]

Funerals of prominent persons were more likely to be held in churches, if for no other reason than that the expected audience could not have been accommodated in a private house. A description of an 1857 Philadelphia funeral indicates how elaborate such an event could be. A long cortege made its way to the church—a "lofty funeral car, draped in black, with the coffin which contained the remains of the dead, [was] strewn with fair white flowers." In the church, the coffin was situated in the center aisle during the prayers, hymns, scripture reading, sermon, and a rendering of Mozart's "Blessed Are the Dead Which Die in the Lord" by "an effective choir."[78]

Most funerals, however, continued to be held in the homes with lay leadership playing a significant role. The minister's part was identified by saying he had "assisted at" or "attended" the funeral. An assistant pastor at the large Bethany Presbyterian Church in Philadelphia, reported in 1894 that he "assisted at funerals frequently, and [went] to the cemeteries, committing the bodies to the grave." A minister in one small Connecticut town, summed up his fourteen year tenure by saying he had married 60 couples and "attended" 145 funerals. One Chicago congregation announced that its pastor "will attend funerals," but cautioned that due to constraints on his time, "he is under the necessity of simply attending the service at the house, except in some extraordinary instance, such as the death of one of the officers of the church or the like."[79]

From cradle to grave, midweek as well as Sunday, worship was an important part of the churchgoer's experience. Carr's Lane, in 1835, had expressed the hope that worship would "check the encroachments of the world, and the increase of earthly-mindedness." Of course, it often did succeed in doing just that, in marking out a realm of the sacred in the midst of ordinary existence. But worship was itself reshaped by its encounter with the rhythms and tastes of nineteenth-century culture, and what was true of liturgy in general was true of its musical dimension as well.

# five

## "A New Song"
### *The Cultivation of Middle-Class Taste*

They had all, members and officers alike, reached the end of their patience with the organist-director and the choir. Two years earlier, the trustees of Second Presbyterian Church, Philadelphia, declared they would supply no additional money until the quality of music was "more acceptable to the congregation." But, tightened purse strings and tactful advice that "more time and attention be devoted by the choir" had not made things better.[1] Now, in the winter of 1895, it fell to the Music Committee to tell Dr. Hugh Clarke that his work, and the work of his quartet choir, was not up to standard.

In a February letter to Clarke, the Committee wrote, "There has been for some time past a very decided dissatisfaction throughout the congregation with the character and quality of the music in our church." Lest Clarke miss the point this time, the Committee specified "that the choirs are insufficiently instructed, that proper care is not exercised in the selection and rendering of the anthems and other music sung by them and that the bass is not qualified for his position." At a face-to-face meeting in March, the Music Committee reiterated its complaints. It told Clarke "frankly" that "the principal causes of dissatisfaction were insufficient practice by the choir, the slovenly manner in which the music was frequently rendered, assigning solos to singers (as instanced in the bass) without sufficient regard to their ability to sing them acceptably, and the apparent indifference of Dr. Clarke himself as to the selection of the music, the manner in which the same is rendered, etc." Clarke "gently demurred," but the Committee was adamant. No matter how much Clarke "blandly assured" them that all was well, their own ears told them it was not. In May, the officers voted to fire Clarke and all the singers, too. At this point, compassion emerged, and they gave Clarke a chance to resign, which he did.[2]

The story might be seen as merely one of dozens of nineteenth-century examples of a congregation struggling with an awkward personnel matter. Examined as an episode in the development of liturgical practice, however, it suggests a remarkable transformation in musical taste among Reformed congregations. Sixty years earlier, this same Philadelphia congregation had no organist or salaried choristers; its entire musical experience was unaccompanied congregational singing. Now, in the mid-1890s, it prided itself in a large pipe organ and a hefty music budget, and it expected to hear fine choral anthems and organ voluntaries. Moreover, its laity were confident enough of their own musical judgment to dismiss an organist-director and four professional singers when they failed to meet the current, heightened musical standards.

Second Church's story was not unique. During the nineteenth century, Reformed congregations in Britain and America moved from unaccompanied psalm singing to ambitious programs employing organists and choristers. The timing varied a great deal; some congregations forged ahead well before midcentury while others clung to the old musical style past 1900. Resources mattered; not only money but access to talent counted. The cultural and social aspirations of the membership were important, too. Not surprisingly, prosperous urban congregations took the lead in a movement which eventually had some impact everywhere.

Sixteenth-century Protestant Reformers shared a determination to make congregational singing an important part of worship. Calvinists, however, distinguished themselves from Lutherans and Anglicans by two prejudices about the types of church music that were permissible. First, musical instruments were forbidden. The human voice was the only divinely created instrument; all others were of human invention. Second, their insistence upon a biblical warrant for every aspect of worship led them to think that only the 150 Hebrew psalms could withstand scrutiny.

To make the ancient psalm texts easier for congregations to render, wordsmiths translated them into metrical form with lines of consistent length, which allowed each succeeding stanza to reuse the same short, simple tune. Because nearly every psalm was translated into one of three standard meters—Short Meter, Common Meter, or Long Meter—tunes and psalms were quite freely interchangeable, and many congregations got along with only a dozen or so tunes that they knew well by memory.[3]

There was, however, a basic tension within the tradition. The taboos against instrumental accompaniment and 'songs of human composure' conflicted with the commitment to lively, powerful congregational singing. By the mid-eighteenth century, not a few were arguing that the early Calvinists had thrown out the two best incentives to congregational praise. Some New England congregations stirred controversy by allowing accompaniment, if not by the pipe organ then at least by a bass viol or flute or clarinet to hold pitch. The psalms-only policy also came under scrutiny. Those afire with the eighteenth-century revival spirit wanted to sing about Jesus' saving grace, and they ached to voice their own spiritual anguish and joy. The hymns of English Congregationalist Isaac Watts or others such as the Wesley brothers provided a remedy wherever they gained entry. Watts's paraphrases, or Christian reworkings of the Hebrew texts, were a less controversial middle ground between the pure metrical psalm and the hymn.

Thus, small modifications of the tradition had already begun well before the Victorian period opened. Hymns, or at least paraphrases, were known, and the addition of new tunes made even the old psalms seem less staid.[4] Musical instruments, however, were another matter, and it was the rare place that found them acceptable. Unaccompanied singing remained the distinguishing mark of Reformed musical practice, and the Metrical Psalms of David, even where they had been augmented by paraphrases and hymns, continued to be sung with deep affection.

Unaccompanied four-part singing was not an easy skill for churchgoers to master, and common sense dictated that a congregation needed someone to give the pitch and lead the tune. This person was the *precentor*. Once, when psalters were scarce and reading skills scarcer, the precentor had 'lined out' each psalm—that is, given out the words to each line just before it was sung. But that practice had long ceased to be necessary, and the precentor now combined the tasks of song leader and singing teacher. The 1836 job description for Mr. Daniel Williams, a Philadelphia precentor, stipulated that "he will conduct the singing on the Sabbath and on Wednesday evenings, and will also instruct in sacred music as many members of the congregation as may attend for that purpose one evening each week."[5]

Precentors might volunteer their work in small or rural congregations, but elsewhere they received a salary. In competitive urban markets, the stipend could be quite substantial. Williams, for instance, was paid $400 annually, a quite princely sum in 1836 for what could not have been more than six or eight hours of work per week. Compensation for precentors in London, Glasgow, and Edinburgh in 1860s, 1870s, and 1880s ran between £20 and £50, but an exceptional singer could command more. St. George's Free Church had to raise Walter Strang's salary to £75 in 1870, and then to £100 the following year, to keep him from being lured away.[6]

Hiring a new precentor was an important decision for a congregation, and considerable care was taken with the selection. To choose a new precentor in 1862, King's Weigh House appointed a search committee which advertised the position, interviewed and auditioned candidates before a vote was taken by the church members. Even in presbyterian churches, the decision was often considered important enough to require a vote of the whole membership rather than the session alone; in 1871, Cowcaddens' members heard five candidates before electing David Johnstone by "a large majority." Typically, the applicants were asked to conduct one or more services before the congregation made up its mind. Most congregations made only a local search, but those that offered a salary large enough to warrant relocation were more ambitious. In 1885, St. George's Free Church advertised in the *Presbyterian,* the *Free Church Monthly,* the *Musical Times,* and six daily newspapers in Aberdeen, Dundee, Glasgow, and Edinburgh, and it netted forty-one applicants for the effort.[7]

The precentors represented the best musical talent that was available, and how superior or minimal this was depended on local circumstances. In rural congregations, the duty devolved to whichever member had the most pleasing, accurate voice and the courage and commitment to accept the responsibility. Once the position was assigned, the incumbent generally kept it until prevented by age. Remembering his boyhood church in Oswestry during the 1850s, Minshall described an elderly precentor whose talents had deteriorated considerably: "The old man who undertook to 'lead' the singing had done it for many years. He was not much of a singer, and I should think he had the very slightest musical knowledge. He would sometimes pitch the tune too high, with a breakdown as the result. His voice was exceedingly shaky and very feeble, owing to age and infirmity."[8]

City churches, such as those in Edinburgh, could do much better. Mr. Craig, of Greenside parish, was twice granted a leave of absence to pursue musical studies in Milan.[9] Both Strang and his successor Walter Hately at St. George's Free Church were professors of vocal music at Edinburgh colleges. Hately was a second generation precentor, his father having been a prominent Edinburgh psalm leader before him; both were important musical editors of psalters, which was a talent displayed by other precentors, too.[10] In Scotland, where precenting remained popular even in the last third of the century, many of the best precentors gained the celebrity status accorded to other virtuoso performers. Three of Edinburgh's stars achieved equal success on the stage—John Templeton of Broughton Place and John Wilson of St. Mary's were operatic tenors, and David Kennedy of Nicholson Street Church gained fame as a singer of Scottish ballads.[11]

While precenting was overwhelming a male occupation, there were female precentors. Miss Nessie Goode, "a lady professional," led the psalmody at St. John's Kensington Presbyterian Church in London from 1869 to 1873. At Fourth United Presbyterian Church in Pittsburgh, Miss Annie Friesel held the position during the 1880s, and Mrs. Woods became precentor in 1913.[12] Quite a few other women, such as Mrs. Marshall at King's Weigh House, conducted psalmody in Sunday School devotional exercises and in children's services.[13]

Whatever the precentor's training and skill, there were limits to what a single person, seated near the pulpit and equipped with no more than a pitch pipe or tuning fork, could accomplish. One voice, even of the best quality, was not likely to hold huge nineteenth-century congregations of several hundred or a thousand people on pitch through an entire psalm. Consequently, in many places it became customary to assemble a "band" of additional singers to assist.

The idea of a band, or choir, was not new; there is a record from 1587 of a Glasgow precentor augmenting his voice with those of four additional males.[14] But bands first took solid root during the singing school movement of the mid-eighteenth century.[15] At Hartford's First Congregational Church during the 1730s, "the better singers, by natural selection, drew together" for mutual support, and in time the nucleus of a choir formed.[16]

By the early nineteenth century, Hartford's band, with assorted flutes and viols, was situated in the rear gallery, which was one common location for these early choirs.[17] Other congregations thought it was better to place the extra singers at the front, either grouped around the precentor or seated before him in the front pews. A group of eighteen volunteers told the deacons' court at St. George's Free Church that they were willing to "assist the music of the congregation if accommodated with seats near the pulpit."[18]

Both volunteer and salaried bands assisted precentors during the early nineteenth century. The volunteers at St. George's Free Church were products of the precentor's weekly singing class, and their sole compensation was a free copy of the psalm book. Most urban congregations, however, paid at least some of their singers. In Edinburgh, St. Andrew's began to pay singers in 1817, and in the 1830s, Greyfriars was budgeting up to £12 per year to hire singers.[19] One appeal of adding a few professionals to a core of volunteers was the guarantee of a qualified voice in each of the four parts. Within a year after its volunteer band had been organized, St. George's Free Church appointed "four leaders of the different parts . . . to assist the congregation in learning to sing in parts." The pay was a token £1 per year, but the principle of compensation had been established.[20]

As choirs became better established, precentors began to take on some of the attributes of a choral director. The more they became singer-conductors rather than merely singers, the better they were able to adapt to changes that were coming. By 1872, the precentor's job description in Govan parish included "training the choir" as well as the traditional responsibility for leading the psalmody and teaching the congregation.[21] A good example of a precentor who made the transition to "leader of the choir," was Joseph Ebsworth, precentor at St. Stephen's in Edinburgh from 1828 to 1868. It was a sure sign that the role was evolving when Ebsworth left the precentor's raised desk and "stood below directing the choir."[22] Ebsworth's choir developed a reputation for fine singing, as did R. A. Smith's band in nearby St. George's parish. Before he came to Edinburgh, Smith's reputation was well established; his band at Paisley Abbey had been good enough to go on tour with a repertoire of works by Handel and Beethoven.[23]

Smith's success led some to worry that if the choirs became *too* excellent, the congregation would simply stop singing and listen. That, plus the egalitarian objection that some singers were being elevated over the rest, kept these early choirs from gaining universal approval. In 1852, the precentor of the Free Church in Airdrie asked permission to organize a band, and he was denied. At Liverpool's Canning Street Church, the precentor won permission to start a choir, but was warned by the session against "the extreme impropriety of having paid singers to conduct the worship who are not members or adherents."[24] These were sharp reminders that congregational singing remained the primary goal, and bands or professional singers could only be justified if they contributed toward that end.

The elevation of congregational praise was the expected outcome of the weekly singing classes, the second of the precentor's primary responsibilities. Few people at the beginning of the nineteenth century could read musical notation, and so they picked up the tunes by ear in the precentor's classes. Church leaders understood that if they wanted good congregational singing, they had to provide a rudimentary musical education. Binney told his congregation bluntly, "Singing is no more to be performed by instinct, or miracle, than any other duty."[25]

The instruction was delivered in two forms, the one-shot course of six to ten weeks and the ongoing weekly psalmody practice. Occasionally a precentor was able to earn extra money for a set course, but the weekly sessions were always considered within the regular duties. Members were rarely asked to pay any fee for their instruction; church budget makers viewed the expenses as a legitimate investment in the congregation's vitality. One Chicago church proudly advertised that "to promote congregational singing, and to enable all to take an appropriate and edifying part in the praises in the sanctuary, gratuitous instruction in vocal music is provided for all children and adults in the congregation."[26] A Philadelphia church, less optimistic that *all* could benefit from lessons, promised only that "those who have voices which are capable of being trained for the purpose should receive a competent degree of instruction in sacred musick."[27]

The old system of precentor-led praise did not survive in the nineteenth century. Its death came sooner in some places than others, but strewn throughout the record is abundant evidence of mounting dissatisfaction—"a general disappointment with our music among the congregation," was the way one church treasurer expressed it.[28] Church boards had recurring discussions about ways to improve the music; members voiced their own complaints and sent petitions advocating this remedy or that. The difficulty was that middle-class musical taste and social aspiration had out-stripped the capability of the old system. Churchgoers now arrived with a definition of quality informed by the concert hall and stage, and there would be no peace until there was a closer resemblance between what they heard elsewhere and what they heard at church. The knowledge that other socially prominent congregations, Anglican or Episcopalian, enjoyed a wide range of musical genres made the unhappiness all the more difficult to bear.

The discontinuity between what tradition permitted and taste demanded made for a great restlessness at the local level. Congregations tried various cures and nostrums, seeking the panacea that would deliver quality. Some proposals actually helped, but more did nothing but eliminate another false hope. In the end, it took two radical changes to satisfy the desire for music of greater quality. First, congregational singing improved measurably once it was accompanied by an organ, the only single-performer instrument capable of supporting such a large number of voices. The capabilities of an entire congregation were still limited, however, even with the help of an organ. The only way to overcome uneven talent and lack of rehearsal was to shift some of the burden to a select group. Thus, in a second great change, the choir gained an independent role allowing it to perform choral selections beyond the reach of the whole congregation. When that happened, the old system was extinct.

Local churches, and advice-givers at the denominational level, began by hoping that less drastic solutions would suffice. For instance, the minister could preach a sermon or the church manual could include a strong exhortation.[29] Some congregations hoped the retirement of an aging precentor would solve their problems, but found they got no more than a temporary lift in enthusiasm.[30] One group of deacons installed a notice board at the front of the church to announce the tune, thinking this might help.[31]

A common recourse was to strengthen the band of singers who helped to lead the praise. Perhaps if there were more voices, or a larger budget, or longer rehearsals, then the rest of the congregation would sing better. St. George's parish engaged a consultant to help it hire the most qualified singers in Edinburgh. Two years later, it thought its problems were solved when it hired Madam Dowland, "a soprano singer of a cultivated and refined style of singing," at twice the salary it gave its other choristers. But within six months, there was further unhappiness, and the expected solution this time was to have the choir turn in attendance cards at each practice.[32] Two other Edinburgh congregations thought repositioning the choir might hold the key. St. George's Free Church moved its choir from the gallery to the front "for greater efficiency in leading the Praise of the Congregation."[33] Greenside parishioners built a platform to raise the choir seats and thought they noticed an improvement, which was "a source of much gratification."[34]

A step that did bear fruit, at least in the long run, was the formation of a Music Committee, or Psalmody Committee. These were actually some of the earliest standing committees that local churches created, well before the proliferation of administrative committees in the 1860s and 1870s. Second Presbyterian Church in Philadelphia in 1837 appointed such a committee—"a standing committee who shall have charge of the musick of the Church." Its duties were the hiring of an organist and precentor, and the preparation of a collection of tunes for local use.[35] Both Old South in Boston and St. George's Free Church in Edinburgh had music committees by the 1840s.[36] Plymouth Church, Brooklyn, formed a music committee during the congregation's first year in 1850 and gave it power to "appoint suitable persons to conduct the Music of the Church; make all necessary arrangements to furnish a well disciplined Choir; and also for the practical development of musical talent in the congregation."[37] By the 1870s and 1880s, such committees were common and useful vehicles for the reshaping of musical practice. In Airdrie Free Church, for instance, it was a "lengthy report" from the music committee that convinced the congregation in 1898 to purchase an organ and start a choir.[38]

Singing classes also drew attention from discontented congregations; it was tempting to believe that more effort or a different teacher or a novel method could rejuvenate the tired classes. In Scotland, where psalmody was most admired and yet in greatest difficulty because of the aversion to organs, popular singing teachers toured and gained wide reputations for being able to work wonders with classes of several hundred. Congregational minister John Curwen had success teaching the Tonic Sol-Fa method, which enabled students to read by sight more quickly. Curwen was also a forceful proponent of four-part singing as an inducement to participation by those with low voices.[39] In a Birmingham church where his methods were adopted, "the whole congregation [formed] a choir of nearly 400 voices, all grouped in their several parts." Curwen himself came to visit in 1861, and called it "true People's Psalmody, carrying us away on its mighty tide."[40]

The happy story of this Birmingham church was, however, not easily duplicated, and the far more common tale was one of frustration. St. George's Free Church had come to a sorry musical predicament by 1881: the worshippers knew so few tunes that they had grown bored by the repetition. Classes to learn more tunes was the obvious answer, but the elders were pessimistic. The precentor had already put "much time and trouble" into teaching, but attendance was low and the results were "shortlived" at best. The elders honestly did not think they dared ask the man to take on any more such "discouraging" work. But something had to be done, and so they contracted for a visiting teacher; perhaps, they reasoned, the "novelty" would "awaken the desired interest." They did get a brief upswing, but by mid-1883 the old habits were back. Attendance at the children's singing lessons was "so small as to almost preclude the possibility of any good result." For the adult weekly practice, there was "a fair attendance of ladies at first, [but] the number soon fell off, & at no time was there anything like an adequate representation even of the members of the choir, not to speak of the congregation."[41]

The greatest boost to musical education came not from within the churches, but from the growing work of the secular schools. Lowell Mason, composer of popular hymn tunes and choir leader at Boston's Bowdoin Street Congregational Church, started the first American public school program in 1838; John Pyke Hullah, editor of an 1843 psalter, initiated a similar movement in Britain in 1841 with music classes for school teachers.[42] In time, as normal schools turned out trained music teachers and public school music spread, it became possible for local churches to place full-staff hymnals in their members' hands with some hope of good results. Beecher's *Plymouth Collection of Hymns and Tunes* (1855) can apparently claim to be the first church hymnal to print tunes together with words, although the model that it set—that of tunes spread across the top of a page with alternate texts in stanza form below and opposite—was certainly not the most convenient for users. American Presbyterians issued a hymnal with musical notation for congregational use in 1866; a version of the *Scottish Hymnal* with tunes appeared in 1872, two years after the words-only edition.[43]

Local church music committees were actually flooded with new hymnals, and congregations often adopted a new one with the hope that it would revitalize the singing. Official denominational products, both psalters and hymnals, became local standards for Sunday worship. A few ambitious congregations edited their own hymnals, or added supplements to a denominational book.[44] Commercially published collections were available, too; the *American Presbyterian* estimated in 1857 that these were appearing at the astounding rate of three per year.[45] In fact, relief from the chaos was one reason local congregations favored denominational standardization. When the Church of Scotland brought out a new authorized collection of psalm tunes in 1869, the editors confidently promised that "one of the greatest hindrances to Psalmody improvement will thus be removed, namely—the use and consequent expense, of a number of tune books, of differing harmonies, in the same place of worship."[46]

The adoption of a new book was an important, and potentially traumatic, decision. There was, of course, an expense involved. Regular attenders were obligated to purchase their own, and the congregation's budget covered a supply for visitors; discarded volumes were transferred to the Sunday School or mission hall, or donated to another congregation that could use them. But cost never seemed to matter if the book was wanted. Committees studied the options carefully, counting the number of old hymns, new hymns, children's songs, and hymns for special seasons of the year. They weighed the sadness involved in giving up old favorites against the promise of improved singing with a more modern hymnal. An 1895 selection committee at Boston's Old South admitted it was keenly aware that "the attachment to certain hymns that have been used in church service is almost a sacred matter and a conservative feeling always manifests itself whenever change is suggested." Yet, the committee argued, "it is also a well recognized truth that the adoption of a new hymn-book is practically a selection for the younger portion of the church worshipers, and however great may be the attachment of those who are older for a [familiar] book, . . . the desire and requirements of our younger members" must prevail.[47]

The hope of reaching younger members caused congregations to consider the wide variety of evangelical and gospel collections popularized by touring revivalists during the last part of the century. Gospel hymns were controversial; not only did they flout musical tradition, but they seemed undignified to the status-conscious middle class. Usually gospel hymnals were relegated to Sunday evenings or midweek prayer meetings, or to youth or mission hall services, but even there they could create division. The use of Moody and Sankey's collection at the second Sunday service drew a protest even in a strongly prorevival community such as Cowcaddens Free Church in Glasgow; revival hymns were fine, but not for Sunday.[48]

The popularity of gospel hymns was but one evidence of the laity's restlessness with the limited musical repertoire in their congregations, and it explains why church leaders thought that new hymnals might improve congregational singing. All the late century hymn book editors made some concession to the lilting gospel melodies. One of the great appeals of the *Plymouth Collection of Hymns and Tunes,* compiled by Beecher and organist John Zundel, was its borrowing of sprightly, secular melodies.[49] The United Presbyterian Church of North America, which alone clung to exclusive psalm singing after the 1880s, knew it had to concede something or risk losing its youth, and in 1901 the denomination published *Bible Songs,* which set traditional psalms to gospel tunes—to "melodies of animated movement" as the editors put it.[50] Such was the attraction of gospel music.

Other routes toward musical variety were more appreciated in socially prominent congregations. Official denominational hymnals drew heavily from the churchly tradition of the Anglicans, and this appealed greatly to those concerned about the dignity of the service. A hymnbook selection committee in Boston expressed satisfaction at finding a good assortment of ancient Latin, Greek, and German hymns in one of the volumes it surveyed.[51] Ironically, many of these hymns (unlike the old psalm tunes) were arranged with organ accompaniment in mind, and their presence added to, rather than alleviated, the restlessness where organs were still unwelcome.

Throughout the Victorian era, psalmody reformers looked with interest on the tradition of chanting practiced by Anglicans and by Scottish and American Episcopalians. Many saw it as a way to reinvigorate psalmody in their own churches. Chanting also coincided with the effort to restore the church's ancient hymns and canticles, such as the Gloria in Excelsis or Nunc Dimittis, to Reformed worship. The 1838 edition of a hymnal published locally by St. Stephen's, Edinburgh, included ten doxologies, three version of the Sanctus, and twenty-six chants.[52] In London, Binney introduced chanting to King's Weigh House worshippers in the 1850s.[53] The *Church of Scotland Psalm and Hymn Tune Book* (1869) provided chants as an option to the traditional metrical tunes. The *Hymnal of the Presbyterian Church,* published by the Old School Presbyterians in the United States in 1866, carried sixty-nine "Scripture selections set to Anglican chants."[54]

In churches seeking musical sophistication, chanting caught on. By 1874, the arrival of a new *Presbyterian Hymnal* (just published by the reunited Old and New Schools) encouraged a Philadelphia session to direct its Music Committee "to secure if possible the more frequent use of chants in our Service."[55] At Lyndhurst Road, London, when the matter came up shortly after the congregation was organized, all favored chanting; the only question was which chant book to adopt.[56]

The last of the moderate innovations—that is, innovations short of admitting organs and performing choirs—was so simple that it is hard to imagine at first why it caused the furor it did. The change was standing, rather than sitting, to sing. Vocal experts explained that a change in posture would help, yet the old habit—stand to pray, sit to sing—was so ingrained that it proved extraordinarily difficult to break. Standing seems to have been the point at which the conservative minority (and it was always a minority when votes were taken) decided to draw the line. It was at least possible to avoid some of the other innovations discretely; if you did not approve of chanting, you could simply refuse to participate, sit silently with your psalter open, and probably few would even notice. But standing or sitting was another matter; you were either up or down, and most visibly so. Thus, traditionalists resisted, perhaps as much for what they feared would be forced on them next as for the habit immediately at stake.

The experience of Greenside parish in Edinburgh was illustrative. In February 1869, session members were given notice that the issue would be considered the following month. At the March meeting, two motions were introduced. The first "invited" the congregation to stand for song and sit for prayer, while emphasizing that "these attitudes shall be entirely optional." An alternate motion, noting that "innovations in the forms of public worship are distasteful to some members of the Kirk Session and of the Congregation," proposed no change for fear of arousing "an element of discord." The alternate failed and the original motion succeeded, nine votes to two.

Three days later, the kirk session was quickly reconvened because Elder Miller, who cast one of the two negative votes, was threatening to resign. After some discussion, his fellow elders managed to calm him by promising to delay pending a poll of the seatholders. So, "schedules in blank" were mailed out with instructions to mark approval, disapproval, or neutrality. The first week of May, with the ballots in hand, the session could see that, although "the great majority" favored standing, a "considerable number" objected. Further delay seemed prudent.

One more month passed. By the time the kirk session assembled for its regular monthly meeting in June, it was faced with two new developments. The majority party had trumped Miller's threat; three who favored standing now said they would quit if change did not go forward. The more surprising event had unfolded the preceding Sunday during worship. That morning, so the clerk noted, "a very great number of the individuals present in church altered the positions usually observed, by standing at praise and not rising at prayer." While the timid session waffled, the congregation had taken matters into its own hands and acted. Realizing there was little choice left, the elders agreed that "such as approve of doing so, may [stand]. Elder Miller was a solitary dissenter, but he did not resign.[57]

Whether worshippers sat or stood, whether the choir sat in the rear gallery or at the front, whether there was more or less psalmody practice, or whether the tune book was old or new, the restlessness about the quality of church music continued until organs and performing choirs were in place.

Organs, as all musical instruments, had been disdained by the Calvinist reformers, and Puritanism had strengthened rather than weakened the aversion. Although references to instrumental praise were plentiful in the Hebrew psalms, opponents could find no explicit mandate in the Gospels; on the contrary, they argued, Jesus had destroyed Temple worship. One Scot, arguing against organs in 1807 described them as "lofty, artificial" aids that had nothing to recommend them other than "novelty." How could anything, he wondered, improve upon the unaccompanied "tones of the human voice, . . . the most simple . . . , the most perfect, the most accurate . . . , the most sublime, and the best qualified to convey the sentiments of the devout heart, in solemn Praise to the Father, the Son, and the Holy Ghost"?[58]

But by the Victorian era, worshippers overwhelmingly had lost faith in the human voice, and they found its unaided efforts anything but perfect, accurate, and sublime. A decision to install an organ typically began, as it did in Dumfries, with grumbling about "the unsatisfactory character of the singing." A Philadelphia session said it was responding to a "considerable dissatisfaction . . . in regard to the manner in which the Psalmody of the Church is presently conducted." A British contributor summed up the sentiments of many when he explained his pledge of £30 to the congregation's organ fund by saying simply, "Something is wanted to make our singing 'go' better."[59]

The organ question took more than a century to play itself out, with the most prolonged resistance found among the Scots, the English Presbyterians, and the small United Presbyterian Church of North America. English and American Congregationalists and American Presbyterians accepted organs earlier and with less disruption to local harmony. Certainly where various string and wind instruments had been called on for assistance during the eighteenth century, it was harder to object on principle to an organ.[60]

Congregational churches had the advantage of local option, which allowed innovative churches to adopt organs without having to battle for nationwide support. In England, Carr's Lane installed a large pipe organ in 1825, apparently because the minister, J. A. James, thought an organ was less divisive than setting apart certain singers as a band. Handsworth Church, also in Birmingham, had an organ in 1832; Fish Street Church in Hull purchased one in 1853. By the 1870s, the last of the English Congregational churches were installing organs. King's Weigh House held off until the 1869 retirement of Binney, who as a Scotophile was an opponent, though by no means a dogmatic one. "There is nothing wrong in principle in the use of an organ," he once said. "There is much that may be useful. But we do not want it."[61]

American Congregational churches used their local freedom to install organs beginning in the eighteenth-century. A congregation in Providence, Rhode Island, possessed the denomination's first organ by 1770, and First Church, Boston, added one in 1785—although the initial two-stop pipe organ proved so unsatisfactory that it was removed before ever being used for worship and replaced by a "large English chamber organ." Hanover Street Church, Boston, lost an organ in an 1830 fire. By then Old South also used an organ, one having been imported from London in 1827 for the extravagant price of seven thousand dollars. First Church, Hartford, put in an organ in 1833, and a larger one two years later. By the 1860s, when Plymouth Church, Brooklyn, paid $22,000 for the largest church organ in America, the use of an organ was taken for granted.[62]

There were organs in the main American Presbyterian denomination as early as 1817 when one was installed in Alexandria, Virginia. During the the middle years of the century, the instruments became typical in urban churches, and by the end of the 1880s, most congregations in smaller towns had installed organs, too.[63]

In contrast, the tradition-bound United Presbyterians forbade organs until 1881, when its assembly finally approved local option. The narrowness of the vote, $620\frac{1}{2}$ to $612\frac{1}{2}$, was reason enough to warn local churches to "abstain . . . from any action in this matter that would disturb the peace and harmony of congregations, or unreasonably disregard the conscientious conviction of members."[64] Peace was nevertheless disturbed. In one rural congregation north of Pittsburgh, the now-redundant precentor became angry and made off with the church's record books, which the elders retrieved only with difficulty.[65] In another western Pennsylvania town, the entry of an organ into the First United Presbyterian Church of Indiana in 1894, led to schism when forty-five dissidents went two blocks away and started a new congregation.[66]

The Scots and English Presbyterians found change difficult, too. Scottish worshippers had long considered unaccompanied psalmody to be a practice that was peculiarly theirs. After removing organs from places of worship at the time of Reformation, they had relived the struggle once when Charles I attempted to rebuild organs and again when James II placed an organ in the Royal Chapel at Holyrood in 1687. Organs, therefore, were tangled in Scottish minds with political as well as religious liberty.[67] Presbyterianism's near-monopoly status north of the Tweed was a second factor in the durability of organless singing in Scotland. Congregations there faced far less risk of losing members to a socially prominent, musically advanced Anglican or Episcopal congregation in the next block. By way of contrast, Old South in Boston stood, at first, a short stroll away from King's Chapel, and then, after its move to the Back Bay, it faced Trinity Church across the square. No Glasgow church faced competition like that.[68]

The first attempt by a Scottish congregation to use an organ was in St. Andrew's parish, Glasgow, in 1807. Members had been using a small chamber organ for their weekly psalmody practice, and the logic of carrying the instrument into the church and gaining its benefit on Sunday was too great to resist. The organ was not permitted to remain, however, because the presbytery insisted on its removal.[69] Not until 1863 did an organ come to stay when Greyfriars Church, Edinburgh, began using a harmonium for two years until its 1865 pipe organ was ready.[70] Other Church of Scotland parishes followed in Glasgow (St. Andrew's and

Park, 1866), in Kilmarnock (Old High, 1869), in Dumfries (Greyfriars', 1873), and in Forgue, where the earliest organ in the north of Scotland was opened in 1872. The most ambitious early project was a very large organ by the French builder Cavaillé-Coll, placed in Paisley Abbey in 1872. The Scottish United Presbyterians opened the door for organs in 1872, and the decade of the 1880s saw vigorous activity among them. Organs were permitted by the Free Church in 1883, and the 1890s were busy years for organ construction in that denomination.[71]

The English Presbyterian synod granted the right to use instrumental music in 1870, and the newly formed St. John's Wood congregation in London had an organ within a year. Over the next three decades, the remaining congregations of the Presbyterian Church of England moved ahead at their own paces. The last to have an organ was Regent Square, London, which held out until 1902.[72]

Having an organ or not became, then, a matter of local decision. Considering the zeal with which theologians had argued the issue nationally, it might have been expected that similar battles would have erupted locally, but they seldom did. Congregations typically introduced organs in stages, which lessened the potential of serious feuds. Canning Street, a Presbyterian church in Liverpool, makes a good example. In 1878, it permitted a small reed organ in the Sunday School, but for practice only, not actual worship. After four years, it was evident that the children sang so much better with accompaniment that the Sunday School was allowed to use it for devotional exercises. By 1888, the Wednesday evening prayer meeting adopted the instrument, too. After four more years, in 1892, the congregation had become comfortable enough to acquire a larger reed organ for regular Sunday worship. By 1893, it had raised enough money to install a large pipe organ.[73]

Victorian churchgoers also became familiar with organs at home. The half century after 1840 was a great age of the reed organ or parlor organ. Half the price of a piano, less challenging to play and more easily tucked into a corner, the parlor organ was a symbol of middle-class refinement.[74] Those seeking respectability wanted organs in their churches as much as they wanted them in their homes. Parlor organs taught a simple practical lesson, too. Home musicians learned how much easier it was to sing a hymn, and how much better their voices sounded, with the aid of an organ, and once they did there was constant pressure for similar help in church. It was the lesson of St. Andrew's choir practice being learned across the land.

By the time local congregations got to a decision about using an organ in Sunday worship, the conclusion was forgone. Their exposure to organs at home and at the margins of church life, their hope of improving Sunday morning praise, and often their envy of other socially prominent churches paved the way. In the end, local opposition to organs turned out to be small, and often easily converted. In Glasgow's Bellgrove United Presbyterian Church, an initial poll of the membership returned 151 in favor of an organ, 66 willing to go along, and 103 opposed. The elders went to see the 103 and also contacted 76 who had not returned their ballot. When they had finished, the division stood at 372 in favor and only 24 in opposition. Of the 24, none objected on the "ground of Scriptural principle."[75]

Other congregations found would-be opponents willing to stand aside for the good of the congregation as a whole, and perhaps even to send in contributions toward the purchase of an organ. One Londoner replied to his minister's fund-raising letter, "I am and always have been opposed to instrumental music in the house of God, but I am willing to forego my own taste and feelings in this matter and if you think that an Organ will be a means of inducing any of the surrounding inhabitants to come within the sound of the gospel I promise you a donation of 1/10/– and pray that you may have success." Another elderly member of the same congregation wrote that he personally was "content" with the unaccompanied human voice and could not fully understand this "Sensual" age's desire for musical "intoxication"; nevertheless, "fossils should not block the way," and he was sending in five pounds "towards your organ Trusting its strains may draw the masses in that ower House may be full and spiritually organised and with Harmony and Grace be filled."[76]

Such conciliatory sentiments meant that when tallies were taken during the last third of the century, they were generally one-sided, even in Scotland. Phrases such as "an overwhelming majority" or "without any dissenting feeling whatsoever" described some results. Gilcomston Free Church in Aberdeen asked members to express any objections to procuring an organ, and after the allotted time had passed, the elders reported, "it is gratifying to say none were given in." Of course, that was in 1898, by which time organs were no longer so strange to Scots. But even those congregations that were pioneers reported healthy majorities. Greyfriars' parish, which built the first organ in Dumfries, netted a 504 to 15 majority in 1873. Glasgow's Park Church in February 1865 was at the very forefront of change in Scotland, yet its pewholders easily approved an organ by 144 to 7 (or, 500 to 14 if total sittings were calculated).[77]

When a congregation's leaders moved too slowly, members and pewholders found ways to speed the process. In St. Stephen's, Edinburgh, minister Norman Macleod's recommendation for an organ was stymied by a hesitant session until a petition from ninety-three male members forced a congregational vote, in which the organ easily won. Frequently, it was the ordinary members, rather than the minister or officers, who first proposed getting an organ. A petition from members did the trick in Helensburgh's Park Free Church, Edinburgh's St. George's parish, and in Philadelphia's Second Presbyterian Church, as similar ones did elsewhere. Lay members on the music committee played the key role in Airdrie, and the choir first raised the issue in Bristo Church, Edinburgh.[78]

Money, or the lack of it, may have limited the size of organ a congregation could afford, but it never stopped a church from getting an instrument of some sort. The standard method of raising funds was a special subscription, but congregations that felt less able to contribute out of pocket turned to church bazaars or other money-making schemes with good results. It never seemed difficult to raise money for an organ. The elders at Lansdowne Church, Glasgow, uncertain whether the people really wanted one, decided to ask for money as a test of support; they soon had nearly £700 in donations ranging from £50 down to 10s.[79]

One advantage of the organ was that it came in all price ranges. Two basic types—reed organs and pipe organs—could be considered. A reed organ, either a harmonium or an American or cabinet organ, was the less expensive option.[80] Prices in Britain ranged from £50 to £80, and in America were about $125 during the 1880s. These were the musical instruments of choice for small churches, lecture rooms, Sunday Schools, and mission halls. In more affluent churches, they served as a temporary instrument until a pipe organ could be installed. Pipe organs were, of course, more expensive, but they too came in a wide range of sizes and prices. A small instrument might be had for as little as £250 to £300 in the 1880s, with a more usual cost to the congregations studied here being £600 to £1000 and a top price being £1500 to £2000. Prosperous city churches in the United States were paying $15,000 to $20,000 for an organ by the turn of the century.

Congregations were invariably happy with their purchases: singing improved, and the grumbling disappeared. After using an organ for about two years, St. George's Free Church noted with satisfaction that "the Public Praise of our Congregation has been conducted with a beauty, a dignity, and an impressiveness that leaves nothing to be desired." At Broughton Place, even the skeptical were convinced. "We do not suppose now," one observer wrote, "that any one would care to go back to the pre-organ days after seeing, or rather hearing, the improvement in the praise which the organ has undoubtedly effected." Lyndhurst Road, which had struggled for some months until the organ in its new building was ready in 1886, reported with relief that "the singing is more hearty and united."[81]

Much of the credit redounded to the person playing the instrument, and talented organists who could elevate worship by their interpretation of hymns were now as much sought after as the best precentor ever was. Zundel, who played at Brooklyn's Plymouth Church, was able to lift the congregation to great crescendos of praise; Beecher "used to say that he inspired his sermons." The opposite could also be true. A frustrated Joseph Parker of City Temple, having suffered through a service with a substitute organist, exclaimed, "Poor creature yesterday! A hammerer, not a player; he battered away upon single stops and had no idea of combination and interblending."[82]

Actually, there were two distinct levels of organists—the talented amateur who worked as a volunteer or for a token salary and the well-trained professional, the best of whom commanded salaries of $1200 to $1500 in Amerca, £120 to £150 in Britain by the turn of the century. Typically, the professional organists also served as choirmasters, which had financial advantages both for them and the congregations; the dual role justified a higher salary for the musician while the church believed it saved some money over what it would spend for two professionals of comparable talent. All of the prominent, highly paid organist-directors were male, but women were well represented among the amateurs and at the lower end of the salaried organists; the parlor organ was, after all, a woman's instrument, and the transition to public performance seems to have been made readily.[83]

While information about amateur organists is too limited to allow judgments about their quality, standards for urban professionals were high, and search committees screened candidates thoroughly, sometimes with the aid of a consultant. As had been the practice when deciding on a precentor, the finalists were sometimes put "on trial before the congregation" by playing a Sunday service.[84] Minshall remembered going "through a searching examination as to [his] abilities, experience, character, etc." before being taken on as organist at City Temple, London.[85] At an 1888 audition for a job at Greyfriars Church, Edinburgh, two experts scored seven finalists in six categories: performing a selection of the candidate's choosing, rendering Handel's chorus "For Unto Us," reading vocal parts at sight, playing a hymn, transposing a second hymn into A-flat, and finally extemporizing on a third hymn.[86]

With this kind of talent at the console, churchgoers were naturally curious to hear the full magnificence of the pipe organ their donations had procured. It was a rather awkward desire to have, however. In congregational discussions, the argument for organs had always been the improvement of congregational singing, not the enjoyment of recital pieces. For some die-hard conservatives, anything beyond hymn playing was a betrayal of what had been promised and agreed. The story is told that when the organist at St. Stephen's, Edinburgh, first started playing voluntaries before the Sunday service, "one dear old lady . . . used to walk up and down the pavement near the door of the church until the sinful sound had ceased."[87]

If she did, she must have been lonely because organ preludes and postludes were popular with churchgoers. Donald Macleod very much wanted the splendid

Park Church organ, the second largest in Scotland, to be heard before and after service, and so he began to ask his parishioners about the idea when he went visiting. To his great pleasure, and relief, he found that with "perhaps one or two exceptions" people were either "decidedly in favour" or at least without objection.[88] By the early twentieth century, a churchgoer anywhere would have been surprised not to hear the organ before worship.

Churches that had large pipe organs wanted to show them off to the town in public recitals, too. As they did so, they learned that the organ was a powerful tool that could enhance a congregation's social status and attract members. There could be, in fact, many reasons for holding an organ concert. There were inaugural recitals, which one church thinly disguised (for the benefit of hesitant conservatives) as a prudent, fiscally responsible "trial and test of the Organ" before accepting the builder's work. Central Presbyterian Church in Rochester charged fifty cents admission and gave the money to the Home for the Friendless; elsewhere performances paid off the last installment to the organ builder or raised money for other church projects. Some congregations encouraged, indeed expected, organists to supplement their salaries by frequent recitals. (Most organists also earned extra money by teaching private students on the church instrument.) At Lyndhurst Road, recitals were primarily a way to gain attention for the congregation, and the public was invited free of charge. When the virtuoso French organist Alexandre Guilmant toured Britain in 1887, Lyndhurst Road gained publicity when he chose its organ for a recital. Not surprisingly, by the end of the century Govan parish had written the obligation to give at least two recitals a year into their organist's job description.[89]

The evolution of the church choir echoed the organ's transformation from psalmody's helpmate to an instrument independently praising God and contributing to the congregation's reputation and growth. The signs were several. Choral anthems and responses appeared in orders of worship. Choirs, together with organs, were moved from the rear gallery to the front of the church, giving them the dominant visual position that worshippers expected based on visits to city concert halls. One London churchgoer, giving his desire a religious rationale, argued that "a visible Choir, reverently taking part in the worship, is a help and a stimulus to reverence and heartiness." A forward location was also, the writer thought, aesthetically attractive, adding "warmth . . . to a cold-looking region of the church."[90] The practice of wearing robes, which followed the move to the front of the sanctuary, usually began with little thought beyond aesthetic improvement—it looked better to have uniform apparel than a motley assortment of street clothing. But it also symbolized the reality that choirs now were distinct from ordinary worshippers and had a role that extended beyond collective hymn singing.

Congregations found that a reputation for fine church music could be a powerful recruiting tool for new members. Like a virtuoso preacher, a stellar choir and organist attracted crowds. Churches used this to their advantage when they prepared advertisements. During the winter of 1885–86, People's Congregational Church was a recently formed congregation in Brooklyn, so new that it was still meeting in temporary quarters while its sanctuary was being constructed. To attract a constituency, it prepared small leaflets to be passed out on the street or during door-to-door visitation. Directly in the center, below the name of the minister, was this promise: "FINE MUSIC UNDER THE DIRECTION OF MR. I. N. SOPER." Underneath were the names of the organist and five professional choir singers—soprano, contralto, "special contralto," tenor, and "basso."[91] When a downtown Philadelphia church was temporarily between pastors in 1895, it reacted by increasing its choir budget, because it understood that the music was going to have to keep it competitive until a new minister was chosen.[92]

By the end of the century, when the evolution of choirs had been completed, there were two types of church choristers—volunteers and salaried professionals. Nearly all town and city churches paid at least some of their singers in order to achieve the quality that was expected by increasingly critical churchgoers. The custom was not without its detractors, especially early in the century; church officers, especially, worried about the morals of singers who were not part of the congregation. One church session, reflecting a common set of suspicions, cautioned the trustees not to hire singers of "doubtful character," but to seek instead a choir "composed of persons members of some Evangelical Church, or children of our own church where practicable; as we regard it a holy office."[93]

By 1900 such pious expressions had disappeared, and ambitious churches sought singers wherever they could be found. Inside each city, the competition for extraordinary voices was intense, and congregations bid against neighboring churches.[94] Those willing, and able, to pay singers enough drew even from outside their own localities. In 1896, one of the singers at Second Church, Philadelphia, was traveling from Camden across the river and another arrived weekly from Chambersburg, one hundred fifty miles to the west. At a church in Ithaca, New York, only two of twenty paid musicians were members of the congregation.[95]

The quartet choir—one singer for each part—was a common, if unpredictable, pattern. In theory, it allowed the available budget to be divided into the minimal number of individual salaries, thereby making it possible to compete for the very top singers. In practice, as young Philadelphia organist Seldon Miller explained to a disgruntled music committee, it was the "worst possible choir." The reality was that four strong voices, however excellent they were individually, might not blend well. Furthermore, Miller continued, "it happens usually that one or another of the singers is suffering from some disability, so that only upon rare occasions can all be depended upon to sing effectively." Miller's solution was to take his budget, a generous $2,300, and spread it out to hire nine good singers rather than four superlative ones. His successor used a slightly larger budget to hire sixteen.[96]

The more common solution was to augment the four lead singers with volunteers from the congregation. This combination of quartet choir and "chorus choir" served many urban churches well. Brick Church, New York City, in 1914 had a choir of eight sopranos, six altos, four tenors, and four basses including one paid singer in each section. Carr's Lane had five paid principals in a chorus of thirteen sopranos, eight altos, eight tenors, and eight basses.[97]

Congregations that mounted all-volunteer choirs were proud of their achievement, but found that these choruses had their own set of difficulties. The most serious problem was that the number of singers fluctuated, and at times dropped to a precariously low level. At Lyndhurst Road, the choir leader was one of the most frequent letter writers to the church news sheet because recruiting volunteers was a never ending task. Some churches accepted both "regular" and "occasional" choir members in order to fill the loft. At Redland Park in Bristol, the situation became serious enough that "for a short time" they laid aside their scruples and hired a few male singers. Most choir directors made do with what they had, but balance was often a problem. Edgbaston Church in Birmingham found itself with twenty sopranos, seven altos, six tenors, and thirteen basses. The director at Lansdowne United Presbyterian Church tried to rectify an imbalance by splitting the women into two groups that sang every other Sunday, while the "gentlemen, from want of numbers, *get no relief at all.*"[98]

Volunteer choirs typically developed social dimensions that were not shared by professional groups. There is some evidence to suggest that they were populated most heavily by young single men and women, and the groups soon took on some attributes of a club or association. The choir of First Congregational Church in Cleveland was organized with a president, vice-president, secretary-treasurer, and librarian, and was listed in the directory along with other social groups. The choir in Govan parish had an annual picnic at the end of the year. A number of all-volunteer choirs were tied to congregational choral societies that performed a more varied repertoire of music than was appropriate for Sunday worship.[99]

Congregations supported their choral programs in several ways. One, of course, was financial. Church budgets will receive a more thorough analysis in Chapter 8, but for now it is worth noting that churches with musical aspirations were directing significantly larger proportions of their local resources into their choral programs by the century's end. The music budget in Glasgow's Lansdowne Church, for instance, absorbed 5 percent of the local budget in 1885, which was fairly typical for a church with an organ but no paid choir. By 1905, however, a more ambitious musical program absorbed 14 percent of the budget. The music portion in First Congregational Church, Cleveland, went from 4 percent of local expenses in 1856 to 19 percent in 1914. A church with a major music ministry such as First Church, Hartford, devoted about 30 percent of its local revenues in the 1890s.[100]

Churches also invested in training for volunteer choristers. At least one church paid for voice lessons for an adult, but most put their time and effort into younger singers. It was the "children and youth" that Third Presbyterian Church, Indianapolis, wanted to groom as future choir members. Lansdowne Church, which relied for years on an unpaid choir, had a class "for the training of beginners and all others also in the elements of singing at sight, and so preparing them for Membership in the Choir." In the 1890s, Lansdowne's children were presenting two cantatas per year, one during the Christmas season and another in the Spring.[101]

Anthems were to choirs what voluntaries were to organists—a chance to praise God by themselves. In its earliest usage, however, *anthem* referred to a piece of music, neither a psalm nor a hymn, that was attempted by the choir and congregation together. Some midcentury hymnals included a few anthems that were deemed accessible to the average singer, and encouraged their use in place of one of the usual psalms or hymns. But it is doubtful that this ever worked well, which is one reason the task was turned over to choirs. At least one report suggests that the midcentury attempts at congregational chanting also amounted to *de facto* anthems by the choir, since so few of the congregation could manage the technique. But the belief that all singing should be *congregational* singing died slowly, and in Scotland there were places in the early twentieth century where the congregation still stood for the choir anthem and thereby kept at least the pretense of participation.[102]

Until late in the century, copies of choral music were difficult to procure, and early choir leaders used manuscript copies or arranged for the printing of their own anthologies. In time, commercial collections were available from publishers such as Novello. Denominations also produced anthologies of authorized music. The 1902 edition of the Free Church *Anthem Book* contained 167 four-part anthems published in both notation and Tonic Sol-Fa versions for 2s. 6d. with cloth binding (or 5s. for leather).[103] A words-only version was available for the pews at 6d. One attraction of a denominational anthem book to church boards was that its exclusive use prevented inappropriate music from finding its way into church. Volunteer choir leaders likewise welcomed the book because of its convenience and because the anthems were so easy to learn, especially when tradition-minded editors chose with the lingering hope that the entire congregation would sing them. An all-volunteer choir at the Church of the Covenant in New York City proudly announced that after having a Scottish anthem book for but a short while, it had already learned twenty of the anthems.[104]

More talented choirs found these anthem books boring and looked for greater challenges, and there is evidence that by the early twentieth century trustees were compelled to build shelving for the growing collections of sheet music. Brick Church, New York, where Clarence Dickinson was organist-director, performed a wide repertoire of church music. Dickinson's annual report for 1914 gave the year's effort as sixteen anthems from the Latin church, seven by French composers, twelve from the Greek church, thirty-two from the Lutheran chorale tradition, sixteen in the religious folk-music category, forty-one by English composers, thirty-four from oratorios, and forty-six by American composers.[105] At First Presbyterian Church, Chicago, the Christmas and Easter services included anthems by Bach, Boellman, Gounod, Schubert, Handel, Arthur Foote, Horatio Parker, Myles Foster, John West, and the church's own organist Philo Otis.[106]

Choirs in large city churches gave grand concerts, as well. First Church, Hartford became famous for the oratorios that its choirs performed under the direction of organist Samuel Cooper. St. George's parish choir in Edinburgh sang Bach's Christmas Oratorio in December 1912. Portions of Handel's Messiah were, of course, frequent choices for holiday concerts in many city churches. For big concerts, extra soloists, choristers, instrumentalists, and even small orchestras were brought in. Wellington United Presbyterian Church assembled a choir of forty-six voices to do Mendelssohn's "Hymn of Praise" before "a gratifying attendance" in 1893. This performance was opened with prayer and closed with a benediction, giving it the context of worship rather than entertainment, but other congregations turned their concerts into occasions for church fellowship, as did Philadelphia's Second Church when it arranged a tea to follow its choir concert in 1896.[107]

The kind of the music chosen for the concerts helped to establish a congregation's identity. When a church such as Cowcaddens Free advertised a "Special Service of Sacred Song" featuring the North Hall Mission Choir, its reputation for revivalistic worship was solidified. Congregations programming Bach, Handel, and Mendelsohn, however, signaled that they wanted to be associated with the elite churchly tradition; string ensembles or harpists rather than brass bands sent the same message. A few congregations sought to emulate their Anglican or Episcopal rivals by establishing men and boys choirs. Organist John Finlay had a boys' choir at Paisley Abbey in the early twentieth century, and in London, King's Weigh House hired T. M. Baker in 1904 with instructions to form "a choir of Men and Boys." Second Church, Philadelphia, established no such permanent choir, but did advertise appearances by two boy soprano soloists in 1900.[108]

In 1910, Minshall was ending his career as organist at London's City Temple, and he looked back over the transformation in which he had played a part. "Church music is very different to-day from what it was forty or fifty years ago," he reflected, "and the leaders of the service of praise are far better equipped than they used to be." What were the changes? At the beginning of his life, there had been few musical instruments, "though a harsh and wheezy harmonium was found here and there." Now, in 1910, there were very few British churches without a pipe organ "of very fair quality." The organs themselves had changed; there were improvements in tone, and with electro-pneumatic action, the instruments "now have an easy 'touch,' [and] the mechanism is more perfect." Fifty years ago, he remembered, "three stave [organ] music was almost unkown," and the organ repertoire was limited to Novello's "Select Pieces," a collection of simple arrangements. But today, Minshall noted, the "choice of organ music is almost unlimited." There was a commensurate improvement in training. When he began his career, proper organ instruction was hard to come by outside the major cities; now it was available everywhere "except in the most remote parts of the country."[109]

The second major change that Minshall observed was the development of a choir tradition in Reformed churches. As a boy, Minshall had hardly ever heard anthems; only "very occasionally" were Cecil's "I will arise," Camidge's "Sanctus," and Farrant's "Lord, for Thy Tender Mercies' Sake" heard; "for Sunday use," he remembered, "these three well-known pieces were the repertoire." Now, by 1910, scores of compositions by Stainer, Smart, Hopkins, Goss and Barnby could be had "at a very moderate price."[110]

> Choirs, too, are now much more efficient than they used to be. Very few people could read music fifty years ago; it was only the upper classes—and not very many of them—who were taught the art. Most people, therefore sang by ear, and under such conditions, harmonies were not always the best. Choir practices were not held regularly. . . . It was a happy-go-lucky sort of arrangement, and the singing—in many places at least—was left to chance. In those days four, or perhaps

five, hymns formed the sole musical service, so there was not much incentive to have regular practices.[111]

How different things were in 1910. At their best, the changes that Minshall and his contemporaries wrought added interest and spiritual intensity to otherwise drab worship; they reconnected the Reformed churches to broader, and older, parts of the Christian tradition; and they made worship an act of the heart as well as the head. If there was a disadvantage, it was that the people threatened to become an audience of connoisseurs rather than a congregation of worshippers. In this sense, the changes only reinforced the focus on entertainment emerging in so many other parts of religious life.

It cannot be said that the transformation of church music occurred without dissenting voices. The excellent choir at St. George's parish church in Edinburgh had to endure Elder Brown, who in 1888 convinced the kirk session to limit anthems to five minutes, and then sat, watch in hand, for the next twenty-two years hoping to catch the choir exceeding its allotment of time so that he could create a furor at the next session meeting.[112] But Elder Brown was fighting a losing, rear guard action, and he knew it. The dominant view was that of a London churchgoer who, in the congregation's in-house newsletter, argued that "the love and culture of music have of late spread so rapidly that, if we do not in our churches keep pace with the growing taste and desire for plenty of good music, we do not satisfy the cravings of the younger members of the congregation."[113] In that one perceptive sentence, the writer had captured the essence of the musical revolution.

# PART III

Life Together

# six

## Becoming a Member
### *Procedures and Expectations*

Early in the year 1830, a young London woman approached the Rev. Thomas Binney, pastor of King's Weigh House, and said she wanted to become a church member. Miss Brown's request set in motion a prescribed sequence of events by which the church assured itself of her "principles and character." Although a written statement detailing her "sentiment and experience" was not required here as it was in some other places, Miss Brown chose to submit one. Binney and two deacons, Dawson and Burkitt, "conversed with" her at length and made inquiries among her acquaintances concerning her "general deportment." At the end of February, her name was announced publicly so that any member knowing cause against her had a chance to speak up (much like the posting of wedding banns). When the allotted month passed and Binney heard no objection from any one, Miss Brown's application was ready to be taken to a meeting of the church.

On 30 March, Miss Brown's written statement was presented to the gathered members, and Binney reported on his conversation with her. "Religious impressions had early been made on her mind by the instructions of pious parents," he recounted, "& though she was unable to specify the precise time of her conversion & had not had those awful views of the evil of sin which some have yet she placed all her dependence on the work of the Lord Jesus Christ & was desirous of uniting herself to the church in obedience to his will." Binney's evaluation was confirmed by Dawson and Burkitt, and then, by a show of hands, Miss Brown was "unanimously admitted into communion with the church." Binney extended to her the congratulatory "right hand of fellowship" on behalf of the church, and at the next celebration of the Lord's Supper, her name was read out with those of other new members.[1]

Joining a church in the 1830s was a *public* undertaking. Prospective members at King's Weigh House and other Congregational churches expected their behavior to be investigated fully and their life story to be laid open to all. If anything,

London's New Broad Street Church was more diligent in assuring that the applicant's "Christian character be certified and unquestioned." There, a written account of religious experience was mandatory, and so were the names of two reliable references—"upright persons in their locality, to whom they are known, who can bear favourable testimony to their moral character."[2] In Liverpool's Great George Street Church, it was "evidence" that members wanted from applicants—"satisfactory evidence that they love the Lord Jesus Christ in sincerity and in truth."[3]

By the end of the century, all of this had changed. Decisions on new church members were neither public nor characterized by a high degree of involvement by other laity. Entry into the church was an increasingly private matter, confined to discussions between the applicants and the pastor. The gradual transformation began early and can be traced through the King's Weigh House minutes. In 1843, the deacons' interviews with the candidate were termed "optional" rather than "indispensable."[4] While this change may well have protected some deacons from overwork, it also protected new members from having their "sentiments and character" examined outside the pastor's study. By the 1860s, the minister's reports to the congregation revealed nothing of his conversations with the applicant. The new, cryptic language of the official record—"the following individuals were this evening proposed for church membership"—made the general meeting sound almost perfunctory.[5] Gone were the references to the minister's "satisfaction with [the candidates'] professed principles and character"; gone was any confirmation "by the testing of the Deacons"; and gone, too, were the candidates' oral or written statements. The process was not yet entirely private. Ordinary members were still given a month to raise objections, and they retained the right to approve an application by vote, although that vote must increasingly have been cast in ignorance. By the early twentieth century, even this much had vanished, and the minutes in January 1904 noted simply, "Dr. Hunter [the pastor] *announced* the following New Members."[6] If a vote was taken, the clerk did not bother to record it.[7] Membership had become a private matter between the pastor and the applicant.

Admissions procedures among American Congregationalists underwent a similar transformation. In Hartford, during the 1830s, both First and Second churches referred applications to an examining committee made up of the pastor, deacons, and several at-large members. This group interviewed candidates, seeking (in First Church's words) "satisfactory evidence of Christian character." If the examining committee found the evidence of personal piety convincing, then the applicant's name was proposed—Americans habitually said "propounded"— from the pulpit, and the entire membership was given two weeks to bring forth questions or objections. If no difficulties arose, the candidates were voted in, and became members by giving "*public* assent" to the congregation's articles of faith and covenant.[8]

But here, too, the process grew less public, more private, as the century wore on. A contrast between the titles of two questionnaires, one printed by First Church, Hartford, in 1835 and another by Second Church in 1860, begins to make the point. Both were intended for the use of incoming members and were actually fairly common aids provided to inquirers. The questions themselves, although from two churches and twenty-five years apart, were not dissimilar. Some, indeed, were identical, such as "You wish to profess religion,—why?" Others led inquirers to examine their sentiments and behavior, or to understand the obligation they proposed to undertake. "Is it your highest desire and settled purpose to be *holy* and walk with God to the end of your life and forever?" "Are you conscious that a union to Christ's visible church adds to your duties and obligations?"

But the titles above the two questonnaires were tellingly different. The 1835 list was captioned, "QUESTIONS FOR THOSE WHO CONTEMPLATE MAKING A PUBLIC PROFESSION OF RELIGION." Whatever value the queries had for the undecided, they must also have been a convenient starting point for the examination itself. One question—"Are you a christian, a disciple of Christ? *What evidence* satisfies you of it?—seems especially designed with that purpose in mind. The wise applicant, one supposes, would have prepared carefully before approaching the examiners. The caption above the 1860 questions, however, denies any such use at all; the questions were identified as being for "private use." The implication is that by the 1860s, the assessment of new members was, if not already, at least becoming a self-assessment carried out by self-interrogation in the privacy of the applicant's own chamber.[9]

By the turn of the century, the change in Hartford was complete. The examiners at Second Church had new instructions that reversed the burden of proof and protected the privacy of applicants. "Unless the committee find good reason to the contrary," the examiners were now told, the applicant was to be approved.[10] In the early days, absence of scandal, in itself, never warranted admission; a committee was expected to search until it found what congregations across America called "credible evidence" or "satisfactory evidence" of personal piety and character. There was no way this could be done, of course, unless the applicant's innermost thoughts and private deportment were open to public scrutiny. A church in Chicago made such an investigation explicit; its committee was "charged with inquiring into [candidates'] Christian history and present religious experience."[11] By 1900, however, the Hartford examining committee had been told that personal matters were off limits. Unless accounts of dishonor reached them, they were not to probe private sentiments or private lives. A decision for Christ was one's own.

Among Presbyterians, admission had never been a matter for discussion by the entire membership; new members were examined and voted in by the elders, and then "announced" to the congregation. On that side of the Reformed tradition, public scrutiny never extended outside the session room. This having been said, American Presbyterian practice had a lot in common with that of the Congregationalists. Sixth Presbyterian Church, Chicago, as an example, listed its membership requirements in language virtually identical to that used by Congregational churches in the same city—"satisfactory evidence of a Christian experience and character."[12] At Central Presbyterian in Rochester, applicants were "examined & rec^d by the Session upon the evidences of their faith in the Redeemer." Afterward, during the ensuing communion service, they stood before the congregation and "assented to the covenant of this Church."[13]

Presbyterian churches, too, grew more protective of the privacy of incoming members. When one man joined Second Church, Philadelphia, in 1832, he "gave an account to Session of his spiritual exercises and of the dealings of God's Spirit with his soul which had led him to entertain a hope of having received Divine grace." His experience was typical; in those early years, candidates came before the elders to be "examined in regard to their spiritual views and exercises." By the 1850s, however, the word "examination" appeared less frequently in the session minutes. Sometimes it was simply omitted; candidates appeared and were admitted, but no interrogation was explicitly mentioned. More often, the clerk wrote down that the elders had "conversed with" the applicants, as distinct from the more traditional word, "examined." Or, in the 1880s, the elders used an even less precise word, noting that there were "meetings" with incoming members. By the early twentieth century, new members' names were simply listed in a column under the heading, "Received on Confession," without comment of any sort.[14]

Much of this was surely a reflection of the general Victorian trend toward private and individual, rather than public and communal, conventions. But these cultural influences were reinforced when repentance and faith themselves (rather than behavior and character as presumptive evidence of repentance and faith) became primary criteria of membership. Traditionally, Reformed theology had considered the true state of a person's soul to be beyond human knowledge, and congregations had been very careful not to claim too much for their examinations. One London congregation in the 1850s noted the limitations of its scrutiny: it would admit those "who are *believed to have* exercised repentance towards God," and it would base that estimation on outward signs—deportment, character, reputation, and spiritual exercises such as daily prayer and Bible reading.[15] First

Presbyterian Church, Philadelphia, had made the same point to its new members in 1841: "We pretend not to know the heart." The congregation was content with "evidence of your personal piety." Whenever this can be furnished to the elders, "we trust that you have been truly renewed by the Holy Spirit."[16]

Slowly, however, this perspective changed under the influence of revivalism; the presence of saving grace itself took primary position. By 1905, First Church, Philadelphia had dropped its earlier criteria and now listed only "saving knowledge of Jesus Christ" and "appreciation of the obligations of church membership."[17] Neither of these was very amenable to the examination of evidence; the second pertained to what might be done in the future, and the first was hidden deep in the private recesses of the heart. The one thing that was capable of examination—past and current behavior—was no longer on the list. It is little wonder that the practice of examining new members disappeared or became perfunctory. New cultural expectations encouraged churches to respect privacy, and at the same time a new emphasis on believing—believing in and of itself—made religion an intensely personal, private affair.

It needs to be admitted here that these developments are more difficult to see in Scotland because the very concept of church membership, as Congregationalists and American Presbyterians understood it, was quite weak there. Residence put a person within a Church of Scotland parish, and any parishioner could ask to be added to the kirk's communion roll—that is, the list of those to whom tokens were distributed for the sacrament. The clergy controlled the process, and in some places it was known as the minister's roll—not the session's or the parish's. In Greyfriars Kirk, Edinburgh, in the 1830s, the minister "conversed" with intending communicants and, if he was satisfied, "laid before the Session" a list of their names. By the 1880s, the procedure had not changed appreciably; if none of the elders objected, the names went onto the communion list.[18] Enrollment never was, then, a particularly public procedure. Nor was it a very probing one; desire to receive the sacrament and a life free of public scandal were generally enough.

In any case, communion rolls seem to have been haphazardly kept, and especially so prior to the 1874 legislation giving communicants the right to vote for parish ministers.[19] When Greenside parish determined in 1871 to put its roll in order, it asked everyone with a communion ticket to fill out a card headed "Revisal of Communion Roll" and then proceeded simply to make up a new roll from the cards. Greyfriars, still scrambling for a "correct Communion Roll" two years after the 1874 law, did the same thing; it "arranged that all applicants for tokens for the approaching Communion be asked to furnish in writing their names and addresses." In practice, the roll mirrored rather than determined who communed.[20]

Free Church congregations at first duplicated the established church procedures. St. George's Free Church, during its first year, added "new communicants" (not new members) simply on the word of the pastor, who "reported" the names to a passive session. It was a half-dozen years or so before applicants appeared in person before session and were registered as "members of this church."[21]

But practice varied among Free Church congregations, depending on how deeply rooted the old established church tradition was. While the clergy continued to handle incoming members at St. George's, the elders of Cowcaddens played a more active role. Cowcaddens was not organized until 1865, over twenty years after the Disruption, and its original officers did not bring established-church habits with them. The congregation, therefore, acted as a gathered church from the start. Applicants were called "Candidates for Church Membership," and each was visited by an elder who reported to the session on his findings. Cowcaddens's early practice had more in common, then, with the Congregationalists and American Presbyterians, and so did its later habits. Here, too, elders learned to respect the privacy of incoming members. By the 1890s, the session records do not carry the names, or even the total number, of new members; there is nothing but a notation that members were admitted and their names entered in the church register.[22]

Before moving ahead, it is worthwhile to look briefly at two groups of incoming members who were handled distinctly—children who had grown up within the church and transfers from other congregations. All local churches accepted "certificates" or "letters" from other congregations. Membership transferred within the Reformed community, back and forth across the Atlantic as well as on either side; Reformed congregations also accepted credentials from churches of other evangelical denominations. Persons arriving from a previous congregation faced a significantly less demanding admissions process. Typically, receiving congregations waived the usual examination, and in some Congregational churches, public propounding was considered unnecessary, too. Although transfer members might be asked to assent to the covenant of the new local church, they were usually excused from a public profession of faith. Sixth Presbyterian Church in Chicago made it clear that they considered transfers a different category altogether; admission was by two routes—you needed either "satisfactory evidence of a Christian experience and character [and] a cordial and unreserved profession of faith in Christ as the only Saviour" or you needed "a regular certificate of dismission from some other evangelical Church."[23] By the turn of the century, two congregations were treating transfers as little more than bookkeeping tasks. At King's Weigh House, the secretary rather than the pastor announced transfers to the church meeting; at Gilcomston Free Church in Aberdeen, arriving transfers were told merely to drop their certificates in the collection plate or send them in by mail.[24]

The system rested on the considerable trust that congregations had for each other. Certificates were not granted casually, and wayward or lax members did not receive them; there was scrutiny on the way out the door as well as on the way in. But there were also good practical reasons to make transferring easy and painless, and as rapid as possible. The reality was that the longer members took to link up with a new congregation, the less likely they were to find a new spiritual home at all. London's Holloway Church expressed what all feared when it warned, "[Delay] leads to a gradual neglect of church-fellowship, and ends in an entire return to the world." Delay also made the issuing congregation's certificate less reliable. How, asked Holloway rhetorically, can a congregation be expected to give "testimony to character after its opportunity of knowledge has ceased?"[25]

As a result, the congregations at both ends of a potential transfer applied pressure for a prompt resolution. One year was the outside limit. Departing members had only twelve months to locate a new church home and write back for a letter of transfer; extensions could be granted, but only for good cause. Members heading out into the American West or across the ocean were encouraged, and sometimes required, to take a general certificate with them; if so, it carried a twelve-month expiration (one congregation allowed only six). At the other end there was equal pressure to settle into a new church. Congregations typically permitted visitors to receive communion with them for no more than a year. Past that point "occasional communicants," as they were called, were not so occasional, and unless there were extenuations, membership had to be transferred.[26]

Children were the second discrete category of incoming members. Youngsters born into the church, baptized as infants, and nurtured in the church Sunday School could graduate to church membership, usually sometime around their twelfth birthday, although there was no common agreement on this age. For Central Presbyterian Church in Rochester the cut-off point was age ten; children younger than that could still be baptized on Children's Day with the infants, while those older could join the church and, if need be, undergo baptism on their own cognisance. But not every congregation dealt with children so young. At Lyndhurst Road, two elders strongly objected that children "less than 14 years of age" were too "young and immature" for membership; the fact that the rest of the officers "acquiesced with much reluctance" likely indicates that this marked the upper edge of what a congregation thought was reasonable.[27]

Children were prepared for membership by training in the home and church. At the time of infant baptism, their parents had covenanted to "instruct" them in the ways of the Lord, and in the early part of the century youngsters would have learned the Westminster Shorter Catechism, some of the metrical psalms, and assorted little prayers and Bible verses at their parents' knees. The lessons had changed by 1900, but home teaching was still expected. Parents in Rochester were urged to prepare their children for membership by "carefully instructing them in Christian truth, by teaching them the Lord's Prayer, the Ten Commandments and The Creed, and by prayerful consecration of them to God."[28] The church Sunday School added another layer of training and encouragement. When the child reached the age of membership, there was further counseling and education from the minister. In most places this occurred informally and individually, but by the 1890s some ministers found an organized "Communicants' Class" more efficient.[29]

The arrival of new members was a significant time in the life of a congregation, and it was celebrated with public ceremony. Early in the century, there were Presbyterian congregations that did no more than announce that new members had been received by the session, but such simplicity was rare. Especially among Congregationalists and those Presbyterians who understood admission as a covenant bond between new and current members, a whole-church ceremony was indispensable, and planners struggled to match the solemnity of the occasion. Lyndhurst Road, shortly after it was formed in the 1880s, wondered what it might do to make the admission of new members "more impressive."[30] It was a common desire even at the beginning of the Victorian era, and one that some ministers had tried to fulfill with awe-inspiring words. Philadelphian Albert Barnes laid full import of the occasion on those who stood before him: "The transactions of this day will live long in your remembrance, and will be followed with everlasting consequences. You are surrounded with 'a great cloud of witnesses.' The eyes of this Church, which now receives you to her bosom, are upon you. The eyes of the world, from which you have separated yourselves, are upon you. Holy Angels, and the everlasting and all-seeing God, witness this transaction. These vows are recorded in heaven. They will meet you again on your trial in the last day."[31] Others embellished their services with hymns: "Just As I Am, Without One Plea" and "Blest Be the Tie that Binds" seemed especially appropriate, as did Philip Doddridge's "O Happy Day."[32]

New communicants in Scotland's established church were received after the sermon during a precommunion preparatory service, when they accepted the church's articles of faith, took for themselves the promises made on their behalf at the time of their baptism, and promised to "submit to all the ordinances" of the church and "serve Him in holiness and righteousness."[33] In the Free Church of Scotland, new members stood in front of the pulpit at a preparatory service, and after being "briefly addressed & admonished" were extended the "right hand of fellowship" and given their communion tokens or cards.[34]

Midcentury American ceremonies tended to be equally straightforward. In a typical ceremony, those joining by profession of faith assembled before the pulpit. Following a few introductory words, the congregation's formal articles of faith (or confession of faith as it was sometimes called) was read point by point, and the new members gave their assent by nodding or, if seated on the first pew, by rising. The church covenant was read aloud, and agreement was again given; those joining by letter of transfer stood in place to add their assent. At this point the entire congregation rose to welcome the newcomers and to own its half of the reciprocal covenant. Both old and new members were admonished to fulfill their promises, a benediction was pronounced and the service ended.[35]

Although congregations shamelessly borrowed or copied what they saw in other church manuals, there was strong local investment in these early services; questions drawn from a congregation's own confession and covenant spoke plainly to what was expected. By the early twentieth century, however, admissions rituals came from denominational manuals that although more liturgically elegant made less specific demands. Opening verses—"Come unto me, all ye that labor and are heavy laden"—supplanted the local minister's wordy introduction. The Apostles' Creed or a denominational statement such as the American Congregational Confession of 1883 took the place of the locally adopted articles of faith or confessions. Questions to new members (now phrased to elicit a verbal "I do" rather than mere nodding or rising) were noticably less precise. Take, as an example, two clauses, each promoting regular worship but written twenty-eight years apart: the modern phrase "to help in sustaining its worship" may have been more stylish than "to assemble yourselves with his people for worship," but it did not carry nearly as much clarity or force. One cannot help speculating that the ambiguity revealed an equal uncertainty about expectations and standards.[36]

Congregations found their own ways of softening the demands that their locally written articles of faith or confessions made on new members. Few statements in use at the beginning of the century made sense by its end. Intellectual currents operating at a level quite distant from the congregation roiled the theological waters and left local churches scrambling to revise or replace their confessions. Boston's Old South Church provides a sharp, if somewhat extreme, example of what happened among American Congregationalists.

The year was 1899, and New England churches had been, one by one for a decade or more, revising or supplanting their local articles of faith. The denomination had written a more liberal statement in 1883, and the New Theology's spirit was spreading outward from Andover Seminary. Congregations, finding that their thoughts were no longer in phase with their words, adjusted. Old South members were a bit embarrassed to admit that they did not even know what was in their articles of faith. Supposedly, their ancestors had written one in 1680, but no one living had seen or could remember it. A senior deacon said he had joined in 1859, and no one ever asked him to assent to any confessional statement at all.

Curious, the deacons decided to look up the old document. When they located it (the last copies had been printed in 1854), not one of them thought he could subscribe to it. "We were not long in coming to a unanimous conclusion," they told their fellow members, "that it was high time for the church to take some formal and final action in regard to this creed." Apparently, the creed had fallen into disuse in the mid-1850s when Manning, Old South's minister at the time, decided it was antiquated. Now, forty years later it seemed superfluous. By a vote of 134 to 6, Old South's members agreed to "set aside this confession of faith or creed hereafter to be discontinued formally as it had been disregarded practically." The church covenant, which emphasized duties and practice, would be enough.[37]

Most American Congregational churches did not literally lose their old confessions, but the trend toward more doctrinal latitude was virtually universal.[38] One route, short of revising or discarding a confessional statement, was to soften or remove the language binding people to it. The church in Binghamton, New York, added a preamble explaining that no "human statement" could adequately reflect divine truth; "there are great divergences of intellectual belief among those whose rightful membership in the Church Universal it cannot and would not question."[39] Beecher's church in Brooklyn left its original articles of faith in the congregational manual, but in 1870, the question "Thus do you believe?" was removed from the admission ceremony.[40] First Church, Hartford, began in 1867 to ask incoming members if they could "assent to these articles as, *in substance,* the expression of your own religious belief."[41]

A more forthright approach was to replace the old-fashioned confession with a new one or with a denominational or ecumenical creed. First Church, Rochester, Masschusetts, adopted a streamlined confession in 1907, shrinking the fifty-five lines in its 1844 confession down to twelve. Second Church, Hartford, discarded a fourteen-point confession in 1874 and decided to require "no doctrinal test of membership other than the ancient confession commonly known as The Apostles' Creed, which is used as a part of worship in the Sabbath morning service." But there was latitude even in this. "Nor does this church require of its members a literal acceptance of even this Confession," the members' manual explained, "but presents and uses it as setting forth, substantially, the fundamental facts of the Gospel and as the common creed of Christendom."[42]

While American Congregationalists moved away from subscription, lay members in other parts of the Reformed community had enjoyed greater latitude of belief from the beginning. English Congregationalists were suspicious of anything that infringed upon freedom of conscience. New Broad Street Church, London, printed a standard set of twenty "Principles of Religion," but quickly denied that this was "put forth with any Authority, or as a standard to which assent should be required." From the English perspective, descriptive statements were permissible, but forced assent was not: "Disallowing the utility of Creeds and Articles of religion as a bond of union, and protesting against subscription to any human formularies, as a term of communion, Congregationalists are yet willing to declare, for general information, what is commonly believed among them; reserving to every one the most perfect liberty of conscience."[43]

Presbyterians traditionally demanded confessional subscription from clergy and elders, but not from the general membership.[44] In places where ties to New England Congregationalism were closest, however, local practice conflicted with that heritage and incoming members were indeed expected to assent to a confession. In Second Church, St. Louis, the reading of the congregation's six-point "profession of faith" was followed by the words, "All this you profess and believe."[45] Barnes's form of admission in Philadelphia included an eleven-part summary (with Scriptural citations) of "the leading doctrines of the Confession of Faith of the Presbyterian Church, to which we expect your assent."[46]

But the stronger tradition, and one shared by the Scots as well, was freedom of conscience on matters of belief. First Church, Indianapolis, explained to its incoming members that while ordained ministers and officers had to subscribe to the church confession, "from the beginning of her history in this country, the Presbyterian Church has received to her Communion all those who, in the judgment of charity, were true believers in Jesus Christ, and who agreed to submit themselves peaceably to the rule of the Church, without requiring as a condition to Church membership the reception of *all* the doctrines taught in the standards of the church."[47]

Thus, national turmoil about theology seldom reached the local level in any concerted fashion. Congregations might divide over whether to stand or sit for prayer, but they were unlikely to do so over theories of atonement; they might discipline members for errant behavior, but rarely for heretical belief. One member of Plymouth Church, Brooklyn, summed it up the prevailing attitude, "Men are taken for what they are, not for what they believe."[48]

Congregational expectations for what the laity should be and do—as opposed to believe—were spelled out in church covenants or lists of "Duties of Church Members."[49] An analysis of how those stated expectations changed between 1830 and 1915 is valuable for itself, but it also begins to illuminate aspects of church life that will be developed in the remainder of this book.

A member's first obligation was a relationship with God. The earliest language emphasized submission and obedience to the triune majesty. Phrases such as "give up yourselves in faith, repentance, and holy obedience" or "give yourselves away in a covenant never to be revoked, to be his servants forever" are typical. So was legal rhetoric calling for members "to walk in all the statutes and ordinances of the Lord" or "to observe all his commandments and ordinances." Members were to "bind" themselves to God, inescapably, forever.[50]

During the last years of the century, the language of submission was replaced by one of decision, devotion, and commitment. Members were not described as submissive; rather they were resolute and determined. They accepted Jesus of their own volition. The language was active; members declared a willingness to "enter into His covenant of grace" or "consecrate your lives" to Jesus. Was this, one covenant asked, "your sincere confession and determination?" The relationship was more personal, less legal. Rather than following God's laws, it was Jesus himself that the members followed. Do "you promise to follow Him in all things, to walk with His disciples in love, and to live for His glory"?[51]

A member's second obligation was a right relationship with the world. In the early statements of duty, this was expressed in terms of withdrawal or separation from an evil, sinful world. Will you "come out from the world, to separate yourselves from its sins and snares," one covenant demanded. Plymouth Church, Brooklyn, asked members to renounce the world and its dominion over them. In 1835, Carr's Lane called for members to "avoid what are called worldly amusements, such as theatrical representations, card playing, balls, and all kinds of gambling, frequenting taverns, fashionable concerts of music, private dancing parties, and fashionable routs, and oratorios." These might not in themselves be evil, but "they abate seriousness and spirituality, promote levity and frivolity of mind, are a great mispence of time, and are a part of that conformity to the world in which christians are forbidden to indulge."[52] Some congregations added a statement on Sabbath observance, others committed their members to total abstinence from intoxicating drink, and English Congregationalists typically included a duty to "act with integrity and uprightness in business."[53]

By the 1890s, this sense of antiworldly piety was quite simply gone. Reformed church members attended the theater as regularly as anyone; indeed, theatrical singers were now likely hired for the church choir, and oratorios performed to an appreciative audience in the sanctuary on Sunday evening. Church picnics, athletic leagues, and dances manifestly demonstrated how comfortable Reformed congregations had become with their place in the world. Except for a continuing opposition to alcohol, about the most that could be expected from a list of members' duties in the early twentieth century was a plea for "an earnest effort toward consistency of life at home and in public."[54]

A member's third obligation was to help the poor. "A life of piety toward God" was to be matched by "benevolence toward your fellow men."[55] "Visit the widow and fatherless, the sick and afflicted," was the advice of the pastor at Great George Street, Liverpool.[56] Despite the national visibility of the Social Gospel movement, social service was not featured any more prominently by the early 1900s. For that matter, despite the considerable involvement of congregations in local mission projects throughout the century (as we shall see in Chapter 9), benevolence was never spelled out with the same specificity given to other responsibilities. But after a fashion it was there—an obligation to support the church's benevolent and charitable work.

Fourth, members had duties within the church. Attendance at worship was primary and was mentioned as frequently at the end of the period as it had been at the beginning, although as we have already noted with less expectation of regularity and certainly with less explicit reference to weekday services. Willingness to submit to church discipline was an obligation that fell out of favor during the century and disappeared from lists. Discipline, in those early covenants, was one part of the members' larger obligation to support and care for each other, to watch over and pray for each other, to amend each other's flaws, to encourage each other in faith, to love each other, to walk together in charity, and to be "kindly affectioned one toward another."[57] Much of this rhetoric remained by the end of the period, but it had a somewhat different significance. The duty to promote the "peace, edification, and purity" of the church related less to the bonds of mutual support than to the pleasures of friendship. Fellowship was the new emphasis, and members had an obligation to get along. Not surprisingly, the newcomers to Lyndhurst Road in 1909 were welcomed with a "New Members' Social Meeting" so that they could become better acquainted with the rest of the church family.[58]

A fifth obligation at the beginning of the period was a devotional regimen— family prayer, personal prayer, reading the Bible. By the early twentieth century, this was still on some lists, but most ignored it entirely. Early twentieth-century congregations prided themselves in their active, rather than contemplative, spirit. And thus a new, sixth obligation was to participate in the activities, associations, and events sponsored by the church. One Massachusetts congregation indicated three, seemingly equal areas of obligation—worship, "activities," and charity work. A Philadelphia church got straight to the point: it wanted from each of its members "an active participation in the work of the church."[59]

A final, and seventh, obligation was one that seldom appeared on lists of duties before the last decades of the century; it was the obligation to contribute money for the work of the church. Its absence early in the period does not, of course, suggest that donations were not sought and expected. They were, and mission projects and the church poor fund depended on them. But, as we shall see in Chapter 8, most churches at that time sustained their own operations by pew rents, not by voluntary offerings. The advent of the free-will offering, however, meant that members' stewardship responsibilities had to be spelled out more explicitly. "Set aside a fair and fixed proportion of your income for sacred purposes" was what one English church put on its list.[60] First Presbyterian Church, Pittsburgh, combined both business-like efficiency and theological rationale when it listed "systematic and regular giving to the support of the church and its benevolence, remembering that God requires that our offerings shall be given ungrudgingly and generously."[61]

Beyond these statements of responsibility, which congregations used for the orientation of new members and the admonition of continuing ones, was an important, if usually implicit, hope—spiritual maturity. The manual for Regent Square Church in London caught this additional expectation when it summed up its members' obligations. What were they to contribute? "Attendance, liberality, service—These are all of urgent importance. But the deeper matter of the inward spirit is a thing more urgent still."[62]

What, to turn the question around, were the expectations of new members as they came through the door? Why did people choose congregational life? What attracted them to a specific church? Why this one rather than that one? For many, perhaps even most, the selection was foreordained; they grew up in a church, went to its Sunday School as children, and as adults joined grandparents, parents, aunts, uncles, cousins, and siblings in the family pews. Brand-name loyalty also was strong, and for those moving to a new town, the presumptive choice was a congregation of the same denomination. Still, after all that is said, populations were mobile, and cities offered multiple churches even of the same denomination. A city of no more than moderate size such as Cleveland could supply some two dozen Congregational churches. Streetcars and other improvements to urban transport meant it was no longer necessary, even within the Scottish parish system, to take the church closest to home. What, then, attracted churchgoers and kept them coming back?

The ministers mattered a lot. Their eloquence and their charisma drew hearers. Most congregations—to judge by the jubilee booklets and church histories they left behind—had a very clergy-centered view of themselves. They were "Dr.

Candlish's church"—or Beecher's or Parker's or Macleod's. Churches caught in the interim between pastors could expect few additions to the roll. Once a new preacher was installed, however, a surge of new members typically appeared. When Charles Wood moved from the Philadelphia suburb of Germantown to Second Church downtown in 1897, there were thirty-one new members in about a month—some of them from his Germantown church. In November 1880, Scott's transfer from one Edinburgh parish to another netted his new charge, St. George's, a quick 105 members, including three elders from his previous kirk, Greenside.[63]

Churchgoers, at least some of them, could be attracted by a cause or by the opportunity for social service. Congregations gained reputations as temperance churches or antislavery churches. The early leaders of Plymouth Church, Brooklyn, were abolitionists impatient with the slow pace of conservative Congregationalism. For them, it was the cause that mattered; among the founders were dry goods merchants whose commercial dealings were jeopardized by their zeal. This was a congregation that sent Sharps rifles to Kansas on one occasion, and purchased a slave's freedom on another. "This little girl is a slave," Beecher said as he introduced Sarah from the pulpit, "and I have promised her owner $1,200, his price for her, or she will be returned to slavery. Pass the basket." One who was there remembered that they got nearly $1,500, with some placing "jewelry, diamonds, watches and chains" into the plate as it passed.[64]

At Regent Square in London during the early twentieth century, the crusade was different, but its ability to attract no less. One young woman, describing the magnetism of that congregation, mentioned its declining urban setting. "Situated as it is in a changing neighbourhood," she wrote, it offered "a place for service." A young man in the congregation found "the darker side to all this—the poverty, the overcrowding, the drunkenness, the absence of religion" to be "an appeal and a challenge." Regent Square stood out, he thought, because it was a "substitute for the stucco and plaster respectability of a conventional suburb." What he found instead was a "pilgrimage," and "broader sympathy with mankind of all classes (and chiefly the poorer class)."[65]

Others came to the church as recipients of its social services. Mission halls, as we shall see in Chapter 9, provided a wide variety of programs ranging from education to recreation, from mutual support groups to assistance with life's basic needs of food, fuel, and medicine. City clerks and shop girls found downtown churches to be a noontime haven for lunch and relaxation. Mothers shared infant clothing and took advantage of day nurseries. Young workers used church employment and lodging registers. As but one example, Regent Square's April 1894 church newsletter carried help-wanted notices for a gardener and a governess; one member advertised in search of accommodations, another for piano and singing students.[66]

The most oft-cited reason for choosing a church was the welcome extended by the people who were already there. New arrivals to bustling late-Victorian cities sought friendship and belonging; when they found it in a church, they stayed. In 1915, a group of young men and women at Regent Square contributed their stories to a sixteen-page promotional brochure, "Testimony of Some Who Have Tried It." The theme that echoed through those stories was finding a home. "My first impression was—this was home," one said. "In the first place, I found in Regent Square a home," another wrote; "I found a welcome. I found people who were kindly and sympathetic." How had they first heard about the church? People again were the key. "A friend . . . told me about the Church," one replied. Another's testimony was, "She invited me."[67]

The fact that Regent Square produced such a collection of testimonies suggests that churches realized, at least by the end of the period, how significant personal connections were. The importance of extending a warm welcome was one reason churches stopped renting pews; a door sign saying "strangers will please apply to the door-keepers for sittings to prevent inconvenience to regular seathold-ers" was hardly inviting.[68] Various innovations signaled a new attitude—a visitor's book in London, a Welcome Committee (including a youth representative) in Massachusetts, a Vestibule Committee in Philadelphia charged with "becoming acquainted with those attending our Church," or the appointment of "stewards" in Birmingham to "provide visitors with seats, give information, and in the name of the Church, make all welcome."[69]

The importance of the initial welcome was one thing Stephen Griswold, a young man who came to Brooklyn to seek his fortune in 1851, remembered about his first Sunday at Plymouth Church. "The large auditorium of the church was thronged," he said, "but I received such a cordial welcome as to make me feel at home, and was shown at once to a seat."[70] Griswold joined the church a year later and served as an usher there for fifty-three years. The story of how he came to be at Plymouth Church in the first place sheds light on the several attractions that huge urban churches held for country lads.

Griswold did not immediately seek out a church when he got to Brooklyn. At first, the excitement of the city and his job as a clerk in a business firm were enough. After a time, however, the "novelty" wore off, and he wanted friends. Lonely, he began to study "notices in the papers and on the fences and bulletin boards." One poster from Plymouth Church caught his eye; he went and, as we have learned, received a warm welcome. On his second visit, he was invited to a Bible class, and "from this time on I had no reason to complain of any lack of social life."

A warm welcome and new friends were not, however, the only things that kept Griswold coming back to Plymouth Church. He was absolutely enthralled by the worship service. Nothing in his country church background had prepared him for what he experienced that first Sunday. "The service," he still remembered some sixty years later, "was a revelation to me, it was in every respect so very different from anything I had ever seen or heard. The singing by the great congregation, the eloquence and withal the helpfulness of the preacher, made a deep impression on me—an impression that stayed with me throughout the week, and I determined to go again the next Sunday."

It must have been difficult for some newcomers to summon the courage to enter one of those great preaching auditoriums or, perhaps more so, the grand cathedral-like structures that Reformed congregations built in the last half of the century. But once inside, they were awed by the stained glass, the organ, the choirs, the sheer dimensions of the building and the packed pews. A big-church experience was at once exotic and familiar. It was adventure and home. It linked new urbanites to their childhood roots and at the same time to the splendor of the city and the new social status to which they aspired.

But beyond the excitement, the friends, the social services, and reforming zeal, members were motivated by their commitment to Christianity. If not always at first, then in the end, membership in a church was an expression of sincere belief. It is important to distinguish here between participation and membership. No one needed to be a member just to attend or even to rent a pew. Membership, as opposed to pewholding or mere participation, provided no particular boost to social respectability; the fact that men joined in remarkably fewer numbers than did women suggests that neither respectability nor economic advancement rested on membership. Supporting religion or participating in church life could deliver tangible benefits in the world, but membership added only obligations.

And yet people joined. There were those who came to belief by childhood training; many a young man headed off to the city with a Bible tucked into his satchel by his mother. For some, Sunday Schools or mission halls or revivals brought them to commitment. Still others were drawn to the church for practical or aesthetic reasons and only later became convinced members. This seems to be the case with the young men and women whose stories filled Regent Square's pamphlet, "Testimony of Some Who Tried It." Friendship brought them in the door, and only later did they gain an understanding of Christianity and become involved in mission projects. Griswold, reflecting on his long attachment to Plymouth Church, mentioned the forceful preaching, Zundel's powerful organ playing, and the "cordial social atmosphere" as the things that caught his attention.

But, in the end, what held him "was the sense that church life was a means to an end, not an end in itself, and that the end was the building up of a true and noble Christian life in all its phases."[71]

Griswold, however, was an atypical member if for no other reason than that he was a man, not a woman. One of the most striking characteristics of church membership rolls was the preponderance of female names. At least for the churches examined here, two-thirds of the members were women. The percentage was amazingly consistent across time, geography, and class. Whether the congregation was theologically liberal or conservative, whether it was rural, suburban, or urban made no significant difference either.[72]

The dearth of male members does not mean that men were altogether absent from congregational life. They were well represented among the financial supporters of the church. Paddock Congregational Church in Huddersfield had, in 1903, a high percentage of female members (75 percent), but a relatively even division of pewholders, 53 percent of whom were men. Most congregations received an even higher percentage of their pew rents from male heads-of-household. In Chicago's Presbyterian Church of the Covenant, 63 percent of the members were women in 1887, but only 17 percent of the pewholders were. In the Congregational Church of Hyde Park, Massachusetts, about 65 percent of the members were women in 1895; of the "additional" persons attending worship or affiliated with the Sunday School, only 24 percent were women.[73]

Men, therefore, were in the congregation. They paid for family pews. They attended worship, although how frequently we cannot be sure. They joined Bible classes; four men's classes at Carr's Lane enrolled 378 men at a time in 1871 when there were only 219 male church members.[74] Their presence seems to have been critical in organizing new congregations, or at least they typically made up a larger percentage of members at the start than they did later. For instance, at Walton Park Congregational Church, which was organized in Liverpool in 1870, women comprised only 55 percent of the members by 1873, and it was not until two years later that they reached a more typical 67 percent. Only 32 percent of the founding members in Boston's Bowdoin Street Church were women, but during the congregation's first eight years, 1826–33, 63 percent of the incoming members were women, and by the late 1830s, women made up the usual two-thirds of the membership.[75]

So, men avoided church membership. They had what historian Curtis Johnson called a "minimalist religious orientation." That much is clear, but the reasons are less so.[76] If men were willing to participate minimally, but not to join the church, it seems plausible to begin by examining the differences between the two statuses. Membership carried two distinct privileges, a vote in ecclesiastical meetings and entry to the sacraments. The first of these does not seem to have been highly sought after by men. Apparently they concluded that the more important votes came in society or corporate meetings, and by virtue of their pew rents or contributions they already voted there. Budgets and buildings counted in tangible ways, and spiritual concerns did not.

Church membership also provided access to the sacraments. The right to have a child baptized was an important benefit of church membership, but as long as a man's wife belonged to the church, there was no additional gain from his joining; if one parent was a member, the baptism could occur. The sole remaining benefit, then, was entry to the marathon communion service and its attendant preparatory services. To many busy men, this must have seemed a burden not a privilege.

Were there disadvantages to membership? The major drawback from the perspective of many men was submission to church discipline. There will be more to say about disciplinary procedures in Chapter 7, but for now it is enough that individualism, independence, and privacy were sacrificed to public, communal standards. A man's business practices, personal habits, and the regularity of his attendance at worship came under constant scrutiny. Many men must have concluded that they earned enough respectability by renting a family pew and attending as frequently as they, not the church, chose. A minimal attachment to the church bought social respectability; an unfulfilled covenant membership meant public censure and the loss of respectability.[77]

Men may not, however, have been so calculating as the preceding paragraphs might suggest. If they were, an increase in male membership should have occurred by the beginning of the twentieth century. The threat of church discipline had disappeared, and the duties of membership were significantly less intimidating. But no such increase in male participation occurred. Indeed, in Jamaica Plain, Massachusetts, the percentage of female members edged up steadily from the low sixties to the upper sixties over the last four decades of the nineteenth century.[78]

The persistent ratio of two women members for every man might be explained, of course, as merely a vestigial continuation of an earlier pattern. Social practices can continue long after the initial reason for their existence is gone, and it is certainly true that men were socialized, from an early age, to regard religion as a woman's responsibility. The gender gap extended all the way back in the children's Sunday School classes. Children's classes in the middle years of the century typically enrolled more girls than boys, although not by so great a margin as that between adult women and men.[79]

Still, it is likely that men's reluctance had less to do with any specific complaint such as church discipline than it did with a fundamental conflict between congregational values and male gender identity. Historian Mark Carnes has argued that American men flocked to fraternal organizations because the lodges promoted rugged masculinity and the churches did not.[80] When church voters (two-thirds of whom were women) selected elders and deacons, they looked for men who were amiable, warm, humble, meek, forbearing, self-sacrificing, and gentle—as we noted in Chapter 2. If this was the ideal Christian gentleman, the model was far from the rugged individualist and hearty "go-getter" that many Victorian men imagined themselves to be. It is perhaps no coincidence that Old South, which had in its Boston pews more than its share of world-wise entrepreneurs, ended up both with very aggressively managed church investments and with an extremely lop-sided female majority among its members.[81]

Church leaders were aware of the gender gap, kept statistics on it, worried about it, and sought ways to reduce it. A session clerk in Rochester kept careful count of the numbers of males and females converted in revivals;[82] annual reports often broke down the membership totals by sex. By the 1880s, Scottish evolutionist and clergyman Henry Drummond launched the "Muscular Christianity" move-ment to give religion a more masculine tone.[83] Christianity was to be related to efficiency and the public sphere, not to sentimentality and the home. At Mayfield Free Church in the Edinburgh suburbs, the Rev. Lewis Davidson, fired by Drummond's vision, began a Young Men's Morning Fellowship Association, a Debating Club, and volunteer work at the Arcade Mission in the city's High Street. Athletic teams were added to church activities and gymnasiums were built. In 1883, the military-style Boys' Brigades began to promote virile Christianity to youngsters. Denominations encouraged men's brotherhoods or guilds. One young man, writing in a local Regent Square publication in 1912, went to great pains to emphasize that church life was adventurous and strenuous and that all Regent Square lads were hearty fellows and loads of fun.[84]

Perhaps, however, it is the wrong approach to ask why men shunned church membership; we can also turn the question around and ask why women joined. The life of service and self-sacrifice idealized by the Victorian church fit easily with the age's prescribed role for women. Starting from the social mandate for women to set aside personal ambition in favor of home and family, it was not a very large step to extend that selflessness to the church family. At the same time, the church provided significant scope for leadership and entrepreneurial activity. Women raised and controlled large sums of money, organized workers, taught, met payrolls, and managed programs and budgets. Both literally and figuratively, they could venture into the city's streets under the auspices of the church.

Through the church, women could also play a central role in setting community standards of conduct, and sometimes enforcing them. With women dominating church membership, it is possible that the enforcement of, say, temperance or sexual mores was seen as a gender-specific threat by certain men. In at least one American church, the possibility of women sitting in judgment of male behavior was considered enough of a menace that the congregation's by-laws stipulated that no man could be censured without a concurrent majority of male voters within the total vote.[85]

Finally, women found in the church unmatched opportunities for sisterhood. In prayer meetings, mother's meetings, mission circles and literary guilds, women made contact with each other. Men were able to build networks in the work place, the middle-class club or the working-class tavern, and the lodge; women connected in the church. What did women find of value? Answering her own question, one young woman put at the top of her list "a common meeting ground." It was "this sense of *camaraderie*," she said, that made church life essential for women.[86]

Once members joined the church, their names were entered on the official roll, a version of which was then printed in the congregation's manual. The typical arrangement of these names suggests that congregations understood a woman's membership to be independent and separate from her husband's affiliation (or lack of it). Although some congregations organized their directories by neighborhood (a method that facilitated visitation) or by date of admission (a style popular for anniversary booklets), the most common format was a straightforward alphabetical ordering by surname. Place of residence was the most common addition in a second column. When congregations used this alphabetized, person-by-person format, women's names appeared as separate entries—"Andrews, Mary" or "Clarissa Brace." Marital status was usually, though by no means always, noted by a bracketed "Mrs." or "Miss" following a woman's forename, or perhaps by a small "m." for married or "w." for widowed. Some entries included the husband's name—"Mrs. John"—along with a title inside the brackets, but a user was just as likely to have to deduce that information by matching street addresses. New Englanders used a variation of the individual-by-individual listing. They printed two completely separate alphabetical rosters, one female and one male, which accented the autonomy of women and men, but at the same time suggested an absolute separation of role.[87]

It is probably wise not to exaggerate the significance of these symbolic arrangements; women were not treated entirely without distinction, as New England's double-list style illustrates. Elsewhere, women's marital status was indicated, while that of men was not (unless it was clear from the wife's adjacent listing). A few compilers were quick to override strict alphabetical order and place a wife's name after the husband's even when her forename would naturally have placed it before. Even admitting these limitations, however, individual alphabetical listings did convey more independence than the family-centered styles adopted in the early twentieth century. For example, the Congregational church in Hyde Park, Massachusetts, chose a family layout in 1915 that drew more attention to women's subordinate marital status than to any independence within the church: the man's name appeared on one line as head of household, and the wife's name was indented below with those of the children.[88]

Whatever the layout, church officers struggled to keep their rolls current and accurate. It was not an easy thing to do, and the best efforts were only imperfectly successful. Occasionally, errors occurred when a new member's name was inadvertently skipped in the copying, or when a careless clerk lost the list of newcomers entirely.[89] But this was not the real difficulty. From London's mushrooming inner suburbs to America's Midwestern cities, mobility and church growth were astounding. Forty percent of a Bristol congregation in 1907 had been members for five years or less. Members came and went so frequently in Rochester that the Central Presbyterian Church devised a blank form to be used for transfers, and then lobbied to have it adopted by the presbytery so there would be "a uniform system of correspondence among the churches with regard to transfer of members."[90]

The midcentury enthusiasm for system and efficiency, which Central's form-making reflects, energized churches in a number of ways. Ministers and church boards resolved to "go over" their rolls more regularly. Congregations approved by-laws requiring themselves to report changes of address or to transfer their membership promptly when they moved from town. They established separate "reserve" or "supplementary" or "absentee" lists to carry the names of out-of-town or missing members. They sent "notes of enquiry" to last known addresses; they appointed committees to track down the lost. An exasperated clerk in Chicago begged to be informed of changes of address, marriages (especially the bride's new name), and deaths. "In so large a membership there will always be a large number of persons who have dropped out of sight," he reasoned; "only by constant diligence on the part of the officers, assisted by the diligence of the resident members, will the list of such be kept within reasonable limits."[91]

But departing members were not as systematic as the roll keepers would have liked. They lost their certificates of dismissal before they arrived at their new home, or they left them in a drawer or a trunk unused. One woman left Rochester in 1870 with a certificate from Central Presbyterian Church; twenty-four years later she returned, with the unused paper in her hand, asking to be put back on the roll (she was).[92] People neglected to, or chose not to, send in changes of address. A St. Louis church in 1857 had no known addresses for sixty-one people, or 12 percent of its membership. In 1863, St. George's Free Church could not find addresses for fifty of its members, which was actually not too bad considering the congregation's size. In 1893, Birmingham's Moseley Road Church dropped fifty-two members who could not be found or who had "drifted away and joined themselves to other Christian Communities without advising us of the change."[93]

The ease with which some members just disappeared was troubling even if the numbers were small, and it was a reminder that entry into a congregation was a beginning only. Sustaining the initial commitment and fostering an enduring loyalty were challenges to individuals and congregation alike. They had, after all, in their admission vows, promised "watch and care" for each other in a covenant without end.

# seveñ

## Caring for Each Other
*Nurture and Discipline*

Community life meant shared responsibility not only for the church as a body but also for each individual within it. The manual of one Midwestern Presbyterian church carried the typical promise: the pastor would come to members' sides whenever there was affliction or sickness, and in better times the elders would faithfully "visit and look after the welfare" of each person. Responsibility did not stop with the pastor and officers. According to a St. Louis church manual, members themselves were expected "*to watch over each other,* and to give and receive faithful counsel 'in the spirit of meekness.'" An English Congregationalist spoke of this reciprocal care as "a mutual helpfulness" within the church: "each is required to contribute something to the good of the whole, and to receive back good *from* the whole, by reciprocal inspection, counsel, watchfulness, caution, comfort, and admonition."[1] Mutual concern took multiple shapes and extended to body, mind, and soul. As this chapter unfolds, we shall look at programs for education and spiritual counsel, for home visitation, for support during times of illness or penury, and for discipline and reconciliation in cases of waywardness. These were all ways that churchgoers cared for each other.

Congregations made every effort to nourish the seeds of faith. Actually, much of the spiritual growth came serendipitously from people's participation in congregational life. Conviction was reinforced when churchgoers heard the word preached or committed hymn texts to heart or stood as witnesses to baptism or partook of the Lord's Supper or bowed their heads in prayer. Commitment grew stronger as it was practiced in local mission programs, temperance crusades, or parish visitation. However true this was, in these next paragraphs we shall focus on more intentional efforts at education and faith formation.

The members' handbooks or manuals, from which we have drawn information so frequently, were themselves means of edification and nurture. This was especially so of the style popularized by Dale in Britain and Beecher in America.

While many other manuals merely reproduced the congregation's by-laws and listed church meetings, officers, and members, Dale's and Beecher's took every opportunity to explain and encourage, often at considerable length. For instance, Beecher included an eight-page "Brief Account of Congregationalism"; his long section on ecclesiastical discipline emphasized both the Biblical foundations and the modern adaptations necessary for a large, urban church. Dale's manual also was generous with advice; for instance, it supplemented a schedule of worship services with "Directions for a Profitable Attendance Upon the Public Means of Grace."[2]

Many manuals provided questions for regular self-examination (or guidelines for "holy living" as a Presbyterian church in Chicago called them).[3] Devout members must have accepted each item as a goal to pursue. A church in Rochester, New Hampshire, recommended that members read its list of twenty questions "at least once every week, and pray God to search your heart in reference to the several points of Christian practice suggested by them." Another congregation recommended that members, with their bedtime prayers, "review every night the transactions of the day."

While the self-examinations varied somewhat in response to local enthusiasms, they showed strong similarities, and indeed much borrowing of language. Typically, lists began with the regularity of private and family prayer, Bible reading, and worship attendance. Other rubrics prompted individuals to assess their "personal efforts to win souls" or their diligence in nuturing the faith of their children. Most lists probed relationships with other churchgoers—"Are you at peace with all who love Christ?" Members were also directed to think about how they spent their money; one list asked, "Is your *property* consecrated to Christ?" Members of a Chicago church asked themselves whether they continually aimed "to please God in all relations and occupation of life; in business, study, politics, social and domestic life and recreation."

Whatever the specifics of the self-examinations, each tried to focus and intensify believers' efforts. The goal was to look heavenward and "to consider the express injunction of Scripture, and the beautiful example of Christ." The hope was that members would continually improve in spiritual health; the final question in one series was, "Am I steadily growing in grace?" The questions guided members as they searched their souls, identified weaknesses, and prayed for more faithful behavior. "If I should continue to live as I now do, till called to give up my account," one list concluded, "could the Judge then say to me, 'well done, thou good and faithful servant?'"

These self-examinations were only one small part of the devotional life that was expected to nourish spiritual maturity. The daily regimen of home prayer and

Bible reading included both family devotions and individual—that is, private or "secret"—prayer. Historian Mark Noll, in his study of American Presbyterian devotional literature, found a wide range of printed material in use—books of sermons, Sunday School lesson books, fiction, hymns, books of directed readings, and collections of prayers.[4]

Both individual authors and denominational committees published devotional helps. *The Sunday Home Service* (1885), by Glasgow minister Donald Macleod, supplied fifty-two family services, one for every Sunday evening of the liturgical year; each week there was an Old and a New Testament lesson, a "discourse" of five to six pages, and several prayers.[5] The Scottish Church Service Society's *Home Prayers* (1879) was an anthology of prayers and collects suitable for morning, evening, Christmas, and general occasions; the prayers were grouped into seventy-seven "services," each comprised of two to five prayers and ending with the Lord's Prayer.[6] Hymnals, too, contained songs that were identified as especially appropriate for "Home and Personal Use" or as pertinent to "Family Life." Advice books and church manuals encouraged mothers to create a "family altar" as a worship center in the home; prominently displayed, of course, was the middle-class family's prized religious artifact and status indicator—the oversized and suitably ornate family Bible.[7]

Actually, the flood of devotional literature during the second half of the century may have reflected the breakdown of home devotional practice rather than its vitality. At least some of the guidebook writers said they were trying to revitalize a declining habit. The Church Service Society, in the preface to *Home Prayers,* admitted that by the end of the 1870s many Scots thought family devotions had been "naturally superseded," and the Society regretted that much of what remained under the guise of home worship was mainly "of the silent sort." Under the circumstances, the Society's editors thought it necessary to begin their book with an argument for the value of home worship to a family, as "both helpful to their common life, and expressive of it."[8] The reality was that work schedules, leisure pursuits, and even a more crowded slate of church activities had began to cut into or reallocate family and personal time. Certainly the appearance of a volume called *God's Minute, A Book of 365 Daily Prayers Sixty Seconds Long for Home Worship* (1916) indicated the precariousness of devotional time by the early twentieth century.[9] Indicatively, historian Colleen McDannell has described how the "parlor Bible" declined in sales after 1870 and by the next century lost its place of prominence in fashionable houses to the photograph album.[10]

The ready availability of published devotional guides also reflected the professionalization that was making its way steadily through various aspects of nineteenth-century religious life. Here, as historian James Smylie has observed, the use of prepared devotional services shifted responsibility for family devotions from parents to clergy. Fathers or mothers could now read a professionally written "discourse" or children's story rather than express their own understanding of the day's biblical passage, and they followed a standardized lectionary rather than selecting their own passages.[11] If so, it can be argued that a similar process of professionalization was underway in religious education, with the advent of congregational Sunday Schools—or Sabbath Schools as many Reformed congregations called them in the nineteenth century.

Sunday Schools had their beginning at the end of the eighteenth century as mission outreach projects that provided basic education and religious instruction to children outside the congregation. Gradually, as government-supported schools made the first function obsolete, mission Sunday Schools put more of their effort into teaching the Bible and the Shorter Catechism.[12] It was not long until church volunteers, who saw mission children happily studying their lessons, wondered why there were not similar places of systematic instruction for the children within the congregation. Thus, the congregational Sunday School was born, the first of many programs invented for mission purposes and then transported back to the home church.

Congregational Sunday Schools replaced an earlier, informal system of parish education that relied on pastors, elders or deacons, and parents. When parents avowed the church covenant during the first half of the century, they had promised to instruct their children *themselves,* not to take their children to a Sunday School. The instructions for Presbyterian clergy in America were to "provide without delay for the stated instruction of the children and youth" in their congregations.[13] In St. Stephen's parish in Edinburgh in 1840, the minister, Dr. Muir, set aside three evenings each week of May, June, and July for "catechizing of the young persons of the congregation, from the age of eight to fourteen." It was the parents' diligence as well as the children's that was put to the test when the youngsters were "examined on the scriptures and the Shorter Catechism, repeat[ed] Psalms and Hymns, and [did] certain exercises in the way of arranging portions of the Bible, according to what may have been prescribed to them in the previous year." For youth beyond catechetical but not yet of communicant age, Muir provided fortnightly "Bible classes" in which he gave lectures "on a variety of subjects," and the students wrote essays which he corrected and returned.[14]

It was this older system of parental tutoring and ministerial catechesis that was replaced by congregational Sunday Schools, and there are just enough hints in the record to suggest that the new approach was not always welcomed by supporters of the old. To allay suspicion, Sunday Schools learned to claim that they only supplemented, rather than replaced, the parents' instruction.[15] Because the original mission Sunday Schools had been created for children whose parents would not, or could not, provide adequate home instruction, some congregations were slow to view Sunday Schools as respectable or necessary places for middle-class children. St. George's Free Church in Edinburgh did not establish a school for its own children until 1886, and then only after a survey to discern whether enough members would send their offspring.[16]

But a delay of this length was extreme. In America, churches began to establish Sunday Schools for their own children by the 1830s. Boston's Park Street Church, for instance, supplemented its "missionary institutions" with a congregational school in 1829. On both sides of the Atlantic, the middle years of the century saw a significant expansion of congregational schools. Middle-class children preferred the schools to an afternoon of restricted Sabbath activity at home. Parents, for their part, came to see the advantages of an organized system with a strong curriculum and to realize that more could be accomplished by coordinated than by individual parental effort.[17]

Congregational schools gathered the church's children on Sunday afternoon or on Sunday morning (usually just before but sometimes immediately after forenoon worship). A few places offered a choice of morning and afternoon sessions, and where they did, some students attended twice. By the early twentieth century, as leisure activities placed more pressure on Sunday afternoon time, the morning hour grew in popularity. Congregational Sunday Schools accommodated pupils from about age five through the midteens. Older students enrolled in "Bible classes" taught by the minister or another highly respected adult; these advanced classes assembled during the week or, more likely, during the hour immediately prior to Sunday evening worship. Although the core text for the Bible classes was still the scripture, as indeed their name implied, some ministers ventured in church history and theology or held discussions on books such as *Pilgrim's Progress*.[18]

Typically, Sunday Schools met only from late September or early October through May or June, and took the summer as vacation. Depending on the vitality of the local school, average weekly attendance in the 1880s and 1890s ranged from 60 to 80 percent of the congregation's children.[19] Especially when allowing for childhood illnesses and other exigencies, these numbers indicate that regular, systematic Sunday School programs had come to enjoy solid support among middle-class churchgoers during the last quarter of the century.

The schools also coincided with the rise of professionalism. While Sunday School teachers could not in any meaningful sense be called "professionals," they usually had some rudimentary training and used professionally prepared instructional manuals and student materials. In any case, their confidence, if not always their competence, surpassed that of many parents. Weekly teachers' meetings were common throughout the century; here the teachers, under the guidance of the minister, rehearsed the upcoming lesson and made plans for Sunday's classes. By the 1870s, American Presbyterian teachers could often avail themselves of training events sponsored by the presbytery or synod. When congregations could, they also drew on the increasing number of normal school graduates for leadership or training. Lyndhurst Road sought out a professor of pedagogy from an Oxford training college and advertised a course of study to its Sunday School teachers in 1910.[20]

Teachers, because they were often recruited from the minister's Bible classes, tended to be young and unmarried; one 1907 study cited by historian Ann Boylan showed most teachers to be between eighteen and twenty-five years of age.[21] More experienced teachers received supervisory roles or assignments to classes of older students. Predictably, given the average age of the workers, schools struggled with a high staff turnover and a constant search for replacements; as young adults settled into their lives, any number of natural events—marriage, children, new employment, new residence—could interrupt their service in the Sunday School.[22] There were, to be sure, exceptional individuals who devoted a lifetime to Sunday School work, and some Bible class leaders achieved such longevity that the classes were identified as "theirs." But congregations could not count on this kind of dedication.[23]

The majority—often the large majority—of teachers were women.[24] While Sunday School officers were predominantly male, it was rare for less than two-thirds of the teachers to be female; three-quarters female was a more common proportion. As one might guess, however, the ratio of male and female teachers was not uniform across the age-graded classes. Teachers for the youngest students were overwhelmingly female (although not 100 percent so), while a more even balance existed among those instructing the older pupils. There was, in fact, a determined, affirmative effort to recruit more men; for instance, an Edinburgh committee reported, not that it needed one more teacher, but that it needed one more *male* teacher.[25] The reason was not difficult to understand. As we have already noticed, fewer boys than girls attended Sunday School, and concerned parents and church leaders blamed this on the want of male teachers. When Govan parish allowed its staff to become heavily unbalanced (85 percent women in the 1890s), its Sunday School Committee received complaints. At one meeting, so the minutes recorded, "Mr Tweedie called attention to the fact that some parents objected to their children being taught by lady teachers, & hoped that more gentlemen Teachers would be got."[26] The reverse was also true; if a church could get its percentage of male teachers up into the mid-forties, as Perth's North Church or

Edinburgh's St. George's Free Church did in the 1890s, then they attracted a more balanced group of students as well.[27]

Whatever the composition of the staff, congregations recruited enough instructors to maintain a very advantageous ratio of teachers to pupils—about one for every ten was normal; with imperfect attendance, class sizes on most Sundays were somewhere between six and ten.[28] The Sunday routine called for the entire school, or department in the case of a large institution, to assemble for opening devotions and then to divide into small circles for the lesson and recitation.[29] Children were expected to memorize Bible verses, the Shorter Catechism, hymns, and prayers. Prizes were often awarded for recitation, or for perfect attendance or scores on examinations.[30]

Over time, the Sunday School curriculum changed in two ways. First, its goal evolved from conversion to nurture.[31] The liberalization of theology had, of course, much to do with this, but so did the beginning of congregational schools. Mission Sunday Schools led unchurched children to a decision for Christ and church membership, and superintendents counted their successes when they prepared annual reports. But the children in congregational Sunday Schools had already been baptized as infants and grown up in Christian homes. They were likely to be enrolled in Sunday School for many years. Not surprisingly, the emphasis shifted to long-term, gradual nurture rather than immediate conversion.

Standardization was a second modification. Out of necessity, early curricula were locally designed. But very early, the growth of organizations like the American Sunday School Union or the Sunday School Union in Britain provided standardized resources. City-wide Sunday School unions and denominational agencies turned out materials, too. After 1872, the international uniform lesson plans swept through the schools guaranteeing that children in Yorkshire and Iowa were studying the same biblical passages on the same Sunday. There was some, but not very much, resistance to the loss of local control and denominational distinctiveness. St. Andrew's parish in Greenock was one congregation that turned down the international lessons in preference to its own "lesson scheme," and other schools continued to rely on the Westminster Shorter Catechism or a children's version of it.[32] But the convenience and quality of uniform lesson booklets was a powerful persuader, and standardization won the day.

Not all the learning came from the formal curriculum; children also absorbed values and behaviors at Sunday School. Printed rules emphasized punctuality, regularity, diligence, politeness, and assorted other virtues. Certainly, children would have noticed that here, unlike in their weekday schools, corporeal punishment was banned. Lessons in benevolence came with the boxes that children filled with coins for foreign or domestic missionaries. Singing lessons and opening devotions prepared children for participation in adult worship. School lending libraries encouraged children to value reading (and to return books on time).[33]

Reading was a habit that was held in high esteem within the church. The books from the Sunday School lending library were not the only religious literature that entered the home and helped to nurture a mature faith. Govan parish for a while sent home a children's magazine called *Morning Rays,* but later decided to give "a good book" at the end of the year instead. Sunday School periodicals were in plentiful supply, and schools that could afford to provide them did so. Lyndhurst Road students got the *Juvenile Missionary Magazine* while the *Children's Missionary Record* went to those enrolled at St. George's Free Church. American children could read the Congregational *Well-Spring* or the Presbyterian *Sunbeam.*[34] The typical middle-class home also subscribed to a religious newspaper or magazine affiliated with the denomination, and these included children's and family pages with games, puzzles, and stories for reading aloud.

Books and periodicals brought the middle-class home into collaboration with the Sunday School's agenda from Monday through Saturday. Parents assisted and encouraged their youngsters' memory assignments and, in general, played an important, cooperative role in promoting the value system that both home and school shared. It is not really very fruitful to worry about whether the school reinforced the home (as its early promoters had promised) or whether by 1900 the relationship had been reversed. The two were partners, playing complementary roles in the nurture of the congregation's children.

The church interacted with the home in other ways, ones that today would come under the label "pastoral care"—home visitation, support in times of illness and distress, and counseling and reconciliation. Although these were certainly pastoral functions in the generic meaning of the word, they were not yet so exclusively identified with *the* pastor—that is, with the congregation's salaried, ordained minister—as they would become, or perhaps even as they once were.

Victorian clergy fell between two archetypes that have been extensively defined by historians—the earlier patriarchal model and the later professional model. By the 1830s, the father-child relationship implied by the first style had already been undermined by a rising democratic spirit and a more assertive laity. Yet during the last years of the era, the specialist-client relationship indicated by the second was only fitfully emerging.[35]

Caught awkwardly between one system founded on deference and a second based upon expertise, nineteenth-century clergy and laity tested a third paradigm characterized by friendship. The "Pastor as Friend" was seldom, if ever, fully realized: aspects of deference still remained and the ideal of expertise soon intruded. Yet its outlines were discernible. Popular pastors were treated to gestures of good will usually associated with friends and family; the practice of introducing a new pastor at a dinner or social reception grew in popularity. When Binney returned to his London charge after a journey to Australia, King's Weigh House rented space in the nearby London Tavern and held a party to welcome him home. The room was "crowded by members and congregation, and some intimate friends," and during the evening's entertainment both refreshment and speeches poured forth.[36] Pastors came to expect conviviality rather than deference, and they felt lost when it was not there. By the early twentieth century most of the members of King's Weigh House no longer lived near the church, and the atmosphere had grown more distant than it was in Binney's day. It was not a change that the minister, F. A. Russell, found to his liking, and in 1909 he resigned, complaining that he did not want a "Sunday morning only" congregation; "I like to meet my people often," he explained.[37]

Some of the strongest expressions of friendship between pastor and people were evoked by the death of a minister. Victorian pastorates were often of long duration, which allowed the bonds of friendship to become strong; when these were broken by death, especially by sudden death, the grief was intense. The Rev. Elias Beadle's sudden death by heart attack while walking home from Sunday morning service plunged his Philadelphia congregation into a sorrow that lasted well over a year. They had lost, they said, "a zealous worker and loving Pastor, and a true and faithful friend." Members elsewhere who confronted the death of a pastor also described it as the loss of a friend. When Archibald Scott died after a long pastorate in St. George's parish, Edinburgh, members penned a memorial minute lamenting the loss of "a personal friend with whom they never had any but the most pleasant relations." The congregation of Plymouth Church, Brooklyn, prayed fervently while Henry Ward Beecher lingered for six days before dying of a stroke in 1887. "No one who attended the services, held almost continuously during the week, can ever forget them," one member wrote later. "The dominant tone was one of the personal loss of a friend."[38]

Friendship and close personal contact emerged as important components of Victorian pastoral model, but at the same time the sheer size of congregations was driving a wedge of distance between minister and churchgoer. While the ideal envisioned a pastor who visited members regularly in their homes, large city and town churches with memberships running to a thousand or more made the ideal impossible. Even a smaller congregation of several hundred challenged all but the most robust clergy.

Beecher, whose Brooklyn church was one of the first giant congregations in America,[39] realized quickly that he could never do home visitation in the same way as his father, a generation earlier. Beecher's recourse was to invent the church social and invite the members to visit him in the church parlor. The biweekly "Social Circle" gave Beecher an efficient substitute for routine pastoral visitation. "In this manner," the church's manual proudly announced in 1850, "the pastor is brought into contact with all the persons of the congregation who may wish such acquaintance."[40]

Plymouth's size made it an extreme case, but the problem was a real one everywhere; "systematic visitation"—that is, every family in rotation on a frequent schedule—absorbed tremendous amounts of time, more than pastors alone had. So what did they do? Together, ministers and congregations devised several ways of coping. Beecher's church social was one such strategy, but there were others. For one thing, churches tried to lower people's expectations. A Congregational minister in Liverpool told his flock that "it is my intention to visit you at your own houses as often as I can," but he cautioned that the "district is large." A church in Cincinnati announced that its minister could get around no more than once every six months. This was actually a quite respectable rotation schedule, but the church manual warned members that in exchange for systematic visitation, the minister had the right to decline "without explanation, any social invitations which would conflict with the attention required by the duties of the church." Such was the burden of "numerous duties pressing upon him."[41] In another approach, two congregations in Britain tried to reduce the minister's workload by allowing members to self-select for visitation: those wishing a house call from the minister had to sign up in the "Minister's visiting book," and then, as London's New Broad Street Congregationalists were told, the pastor would see then "in their turn" (but only, they were cautioned, "as his time allows").[42]

Another common strategy was the adoption of more efficient, time-saving procedures. For instance, scheduling the visitation by neighborhoods saved travel time. Congregational churches in Manchester and Huddersfield announced the evening when the pastor would be in a district, presumably to encourage residents to stay home and reduce the need for follow-up visits. St. George's Free Church asked neighbors to assemble in one home so that the minister could converse with more than one family at once. The weekly *American Presbyterian* urged its readers not to throw the minister off schedule. "His time is precious," the editors reasoned, "and he cannot afford to wait for you to dress, perform your toilet, and put things to rights."[43]

Other congregations, foreshadowing twentieth-century medical tactics, tried to substitute office visits for house calls. Members of Chicago's Sixth Presbyterian Church were welcome to come to the minister's office any afternoon or evening (but not morning which was "devoted to the work of the study" and hence "should be free from interruption, except for urgent reason"). In return, the minister promised to call upon members when they were sick, but he gave no pledge of routine house-to-house visiting.[44] First Congregational Church in the same city made the same policy explicit. The members, by official vote, had decided that their pastor was too busy for routine visiting, and a notice in the 1859 handbook reminded them not to expect the minister to come except for "reason of affliction, illness, religious inquiry, or recent arrival among us"; members who had non-emergency needs could find the minister in his study at the church on Monday evening and during every forenoon. (With typical Victorian concern for efficiency, the handbook entreated members to keep their office visits "brief, . . . to avoid loss of his time.") First Church seemed to recognize that its new efficiency might come across as cold and impersonal, so it advertised a less formal opportunity that was expected to "compensate in part" for the end of pastoral home visits. Taking a page from Beecher's book, First Church held "a monthly sociable, for social and Christian intercourse with one another and with the Pastor."[45]

What has been said so far may imply more than is meant. First Church ended non-crisis house calls *by the pastor;* it did not stop *all* ordinary visitation. What it did was shift the responsibility for conventional home ministry to lay workers. This is what was happening at Beecher's church, too, and indeed throughout the Reformed community.[46] Ministers continued to rush to the bedside at the onset or crisis point of an illness, and they came at other times of special need such as bereavement.[47] Nearly every church manual carried instructions for summoning the pastor when someone became ill. "In sickness, when physicians and nurses are wanted," one manual said bluntly, "they are notified; be equally considerate towards the pastor."[48] But, lay workers picked up the largest portion of home care, both the ordinary household calls and the special attention given to the chronically infirm.

Actually, it would have been quite unthinkable to have eliminated all visits to churchgoers' homes. Calling, we must remember, was a social ritual in Victorian times; it was expected of friends and social acquaintances, and the church could hardly excuse itself from the custom. Even if calling had not been dictated by social propriety, the churches themselves would have done it because they considered it an essential part of their care for people. Whatever public exchanges there were between church and people, those that occurred in the home were understood to be different. The home was private space, and there people could be approached as they truly were. Thus, calling was critical work, and when it was too much for the minister, it had to be done by someone else. Growing congregations sometimes did hire a second ordained minister, but this person was usually contracted for extra preaching or teaching or for a specialized mission project. Home visitation was a task that lay people seemed perfectly capable of doing.

Congregations used two kinds of lay workers—salaried and volunteer. A number of congregations hired a paraprofessional, variously titled the "church missionary" or "church visitor" or "parish visitor." Men occasionally held these positions, but they were more likely to be occupied by women, such as Mrs. Sophia F. Orton who was the church visitor for First Presbyterian Church, Chicago in the 1860s.[49] As the "Lady Visitor" made her rounds, she performed, *de facto,* many implicitly pastoral responsibilities—praying, reading and interpreting scripture, exhorting, and counseling. Whatever scruples barred women from ordination apparently had more to do with preaching and the exercise of authority in the public sphere than with pastoring.

More often, the visitors were volunteers. They included both church officers who did visitation as a standard part of their job description, and other lay workers who were recruited specifically for this task. Virtually every church organized itself in the same way for visitation by its church officers; it divided the congregation or parish into neighborhood "districts" and assigned an elder or deacon to each. The idea of geographical division grew very naturally within the British parish system, where Chalmers had pioneered the concept in his Glasgow charge at the beginning of the 1820s,[50] but its wider appeal came from the age's eagerness for system and efficiency. Philadelphia's Second Presbyterians admired districting because it was "systematic." Elders at St. George's Free Church said it accomplished the task more "effectively."[51]

Visiting members quickly adopted techniques that added to the aura of system and efficiency. In Greenock, St. Andrew's kirk session members kept books in which they methodically recorded the vital statistics—the total number of families residing in the district and the church affiliation of each, the number of families affiliated with St. Andrew's and whether they were seatholders, the number of communicants in each kirk family, the state of education of each, the number of children available for the Sunday School, the names of potential Sunday School teachers, and contributions to mission projects.[52]

The work of the elders and deacons was pastoral. They conferred individually with communicants before distributing tokens or tickets to the Lord's Supper. They ministered in cases of sickness or bereavement; they exhorted absentees and conferred with any accused of indiscretion. They sought out prospective members. They led prayers and read the Bible in homes, and sometimes held district-wide prayer meetings. When Elder John Scott Ferrier died in Edinburgh in 1910, his obituary noted that "his intimate knowledge of all the families of his district, and his annual precommunion prayer meeting of his district people, set a pattern that many other elders have followed out."[53]

A great many churches also used a special committee of lay visitors, either as a supplement or an alternative to the work of the church officers. Typically, these additional visitors were women, the sex that enjoyed the more flexible daytime schedule and that seemed to Victorians especially suited for house-to-house calling. Withington Church's committee in Manchester included fourteen women, twelve of whom were married; if young, single women tended to fill Sunday School teaching positions, more mature women apparently went visiting.[54] These committees—variously known as the "Ladies' Visiting Committee" or "Female Parish Association" or the "Pastor's Aid Society"—assigned visitors to the congregation's established districts, so that it was common for a district to have both a male elder or deacon and a lady visitor at work within it. The pair worked as a team; the women, for instance, found that they could without hint of impropriety visit single shop girls or servants in their lodgings or quarters.[55] In general, the women were able to cover the district homes more frequently, and they added their prayers, Bible reading, exhortations, and counsel to those of the elders or deacons. They reported crises to the minister, pursued absentees, assessed cases of penury or need, searched for new members, and in one instance even offered to "lend and exchange" library books for shut-in members.[56]

The work of the lady visitors often included special attention to the church's needy members. Every congregation made provision for its own poor and kept a separate poor fund for alleviating need. Church officers or lady visitors noticed worthy cases during their visitation rounds, or they investigated appeals for aid initiated by the needy themselves. The Church of Scotland's situation was unique because it was, by law, responsible for the poor residents of the parish until 1845, and even after that it continued as the administrative unit for poor relief.[57] Elsewhere, poor fund expenditures were limited to those connected to the congregation. Congregations had other funds and programs for those beyond the congregation, but the "poor fund" was for taking care of its own.

Money for the congregational poor fund was raised in several ways. In Scotland, the standard practice was a weekly "church door collection," one-half of which was designated for poor relief.[58] Elsewhere, the usual source was a collection taken up at each celebration of the Lord's Supper. Besides these basic fund-raising techniques, congregations occasionally employed other methods. For instance, if door or communion collections fell short of anticipated need, officers might circulate a subscription for more money. In Scotland particularly, it was not uncommon for members to leave legacies for "the poor of the congregation."[59]

Hartford's Second Church, had an unusual by-law that authorized the deacons to "assess and collect of each member of this church, such a sum as shall be a fair and just proportion of the amount necessary . . . for the indigent of the church."[60] For unusually large needs that the poor fund could not supply, congregations made special appeals, as Central Church, Rochester, did in 1876 to raise "$150, for a Life Support, of Mrs. Matilda Bell, in the House of the Friendless." In Edinburgh, "ladies of the congregation" raised an additional £50 in 1879 for a member, "who from age and infirmities was unable to provide for herself."[61]

A significant amount of congregational poor relief was given in kind. The most frequent items charged against the poor fund were fuel (wood or coal) and food (meat, meal, flour, bread, tea, and sugar). At least until the onset of the temperance movement, some congregations gave their leftover communion wine to the poor. Clothing, often sewn by church women, was another common item, as were blankets. But virtually nothing was considered out of bounds if the need were legitimate. Poor funds contributed to children's school tuition, to college tuition, to funeral expenses and burial plots, and to bed and board at asylums. They covered medical expenses, remitted unpaid pew rents, and in one London congregation even subsidized passage to Australia for a couple and its eight children.[62]

Cash was the most straightforward form of assistance. Needy members could be given either intermittent subsidies or a perpetual pension. The number of weekly, monthly, and yearly pensioners—almost invariably elderly widows—was never large. In Philadelphia in 1839, Second Presbyterian's list included one person whose private board was paid, three annual pensioners, three monthly pensioners at two to six dollars, five occasional grantees, plus four others who received cash only and six who received fuel only.[63] The amounts involved were usually not large. In Britain, an Edinburgh church in 1870 was allotting one widow a shilling per week; King's Weigh House gave a male pensioner a pound per month in 1853.[64] But even by 1850 perpetual pensions were rare, and soon after they were gone entirely. The session of St. George's Free Church, Edinburgh, reported with satisfaction in 1885 that it no longer had a "permanent pensioner list"; instead, the dispensing of funds was at the recommendation of the lady visitors and the minister because they were in the best position to know the true need.[65] The new system undoubtedly did give the church more flexibility to tailor grants to circumstances, but it also made the congregational poor less independent. Visitors' roles also were changed, as they took on some of the behaviors of social workers, such as the keeping of case files. Indeed, in 1891 Rochester's Central Presbyterian Church began sharing its assistance records with the city's Charity Organization Society to achieve better coordination of benefits.[66]

The final piece of the congregation's internal care system was ecclesiastical discipline, the procedure by which the church dealt with deviant behavior. It is a part of nineteenth-century church life that most modern minds reflexively regard as censorious, humiliating, and oppressive. Yet its survival through three-quarters or more of the century, and the acquiescence or even eagerness of many who fell afoul of it, suggests that the reality was more ambiguous. By examining how discipline functioned within a congregation and why it fell ultimately into disuse, we shall be able to learn something about the shifting of focus from community to self, and the passage from a religious to a therapeutic understanding of deviance.

The basic outlines of the disciplinary system are not hard to grasp. Members, when joining a congregation, promised to submit to the judgment of their peers. The available penalties varied slightly from denomination to denomination, but basically they consisted of admonition or warning, rebuke (either private or public), suspension (either indefinite or for a fixed term), and exclusion or excommunication. Among presbyterians, the elders and minister meted out discipline as representatives of the congregation; among congregationalists, the whole membership decided. The first system would seem to have carried the greater potential for handling matters discretely, but perhaps also the greater risk of judgment by a small, aging session out of touch with changing mores. Yet, the differences meant less in practice than in theory. The church committee, which among Congregationalists screened cases before they reached the church floor, held nearly as much power as a presbyterian session, and presbyterian elders do not seem to have been either more or less compassionate than those who voted in Congregational church meetings.

The offenses chosen for prosecution fall into several general categories, although with some noteworthy differences among denominations or individual congregations. Nonattendance was the most frequent cause for censure everywhere except in the Church of Scotland, which with its parish orientation rather than gathered-church mentality ignored the matter. Sexual and marital indiscretions—adultery, bigamy, desertion or abuse, fornication, unwed parenthood, and "antenuptial fornication"—made a second category. While extramarital violations were dealt with everywhere, the same was not true of premarital transgressions. Outside of Scotland, premarital behavior was either ignored or infrequently noticed; in Scotland, however, it was by far the most prevalent offense and for the Church of Scotland virtually the only censurable offense.[67]

Alcohol-related violations were the third most mentioned category; nearly all congregations cited members for intoxication and disorderly conduct, and depending on their temperance zeal perhaps also for liquor selling or all consumption of alcohol. A fourth group of offenses included theft, fraud, and financial dishonesty; English Congregationalists stood out here because of the special care with which they investigated bankruptcies for any hints of dishonesty.[68] In a minority of congregations, Sabbath violations, such as opening for business or riding public transportation, were a fifth category. Specifically ecclesiastical offenses, such as trying to slip in a communion token from another denomination or misbehaving during worship or joining the Roman Catholic Church, brought censure, too. Here and there, a congregation cited members for gambling, dancing, profanity, slander, or libel. And, there was one overly enterprising Edinburgh man who got himself into trouble for sub-letting his church pew at a profit!

Lest this lengthy listing of censurable offenses give the wrong impression, it should be noted that disciplinary cases were not abundant, and in many congregations they were extremely rare. King's Weigh House started only six cases between 1830 and 1866, and only two of these progressed to a formal verdict. At First Congregational Church in Chicago, only a little over 2 percent of the 2,948 persons who were at one time or another members between 1851 and 1883 came under church penalty. Evangelical congregations processed more cases, but even a large evangelical congregation like Central Presbyterian Church in Rochester averaged only about one case per year between 1858 and 1900. Second Presbyterian Church in Philadelphia, without the same evangelical zeal, brought only nine cases of discipline between 1836 and 1882, and none thereafter. The greatest number of cases came in the parishes of the Church of Scotland, but if ones relating to premarital sexuality were removed, the number would dwindle to almost nothing. For married adults, then, discipline was no longer a relevant danger.

The point is not that discipline was so infrequent as to be inconsequential; on the contrary, even an occasional judgment could focus the possibility in the minds of other members, or convince certain male churchgoers that it was safer to remain a nonmember and hence beyond the reach of discipline. But, it is still important to remember that discipline was not a widely used sanction. Nor was it something that the great majority of members lived in constant fear of confronting. Having internalized the church's moral code, they could not easily imagine themselves ever to be guilty of public drunkenness, sexual immorality, or long absences from church. Thus, they lived as unselfconsciously under church discipline as they did under civil laws against burglary, murder, and rape. But discipline was there as a last resort, to be taken up when the normal bonds of the community failed.

Where there were church manuals, they set out in general terms the violations subject to discipline, and they explained how cases were conducted. There were, in reality, two types of situations. First, there were the great public sins we just described above. Since all members were expected to watch and care for each other, whoever was "first cognizant" of an offense had the obligation to call it to the attention of the authorities. Of course, in many cases, this was not necessary because by the time one person knew, everyone did. Official records of cases often began with a remark that the wrongdoing was a "matter of public notoriety" or "common fame," or that "reports have long been in circulation" about a certain person.[69]

The second situation was the personal grievance or complaint by one member against another. For instance, a Philadelphia woman in 1836 thought she was being treated unfairly by her mother-in-law; or, another woman in the same city claimed that a box of linen she had given to a friend for safekeeping had been returned incomplete.[70] These "unhappy differences,"[71] as several Congregational manuals called them, usually did not involve any censurable church offense (although the case of the missing linen was open to an interpretation of theft as well as of negligence or misunderstanding). But even when there was nothing more than bad will, members were permitted to use the disciplinary system for adjudication; no one wanted such feuds to end up in the civil courts. Congregational church manuals provided Biblical guidance for members who harbored grievances against fellow churchgoers. Following the prescription of Matthew 18:15–18, they were first to speak privately to the person. If this failed, they were to take "one or two others" along and try once more to resolve the question. If this also failed, then they were justified in placing the matter before the church.[72]

Once a matter, either a public sin or a personal dispute, came to the attention of the community, it progressed by procedures carefully designed to discourage abuses. Congregationalists placed these in their church manuals, and indeed some churches titled the disciplinary section "Rights of Members," emphasizing that a person could not be "deprived of church privileges except by regular process."[73] Usually accusations had to be presented in writing through the Church Committee which acted to verify evidence and screen out frivolous complaints. The accused person had a right to a copy of the charges and a list of the witnesses, and enough time to prepare a defense; in many places a two-thirds vote was needed for conviction. Presbyterian procedures included similar safeguards, and verdicts by local sessions could be appealed to the presbytery and the synod.

The inclination of those holding power in both presbyterian and congregational systems was to avoid disciplinary action as long as possible. No one relished taking on a difficult, troubling case. Once engaged, lay leaders moved slowly and cautiously, occasionally extending proceedings over months or even years. Take, for instance, an 1830 case in Boston's Old South Church involving a Mr. Carrier whose business had failed. That in itself did not require investigation (as it would have done among English Congregationalists), but this case was worrisome. Almost from the day he had joined Old South, there had been "rumors" about Carrier's "veracity." He had always been given the benefit of the doubt, but now, the Church Committee reported, "during the last year, rumors of this kind were greatly multiplied, & become very public so as materially to affect the standing of Mr. Carrier, & the cause of religion."[74]

The Church Committee had, in effect, delayed as long as they could. But now that the matter was out in public, they felt "impelled" and "under powerful necessity" of taking some action. Still, they were in no hurry. The pastor met with Carrier, and two deacons "called on several persons who were known to have dealings with Mr. Carrier, or to have been intimately acquainted with him." What the deacons uncovered was "that confidence could not be placed in his veracity, & that there were several specific instances of charge [sic] of falsehood." The Church Committee met with Carrier and he tried to explain himself. Perhaps, he admitted, "he had not in all respects done right," but he pleaded that his "circumstances had been peculiar" and that he had behaved no differently than "other professors of religion had done, when they failed in business."

At this point, the Church Committee decided to delay, "to give time to Mr Carrier for reflection, & to further inquire." The pastor continued to counsel with the man, and the deacons sought out the six persons Carrier had given as character witnesses. Unfortunately, however, these people either pleaded insufficient information or confirmed the negative allegations. The Committee met a second time with Carrier and found him unchanged. He continued to make excuses, and "did not manifest anything of a spirit of contrition." In these circumstances—"painful circumstances," the Committee called them—there was nothing left but to take the case to the whole church and recommend suspension. Carrier was told he had a right to be heard at the church meeting, but although he said he would come, he did not. After "deliberation," the church meeting voted to suspend him. Two years later, after further efforts failed to secure any hint of repentance or to nudge Carrier toward "some reparation for the injury he had done to the cause of religion," he was excommunicated.[75]

In Edinburgh, some fifty years later, the kirk session of St. George's Free Church proceeded with equal deliberation. The case involved a man named Norval, who was named as a principal in Mr. Wilson's divorce case against Mrs. Wilson in the civil courts in December 1881. Before the elders did anything, they consulted the presbytery to make certain they would make no procedural missteps. The result of the first civil trial was not in Norval's favor, but an appeal was. The kirk session, however, took neither the court verdicts nor the newspaper accounts at face value, and the elders conducted their own investigation. When they finally met with Norval in July, his story was that although he had spent the night with Mrs. Wilson in Lamb's Hotel, nothing had happened—the room "was a double bedded one." It was an explanation, the session concluded, that "could not be accepted" as satisfactory, and Norval was suspended. The case did not stop here, however. Over the next weeks, the minister and elders continued in conversation with Norval. Six months later, Norval confessed, expressed penitence, was forgiven, and in April 1883 received a favorable letter of transfer to his new congregation in Grangemouth where he had relocated.[76]

Not every case took two years to unfold, of course, but the overriding tendency was caution rather than a rush to judgment. As these examples also suggest, the studied pace with which the sessions and church committees moved came from a commitment to thoroughness and equity, too. Lay leaders took time both for counseling and for investigation before a case was decided. The disciplinary regulation at Great George Street Congregational Church in Liverpool specified that "if any member be found walking disorderly, he shall be visited by two Deacons, or other members of the Church."[77] In the case of an unwed mother in 1868, the session of Cowcaddens Free Church sent two elders, including her regular district elder, to "visit & deal with her, & to report." A month later, the two reported that they had "dealt with"—that is, met with, counseled with, stayed in touch with and not shut off—the young woman and found her in "a penitent and hopeful state." They promised to continue to work with her and bring her to the next monthly meeting.[78] Clergy usually made contact with the erring member, too, but much of this preliminary counseling was done by lay leaders.

Elders and deacons also investigated the accuracy of the charges. This was partly because they believed truth-telling was the start of repentance. But it was also because they did not want to jump to conclusions. Since most of these cases started on the basis of "rumor" or "common fame," the preliminary inquiry could be quite important. Not all allegations bore up under scrutiny. Hearing whispers that a member was guilty of bigamy, Pittsburgh's Fourth United Presbyterian Church sent an elder to "inquire into the circumstances," and the matter ended quickly when the accused member readily produced a certificate of divorce.[79] In a small western Pennsylvania town in 1859, "common fame" had it that two youths were guilty of "scandalous and offensive conduct with each other . . . at or near the Presbyterian house of worship," but the gossip turned out to be no more than half true. The two had been "indiscreet" and deserving of an admonition and suspension from one communion service, but there had been no "lewdness" at all.[80]

The investigations sometimes extended beyond the usual interviews with local witnesses. When a King's Weigh House member stood accused of fraud in connection with a bankruptcy, the deacons interviewed him and his creditors, examined his books, and sought advice from others in the same field of business to be certain they understood the boundaries of acceptable behavior.[81] Greyfriars kirk session in Edinburgh listened to Margaret Allen's tale that her child had been fathered by John Thompson, who had gone off soldiering and died. Sensing from her demeanor that the story did not quite add up, the session wrote to the regiment for verification and learned, unfortunately for Allen, that no such person ever existed.[82] While in this instance, the search for the responsible male led to the army, in many cases it led simply to another parish in Scotland, in which case the inquiry drew on the cooperation of a second kirk session.[83]

After all the counseling and investigation, the session or the church meeting came to a decision. Some people were acquitted. Phrases like "not well founded" or "nothing had transpired" or "no evidence had been brought forward to support a charge" signaled an end to the matter.[84] If the person was found culpable, the result could be only a warning. For instance, a church official in Greyfriars, Edinburgh, was found guilty of issuing fraudulent marriage banns, and "was solemnly and severely rebuked by the Moderator, and admonished to be cautious and circumspect as to his future conduct."[85] Especially in relatively minor cases, cooperation went a long way toward earning good will. Two men were summoned before Rochester's Central Presbyterian session in 1858, accused of identical charges of "covenant breaking and neglecting the ordinances of religion." One showed up, confessed, and promised to do better, which the elders accepted as "satisfactory." The second man did not respond either to the initial citation or a second; the session tacked on the additional charge of "contumacy" and suspended him.[86] Temporary suspensions or permanent excommunications were read to the congregation at the next communion. Suspension barred the person from the sacraments, from transferring membership, and voting. When the suspension was lifted, the "church privileges" were restored and the right hand of fellowship extended to the repentant member as a sign of welcome.

Although congregations did not do so perfectly, they tried to act with compassion. A manual from Jamaica Plain Congregational Church near Boston reminded its readers that "all such proceedings should be pervaded with the spirit of Christian kindness and forbearance."[87] An 1830 Boston case provides an example of what many churches must have imagined to be an ideal outcome. The church organist "had fallen into immorality, grievously wounding the cause of religion, in violating the seventh commandment." He immediately "professed sorrow & shame for his conduct," and "voluntarily addressed a letter to the committee, expressing these sentiments," agreeing to abide by whatever the church decided, and asking for its prayers "that he may receive God's merciful forgiveness, and be enabled hereafter to lead a virtuous & holy life." The congregation was clearly torn. On the one hand, they were so angry at the injury he had caused his wife and the church, they were of a mind to throw him out. On the other hand, he was so truly sorrowful that they could not bring themselves to do it. They remembered their "desire to deal as gently with offenders as a due regard to the honor of religion will admit," and the organist was only suspended. Eighteen months later, he was restored to church privileges—reconciled, it appeared from the deacon's inquiries, not only to church but to his wife.[88]

Restoration of right relationships between the erring member and the community and between the member and God—not punishment *per se*—was the overarching goal of the disciplinary system. This was the purpose of church intervention into personal, private disagreements between members. In 1843, for instance, a Philadelphia session approached one of its members to find out why she had skipped communion for the last five or six years. The problem, it turned out, was "a difficulty" existing between her and another woman in the church. The elders, by settling the feud, regained the woman's participation.[89] A case in Rochester, New York, reached a similarly happy solution; the session minutes recorded that after a "patient and thorough investigation and a conference with the parties immediately concerned, . . . an amicable adjustment of the differences between these persons had been arrived at," and no further action was needed.[90] This was the hope in every case.

Disciplinary action also functioned as a way for the congregation to mark its ethical boundaries.[91] The choice to prosecute certain cases rather than others represented a congregation's judgment about which of its boundaries most needed defending or had been called into question by external events. For instance, a United Presbyterian session in Pittsburgh, after a discussion of the low "state of religion in the congregation," decided to initiate proceedings against five persons for nonattendance.[92] Or, as another example, the suspension of twenty Southern sympathizers from a rural United Presbyterian congregation in western Pennsylvania in the months after Lincoln issued the Emancipation Proclamation was a forceful reiteration of that denomination's long-standing opposition to slavery.[93]

Such boundary-marking also helped to establish the outlines of Victorian middle-class morality as it was being invented during the first half of the nineteenth century. The extraordinary wariness of bankruptcy among English Congregationalists clarified the limits of acceptable business practice in a denomination where many members were just beginning to flex their entrepreneurial muscles. Prosecution of members for intoxication joined with other temperance activities to establish sobriety as an essential criterion for acceptance into the middle class. In

Scotland, the compulsive concern about antenuptial fornication coincided with the transition from rural folkways to urban, middle-class expectations.

Congregations also understood discipline as a necessary safeguard against charges of hypocrisy. So long as infractions remained out of the public eye, church leaders believed they had the option of leniency. Once tongues began to wag, however, they had no choice but to deal with the allegation; either it had to be shown false or the wrongdoer had to be brought under discipline. As the session of Central Presbyterian Church in Rochester put it, the crime now had become "a scandal upon the cause of Christ."[94] St. Paul's Chapel in the Kentish Town suburb of London felt it had to exclude anyone "who brings discredit on the Christian Society by grave misconduct in family life, by fraud or injustice in trade, by impurity, by intemperance, or by notoriously slanderous speech."[95] In St. George's Free Church, midcentury penitents routinely expressed regret for the "scandal [they] had brought on the church."[96]

Congregations hoped, of course, that discipline would lead to changed behavior. In certain kinds of cases, it often did. In one Pittsburgh congregation, pressure brought on nonattenders seemed to cause improvement. The most common notation in the session's minutes was, "Promised to do better. Promise kept." In Boston, a woman suspended for adultery in 1828 had "conducted herself with propriety" for four years, and so was restored to good standing.[97]

There were, however, no guarantees. Cases of intoxication, as any twentieth-century expert on addictive behavior could predict, had a higher probability of recidivism than those relating to church attendance. But even in cases of lax participation, congregations could meet with frustration. Rochester's Central Presbyterian Church finally suspended seven members after trying for several years to encourage more faithful attendance; the elders lamented that "diligent means have been used to bring them to repentance, with no effect." In Boston, when deacons went to ascertain why Mrs. Murray did not come to communion, they were met with nothing but "anger & bitterness" and were accused of not paying attention to her during an illness. She said she had no religion and wanted none and asked to be "discontinued from Church."[98]

Some accused members refused any participation in the disciplinary process. When King's Weigh House called Mr. Blackadder to answer "rumours" concerning his relationship with a married woman, he simply withdrew his membership. Central Church, Rochester, found that on occasion its summonses were treated with "contempt" or "utter neglect." Cowcaddens Free Church sent two elders to visit a young woman accused of fornication; they found her at home, but before they could speak with her "she left the house." An Edinburgh woman accused of intemperance had one meeting with her minister, and then was listed as "fleeing from discipline."[99]

Yet others did exactly the opposite and sought discipline voluntarily. In a few instances this turned out to be no more than a person trying to be a step ahead of the law; the man who wrote to King's Weigh House saying that news of his bankruptcy was soon to appear in the daily newspaper was no doubt calculating that it might be better if the deacons heard it from him first.[100] But many requests to be put through the disciplinary process, especially the omnipresent premarital violations in Scotland, seem less devious. Marion McCallum's story is an example. At the end of December 1861, she "voluntarily compeared" before the session of Park Church, Glasgow, confessing that she had committed fornication. As her tale unfolded, she "declared that Archibald McKinnon, an unmarried man also residing in the Port Dundas District had been guilty with her, and was the father of her child, which she then had with her; that the said Archibald McKinnon, while he had failed to keep his promise to marry her had acknowledged the paternity of her child, and had partially contributed to its support." The young woman's father was with her and upheld her narrative, as did the parish missionary who had been counseling her. As she finished, she "confessed her deep sorrow for the sin of which she had been guilty, and her resolution henceforth through Divine Grace to walk in newness of life and endeavour to adorn the doctrine of God her Saviour." Then, the minister, "after a serious rebuke and solemn Admonition, did in the name of the Lord Jesus Christ and on behalf of the Session absolve her from the scandal of her Sin and restore her to the privileges of the Church." Before she left the room, her child was baptized.[101]

What are we to make of such episodes, repeated by the hundreds throughout Scotland as newlyweds with inexplicably early births, unwed mothers, and a few unwed fathers stepped forward to meet with kirk sessions? Certainly in the huge urban parishes, the church had no sure way of discovering the offenders, let alone forcing them to come in. The ritual of ecclesiastical discipline must have served a function for the accused as well as the church. They, too, sought reconciliation and wanted their lives put right. The story of Marion McCullum likely had as much to do with reconciliation with her father as it did with her relation to the church, and we should not underestimate the tension between the two that was broken when the church, by its absolution, declared her whole.

The absolution sought by others was individual. Certain believers, plagued by a guilty conscience, seem to have found truth in the adage that confession is good for the soul. Two young members of Cowcaddens Free Church provide an example. In 1898, a young deacon and his girlfriend came forward "voluntarily" and confessed to have "sinned." There is no evidence of a child or a pregnancy, nor of their having been found out. The session, for its part, determined "not to throw any barrier in the way of their return to the Saviour, but [to] deal with them as the Saviour Himself would have done." The man was suspended from his deacon's duties for six months, but not from the church. Both were given the ritual "serious rebuke and solemn admonition" and then "absolve[d] from the scandal of their sin."[102]

Some who came forward had more practical reasons in mind. Baptism of the child was one consideration. In a community where infant baptism was expected and traditionalists worried about the ultimate fate of unbaptized infants, there was significant pressure on parents to present their children for the sacrament. So long as the churches made confession of sexual indiscretion a prerequisite, parents would do what was asked. The story of a couple who approached Edinburgh's Greenside Church in 1872 was not unusual. Stating that they had never been affiliated with any congregation, they now "professed their anxiety to join the Church & have their child baptized."[103]

Unwed mothers often had another hope: they wanted the church to pressure the father to acknowledge paternity and pay support; in some cases, the church's help was wanted to find a man who had escaped to another parish. A number of these cases eventually ended up in civil court, but kirk sessions, which offered their services without charge, were often the courts of first recourse. And in some cases, they succeeded in setting matters right. Because of the Victorian view of women as sexually passive and males as aggressive, the girls could usually count on being received kindly, as victims sinned against as much as sinners.[104] The reverse was also true; males who refused to acknowledge paternity or sought to escape responsibility received less forbearance than any other culprits to come before kirk sessions. While unwed mothers, such as Marion McCallum, usually received absolution on the spot, unwed fathers could not always expect the same sympathy. In one striking case that came before St. George's Free Church session in 1853, neither mother nor baby survived childbirth. When the father tried to deny responsibility, the elders were as set on judgment as they ever got. They took advice from presbytery to see just how far they were allowed to go, held a formal trial with witnesses, found the man guilty, and even after he confessed they kept him under suspension for five years.[105]

Issues of paternity were not the only occasions in which congregations used the disciplinary process to set matters right; the restoration of people's lives was included in the understanding of reconciliation. This was what so frustrated the session in the preceding paragraph: the young woman and the baby were dead, and the elders could do nothing to change that harsh reality. Usually church leaders had more cause for hope. When Lyndhurst Road was confronted with the bankruptcy of Mr. Sewell in 1885, their concern ranged beyond ascertaining whether his behavior had been ethical. To resolve his family's immediate need, they offered him £50 from the poor fund, which he accepted "as a loan." Beyond this, they arranged for an expert consultant to help him reorganize his business, and they discretely solicited enough donations to pay the school tuition of his children for two years. In another case at St. George's Free Church, when the elders heard that a young woman was going from member to member borrowing money, they decided they had better find out the reason. Ascertaining that the girl's father was seriously ill and temporarily unable to work, they promptly appointed a committee "to get the matter put on a satisfactory footing." In yet another case, a resident of Glasgow's Govan parish came to the kirk session in 1856 complaining that false rumors about him were circulating in the community; he had already won a libel suit in the civil courts, but the tongues would not be still. The church, after its own investigation, agreed that he was being "falsely assailed," and declared to the congregation that he was "free from any scandal."[106]

The ritual use of the phrase "free from any scandal" expressed in Scotland what those who sought out the disciplinary process hoped for everywhere. Church discipline could be an act of restoration. In the Church of Scotland, the usual language was "absolved from the scandal and restored to the privileges of the Church." In the Free Church, the final phrase was often "restored to the fellowship of the Church." Either way, as Greenside parish put it more succinctly, "the Scandal was removed." Ecclesiastical discipline, understood within the church as a form of reconciliation, did not stigmatize a person; the deed itself and the public gossip and common fame had done that. What hundreds of unwed mothers in Scotland came forward to hear was that the scandal was no more.

By the beginning of the twentieth century, ecclesiastical discipline as a form of pastoral care was gone, or if not eliminated at least much enfeebled. The practice endured longest in the most evangelical congregations; in many other places it had not survived the 1870s or 1880s. Why had this happened? For one thing, its role as a marker of moral boundaries was less important. The boundaries themselves had become, paradoxically, at once more clear and less clear. Early in the century, when the emerging middle class was still struggling for identity, its characteristic moral code was not yet fully defined. Later, middle-class morality triumphed as accepted convention, if not practice. In one sense, then, the code could be taken for granted, and needed less support from the church. But in another sense, Victorian morality by the end of the century had been significantly weakened by the growth of commercial culture and leisure activities. Congregations that once railed against picnics and worldly amusements were now running a full program of church socials, bazaars, and outings themselves. Many would no longer have known quite where to draw a line had they wanted.

Discipline had always assumed that members were under each other's "watch and care." It assumed that members lived in proximity to each other, knew each other's movements, and interacted daily. This is what lay behind phrases such as "common fame" or behind the concern that a public scandal would reflect negatively on the church. The reality, however, was that in large urban congregations, members might not even recognize each other. Nor, with the advent of better transportation, did they necessarily live together in a neighborhood. The community that discipline sought to protect and restore was artificial, if it existed at all. Among the last cases of discipline in a congregation's history were usually those who had landed in jail or whose names appeared in the newspaper; perhaps these were the only cases that were truly public any more. Church officers were often subject to disciplinary action after cases against ordinary members had ceased. Their prominence in the church made their behavior more public. A Philadelphia organist discovered housing a mistress or a Glasgow elder reported distributing communion cards while in a state of intoxication still caught the attention of the church, but much else passed unnoticed.[107]

Public discipline also declined because it conflicted with the increasing value that was placed on privacy. We have already seen in Chapter 6 that public examinations of incoming members waned; so did public scrutiny of behavior inside the church family. Public punishments of all kinds—stocks, whipping posts, public hangings—disappeared in the nineteenth century; the church was no exception. Manuals or anniversary booklets that listed all members since the founding of the church stopped placing asterisks beside the names of those who had been excommunicated. In 1874, Plymouth Church in Brooklyn no longer read from the pulpit the names of those removed from the roll due to lack of attendance. Union Park Congregational Church in Chicago decided in 1887 to abandon the denomination's traditional practice; henceforth in "cases of peculiar delicacy" all details would remain within the Standing Committee which would relay only the "substance" and its recommendation to the full church meeting.[108]

Where discipline continued, official records often protected the privacy of members; either the offense or the name would be entered, but not both. It was "the case of Miss Jeannie Whyte" or "the Richardson case" only. Or, it was an "alleged case of intoxication" or "an alleged erring member" or "two members of this church." Euphemisms replaced traditional language; members might be "dropped" from the rolls for nonattendance; they were no longer excommunicated or excluded for breaking their covenant vows. In a extreme example of concern for privacy, Old South Church in 1875 voted to destroy old files relating to disciplinary cases.[109]

The desire for privacy coincided with the emergence of ordained ministers as the professional care givers within the congregation. The old system had not only been more public, it had relied on lay judgment and counseling. If the minister intervened alone, both privacy and expertise were achieved. In most congregations the transition from discipline to pastoral counseling occurred gradually, with elements of each coexisting for decades. In Glasgow's Govan parish, however, the dividing line was sharp and visible. When John Macleod came to his first session meeting in January 1875, two cases of antenuptial fornication awaited action. Macleod asked for a postponement "on the understanding that the parties should in the first instance meet with the Minister in private." Macleod never brought the cases back, nor did any other case of discipline reach the session during his twenty-four years as pastor. Just that suddenly, ecclesiastical discipline was replaced by pastoral counseling.[110]

As with every historical change, there were gains and losses. There is no question that confidentiality benefitted counseling. The clergy's skills did outstrip those of amateurs, if not immediately, certainly later as seminary curricula were strengthened. Undoubtedly, some lay leaders were unbearably self-righteous and did more damage than good by their well-meaning interventions. And, the old system had always driven some members from the church and discouraged others from entering.

But without the disciplinary process, there was no sure way for the accused to receive the community's absolution. In civil cases, payment of a *fine* meant— according to the word's medieval derivation—a finish, an end to the matter. It was more difficult, in the minister-centered model, for the church to declare an end to further censure or to say, as it once could, that the scandal had been removed. Also, because the therapeutic model was better suited to cases involving intimate behavior than to matters of public ethics, such as the boundaries of acceptable business practice, those latter offenses received less attention from the church than they once did. The congregation, too, lost the opportunity to speak *as the church* about morality. Lay leaders were shut out of conversations about ethical standards. As a result, church board meetings devolved increasingly to discussions about organization and finance. Here, too, claims of expertise would be raised, but this time the advantage was with the laity.

# eigh͏̈t

## The Business of the Congregation
### *The Pursuit of Efficiency and Financial Stability*

Archibald Scott was well known in Scotland as a pastor with a mind for business. Like the worldly entrepreneurs of his day, he gained a reputation by founding a new enterprise. In 1865, Scott assembled a congregation in Maxwell, an elegant southwestern suburb of Glasgow. The church flourished under his leadership, and within a few years it had a substantial building, an organ and paid choir, a mission station, a thriving membership, a sound financial statement, and a healthy endowment. Scott built well, and he could have remained there comfortably until retirement. In an earlier age he might have done so, but in 1871 Scott followed a professional career path to Edinburgh. He went first to Greenside parish and then, ten years later, to a fashionable New Town parish, St. George's. Recognizing financial acumen when it saw it, the Church of Scotland soon made him chairman of its General Assembly Business Committee.[1]

Scott's years at Greenside provide a case study of the corporate model that congregations all over Britain and America were copying after 1860. The Greenside example was unusual only in two ways: the initiative came from a member of the clergy rather than lay business leaders, and the changes emerged less gradually and piecemeal than they did elsewhere. In under four and a half years, Scott retooled the parish administration for systematic efficiency. The church's communion rolls and baptismal records were put in order. Its benevolence causes were placed on a one-per-month schedule, and printed copies of the calendar were distributed to the congregation. Instead of placing a collection box by the door, a plate was passed through the pews so that no one escaped the opportunity to give. Procedures were revised to insure that all money was "passed through [the] Cash Books." Auditors were appointed, and there was a new bookkeeping system, with "books to be so ruled & headed as to shew the operations on each separate Scheme." The session now received monthly financial updates in the new format, and an annual financial report was printed and distributed to the congregation. Bank balances were "slumped together" to alleviate cash flow problems in some of the accounts. The elders, rather than working as a committee of the whole, were organized into six standing committees. The typical session agenda soon consisted of committee reports, each submitted in writing and circulated prior to the meeting; significant motions had to be handed out one month prior to action. Tighter budgetary restraints were instituted to hold committees within their allocations, and steps were taken to reduce long-term debt. District visitors were given "diaries" in which to record their contacts, and now had to turn in monthly reports summarizing their activity.[2]

Historians have described how the managerial revolution with its new understandings of time, discipline, standardization, and organization affected factory and office. And, they have also noted how the same desire for order and system was transferred to other aspects of life such as government or home management.[3] Churches, too, adopted corporate characteristics; as historian Paul Heidebrecht's study of Presbyterian businessmen in Chicago demonstrates, lay leaders had a "keen desire to apply notions of business efficiency to religious activity."[4]

We have already noticed the craving for efficiency and foolproof systems that was exemplified by communion tickets, standardized forms for membership transfers, and visitation by districts. Many church manuals sprang from a compulsion to organize congregational life and standardize procedures, and as the century progressed they were increasingly revised to mirror corporate annual reports. As we shall see in Chapter 10, the mushrooming number of church clubs and societies in the 1880s led to its own merger movement that mirrored the objectives, if not the viciousness, of business consolidation. A few churches, by the early twentieth century, were actually printing corporate-style organizational charts in their handbooks.

It was not, then, simply that more and more congregations took advantage of civil laws by incorporating—that is, by literally becoming corporations. It was a matter of values and attitudes. Denominational quarterlies published articles promoting more competent church administration.[5] The word "efficient" became one of the church's most admired adjectives. Improved plans for seating overflow crowds brought "order." Sunday School teaching became "more efficient." Even prayer meetings could be "sustained with much efficiency."[6]

The rise of "systematic benevolence" illustrates this desire to bring rationality to what was perceived to be inefficient and out of control. Benevolent giving was money passed through the local congregation but intended for denominational mission agencies and other charitable societies. These contributions were kept separate from local operating budgets, and people gave the money separately. A problem arose, however, when the rapid growth of voluntary associations during the first half of the century confronted local churches with a abundance of good causes. No single congregation could reasonably support them all, however worthy. The situation was less awkward in poor or rural areas, but urban churches—especially those known to be affluent—were flooded with requests; by the 1860s, King's Weigh House was turning down two or three for every one it accepted.

At first, local leaders took up each request for support as it arrived, but the consequences were not very satisfactory. Collections could come too close together, blunting their effectiveness. The amount of money collected sometimes had more to do with luck than with the magnitude of the appeal. The session of Second Presbyterian Church in Philadelphia was not the only board that was "deeply impressed with the importance of a more systematic plan."[7]

These Philadelphia elders sat down and worked out a yearly schedule of collections. They were not the first to do so, nor by any means alone. Beginning about 1850 the yearly schedule plan caught on as religious newspapers and denominational leaders took up its advocacy. Although some flexibility to respond to emergency appeals may have been lost, most church boards viewed the new method as a welcome relief; Rochester's Central Church, for instance, could now decline additional appeals "on the ground that we do not wish to change our regular plan."[8] The usual pattern was one cause per month, although a strong mission-oriented congregation such as St. George's Free Church had a fortnightly spacing.[9] Because some months were conducive to stronger collections, church boards found they could establish funding priorities by the way they put a schedule together. Once the schedule was established, it was publicized to the congregation by a circular sent to the home, a pew card, or a notice in the church manual.

Almost from the start, "systematic benevolence" meant more than just establishing an annual schedule. If the church planned ahead, so should individual members. Beecher, one of the early advocates of systematic *giving*, told his people, "It is very desirable all the members of the congregation should adopt some regular system in giving, decide what sum can be spared during the year, and how much to each particular cause."[10] Regent Square Presbyterian Church in London was also quick to see the merit in systematic contributions. "The duty of giving to Christ's cause should be *systematically* discharged. Hitherto it has been too much the custom to leave the service of God's house to be provided for, so far as the great majority of Christians are concerned, by accident. . . . [F]inding himself in his pew, with a purse almost empty, the worshipper persuades himself that a trifle will suffice; or if he deems the trifle shabby, he gives nothing at all." Regent

Square urged its members to consider benevolent giving in four steps. They should prayerfully plan their giving ahead of time, think in terms of a minimum rather than maximum gift, divide their gifts among the agencies according to the need, and give some money to their children to allot in their own names so they learned the habit of systematic benevolence.[11]

If members were to make well-conceived family benevolent budgets, they needed information, and church schedules gradually expanded to include not only the name and date of an offering but also a paragraph or two of explanation. Experience taught church boards that members would increase their giving if they knew how the money was to be used.[12] Supporters claimed that the method actually did increase donations; the American Systematic Benevolence Society, an association formed to promote the idea, reported in the 1850s that Old School Presbyterians, a group that heavily promoted the scheme, averaged an annual $2.50 per member, which was a very healthy $2.00 higher than other evangelical churches in the United States.[13]

Victorians generally believed that efficiency was well served if a blank or form had been filled out. Regent Square, as early as 1848, placed a family planning sheet with twelve columns, one for each cause, at the very front of its church manual. King's Weigh House in 1862 decided "to try the experiment" of distributing "a List of these Societies and requesting the members of the Congregation to insert [opposite] one or all of them whatever am$^t$ they might think proper to give." Most congregations used more insistent language than that. Bible verses—"It is more blessed to give than to receive," "Give and it shall be given unto you," or "Every man shall give as he is able, according to the blessings of the Lord"—were popular embellishments. In the 1880s, Rochester's Central Church was coyly mentioning how much money would be raised if the average donation were ten cents or fifteen cents or twenty cents. Once a systematic benevolence paper was filled out, signed, and submitted, it was understood as a "subscription"—a promise to pay the set amounts when due. For emphasis, some congregations began to call the benevolence sheet a "pledge card."[14]

Churches were divided as to the best way to gather the money. The older system, and one still used in some places after 1900, called for house-to-house collections. Armed with blank forms or a "collecting book," the visitors fanned out to canvass the members and return with donations to that month's cause. Although church officers were sometimes the designated collectors for their districts, it was more common to use "female collectors." The collectors were almost invariably volunteers, but in the 1850s St. George's parish in Edinburgh was paying a commission on the money collected. Organizing the campaign was sometimes the responsibility of a "Missionary Association" or a "Parochial

Association." Old South appointed a committee for each monthly cause, and each in turn was responsible for publicizing the need as well as collecting the money.[15]

Although some congregations continued to find house-to-house collections expedient, this method grew less popular as members guarded their privacy more jealously. Presumably, it would have been difficult to turn a collector away without making a respectable gift, and by the 1850s, some members were complaining of "too many calls."[16] The alternative, of course, was to trust members to bring their contributions to the church. James, whose ministry at Carr's Lane in Birmingham ended in 1859, was an innovator among English Congregationalists in substituting church collection boxes for what his flock remembered as the "old and objectionable custom of collectors calling . . . at private houses or business premises."[17] First Congregational Church, Hartford, was another of many churches that switched; a new plan adopted in 1864 designated the second Sunday of each month as the time for members to bring their money to church.[18]

Congregations could choose between two opportunities for collecting money—a plate by the church door or an offering integrated into the worship service. In the end, the second method won the assent not only of the liturgically minded, but also of the business minded: it produced larger collections. As one Scot cannily observed, passing a bag or plate through the pew "possesses the advantage of direct application being made to each individual."[19] In Rochester's Central Church, a short prayer both before and after the offering helped to impress upon members the religious obligation involved.[20]

It was the Scots who were most wedded to door collections, and some congregations continued the practice into the early twentieth century. They tried various techniques to make it work, such as situating the plates more prominently at the door or putting a sign over the plate to remind contributors of that day's cause or assigning an elder to call attention to it.[21] But it was a losing battle. Within months after Scott's Greenside parish started pew collections in July 1872, other Edinburgh parishes copied. Greyfriars was circulating a collection bag by early 1873, and although there was some grumbling by churchgoers, the elders resolved to keep doing it because, compared to door collections, "the amount of the collection has been found to be thereby increased." Word spread, and St. George's parish, hearing that others had found the pew method "largely increasing the collections," ordered twelve bags for "the Elders going round." Old habits, however, were hard to break. After St. Stephen's parish in Edinburgh switched to pew collections in 1894, one man recalled that "for at least a dozen years thereafter [he] found himself fumbling in his pocket as he neared the head of the entrance stair," which illustrated, he confessed, the "haphazard" nature of the old unsystematic method.[22]

Placing monthly benevolences in the Sunday offering plate or bag created a new puzzle for treasurers, however. Churches were already taking up weekly door or pew collections to augment operating revenues and perhaps the congregational poor fund as well. If, say, on the third Sunday of the month, people now tossed in not only their "ordinary collection" but their benevolence money as well, how was the counter to know which coins were meant for which fund? The standard solution was for the treasurer to establish an average for the Sundays when only ordinary money was received. Then, on Sundays when contributions were mingled, the average was allocated to the ordinary fund with the excess going into the benevolent fund.[23] The system worked, but it was imprecise.

The better solution was to have contributors place their systematic benevolence into envelopes so that it would stay separate. An envelope system turned out to have other advantages, too. Preprinted packets of envelopes could be prepared, one for each cause on the congregation's schedule; they could even be prepared with members' names or an identifying number. Since the money was now easily separated from ordinary offerings, benevolences could be brought on any convenient Sunday of the month rather than only one. A sealed envelope shielded the contribution from the eyes of others nearby in the pews, and this coincided with the century's growing preference for privacy. At the same time, however, a name on the front of the envelope meant the contribution was no longer anonymous to the accountant. When opening the envelopes, the church treasurer could compare the amount to the figure pledged on the members' systematic benevolence card. In this sense, envelopes restored the accountability that house-to-house collections had provided.

Benevolence contributions constituted a high proportion of the congregation's total yearly giving. It was not unusual for benevolences to exceed the amounts given to cover local operations. Large, prosperous churches donated two or three times as much to charitable work as they kept for their own needs; most congregations seem to have divided their giving about equally between missions and home costs. The exceptions are not difficult to explain. A weak, struggling church like First Congregational in Cleveland, which was having trouble paying any of its bills, could manage only 21 to 29 percent for benvolence during the 1880s. Very small congregations, with fewer people to share the overhead, also sent less money away, perhaps no more than 5 or 10 percent. A major local building project could temporarily pull contributions away from missions. And, benevolent contributions were usually lower during the first few years of a church's existence while it was getting its feet on the ground.[24]

Systematic benevolence's employment of simple budgeting techniques was only one example of the churches' efforts to follow more business-like practices. As early as the 1860s, more advanced congregations began to adopt annual line-item budgets for their general operations; for instance, Old South's Standing Committee now for the first time wrote out in advance its "Estimate of Expenditures" for the fiscal year.[25] By the end of the century, it would have been a rare congregation that did not try to follow a budget. Preparing one in advance, and then sticking to it, freed people from emergency appeals when the money ran out in mid-year. With formal budgeting came more modern bookkeeping practices, stricter fiscal accountability, regular audits, and end-of-year reports.

Corporate-style annual reports to the membership came to be standard practice. Before midcentury, churchgoers had on occasion received printed summaries of church expenses and income, but the practice was intermittent and usually meant to prove the necessity of an accompanying emergency appeal. Now, the release of information was dictated by the calendar, not by a crisis. The deacons at King's Weigh House discussed in 1860 the "desirableness of presenting to the Church and Congregation *periodically*, a statement of the Income and Expenditures of the various Societies in connexion with the Church." By 1862, this report had been added to the church manual, which now appeared in a "remodelled form."[26] In the 1840s, no church yearbook would have routinely carried detailed pages of financial information; by the 1890s, none would have ignored it.

The compilation of financial and demographic data was also prompted by requests for information from governmental and denominational bureaucracies. Scottish parishes, for instance, were obliged to send to the House of Commons totals of male and female members. Some official minutes made it quite clear that the motivation was not local. As the clerk at Fourth United Presbyterian Church in Pittsburgh wrote down in 1878, "The Session then filled out the blank sertistic [sic] of the Church for the meeting of Presbytery."[27]

In time, the statistical mode of expression became dominant and threatened to drive out alternate ways of understanding. On New Year's Eve 1913, the clerk of Cowcaddens Free Church provided an entirely statistical evaluation of the elders' faithfulness that year—there were forty-three elders, twenty-two meetings had been held, the average attendance was twenty-one, the average number of meetings attended per member was ten, the highest attendance was twenty-eight, and the lowest was nine. Numbers replaced narrative elsewhere, too. Back on New Year's Day 1846, when the elders of St. George's Free Church summed up the previous year, their report certainly included some numbers—total children in the Sunday School, number of pewholders, amount raised for the poor fund, and so forth. But the report was primarily narrative, not quantitative. It did not count the number of visits elders made in their districts, but instead mentioned "meetings for prayer and reading the Scripture." Sections of the 1846 report described the "spiritual state" of the congregation and called attention to the "marked increase of seriousness" among the young men of the church. A generation later in the 1880s, first-of-the-year reports had lost these narrative qualities entirely. A straightforward listing of the current year's worship attendance together with the previous year's total was as close as the report came to the once traditional assessment of the congregation's spiritual state.[28]

As congregations expanded in size and function, church leaders needed to work harder at internal communication. Before midcentury, there was little need for extraordinary effort. Announcements were made by verbal intimation from the pulpit or a printed notice left in the family pews or affixed to the church door. Word-of-mouth was naturally important, too, and especially so in congregations knit by close residence and kinship. Only on rare occasions—such as the selection of a new minister—was it thought necessary to place a notice in the newspaper or mail a circular to homes.[29]

By the last decades of the century, large congregations—like large corporate structures—needed more intentional steps to insure that information reached members. Cheaper printing opened up several new opportunities. Printed orders of worship, which started to appear at the end of the 1880s and became quite common by the first decade of the twentieth century, offered a chance to place weekly announcements on the reverse side or on a second fold. (One group of clock-watching elders was pleased at the chance to "economize in the time heretofore used in reading such notices."[30]) Church bulletins or calendars, as they were called, had the advantage of a weekly printing schedule, but space was limited, and they reached only those who were in church.

Beginning in the 1880s, some congregations began to publish a newsletter intended for home reading. Congregations that subscribed to denominational magazines could sometimes arrange for a few pages to be separately printed with whatever local text they submitted. For instance, Regent Square's local newsletter came out as a supplement to the *Presbyterian Messenger*. The Church of Scotland's *Life and Work,* which started publication in 1879, gave parishes the opportunity of adding their own pages. After it was redesigned in 1882 along the lines of *Life and Work,* the *Free Church Monthly Record* was also prepared to print the inside covers with locally submitted text.[31]

But many congregations ran an independent operation. In 1887, the Lyndhurst Road deacons decided "to try the issue bi-monthly of a simple notice-paper to Church members—to be taken round by the visitors." Ten months later, they reported that "the lithograph circular" had "proved very satisfactory so far." By the 1890s, Lyndhurst Road had switched to a quarterly ten-page news sheet filled with the names of new members, obituaries, changes of address, a "diary of church events," a minister's letter, brief financial updates, paragraph reports on the activities of church groups, a children's corner, and letters to the editor. In Chicago's Forty-first Street Presbyterian Church, it was the Young Men's Bible Class that in 1899 took on the *Church News* as a project and turned out monthly issues crammed with news, upcoming events, financial reports, summaries of group activities, a column by the pastor, news of the Chicago presbytery, and excerpts from national religious magazines.[32]

From the world of commercial advertising, churches learned yet other methods of communication. By midcentury if not earlier, churches used posters and handbills to attract attention, and they placed what they called "notices" in local newspapers. By the last third of the century, however, local churches sought to entice as well as inform. A Regent Square poster for an evening evangelistic service proclaimed "Sankey's Hymns are Used" and as a further inducement, "Hymn Books Provided—All Seats Free—No Collection." Another of this congregation's posters displayed a map with the church's location and specific directions for access by bus, tram, and railroad. First Presbyterian Church in Chicago also included transportation routes on its advertising. It was touting a different style of service, however, when it announced music from organ, violin, and a "selected chorus of trained singers," and promised that "a printed programme with the anthem, hymns and music, responsive readings, Apostles' Creed, and responsive chant will be put into the hand of each attendant."[33]

By the 1890s, large city churches bought space in daily newspapers and advertised their regular Sunday services. They watched the results carefully, and deleted or added papers to get the most return. Lyndhurst Road, which had advertised only in the local *Hampstead-Highgate Express* during its first year of existence in 1882, began casting a wider net in the city in 1911 by purchasing space in three and eventually four major papers; Govan parish took the opposite course; it concluded that in the Scottish parish system there was no reason to go beyond the *Govan Press,* and therefore it could eliminate the *Glasgow Herald.* Cowcaddens Free Church switched in 1893 from the *Evening Citizen* to the *Glasgow Echo* in the expectation that they would reach their target audience more effectively.[34]

A final form of advertising was the erection of exterior sign boards. Most churches had rather modest construction in mind. Lyndhurst Road put up a "notice board" in 1884 that announced the name of the minister and the times for worship, communion, and Sunday School. St. George's parish, Edinburgh, probably expected about the same thing when it discussed in 1907 "having a Board put up in front of the Church giving information as to the Services." Cowcaddens, however, with a more evangelistic spirit, meant to have "a large Board." In Rochester, Central Presbyterian was even more adventurous; it thought its 1889 sign should be "illuminated." In 1908, the same church decided it wanted an "electric sign" affixed to the building. After some investigation, it backed away from the idea, citing the cost and "the danger on account of its size." But five years later, the temptation to see the church's name in lights was too much to resist, and the sign went up.[35]

The relationship between religion and advertising went two ways: churches not only bought advertising, they also sold it. The young men in Chicago who published the *Church News* for Forty-first Street Church financed the newsletter with several pages of paid advertising. Rochester's Central Presbyterian elders set out to make its news sheet "self-sustaining," too. Astute leaders elsewhere calculated that they could put the printing of church manuals or annual reports on a paying basis if they sold advertising space. Chicago's Fifty-second Avenue Presbyterian Church put out a 1903 year book in which advertising was prominently featured. On the inside front cover, readers saw two drawings showing how "featural surgery" could improve the shape of a nose. Other pages declared the advantages of miscellaneous shops and professionals—milliners, banks, candy stores, coal merchants, "the little store round the corner," barbers, dentists, osteopaths, and embalmers, plus a selection of patent medicines and an opportunity for Panama land investment. The church, borrowing a tactic from its advertisers, displayed its own pithy slogan, the biblical "We, being many, are one body in Christ," on the title page.[36]

The realization that a church could turn a profit on something that had previously been an expense alerted enterprising trustees to consider other commercial ventures. Church manuals and annual reports could be sold rather than given to members. Scott charged his Greenside parish three pence each for the annual report in 1874, and Redland Park Congregationalists purchased their 1890 manuals from the sexton at the same price. Lyndhurst Road found it could make money by printing the minister's sermons, although with a twinge of conscience it decided it was best not to sell them on Sunday. When Lyndhurst Road had opened its new building in 1884, an artist approached them with a percentage scheme to profit from pictures of the edifice, and the idea was referred to the planners of a forthcoming bazaar.[37]

Church bazaars or festivals were the most manifest examples of congregations' entry into commercial culture. These church fairs were capable of raising large sums of money, quite enough to have a noticeable impact of the congregation's ledger sheet and wipe out troubling deficits, as we shall see later in this chapter. They were deemed particularly effective for raising money for special mission projects or capital expenses such as a new building, an organ, or a major renovation. In style as well as in revenue, they were far removed from the days earlier in the century when ladies discretely sold a few pieces of fancy work to raise money for missions. Many of these bazaars were real extravaganzas with elaborately decorated stalls. While the events recalled some attributes of medieval town fairs, the festivity was contrived rather than spontaneous. A proper Victorian bazaar had to have a theme around which everything was organized efficiently. One four-day festival in Birmingham, for instance, followed a flower theme, with booths called "Violet Vale," "Ivy Bower," and "Lilac Lodge."[38]

The Cavendish Street Congregational Church in Manchester rented out the Hulme Town Hall for a four-day "Grand Bazaar" at the end of October 1909. Once visitors paid their admission of one shilling (down to six pence for the third or fourth day, or discounted to five shillings for a "season" pass admitting the whole family) and purchased a copy of the stylish art nouveau program booklet (printed by William Morris Press), they could wander magically through "An Old Cheshire Village." A printer's booth published a daily "Bazaar Chronicle" and sold personalized business cards or stationery, printed on the spot. In addition to the stalls selling crafts, flowers, fruits, sweets and ices, and "refreshment and tea," consumers could take in the entertainments and competitions. The Albertini Band was there daily, and there were dramatic performances, recitals, animated wax works, children's dancing shows, and "phrenological delineations." The more daring souls could enter competitions that gently spoofed traditional gender roles—ladies' nail driving or whistling, men's laundering. For a penny a dip, a child could search for a prize in a bran tub. For three pence, adults could view a "model doll's house . . . furnished throughout and lit by electricity." The younger set no doubt made good use of the "bazaar post office," where they could send a card or package to anyone else in the hall—"a happy medium for the shy gentlemen who desire to make presents to the ladies."[39]

Such events were tremendously popular between 1885 and the Great War. Consumption, churchgoers were learning, could be pleasant and entertaining—and enjoyed with much better conscience when presented in the cause of religion. A Congregational church in Huddersfield reported that its annual three-day sale and entertainment had been "very successful, and proved a time of happy intercourse and social re-union."[40] In many congregations, "entertainments" became an additional type of fund-raising event, distinct from the bazaar or fair with its retail booths. There might be a concert to benefit the unemployed, or a garden party, banjo entertainment, "Tom Thumb Wedding," or a "Martha Washington Tea Party."[41] The ability to have fun and raise money at the same time proved irresistible. After Withington Congregational Church in Manchester held an 1889 bazaar modeled on an Oriental town, "at once novel and picturesque," its members could hardly wait for the next one: "The one absorbing topic during the past year has been the *Bazaar*. At home or abroad, in London, Paris, or by the sea, wherever the heads of stalls have passed a few days or spent a longer holiday, observant eyes and active brains have been at work in search of novelties in materials and design to be deftly turned into account for the *Great Event*."[42]

As congregations grew in size, diversified their activities, and acquired larger physical plants, they became more difficult to administer. In a manner similar to what was happening to business corporations, church management was restructured to allow for differentiation of task and more precise lines of responsibility.[43] One striking evidence of this was the rapid growth of church committees. Beginning in the 1860s and continuing through the next decades, governing boards systematically divided themselves into committees for the conduct of business. In the 1840s, church officers had established short-lived *ad hoc* committees or had delegated care of one or two tasks, most likely music or seat letting, to subgroups. But in the second half of the century, they apportioned all of their business among standing committees and acted only in response to reports. There was no uniformity to the way work was divided; church boards followed their own inclinations and tailored their plans to the activities of the congregation. For instance, Cowcaddens Free Church reflected its distinct style when it included among its seventeen standing committees in the early 1890s not only the usual building and finance committees, but also one on open-air evangelistic services. The Boylston congregation in Boston had no desire for an evangelistic committee, but it did have ones for music, administration, benevolence, pulpit supply, discipline, spiritual affairs, finance, and building.[44]

Administrative staff grew along with the number of committees. Beecher, in 1870, finally asked for an assistant, and by the end of the century most large churches had an assistant minister or two.[45] Expenditures for occasional stenographic or clerical services began to appear in the ledgers of sizable, urban churches in the 1890s, and although in the early twentieth century full-time secretaries were still atypical, they slowly arrived to operate typewriters and telephones in the church office. Written job descriptions and industrial terminology helped to define roles, as when one board of trustees reorganized its janitorial staff and designated one person as "building manager."[46]

The explosion of committees and employees meant a longer directory of officeholders at the front of church manuals. Between 1858 and 1888, First Congregational Church, Hartford, went from one to three pages of names, from fifteen individuals to seventy-one. Chicago's Second Presbyterian Church, in 1856, listed only the pastor, elders, trustees, and a Sunday School superintendent. By 1906, the same congregation had, in addition to the pastor and officers, a Sunday School director, deaconesses, parish missionary, "executive secretary," lay-worker, kindergartner, organist and choir director, sexton, and under-sexton; in addition, the session was now organized into seven standing committees.[47]

Not surprisingly, the proliferation of committees and jobs risked confusion if lines of responsibility were not clear. By 1913, Central Presbyterian in Rochester thought it wise to create still another committee, one "to prepare a system of charts, showing the organizations of the church and their work, to be on exhibition at the coming Church Day."[48] Brick Presbyterian Church in New York City published a fifteen-inch by twenty-inch fold-out organizational chart in its 1911 annual report.[49] Another approach in a few large churches was to create a committee on committees, such as Brooklyn's Plymouth Church established "to promote harmony and cooperation among the branches of the church."[50]

The proliferation of church administration from a single board to multiple committees gave women more access to power. Although women were still barred from positions on sessions or boards of deacons, they could be appointed to the standing committees where fundamental decisions were made. In one instance, this was a result of deliberate policy; Cleveland's First Congregational Church, when it set up standing committees in 1869, specified that they be "composed of male and female members of the church, so as to enlist as many as practicable in active service."[51] In most cases, progress along these lines was more inconsistent and limited to instances where the need for women seemed demonstrated. Women might be invited to a property committee when new carpeting was to be selected without any implication that they should be on other committees or even on this one at a later time. Plymouth Church in Rochester put two women on its music committee in 1877, but none elsewhere.[52] In some cases, the women were appointed not as individuals (as men were) but as representatives of women's associations; for instance, Rochester's Central Presbyterian added two women from the Women's Missionary Society and two from the Young Women's Missionary Society to its Systematic Benevolence Committee in 1897. Women in some Congregational churches gained seats on the church's central administrative committee. King's Weigh House placed a Ladies' Committee representative on the congregation's important General Committee in 1903, and by 1917 women held one-third of the seats on the Prudential Committee at Second Church in Hartford.[53] Slow and halting as change was, the expansion of committees did increase women's voice in church governance.

The lay leaders who used their business sense to remake church practice did not bring identical commercial experience to the task. A Boston merchant was not a Cleveland shopkeeper, and it mattered which gave direction to the congregation's finances. The contrast will become clearer as we continue to examine how congregations raised and spent their local operating money; it will be enough for now to indicate the dissimilarity. The manner in which leaders at Boston's Old South Church and at First Congregational Church in Cleveland thought about indebtedness makes an initial example.

The men who managed affairs at Old South brought an aggressive, entrepreneurial confidence to the task. While they did not incur debt rashly, they understood it primarily as a means to an end. Debt was not an obstacle, but a pathway to opportunity. They never flinched at borrowing for a significant capital improvement, whether a new mission hall or a splendid sanctuary in the Back Bay. It is true that the church's significant real estate holdings in the city gave these trustees a financial cushion that other congregations did not have. But in the mid-1870s they did not hesitate to assume obligations in excess of a half million dollars, approximately double the insured value of their assets. Indeed, they knew from experience with their commercial real estate that borrowing money to replace smaller properties with larger multistory buildings had more than paid off in higher rental income for the church. If they had ever gotten the church debt down to zero, they would have been embarrassed not to be stretching themselves for the advancement of the Kingdom.

In contrast, the trustees in Cleveland were paralyzed by their fear of debt. At the end of the 1870s, First Church was perennially short of cash because its building was too small to generate enough pew rent to cover the bills. If it borrowed money and built a larger sanctuary, it was certain to escape its predicament: there were ready applicants to fill the added pews, and the newcomers would bring in enough pew rent to cover both routine costs and loan payments. But the congregation remained frozen. They could not seize the opportunity because they saw debt only as a burden, not a tool. The world of finance in which the Boston trustees moved with swift self-assurance was to these people a place of danger and ruin. Debt was something a church got out from under, not something it used to advance Christ's cause.

Although the exaggerated inactivity of the Cleveland trustees was unusual, their negative view of indebtedness was not. Church records elsewhere echo their anxiety. The treasurer of St. George's Free Church in Edinburgh, speaking to the deacons' court in 1844, "expressed strongly his views of the necessity of clearing off the whole debt of the church and using the utmost exertion to accomplish this without farther delay." A half century later, as the Congregationalists at Moseley Road in Birmingham paid off the last cent of their debt, they rejoiced because the church was now free to "support a programme of Christian work of a more aggressive character." Their treasurer said he could "urge nothing stronger" than a recommendation that the church now stay out of debt and avoid throwing money away on interest.[54]

The affluence—and financial stability—of congregations varied significantly, as we shall continue to see in the next sections that examine sources of income, patterns of allocation, and strategies for bringing receipts and expenditures into balance. The disparity between the richest and poorest congregations shows up in the total amount of money available for allocation, as even a few examples will indicate. In the 1890s, the annual total budgets (benevolences plus local operations) of two Scottish Free churches in Glasgow showed nearly £8 per member at College Church, but less than £2 at Cowcaddens; midway between, Mayfield Free Church, Edinburgh, had a bit less than £5 per member to spend. Turn-of-the-century American budgets ranged from less than $18 per member at Rochester's Central Presbyterian Church and Cleveland's First Congregational Church to $93 at Philadelphia's Second Presbyterian Church and an even higher $143 at New York City's Brick Presbyterian Church.[55]

Nearly all of this variation can be accounted for by the relative economic standing of a congregation's current members. But in some instances, a church benefitted from the largesse of its forebears. Boston's Old South Church was perhaps as blessed as any in this regard. A 1669 bequest from Mary Norton gave them control of land that two centuries later turned out to be some of Boston's most well-situated commercial real estate. In the 1860s the church's rental properties earned about $70 per member, which was a very significant augmentation to the approximately $40 per member derived from current churchgoers' pockets.[56]

Wealthy congregations typically lavished some of the abundance on local operations, but proportionately more of it went to benevolence. For instance, Great George Street Church in Liverpool raised almost twice as much per member as did Carr's Lane in Birmingham; with its greater affluence, Great George devoted 50 percent more than Carr's Lane to local expenses, but nearly 300 percent more to benevolent causes.[57] During the early 1870s when the local expense account at Plymouth Church, Brooklyn, was running a surplus annually, some $79,000 was reallocated to mission purposes during one five-year period.[58] The reverse was also true; a congregation that was financially pinched could more easily reduce charitable giving than allow salaries and fuel bills to go unpaid. The tiny seventy-member Handsworth Congregational Church in Birmingham raised a respectable seven and a half pounds per member in 1899, but after its quite modest local expenses were covered, little was left for mission.[59]

Prosperous congregations found ways to share their wealth with weaker siblings; this was done both on an independent basis and as part of a concerted denominational plan. Carr's Lane in the 1870s was aiding two other Birmingham congregations and four village chapels.[60] Beginning in the 1890s, Old South sent between a quarter and a third of its real estate profits as "gifts" to some thirty-five churches in eastern Massachusetts.[61] In New York City, Brick Church, like many urban churches, continued to support congregations that had once been its mission stations.[62]

The most ambitious denominational program of support for weaker congregations was the Free Church's Sustentation Fund.[63] Money raised across Scotland was used to guarantee a minimum stipend of £150 to each Free Church minister. Congregations that were able, and hoped to attract prominent pastors, added supplementary salary from their own resources, but the redistribution of money from affluent to poor congregations insured a minimum of support everywhere. Although they were not so well known, nor so zealously supported, similar funds existed in other denominations.[64] Of course, these funds, even while they allowed weaker congregations to survive, did not create equality; affluent congregations still offered higher salaries, ran more ambitious programs, and worshipped in more luxurious buildings.

Nearly all Victorian congregations used pew rents as the primary funding for local operating costs—salaries, building maintenance, and program expenses. Churchgoers contracted annually for a whole pew or, depending on need, for single "sittings," measured at a standard eighteen inches (a few churches allotted as little as seventeen-and-a-half or as much as twenty). Although most congregations thought of this as a rental system, it functioned somewhat like the purchase of a season ticket for the theater: payment in exchange for reserved seating. A few congregations ran on a purchase rather than rental basis. They sold their pews for a substantial one-time payment (often as a way of covering initial construction costs) and then charged a yearly rate on the assessed value of the pew.[65]

Seats carried higher or lower prices depending on their perceived desirability. Seating was more expensive on the floor than in the gallery, and aisle seats went for more than interior seats. People wanted to be able to see and hear, and thus seats in back corners or behind pillars had low value. The opportunity to *be seen* was apparently important, too. Old South raised the valuation of its center aisle seats in 1861 when they rose in popularity; the Standing Committee grumbled, however, that "in bygone times, this desire for prominence in location in the House of God was less intense than at present."[66]

There was an intense desire to be fair and just in determining the prices of sittings. Churches wanted to get as much income as possible from their seats, but they were also concerned about access for poorer members. The result was a graduated scale that not only apportioned the best locations, but also worked as a progressive tax on wealth. In a place such as Paddock Congregational in Huddersfield where worshippers' economic situations were relatively equal, the most expensive seat was only three times as costly as the least. Where differences in wealth were more extreme, as in Glasgow's Wellington United Presbyterian, the differential was six; Boston's Old South and Chicago's Union Park churches assessed the affluent sixteen and twenty times the bottom rate.[67]

Congregations tried to maintain access for low-income worshippers. Increases in seat rents were usually scaled to hit the more affluent harder, as in Rochester's Central Presbyterian in 1884 when it placed the entire addition on the top-paying seatholders. Glasgow's Park Parish adjusted rates in 1865 and, with the needs of servants in mind, held the line on the lower priced seats.[68] Commonly, churches designated a block of free seats for those who could not afford to pay. It is unlikely that many of the city's very poorest ventured into middle-class churches; more likely the free seats were occupied by the marginally or temporarily poor— widows, students, servants, shop girls, or what a King's Weigh House historian identified as "young men starting their training or careers in business."[69] Church leaders knew that accessibility was important and that it could be destroyed by high pew rates. Partly because accessibility was a widely shared goal, it seldom became a matter for debate or articulation.

Kirk sessions in the Church of Scotland, however, dealt with government officials who were often more interested in balancing budgets than ensuring access. The town council or, later in the century the city's Ecclesiastical Commission, garnered the pew rents and one-half of the door collections and, in return, paid the minister's stipend and the costs of maintaining and heating the building. Historian Callum Brown's study of ten Glasgow congregations demonstrates, however, that with the new competitive mentality that accompanied the rise of a market economy, the town council increasingly conceived of its churches as "a corporate business" of which it was the "commercial operator." By maximizing rental income and holding down maintenance expenses, it might hope to turn a profit on the operation of the town's churches. Its eagerness to do so brought it into repeated conflict with kirk sessions, and ultimately alienated many of the working poor.[70]

The relationship between town and kirk was no more cordial in Edinburgh. By the 1840s, the Greyfriars kirk session, frustrated with the council's policies, was using its own benevolent money to operate Magdalene Chapel for those "totally unable to pay seat rents" in the parish church. In 1879, when the same session proposed raising £20 more from current seatholders to defray the cost of "free seats for the poor" in the parish church, the city's Ecclesiastical Commission proved inflexible and the plan came to naught.[71] St. George's kirk session pressed the town council in 1848 to lower "such a portion of [seat rents] as may enable the poorer members of the Congregation to secure full accommodation for themselves & family." Later, in the early 1860s, it protested without success the traditional practice of charging reduced rates to royalty.[72] In other denominations, of course, church boards had control of their own pew rates, and such conflicts did not arise.

The annual seat letting was a major event in the life of a congregation. January or May were frequently chosen months in the United States; in Britain, Martinmas in the fall or Whitsunday in the spring were normal times for renting pews. The details varied from place to place, but current seatholders were typically given an opportunity to renew their same locations first. Then, on a specified evening, new renters and those hoping to improve their location gathered at the church and selected among the vacant sittings. During the last third of the century, the annual seat letting night became a festive occasion, often with a light supper and entertainment organized by the ladies of the church.

Beecher perfected a variation at Plymouth Church that was calculated to extract the maximum money from the congregation's wealthiest churchgoers. No rentals at Plymouth could be automatically renewed by the current occupants; each pew was auctioned annually, and members were encouraged to bid against each other for the right to sit in the choice locations—and to make the largest donation to the church. One participant remembered it as "a sort of gala time, when loyalty to Plymouth and its pastor and good-natured rivalry had combined to bring from the more wealthy members sums mounting into thousands of dollars."[73]

Seat rents were paid quarterly, in some places half-yearly. An agreement to rent was considered a contractual obligation to pay, and congregations energetically pursued delinquents and, in a few cases, turned accounts over to a collector.[74] But, with a few exceptions, churches did not seem to have particular difficulty with collection, although timely collection was more elusive. At a meeting of a congregation in Pittsburgh in 1872, the auditors talked about "some of the existing evils, the most prominent being tardiness in paying pew rents."[75] Occasionally, there were instances of a family's asking to be excused from its commitment because of a death or an unfortunate turn in family finances; in these instances, church officers were sympathetic, often allowing the occupants to stay in their pew without fee. At Central Presbyterian in Rochester, a man whose father had died wrote to the trustees asking that his parents' pew be cancelled, as his mother would now sit with his family; the trustees concurred, but offered that the widow could continue to sit in her same pew without further payment if she preferred.[76]

Because rents were due at three or six month intervals, however, churches frequently struggled with cash flow. Quite a few congregations owed their treasurers money or had floating loans or overdrafts from the bank before the next installment arrived. One solution was to encourage, or to specify, that the rent be paid in advance. But a quarterly or half-yearly payment schedule almost guaranteed that individuals on tight family budgets would have difficulty coming up with a quarter or half of their church payment at one time. Later, as congregations adopted more efficient business practices, it was more usual to ask for rents weekly. Rather than taking the money to the church on "rent night," pewholders placed the appropriate sum in an envelope and dropped it in the collection plate. This way the church received a steady stream of revenue, and members paid in convenient installments. The Congregational church in Binghamton, New York, touted the envelope system in 1875 because it reduced collection costs, ensured promptness, put less strain on the family budget, was more certain to be paid, made giving a part of worship, and therefore was more scriptural.[77]

The pew rent system persisted because it worked well. Worshippers liked it because a reserved seat was worth a great deal in a day when churches were overflowing. Church leaders could trust the system to produce the necessary local revenues, and when a church needed more money, an increase in seat rents brought more predictable results than an appeal for extra voluntary contributions. Pew rents also seem to have been accepted as a fair way of raising money; affluent members got to sit in the more desirable locations, but they also paid more.[78]

This system, so fraught with class distinction as it was, has not found much favor among twentieth-century church leaders or historians. The system did, without question, echo and reinforce class divisions, but this criticism was seldom mentioned as a drawback at the time. Less affluent churchgoers do not seem to have been affronted or humiliated by a system that placed them in the back or in the galleries. These churchgoers seem not to have resented or even thought much about sitting in the seats they could afford—any more, one supposes, than the twentieth-century sports fan devotes much conscious attention to the class implications of bleachers and luxury boxes. Indeed, churches continued to report the highest demand for the least expensive seats, and some restructured their pricing to create more seats in this category by raising rates on the top-priced seats.

From the nineteenth-century perspective, the potential for social disgrace rested not on the poor, but on any persons of means who would have sat in pews less expensive than their social station indicated they could afford. The system used the wedge of social respectability to guarantee large contributions from those who could afford them—especially if the bidding on seat-letting night was manipulated to its fullest by someone like Beecher. Ironically, for all of the class distinctions built into the system, an end to pew rents likely shifted more of the burden for supporting the church onto people of modest means. At very least, it became possible for prosperous churchgoers to give meager contributions or shirk responsibility entirely without embarrassment.

The method that gradually replaced pew rents as the primary source of local operating revenues was the voluntary or "free-will" offering. Even where pew rents raised the majority of local income, offerings had been used as a supplement. Some congregations designated the pew rent for the pastor's salary and used offerings to pay for heating and incidentals; others pooled the money and allocated it as seemed best. In time, quarterly offerings—like quarterly pew rents—gave way to weekly envelope contributions as churches attempted to improve cash flow and make payment more convenient.

From the beginning of the period, there were a few Reformed congregations that dispensed with pew rents and relied solely on voluntary contributions.[79] These opponents of seat rents occasionally voiced objections to pew-letting's class implications—what one congregation referred to as "an aristocratic exclusion spirit and . . . a distinction between the rich and poor in a place in which no such distinction should be recognized—,"[80] but usually objectors raised a more fundamental concern. The abuse lay not so much in graduated assessments and class-determined seating, but in the idea that *anyone* should have to pay for access to the Gospel. God's grace came free, and so should the church. Congregations that emerged from the Second Great Awakening, in particular, wanted to sustain themselves on the gifts of converted hearts, not rental contracts.

Many of the newly formed churches of the nineteenth century were "free-seat" ones; Lyndhurst Road, for instance, stated bluntly at its founding in the 1880s that "the system of Pew-rents as such does not seem in accordance with the spirit or principle of the New Testament."[81] From the 1870s on, a growing number of long-established congregations converted from rents to offerings. The Withington Congregationalists in Manchester rejoiced in 1887 to see that "older Churches than our own . . . are taking up one by one the more excellent plan, as it seems to us, which we have all along adopted, and with results as satisfactory as they have been in our case."[82]

Despite such expressions of optimism, churches were reluctant to give up a system that worked, and many thriving congregations continued to collect rents until the 1920s and 1930s. Of those that shifted, some did so because they agreed that offerings were more biblical, that giving should be cheerful and worshipful rather than obligatory and commercial. Particularly as congregations tried to understand their relationships to the larger commercial culture, selling what amounted to season passes—as if worship were but one more amusement—became a matter of conscience. Other congregations that were trying to redefine themselves as communities based on friendship and openness understood that yearly rents and reserved pews were contrary to their new spirit.

Pew rents also declined in popularity when they became less effective in raising money. The system, counting as it did on the value of a reserved seat, assumed a full sanctuary. Pew renting and attendance reinforced each other. Once a pew was let, there was an incentive for the renter to use it often. At the same time, where attendance was high, a seat reservation was worth its price and renting thereby encouraged. The system began to fray when Sunday evening attendance declined and churches declared those seats free; when Sunday morning attendance became erratic also, the system fell apart. Once pew rents were no longer effective, churches turned to the only other system they knew—the combination of subscription cards and offerings that had already proved it could raise large sums of money for charitable and mission causes.[83]

Congregations that employed a voluntary or "free-will" offering system borrowed much from their experience with systematic benevolence. Weekly envelopes became the common method of collection, with care taken to be sure people knew to put in "two envelopes or double the amount" if they were absent for a week.[84] Congregations also used pledge cards or subscription papers so that budget makers knew how much to anticipate. The Congregational Church in Binghamton, New York, which stopped rents in 1894, explained to its members how the new "voluntary offerings of the people" would work: "It is desired that every member and attendant should contribute regularly. . . . To become a contributor, fill out one of the Pledge Cards in the pews, and place it on the collection-plate, or mail it to the Treasurer of the Society, who will send you a package of weekly-offering envelopes."[85]

Some offering plans still provided for reserved seating. When Lyndhurst Road was founded, it tried for a short while to leave all seats open, but the resulting anxiety and inconvenience of fighting for a seat caused them to pair the voluntary offering with a seating plan. Central Presbyterian in Rochester converted to offerings in 1891, but still instructed a committee to "assign seats to all persons who have signed pledge cards, and . . . arrange the audience substantially as now located." Actually the Rochester plan was even more of a hybrid: the letter soliciting pledges the second year stated what the sitting would have cost under the old rental system and strongly recommended that "the amount on the pledge cards be made to correspond to the schedule valuation of the sittings."[86] Churchgoers who filled out King's Weigh House's first pledge cards in 1912 indicated not only how much they promised to pay but which seats they wanted; everyone was to "self-assess . . . according to his or her means," but the mental link between the pledge and the value of the pew remained.[87]

Not every conversion from seat rents to offerings was a happy story. First Congregational Church, Cleveland, changed to voluntary pledges in 1886. The results were disappointing; revenue fell from $3,011 the first year to $2,904, then to $2,576, and to $2,137 the fourth year. Indeed, that fourth fund-raising campaign in 1890 had been a disaster; 39 percent of the families neglected to return a pledge card. This was "not owing to lack of opportunity or notice," the frustrated committee lamented. The pastor had preached on the subject, and pledge cards were given out in church and sent to homes "accompanied by an urgent written request." Those who failed to respond "were seen personally." Still, many did not cooperate, and revenue continued to drop. Whatever the case elsewhere, the committee concluded, "the plan in its practical workings in this local church is ineffective."[88]

So these disillusioned trustees—"as business men looking at the financial affairs of the Society as they would other business and financial matters"— recommended a return to seat rents. Whatever the theological difficulties with rents, they were convinced that "a well-filled treasury is as indispensable to the prosperity of the Church as purity of doctrine." The offering system "unjustly" penalized and weakened the "moral enthusiasm" of those who contributed gener- ously because they still had to face an insolvent church. A return to rentals meant the burden of current expenses would be more equally borne, no one could escape, people would feel a "greater legal obligation" to pay, and renters were more likely to participate in worship.[89]

The experience of these Cleveland Congregationalists suggests that volun- tary offerings, unlike obligatory pew rents, depended heavily on commitment and motivation. Other churches experienced similar frustration; a church in Pittsburgh, after analyzing its giving patterns, found that "there are some members who attend regularly and occupy their regular pews who do not contribute anything." Worse, the trustees lamented, these were the same ones who were "loudest in fault finding about continual begging, &c."[90] Although it would be virtually impossible for a historian to measure, it seems a good guess that the amounts given under the voluntary system correlated more with the depth of members' commitments than the depth of their pockets.

Motivation became a key factor for congregations using the voluntary system. Quarterly statements kept pledgers abreast of their progress, and reminder cards jogged those who fell into arrears. Annual reports, letters, and brochures tried to clarify exactly why the money was needed; it was not surprising that Lyndhurst Road's newsletter was the responsibility of the fund-raising committee. In Rochester, there was an "every member canvass" to carry the message of giving to each home.[91] Sunday Schools sought to inculcate the habit of giving among the young; one congregation even put out a children's annual giving report, itemizing the mission offerings the youngsters had brought during the year.[92] The primary strategy of the motivators was to associate giving with religious duty—that is, to substitute a spiritual obligation for a rental contract. Bible verses adorned pledge cards and buttressed pleas in letters or church manuals. Churchgoers in London were told that supporting the Congregational Fund was a "*sacred duty*" for "*every regular attendant.*"[93] A letter to the members of Fourth United Presbyterian Church in Pittsburgh made a similar point: "Friend, you are personally responsible for the amount you pledged yourself to give towards carrying on God's work in our Church. You don't owe it to the Pastor, you don't owe it to the Trustees, but you do owe it to God."[94]

Throughout the nineteenth century, financial commitment to the church was tangled with the matter of privacy. At least into the 1880s and 1890s, and occasionally beyond, congregations published names of contributors together with the specific amounts given. This was true of benevolent donations, special building campaigns, and free-will offerings; individual giving patterns were public information. Pew rent contributions were, of course, readily apparent to anyone who noticed where people sat on Sunday.

As long as church contributions were published in annual reports or noted in membership directories, the free-will offering system provided wealthy church-goers with incentives equal to those under the pew rent system. Respectability still required generosity. But gradually, an expectation of privacy prevailed here as elsewhere in the church. Some congregations continued to list contributors, but without amounts; more dispensed with lists entirely and advertised that gifts were confidential. A Birmingham congregation was assured that only the treasurer would ever know how much had been put in an envelope. In Manchester, the concern for privacy went farther. Envelopes were numbered only, and the person who recorded the amounts had no access to the corresponding names; it was "an essential part of the system that the Weekly Offering Stewards do not disclose to any one the sum contributed by individual subscribers." In 1911, Regent Square told contributors simply that "giving is secret."[95] However much the removal of public scrutiny was appreciated by others, its greatest beneficiaries were apt to be respectable churchgoers looking for an opportunity to reduce their contributions.

Whatever means was used to raise local operating revenue, the amount was sometimes insufficient. How did congregations deal with financial adversity? In the early days before churches planned yearly budgets in advance, crises were virtually guaranteed to arrive without much warning. The treasurer would announce that the money had run out, and the congregation would hurry into action to escape embarrassment. But even with foresight, most congregations lived close enough to the edge that any unexpected turn could throw the budget out of balance. Problems came from overdue pew rents or offerings, suddenly rising costs, unanticipated expenses, mid-year program expansions, and occasionally from national depressions or local demographic trends. What, then, was done about the resulting deficit?

Churches could employ one or a combination of three strategies: borrowing, reducing costs, and increasing income. Some boards faced crises with such regularity that they knew immediately from experience what course they wanted; others debated, or asked a committee to make a recommendation. The officers' first concern was to get past the immediate difficulty, but they also looked for ways to avoid a recurrence. To quote an Edinburgh kirk session, the ultimate goal was the "equalizing of the Income & Expenditure in the future."[96] Fiscal emergencies thus became occasions for implementing better financial controls, changing to an alternate method of funding, restructuring church organizations, or even relocating to a new neighborhood.

Borrowing was often a necessary first step. A commercial bank loan was one possibility. Quite a few congregations, in anticipation of the sort of repeated deficits that came from uneven cash flow, negotiated the right to overdraw their accounts with interest due on whatever portion of their credit limit they used. A severely strained congregation, such as Cleveland's First Congregational Church, might find itself carrying a loan on which it was capable of making only interest payments. A further complication for officers of unincorporated congregations was that they bore personal responsibility for the loan. When an interest payment was due in 1860, Cleveland's trustees pleaded for its "prompt payment" because they "had become individual [sic] liable for the amount." The congregation, taking the point, quickly circulated a subscription to raise the amount and rescue the credit of its officers.[97]

Church officers were, in fact, often the ones who provided temporary financial backing for a congregation. More than one treasurer quietly covered a deficit from personal funds.[98] In 1867, when a Pittsburgh congregation needed two hundred dollars for the pastor's salary, one of the trustees took the money from his own pocket in exchange for a promissory note. It was not the first or the last time that this happened, and the trustee eventually settled—not too happily—for only partial repayment.[99]

Pastors were another, generally unwilling, source of emergency funds. Congregations that deferred scheduled salary payments in effect borrowed (although ministers might have chosen a less charitable word). In 1869, when the president of the Fourth United Presbyterian Church's board of trustees reported "the finances good and the prospects encouraging," the minister objected. "It might be so," the clerk reported his saying, "but it did not appear so to him, inasmuch as he had preached about fourteen months and received only $1,200 [twelve months salary]." The clerk added that "this lead [sic] to an animated discussion." Before the meeting was over, the treasurer had been instructed to make "immediate payment" of two hundred dollars "for the purpose of peace and harmony between Pastor and people."[100]

Churches sometimes found other ways to borrow internally and escape a commercial loan. Cleveland's First Congregational negotiated a small loan of $177 from the Ladies Sewing Circle; the women, perhaps appreciating all too well the congregation's shaky fiscal record, made it a formal note at "10% payable on thirty days notice." Other congregations were fortunate enough to have endowment funds that could be tapped. Edinburgh's Greenside parish turned to "Miss Sunderland's legacy" to pay off accumulated debts in 1876. King's Weigh House, finding that it owed the treasurer over five hundred pounds in 1874, sold some of its investments to clear the balance.[101]

Congregations naturally preferred to avoid borrowing entirely either by cutting expenses or by increasing revenue. There was usually not much that could be done to reduce costs. The deacons at St. George's Free Church resolved in 1904 to follow sound business practice and seek "competitive estimates . . . whenever practicable"—with what success the minutes do not reveal.[102] But there were few items that could be removed from a budget or pared significantly. The difficulty was that typically 90 to 95 percent of the budget was tied up in a combination of fixed building costs (fuel, light, insurance, and cleaning) and contracted salaries paid to the minister, lay missionaries, and musicians.[103] Building repairs of any magnitude were funded by separate subscriptions. Benevolence money was off-budget, and so was virtually all program money. Sunday Schools, women's associations, youth groups, church libraries, local mission projects, and other activities were self-supporting; they raised their own money, and deposited and spent it through their own treasurers. At least until the early twentieth century, churches did not spend enough on postage, printing, or office supplies to make much difference in a budget crisis. Even when church officers tried to trim costs, they met resistance. For instance, when the kirk session of St. George's parish, Edinburgh, proposed to reduce the number of choir singers to save fifty pounds in 1908, the music committee quickly stepped forward to launch a subscription for the wanted amount.[104]

Revenue enhancement, then, was the more likely course of action for most congregations facing a deficit. Congregations at various times sent reminders to delinquent contributors, dispatched more women door to door, sought contributions from regularly attending nonmembers, made a "strong appeal to the young men & women," raised pew rents, took up special collections, read notices from the pulpit, and sent letters urging "every one to give as God has prospered him or her."[105] The most common way of raising emergency money was a subscription—that is, circulating a paper and asking individuals how much they would "subscribe." For instance, as the year neared its end in 1877, Greyfriars parish in Edinburgh made a "special appeal . . . for subscriptions for the Congregational funds . . . with a view of making up the deficiency." Rochester's Central Presbyterian Church asked the pastor to preach a special sermon starting a subscription of "weekly pledges to pay off the debt" and had half the goal by the next day.[106]

By the last quarter of the century, as we noted above, congregations discovered a new method for eliminating deficits—the church fair or bazaar. Some hard-working groups raised extraordinary sums. The parish church in the small Scottish town of Dalbeattie not only achieved its goal of clearing a four hundred pound debt, but had enough extra money to repaint and "decorate" the church. In the mid-1890s, the Congregationalists in Moseley Road, Birmingham, earned over £1,200, more than eliminating the church debt.[107]

Fourth United Presbyterian Church in Pittsburgh more or less stumbled upon church suppers as a solution to perennial budget problems. At the congregation's annual meeting in January 1871, one elder suggested an "oyster supper." His primary interest was to help people "become better acquainted one with the other and become more sociable and to exhibit a more Christian spirit towards one another"; if at the same time it helped to "replenish the treasury," then so much the better. The supper was a smashing success in both departments; a good time had been had by all and they cleared $675 after expenses. To put that profit into perspective, the pastor's annual salary was only $1,500, and a recent contract for roofing, tinning, and spouting the church was less than $500. The congregation, populated by people of modest means, was suddenly rich.[108]

Thereafter, Fourth United Presbyterian's oyster supper became an annual event. The church became quite adept at merchandizing its product; it gave free tickets to any minister in town who would promote the dinner from his pulpit, and prizes to the Sunday School boy and girl who sold the most tickets. By 1886 the supper had been expanded into a full-fledged "fair" with stands selling flowers, glassware, fruit, ice cream, and fancy work. That year's activity netted $1,683, a fantastic sum surpassing combined pew rents and offerings. The money-raisers continued to be part of Fourth Church's life into the early twentieth century, and for much of that time they were responsible for keeping the congregation afloat. After the congregation relocated to a more prosperous area of the city in the 1890s, the need and eventually the enthusiasm for the annual supper diminished. Finally, in 1908, one man suggested that it would be a lot easier if each person donated three dollars and saved all the hard work. With the threat of deficits no longer imminent, the members heartily concurred.[109]

In their quest for financial stability an increasing number of churches built endowments. The Scots, with a long tradition of endowed chapels and parish churches, were quickest off the mark. St. Stephen's in Edinburgh, between 1848 and 1914 received forty-three legacies ranging in size from five to five hundred pounds; most of these gifts were designated for missions or the relief of the poor, but some were for general parish support.[110] Although the custom was less common, members of English and American congregations also left money or property to their churches.

After midcentury, churches located in the centers of major cities watched their members scatter toward the suburbs and realized that adequate endowments were essential to survival. Consequently, they embarked on organized, systematic campaigns to build assets. Beecher was one of the first to see the need, and in 1872 Plymouth Church started a fund with forty thousand dollars raised in honor of his twenty-fifth anniversary as pastor. What Plymouth grasped, according to one recollection, was that the "problem of a city church" in the last years of the century was "far different from that faced by its founders." With a large building to maintain, an ambitious program of activities and mission work, high standards for music and preaching, and a limited membership base, a downtown church needed a "permanence of financial basis." By the first decade of the twentieth century, Plymouth's fund had reached one hundred thousand dollars.[111] The endowments of other urban congregations climbed, too; by the World War I era, Second Church in Hartford was two-thirds of the way toward a goal of one hundred thousand dollars, and Brick Church in New York City was nearing three hundred thousand. A decade later, in 1928, the capital fund of St. Stephen's, Edinburgh, had risen to nine thousand pounds. Most endowment money came from bequests or special gifts, but occasionally a congregation got a windfall from the city's exercise of eminent domain, such as the $110,000 that Old South received as compensation from a street-widening project in 1904.[112]

The management of endowment funds plunged church boards even more fully into the world of commerce and banking. Old South's trustees managed large, multi-storied commercial properties in the heart of Boston that were, by 1914, generating seventy thousand dollars in annual rent. Old South's position was unique only in scale; other urban congregations, such as Hartford's First Church, Pittsburgh's Fourth United Presbyterian, and Edinburgh's St. George's Free Church, had real estate interests, too.[113] Other congregations—St. George's parish in Edinburgh and Fourth United Presbyterian in Pittsburgh—owned bank stock. St. George's Free Church invested in an insurance company and the Scottish-American Mortgage Company. Glasgow's Govan parish held railroad stock. King's Weigh House invested in a mix of 2.75 percent consolidated bonds, government bonds issued by Canada and the London County Council, and various British or colonial stocks.[114]

More than ever, then, congregations were immersed in the commercial culture around them. They managed real estate, invested in stocks and bonds, wrote advertising copy, and earned retail profits from church fairs. Their financial practices and fund-raising procedures had been redesigned for smooth operation and business-like efficiency. The mark of the corporate-style church was stronger on some congregations than others, but none escaped its impress entirely.

The change was noticeable in the tone of church board meetings. In the 1830s, there was a piousness—admittedly formulaic—to the discussions. In some congregations, elders and deacons referred to each other as "brother." A meeting of financial officers in Rochester in 1859 paused "to acknowledge the Divine Blessing in the Signal prosperity which had marked our progress since the work of church erection commenced"; the gathering ended with the trustees singing the doxology. But, by the 1880s minutes ceased to include topics such as "the state of religion in Scotland" or "an exchange of views on the spiritual condition of the congregation."[115] Where these topics still survived, their mention was perfunctory and unelaborated. With the end of disciplinary cases, discussions of community mores disappeared as well. What remained was the management of church finances and congregational activities.

Church manuals, once handbooks for pious living, became corporate style annual reports, dominated by balance sheets and other financial data. Carr's Lane's publications make a striking example. In 1835, the manual included a form of admission to membership, religious opinions of the church, principles of church order and discipline, duties of members, "directions for profitable attendance upon the public means of grace," meetings of the church with reasons for attending, the "ends of church fellowship," questions for self-examination, and a list of the church societies. There were no financial reports at all. By 1871, the manual had changed dramatically. It opened with a brief letter from the pastor (the corporate executive's standard introduction), and then came membership statistics, financial reports, church organization reports, a list of all donations, and a membership directory. By 1903, there were thirty-nine pages of financial reports—fully 44 percent of the total.[116]

Not everyone submitted easily to the corporate-commercial model. When an individual at Cowcaddens Free Church suggested that a bazaar would be a good fund-raiser for missions, the elders demurred; a sale, they said, had "in it elements unfavourable to the workers and to the work."[117] The Rev. George Critchley, a Congregational minister from London, wondered whether the church had inverted its priorities: "We, it is to be feared, reverse the order, and instead of looking at the spiritual condition first, and making it the measure of the material prosperity that we expected to see, we look at the material prosperity, and think little of that which is esteemed better than riches or power in the sight of God. . . . Will you, therefore, dear friends, each one of you before entering upon the question of the material prosperity of the Church, examine yourselves?"[118] Critchley hoped for a model of the church other than that based on corporate efficiency and commercial culture. As we shall see in the next chapters, there were two competing visions from which he could have choosen—a church that served the poor and a church sustained by friendship among its members.

# nine ✠

## Caring for Others
### Social Christianity and the Local Congregation

Pilrig Free Church stood part way down the slopes that led away from central Edinburgh to the Leith docks. A simple preaching station in the beginning, it became in 1843 an organized congregation. Its first minister was William Garden Blaikie, later professor of apologetics and pastoral theology at New College. When Blaikie began his visitation rounds, he was "shocked" at the blighted dwellings he encountered in the district streets. Why, he thought, should not the Pilrig congregation undertake "improving them in a practical and systematic way" as its mission project? By 1849, a site had been found and the "first row of the Pilrig Model Buildings was ready." Over the next dozen years, the congregation invested some seven thousand pounds and built sixty-two cottages, "each with its own street door and garden plot" and "place for private devotion." Economically successful, Pilrig's housing project continued to operate until 1892 when the deaths of key contributors and directors brought the experiment to an end.[1]

Pilrig's venture into Social Christianity[2] was unusual only in its choice of model housing for a project: as we shall see, education, banking, insurance, retailing, medicine, or family services were more common sectors of activity. In other ways, however, Pilrig was more typical than unique. Its entry into urban reform in the 1840s was not especially early; Social Christianity at the local level was a product of the early, not late, nineteenth century. Indeed, as the termination of Pilrig's enterprise in the 1890s suggests, much local energy was fading or being redirected into other forms of mission just as the national debate about a "social gospel" reached its peak. Pilrig's interest in cooperative, nonprofit, or subsidized schemes to protect individuals from the harshness of the marketplace was also a common rather than unusual local strategy. Finally, Pilrig's ability to attend both temporal and spiritual goals simultaneously—supplying sanitary houses *and* family altars—was a noticeable characteristic of nineteenth-century city reform.

Although traditional histories have divided nineteenth-century religious history between an early neglect of urban distress and a quickening of social commitment at the end of the century, local activity suggests more continuity than change. From the beginning of the Victorian period, congregations understood Christianity in a way that required local mission. Involvement came a decade or two sooner in Britain than in America, but so did industrial growth. As the years passed, churches became more astute about the nature of poverty and their programs grew more elaborate, but on both continents an active Social Christianity was a well-established part of congregational life long before the end of the century. St. George's Free Church's mission work on Rose Street in Edinburgh dated to the 1830s before the Disruption; its Fountainbridge Mission was founded in 1849. Carr's Lane started a Town Mission in Birmingham in 1837. King's Weigh House organized a "Domestic Mission" in 1831 in Rosemary Lane about a half-mile from the congregation's Fish Hill Street meetinghouse. Bethel Mission, which was adopted by Plymouth Church, had its start in Brooklyn in 1841. First Presbyterian Church in St. Louis became actively involved in city mission work sometime between 1859 and 1861.

Congregations that were founded later in the century sought an off-site city mission as quickly as possible. Highgate Presbyterian Church was organized on the north side of London's Hampstead Heath in 1887, and after three years the minister, already impatient, urged, "It is desirable that, as soon as may be, we begin direct mission efforts of our own. . . . Though our neighbourhood does not show any likely field which is at present unoccupied, it is desirable that, as soon as an opening shows itself, we be in a position to take advantage of it. Let us keep this aim steadily in view."[3] In 1891, Highgate located a site and opened Thrift Hall. Young congregations worried that without a mission project their growth would languish. Norwood Congregational, a new church development in 1870 on West Darby Road leading out of Liverpool, was blessed with a solid core of members who had quickly, and easily, gotten it firmly established and even paid off its building debt. But, ironically, it was more worried than satisfied by these advantages. Its first manual cautioned, "We must resolve to spend the same amount of energy or of funds on new objects, if we would really profit by our advantages." Within two years, Norwood set up the Every Street Mission, complete with a missionary, Bible woman, savings bank, and evening school for working boys and girls.[4] A local mission project was simply an expected, natural part of organizing a church.

Once established, city mission halls added or expanded programs according to the circumstances they encountered and the resources they had. Information was shared among congregations, and where conditions were similar they copied programs that were working elsewhere. But new directions came just as often from workers' own observations once they were on the site. Without a lot of attention to theory, volunteers simply saw needs and tried to meet them, letting each experience suggest the next step. When younger siblings tagged along with their sisters to sewing class, the women at Chicago's Third Presbyterian mission hall organized a new activity to get them out from under foot; there would be "drawing cards and materials" for the littlest ones. When the girls' older brothers— unattracted by either stitchery or art—stayed out on the street, then there had to be "tools and work benches" and a woodworking teacher for them.[5] After Glasgow children repeatedly showed up for Sunday School without breakfast, the workers from Lansdowne United Presbyterian found a way to feed them before class.[6] In London, the mission workers from Lyndhurst Road went a step further and "consulted" with the children's week-day school teachers. Their suspicion was confirmed: the children did not eat during the week either, and sometimes even "fainted in school, from want of proper nourishment." There was soon a daily breakfast program serving between five and six hundred morning meals per week.[7]

Local mission workers did not set out to overthrow or even radically alter existing political and economic orders. Individual congregations were not very probable venues for launching national crusades in any case—which may say something about why the Rev. Norman Thomas left his assistant pastorate at New York's Brick Church for socialist politics. Their direct power was certainly limited; a majority of church members—as women—were denied political vote, and in Britain, property qualifications prevented many men from voting, too, at least until the Franchise Act of 1884. The subtler political arts, such as moral suasion, were available and were used, but immediate power to change the political and economic systems was beyond the reach of any single congregation working alone. By the early twentieth century, denominational agencies or interdenominational associations provided better access to national policy makers, but this work went on largely apart from the local scene.

Congregations did discuss national issues in their own temperance societies or literary and debating clubs; for instance, a "general Bible Discussion Class" at New York's Brick Church listed "The Disposition of Disputes between Capital and Labor" among its topics for 1914.[8] National groups like the Women's Christian Temperance Union were permitted to use church facilities, if there was no interference with ongoing activities.[9] But local churches acted locally. Beecher's congregation in Brooklyn, for instance, could not by itself reach the Southern slave power, but it could and did purchase the freedom of a slave girl. The crusade for national prohibition was mostly unmentioned in American church board meetings. Instead, congregations established Bands of Hope for the children, collected total abstinence pledges, or ran Saturday evening men's clubs as a non-alcoholic alternatives to the local taverns.

Congregations did not eschew political activity entirely. When they could identify a local issue that seemed within their reach, they sent petitions or organized opposition or lobbied for change. Any number of congregations raised protests when neighborhood saloons became too numerous or came too close to church property.[10] New York City's Brick Church organized "Neighborhood Associations" in Chelsea and Kips Bay that applied pressure to local governments for recreation facilities, inspection of "uncovered food stuffs," closing of "disorderly houses," and opening of school doors for recreational use.[11] The Hampstead and St. Pancras Sanitary Aid Committee, started by Lyndhurst Road's Social Reform League, fielded complaints about substandard housing and, if a private word to the owner did not bring a remedy, took cases to the government.[12]

At the same time, however, even purely local mission projects could challenge the hegemony of property and profit, if only in limited, indirect ways. By organizing cooperative banks or retailing activities (described in more detail later), mission halls effectively circumvented, without replacing, usual commercial practice. As historian Gary Smith has pointed out, nineteenth-century Calvinists distanced themselves from competitive Darwinism and its religious equivalent, the Gospel of Wealth; "benevolence and service" were higher ideals than "productivity and profit."[13] Local mission work grew from a Calvinist understanding that wealth was an gift of God, not a reward for righteous behavior. An 1852 committee report urging that Boston's Old South take "aggressive action" to assist a "less favored portion of the city," spoke forthrightly of the obligations of wealth: "A wealthy church is indeed a rare sight—ours may be said to be such. Shall the wealth be a blessing to ourselves, our children, this community & the world, or shall it be a curse? Shall Christ be honored by its wise charitable & benevolent use, or shall Satan rejoice in its perversion? These your Committee feel to be solemn questions. You all profess to belong to the Master's household—you have wealth—how will you use it? The responsibility is on you—you cannot throw it off if you would."[14]

While mission workers rejected the extremes of competitive capitalism on the one hand, they rejected the necessity of class conflict on the other. In the community as well as within the congregation, they valued meekness and compromise over power and confrontation. They believed themselves to be in the business of reconciliation, of building community. As a result, they looked for ways to promote contact between the "classes"—a term they used imprecisely to mean little more than a division between those like themselves and those with less education, skills, and income. Thomas Cochrane, who spent a half century in city mission work in Edinburgh first as a lay missionary with Thomas Guthrie at St.

John's and later as the ordained minister of the Pleasance Church, remembered Chalmers's "clear and strong conviction that the various classes of people in this city—the rich and the poor, the educated and the uneducated, they who live at ease and they who live in the midst of difficulties or on the earnings of hard and honest labour—have hitherto kept at far too great a distance from each other."[15]

Cochrane was encouraging middle class churchgoers to volunteer for mission hall service and to join teams of house-to-house visitors. H. M. Ross, who headed the Fountainbridge Mission in Edinburgh, pressed "men & women of culture & spirituality" not only to volunteer, but to "take up their residence in the District, and thus help in the work."[16] Many efforts at contact were sporadic, and likely somewhat artificial. Children from the mission and the sponsoring congregation were taken on joint outings, mission Sunday School teachers brought their classes home for holiday parties, or Mothers' Meetings were invited to the manse for tea. But a few activities promised more continuous contact. Early in the twentieth century, for instance, Lansdowne United Presbyterians had only one Young Men's Club which was "open both to young men in the Congregation and to young men resident in the mission district." All the activities were held at the mission hall, and every Friday evening, the group met for physical drill and lectures or debates; on Saturday mornings, there was a football club in the Glasgow church league, and on Sunday afternoons, a Bible class.[17]

City missionaries did not articulate very clearly what benefit they expected from the interaction of classes. Certainly a raised consciousness—and increased donations—on the part of the middle class was foreseen. Speaking of its own members' involvement in mission work, Mayfield Free Church noticed that "not a few have found here opportunities for service which has developed their religious life, broadened their sympathies, and strengthened their faith, by their experiences among those in less fortunate circumstances than their own."[18] Mission advocates were also confident that middle-class values would rub off on the mission hall youth. Although local churches acted as if everyone were a potential convert, they held particularly high hopes for the children—"the plastic young minds," as Old South's 1859 mission report called them.[19] Many of the mission stations originated as district Sunday Schools, and children's activities continued to be important aspects of their work. It was not without reason that the Lansdowne United Presbyterians referred to their Springbank and Garscube missions as the "Lansdowne Church Mission for the Young."[20]

The objective was self-reliance and self-sufficiency, both for the hall itself and for the individuals served. Quite the opposite of control, the purpose was to turn the mission into a self-sustaining community as quickly as possible—and then move on. Congregations were trying to plant enough new, independent churches to keep up with the burgeoning urban population, and to have lingered unnecessarily in one location would have been irresponsible.[21] In the mid-1860s, St. George's Free Church's Fountainbridge Mission had become an independent congregation. Actually, Fountainbridge still needed financial support and volunteers, but St. George's was already planning another mission west of Haymarket Station in the Roseburn district, "where numerous houses for the working classes have lately been erected." They acquired temporary space for a school and preaching, and wisely secured a site for a future church while land was still available. In a fund-raising letter to the congregation, Candlish wrote, "Let us go among them in a friendly spirit; not in such a manner as to wound in the least their self-respect, but rather with the avowed object of aiding and encouraging them in working out their own welfare. We aim at their being as independent of us as Fountainbridge has for some years been. The School and the Church will be theirs, not ours."[22] The first worship services at Roseburn were held in 1866, and by 1869 the fledgling congregation had its own self-governing Deacons' Court.

Thus, mission work and new church development were complimentary tasks. Carr's Lane spun off five Birmingham congregations before the end of the century, and St. John's Wood had an equal number of "daughter congregations" in London between 1887 and 1920. Before Govan parish built a new edifice for itself in the 1880s, it had already devoted £37,000 to erect "two temporary mission churches, and three large permanent churches, meeting for our generation the needs of the poorer districts." At the turn of the century Brick Church's two New York "affiliated" congregations—Christ Church and Church of the Covenant— each had their own pastors and sessions.[23]

Mission workers sought self-reliance and self-sufficiency for individuals, too. They sought to empower, not to control. They imagined themselves providing the education and habits that would lead out of poverty, or would at least allow people to gain the most from what they had. Church workers were not quick to see structural problems with the economy or with industrial practice, but when they did, they tried to circumvent the difficulty. They could easily see the inequalities that young children faced, and they tried to provide the literacy, skills, and attitudes that they expected would open opportunity. They were also able to recognize the negative implications of alcohol abuse for family life. Occasionally someone understood alcoholism as a response to oppressive poverty, or at least saw the ambiguity of cause and effect; Deacon Lathrop's 1861 report on Old South's mission endeavors in Boston argued that "a sinful life induces poverty, and poverty tends to a sinful life," and he added that he had "seen most saddening examples of both."[24] More often, alcoholism was interpreted as a cause of distress, or at least as a barrier to escape and comfort.

Congregations understood their mission work to be liberating in the sense that it broke the chains that bound people not only to sin but to poverty, and empowering in the sense that it offered not only spiritual salvation, but the tools of economic betterment. There could be, therefore, no inherent conflict between the work of evangelism and the work of social reform. Victorian congregations spoke of the two as twins, not enemies. When the members of Newington United Presbyterian Church in the southern extremities of Edinburgh began a mission project in Duncan Street in 1840, they explained their aim as "the religious and social improvement of the inhabitants of Causewayside."[25] Cochrane, speaking from his long years of experience working in the slums of Edinburgh, believed social work could not succeed without a strong religious dimension; "the defect of all such purely city mission labours" was the lack of word and sacrament "to bind converts together."[26] Charles Booth, recording his observations of Lyndhurst Road's mission hall in London, concluded that while "the ultimate aim is undoubtedly religious . . . , comparatively little of the work is primarily religious"; rather, the missionaries understood "religious and social work as inextricably mixed."[27]

The same congregations and individuals promoted, without a hint of conflict, both evangelistic meetings and social services. By the early twentieth century, as we shall see, the union of these aims was dissolving, but for now the two were partners. It was Moody's 1876 revival in Chicago that stimulated Third Presbyterian to open the Foster Mission with an "industrial school" to complement its evangelism. Bethany Presbyterian Church in Philadelphia operated a medical dispensary, savings bank, home for the unemployed, consumer cooperatives and a host of other services while minister J. Wilbur Chapman earned a national reputation as a revivalist. In Glasgow, lay missionary William Agnew led the Springbank Mission for nearly forty years before his death in 1907. Almost every year there were one or two weeks of evangelistic services, but there were also free medical services and cooperative buying schemes for coal and cloth.[28] In the minds of missionaries such as Ross, the spiritual and practical were one.

Churches cooperated, rather than competed, with each other in starting city mission work. Most cities had an nondenominational mission society that provided coordination; in Boston, the City Missionary Society actually "allotted" districts to the various churches so that efforts would not overlap. There was an unwritten code that congregations would stay out of each other's way, and Roman Catholic boundaries seem to have been respected as much as those of other Protestant denominations. By the last quarter of the century, some congregations were conducting systematic city or district censuses to assist local mission work, and one of the reasons that such surveys tallied religious preference as well as existing services and needs was the desire to locate among Protestant rather than Catholic residents.[29] Guthrie, when thinking about the best site for the Pleasance mission in Edinburgh, wanted "a place with a sunken Protestant population."[30] Partly this was a matter of efficiency: where there was so much need, duplication of effort was senseless, and of course unaffiliated Protestants were more likely converts than either attending or nonattending Catholics. Partly, however, it was the lay churchgoers' lack of concern with dogmatic distinctions in the face of urgent poverty.

As time went on, it became more difficult to find a mission field that was not already being worked. Third Presbyterian Church in Chicago was searching for an additional site in 1872 and thought it had found one in the section lying north of Fulton and west of Halstead streets, but "after careful inspection it was found that to plant a mission there would be to encroach upon work of the same kind." Philadelphia's Second Presbyterian looked for more than a year in the mid-1880s to find a location. The church almost had one in West Philadelphia, but it was slow off the mark, and Woodland Presbyterian Church beat them to it. The congregation dismissed several other spots as "inexpedient" and took the advice of presbytery before settling on a satisfactory place. When Mayfield Free Church was founded in 1875, it discovered that "the area in the southern part of the Causeway-side was already worked by other congregations"; a bit at a loss as to what to do, Mayfield was helped out by Buccleuch Street Free Church which gave them the southern part of its district in 1881.[31]

Start-up costs for mission work were usually minimal, although with a full-fledged program expenditures were certain to grow. When Fifth Presbyterian Church in Chicago started a mission in June 1875, it rented a house and furnished it inexpensively by relying on gifts and volunteer labor. According to the year-end report, "lumber for the seats and battening the house was kindly donated, and ready hearts and hands found time to make the seats, and make the house comfortable." Others donated lamps, chairs, tables, a parlor organ, and sixty-five books for the library.[32]

Funding for mission work came primarily from special collections or subscriptions. Wealthy congregations, of course, could afford to use money from investment income or from local revenues. When Plymouth Church built a new facility for its Bethel Mission in Brooklyn, two-thirds of the $75,000 was from a "surplus of the pew rents"; $20,000 came from a subscription drive and the remainder from "a fair held in Plymouth Church."[33] In 1905, Second Presbyterian in Philadelphia used some of its Sunday collection money for its "Settlement."[34]

Because churchgoers contributed more readily to specific causes, most of the program money, such as supplies for the sewing class or subsidies for various mutual aid schemes, came by separate collections, which left the mission station's main budget to cover personnel and overhead. Old South's Chambers Street Mission had a budget of $6,620 in 1862, including $2,800 for a "superintendent," $500 for a sexton, $600 for teachers in a summer "vacation school," and $300 for music; rent came to $1,900, and another $300 was allotted to coal and gas.[35] Fountainbridge Mission in Edinburgh owned its building, and thus there were no rent charges in its £546 budget for 1909; however, custodial services, heat and light, repairs and insurance amounted to £170. The lay missionary earned £200, the Bible woman received £50 plus lodging, the part-time organist got £20, and the mission spent £33 for a part-time assistant. Fountainbridge's budget did show £30 for poor relief, and £76 went for costs of "treats," the Boys' Brigade, the Sunday School, additional Bibles and hymnals, and miscellany.[36]

A significant portion of the mission money was raised by women, sometimes acting as "lady collectors" for a congregational association, but quite often as part of a women's home missionary society that raised and expended money independently and apart from the mission's general budget. The "Ladies Association for Christian Work and Beneficence" at Glasgow's Lansdowne Church had enough money to fund the mission's relief work, Mothers' Meetings, Girls' Club, medical services, coal-buying cooperative, and the salary of the Bible woman.[37] Women gained additional prominence in city mission work because they provided more than their share of the volunteers, and the salaried on-site director was almost always female.

The women's energy and resourcefulness in raising money and directing mission activities was not always accepted comfortably by their congregations' male officers. When Philadelphia's Second Presbyterian Church was between ministers in 1908, the trustees prodded the elders to ask whether the Beth Eden Mission needed additional guidance now that the church was pastorless. Mrs. Audenried, the president of the Church Settlement Society, together with head resident Miss Kemp and superintendent Mr. Patton showed up, as summoned, to reassure the elders that they were managing quite well, as they always had. One supposes the trustees meant well, but the mission leaders must have been bemused, or worse, at the suggestion they were unable to tend the work on their own.[38] At least one reason that Jane Addams cooled toward organized Presbyterianism in Chicago was her sense that the pastor at Fourth Presbyterian Church was afraid of strong women.[39]

Volunteer workers were the lifeblood of every mission. "Lady visitors" went door to door weekly through the district, identifying needs and providing assistance where they could; male visitors were dispatched on Sunday afternoons to the men's lodging houses. Mrs. King, the Bible woman at Lyndhurst Road's

Kentish Town Mission in London, claimed that her sixteen ladies' weekly calls came to be anticipated because they met real needs.

> A ticket for a Hospital may be wanted, or some neighbour may have brought a sick child to be seen by the lady. At another house the mother shows the School Certificate of her boy who has just left School, and they talk over what he can do and what can be done to help him, the mother telling of her hopes and anxieties. Upstairs she enters a room, a young mother has her first baby to show, dressed, perhaps, with a little more care, because it is Tuesday, and "the lady is sure to call." . . . Another family in trouble is visited, there the father, though a steady man, is out of work, has walked miles for a half-day's work, has toiled hard but earned little, he is unskilled. What can be done? is considered. A ticket for some needlework is given the wife, this, if she is competent, leads to more or some temporary work may be found.

An idealized portrait perhaps, but Mrs. King did not claim that every story had a satisfactory ending. "Often there seems no way open to relieve the sorrows they tell of," she lamented, "and the Visitor pauses and marvels as she sees the patient endurance of suffering." Overall, however, Mrs. King insisted that the visitors gained a welcome because of the aid they provided; "there is a growing feeling amongst the people that the Visitors are their friends—they look to them in their trouble, and proofs of their gratitude are not wanting."[40]

Cochrane called such "persistent visitation" the "basis of all true work." "Begin at the doors of the first landing," he recommended, "and thus upwards to the summit." Cochrane's volunteer visitors met weekly "for prayer and conference"; "individual cases were discussed, overlapping was avoided, and the brethren and sisters went forth again with renewed strength." It was important, Cochrane advised, that "our manner should be natural, and unaffected, maintaining a calm tranquility amid severest trials and tribulation, endeavouring to wear a happy and placid countenance." Following the pattern Chalmers had established for parish visitation, each of Cochrane's volunteers had a district and responsibility for about twenty families. The workers visited faithfully, "making themselves," according to Cochrane's ideal, "not almoners, but friends in each household, trying by weekly visits to earn good-will and induce them to accept the Christian verities."[41]

Volunteers performed a variety of other tasks. Much of the work involved teaching Sunday School or basic literacy or household skills or woodworking. Other volunteers organized recreation or managed social services. Lyndhurst Road was advertising in 1892 for teachers of educational and technical classes, a piano player for musical drill and social meetings, a man to lead gymnastics, and various "general workers."[42] The workers were mostly young, mostly female. Men were admittedly harder to recruit, in part because of less flexible schedules, but in part because male gender roles accorded less easily with care giving. A Glasgow mission reported that it had plenty of young women to work with the girls and junior boys, but "it is to be regretted that the absence of a sufficient number of gentlemen of ability to interest and instruct the senior boys spiritually and educationally has retarded progress in that important department." When King's Weigh House specified that "both Ladies and Gentlemen of the congregation are earnestly invited to join in the work," the emphasis was certainly that males were welcome.[43]

Volunteers were motivated primarily by the religious teaching of the home church. Just as no congregation felt whole without a mission project, neither did many high-minded individual members. Old South identified those who volunteered at its Lowell Street Mission as "the philanthropic and benevolent young ladies and gentlemen whose sympathies with suffering humanity prompt them to forego their own ease and comfort and labor to clothe the naked, instruct the ignorant, and reclaim the wayward and neglected of our Lanes, Alleys, and places of obscurity."[44] There was, undoubtedly, a sense of personal fulfillment to be gained from the work, too; Cochrane, who started out as a young lay volunteer, found the work so satisfying that he turned to it full time. One can also imagine the camaraderie and spirit of adventure experienced by the young women of Third Presbyterian Church in Chicago: "every Saturday, for twenty-two weeks an omnibus loaded with ladies has been seen to leave our church going north . . . [into] one of the dark places of Chicago." Pelted in season with street boys' snow balls, the young women nevertheless arrived at the Mission and Industrial School to teach sewing to 247 girls.[45]

Mission halls employed full-time and part-time paid workers, too. An ordained or lay missionary, or in some cases the sponsoring congregation's assistant minister, provided preaching and led religious services; a resident director— variously called a Bible woman or lady resident or superintendent or female missionary—organized the social services. In the popular mind, the two positions "were ranked very much together" in status.[46] In at least one locale, the women were commissioned by prayer in a special worship service. Norwood Congregational Church in Liverpool installed Miss Browne as a female missionary in 1871, and "before entering on her work she was specially commended in prayer to God at a meeting at which the Rev. John Thompson, Superintendent of Liverpool Town Mission, delivered an appropriate address."[47]

Some women made life-long careers of mission work, taking better job offers as they came along from other congregations or serving long years at the same charge. When Miss Lang died in 1889 at age seventy, she had been at her Glasgow post for over twenty-two years. By 1914, Miss Anna Juppe was in her thirty-second year with Brick Church, New York City.[48] Their annual reports evidence a hectic pace and great variety of personal activities in addition to the general management of the mission hall and coordination of volunteer work. Mrs. Shepherd, employed by First Congregational Church in Hartford, made 1,466 calls and received 232 calls in 1884.[49] Lang's 1873 report showed that she had visited, read to the "sick and aged," led a worship service for mothers, distributed relief and Bibles, wholesaled coal and flannel, ran a Total Abstinence Society, and directed the work of the lady visitors.[50] Miss Ziesse at Christ Presbyterian Church in New York City simply listed her visits in 1914 as "too numerous to count"; she also distributed relief, ran an employment society, made loans, organized fresh air outings to the country, and led a temperance program.[51]

The earliest missions of the 1830s and 1840s were small and simple compared to the multifaceted settlements with spacious classrooms, medical clinics, social halls, and gymnasiums of the 1910s, but there is a direct line between the two, and most types of social services can trace their roots back before midcentury. Five programs that became mission standards on both sides of the Atlantic were in place in St. Stephen's parish, Edinburgh, during the 1830s: a lending library, an evening school teaching basic literacy skills to adults, a "work society," a savings bank, and a mutual insurance society. The work society—called an "employment society" in some places—hired needy women, who were given tickets entitling them to a number of hours of paid knitting or sewing. The society's expenses, essentially fabric and wages, came partly from donations and partly from income earned by selling the finished clothing at reduced rates to the poor or at full price to "benevolent individuals" for distribution to the poor. The savings bank—or "penny bank" as some missions called it—pooled small deposits, placed them in a commercial bank, and returned interest to its users; the scheme was popular everywhere because commercial banks were often inconveniently distant from mission districts and did not welcome small depositors in any case. St. Stephen's insurance scheme, or "Yearly Society," collected membership fees and returned them as "mutual relief in sickness" and help toward "defraying funeral charges."[52]

Other early mission activities showed a typical mix of evangelism and mutual aid. In the 1840s, the Rose Street Mission operated by St. George's Free Church offered, in addition to preaching and visitation, a "yearly savings fund," medical aid, a savings bank, and a "Society for providing work for unemployed females."[53] American city missions started with similar programs. About 1860, First Presbyterian Church in St. Louis offered "public worship" and "Sunday

School" plus a variety of social services: "By encouraging industry and frugality; by dissuading from intemperance and other vices; by helping persons to find employment; by visiting the sick; by providing food, fuel, clothing, medicine and nursing, for those who need and cannot procure them for themselves; and by giving aid and sympathy at the burial of the dead, we wish to do all that we can to prevent or to relieve the miseries of poverty, and to alleviate those sufferings which are unavoidable."[54] Old South's mission on Chambers Street in Boston in 1863 offered worship on Sunday evening, a Sunday School, a sewing school, an evening school where child laborers were taught to "read, write, and cipher," and what modern readers might recognize as a sort of early day care center—a Charity School that took in children "too young to attend the public Schools, and whose parents have to work during the day."[55]

As church missions matured and expanded during the second half of the century, their programs expanded and—simply for our convenience as we examine them—can be grouped into seven categories: (1) religious services and evangelistic work, (2) direct relief to the needy, (3) educational classes, (4) self-improvement efforts, (5) mutual aid societies and cooperatives, (6) medical services, and (7) programs for women. By the very end of the century, an eighth category, recreation and entertainment, was added.

No single mission attempted all that was possible, although some large, ambitious congregations such as Bethany Presbyterian Church in Philadelphia came close to doing so. Kings' Weigh House's mission directory listed thirteen activities in 1885, and First Church, Hartford, advertised fourteen programs three years later.[56] Most churches put together a selection that seemed best suited to meet local needs and that were within the reach of their budget, space, and volunteers. Space was often a limiting factor, and mission workers frequently complained about being held back for want of adequate room. Churches that could afford to do so went to considerable expense to acquire or build proper facilities. To take two extremes, there was a very considerable difference in what could have been accomplished by King's Weigh House when it first opened its Darby Street Mission in 1841 in two rented rooms and by Christ Church in New York City after its sponsor, Brick Church, built it a new "Church House" in 1899 including meeting rooms, a gymnasium with showers and lockers, a kitchen, a library, well-equipped classrooms, and residences for the superintendent and the janitress.[57]

The mission halls were, without contradiction of their temporal objectives, committed to evangelism and public worship. Tract distribution, "kitchen meetings," week-long or once-a-week evangelistic services, and outdoor preaching were all standard tactics for gathering converts. Teams of tract distributors worked street corners or went door-to-door; in Glasgow, each Sunday between forenoon and afternoon worship, "12 ladies and gentlemen" from Free College Church handed out pamphlets in the tenements of the congregation's mission district.[58] Kitchen prayer meetings were held in neighborhood homes. Springbank's evening gatherings lasted one hour and included praise, prayer, reading, and a "homely explanation"; male volunteers presided, and "several young ladies assist[ed] in leading the praise or sing[ing] sacred solos . . . , while others help[ed] by visiting the families and announcing the meeting half-an-hour previous to its being held."[59] Prospect Street Presbyterian Church in Hull held regular preaching services in men's lodging houses, packed bags of "carefully selected books and periodicals containing Gospel truth" for departing seamen, and distributed tracts to Swedish emigrants passing through on their way to Liverpool and thence to America.[60] Most missions held a weekly evangelistic service, usually on Sunday evening. Although almost all the evangelistic preachers were men, there were a few instances where women led services; Miss Kate Glover led an "evangelistic mission" for the Free Church in Airdrie in 1900, and during the late 1880s, Miss Tyson conducted evening evangelistic meetings at Springbank mission in Glasgow.[61]

A number of missions went into the streets and parks to reach potential converts. Prospect Street Church held dock-side services for sailors. Regent Square held "open-air" services in the middle of King's Cross, at least until the London police moved them away from the "main thoroughfares." Lyndhurst Road's Kentish Town Mission had its "street services," and the Broughton Place United Presbyterians organized "open-air services to reach the non-churchgoing classes" on Edinburgh's Calton Hill.[62]

Mission halls learned that they needed to adjust the hour and style of their worship services to fit working class requirements. The traditional ten-thirty or eleven o'clock forenoon hour had to be changed to accommodate workers' schedules. Sunday evening was the typical time for mission hall worship, although the Spring Road Mission in Birmingham succeeded with an early service at seven o'clock Sunday morning before the work shifts began. A mission in Bristol held an early eight o'clock "Working Men's Bible Class and Prayer Meeting" on Sunday. Some mission halls found that they could attract more people with separate services for men, women, and children than with family services. This was partly an appreciation of the difficulties of infant care in families without the luxury of servants, but a service entirely for men also countered the perception that religion was a woman's activity. Early in the twentieth century, First Presbyterian Church in Pittsburgh drew a good attendance to a Sunday afternoon working men's "club" that offered music, a "gospel address," "a social hour . . . [with] light refreshments," and an "employment bureau."[63]

The style of mission hall worship catered to more popular tastes. Sankey hymns and "evangelistic choirs" replaced the music of Watts and Mendelssohn. Over and over, worship leaders, such as those at the Buccleuch Street Mission in Edinburgh, promised to make services "as bright and attractive as possible."[64] Cochrane advised other mission preachers to limit their sermons to twenty minutes and to emphasize practical application. Workers, he concluded, "preferred a preacher speaking to the heart before one of flash wording . . . ; working people want the old story plainly told, with sympathy and kindness."[65] The Garscube Mission in Glasgow was among those halls that specifically advertised their worship as a "working-dress meeting" or a "Forenoon Meeting for People in Working Dress."[66] A number of Scottish missions held a church service for child laborers patterned upon the "Foundry Boys Religious Society" model. Springbank Mission's service eventually drew an average attendance of 683 boys in 1887 with crowds sometimes passing 900 (seated with one adult "monitor" per pew); the one hour and twenty minute service included song, prayer, scripture, and an "explanation" embellished at times by "coloured cartoons or by blackboard sketches."[67]

Direct relief was a second part of every mission's work. Most congregations had a Dorcas Society that sewed clothing for the poor. The society of Glasgow's Lansdowne Church worked with five lady visitors at Miss Lang's Springbank Mission to dispense aid; in 1869, one hundred pieces of clothing went to fifty people.[68] Mission workers tried to meet emergency needs as they arose. Loads of coal, boxes of food, medicines, rent payments, bundles of clothing, shoes, and blankets went where they were required. Some congregations ran soup kitchens or provided housing for the homeless. In 1895, Bethany Presbyterian Church, Philadelphia, opened a "Men's Friendly Inn" giving meals and lodging to unemployed males; Lyndhurst Road Congregational Church in London supported the Hampstead Women's Shelter, which provided similarly for homeless females. The Friendly Hand Relief Association, which also operated out of Bethany, provided food to thousands. In a two-month period during the depression winter of 1894, aid went to 7,924 families (42,394 persons); the totals included 13,949 loaves of bread, 5,185 gallons of soup, and 230 gallons of milk.[69]

Mission workers recognized that relief was, at best, a stop-gap measure. The *American Presbyterian,* in an 1869 issue, acknowledged that giving clothing and food was needed "in extreme cases," but asked whether permanent skills and jobs would not be better. The article approvingly noted that one church had replaced its Dorcas Society with an "Industrial School." The same women, it explained, ran the program, but rather than meeting on Wednesday to sew and sort clothing, they met on Saturday to teach the skills needed for economic independence.[70]

Mission halls poured money and energy into education. Religious education—Sunday Schools and Bible classes—was, of course, central to the work from the very first, and nearly every mission reported its Sunday School full to overflowing. But the earliest history of Sunday Schools had been one of basic education—reading, writing, and arithmetic—, and this tradition survived, too. Even after the state assumed responsibility for primary education, in the 1830s and 1840s in the United States and in the 1870s in Britain, work remained to be done. Mission halls welcomed students who were ignored by the public system. Second Presbyterian in Philadelphia ran a school for African Americans in the 1830s.[71] Later, missions in the United States provided educational opportunities to immigrants from Europe and Asia.[72] In the 1860s, Regent Square provided a class for the blind at its Middlesex Street Mission in London.[73] Old South's Chambers Street Mission offered a place in its Charity School for children "too weak mentally or physically to endure the routine of the public system."[74]

Evening classes offered basic literacy and computation skills to adults and to child laborers. Old South opened an evening school—which boasted that the "individual teacher acts directly upon the individual pupil"—for "young servant girls employed in families, news boys and errand boys for offices, and young apprentices of both sexes . . . , and also young men and women whose early education has been neglected"; by 1870 the enrollment had reached five hundred. Regent Square had evening classes for girls aged ten to fifteen "who are kept at home during the day to take care of the house, or of the younger children," and Springbank Mission in the 1860s taught the three R's to a class of eighteen "boys who are employed during the day."[75]

Mission stations also provided what were called "industrial classes." Training for girls appeared first, since most mission volunteers were women. From about midcentury on, young girls filled classes in sewing, needle work and knitting, cooking, baking, kitchen gardening, washing and ironing, and other domestic pursuits. Classes in sewing, requiring less equipment, were generally the first to be offered; later, as kitchen facilities were available, cooking was added. A few missions trained girls specifically for domestic service, and at least two New York City missions were teaching stenography and typing by the early twentieth century.[76] Boys learned the manual skills that the nineteenth century associated with men. Woodworking was most common, but when young men from Springbank Mission held an exhibition of their products in January 1876, the crafts of carpentry, iron molding, tin work, and masonry were displayed.[77]

Beyond formal classes, missions encouraged "self-improvement" efforts aimed at inculcating the habits and tastes that defined middle-class respectability. For instance, Erie Mission Chapel in Chicago organized a weekly "Chautauqua

Literary and Scientific Circle," and its leaders were pleased that the young people who attended were now reading "the best books and magazines." At the Springbank Mission in Glasgow, there was in the 1880s a "Mutual Improvement Society for Young Men" (later called the "Young Men's Literary Association") that undertook "reading of essays or taking part in debates." Libraries were standard features of mission halls, and while some were only modest in size, others were quite substantial. Bethel Mission in Brooklyn owned two thousand volumes in 1874 which it claimed were "constantly resorted to by numerous mechanics and other laboring men."[78]

In various and subtle ways, mission workers fostered the traits and behaviors they associated with success. Although they did not articulate the distinction, they seem to have had some sense of which so-called middle-class attributes had market value. To take one example, a preference for gospel hymns over chanted psalms did not affect employability, so on that point mission workers adapted themselves to popular tastes rather than pressing for refinement. But other habits—punctuality, cleanliness, sobriety—could arguably be related to the ability to secure a position, and here mission teachers pushed ahead with evangelical zeal, especially with the children. A Pittsburgh church expected its Sewing and Industrial School not only to teach manual skills, but to "inculcate ideas of neatness and refinement and good manners in those who attend."[79] The superintendent of a Chicago mission reported that "the first improvement noted in these children was the increased cleanliness both in person and dress." She went on to recall one eight-year old boy's arrival at the school: "Observing that the children were about to march to music, [he] demanded to lead the procession. The teacher quietly remarked that only boys with clean faces could lead the march. The next Saturday Jimmy appeared radiant, ready to take the coveted position, after having made an almost pathetic attempt at washing his face, as was shown by the water mark under his youthful chin. His efforts, however, were rewarded as desired, and he stepped proudly forth in all the unaccustomed glory of a clean face."[80]

Mission workers considered sobriety a prerequisite for economic advancement and family stability, and they went after alcohol as enthusiastically as a twentieth-century social worker pursues heroin or cocaine. Considering the threat that an alcoholic spouse could pose to the stability of a working-class family, many women considered themselves more than justified in their fervor.[81] On-site temperance societies—or total abstinence societies if the missions were more zealous—joined moralism with hard-nosed realism in making a case against liquor and saloons. Temperance crusaders collected pledge cards from the converted, held lectures and marches, and organized the children into Bands of Hope, where the little ones made their own promises never to touch alcohol.[82]

Missions did more than merely condemn strong drink; they also tried to create alternatives to the saloon. Because British temperance champions in particular recognized that persons living in cramped rooms truly needed a 'public house' for space and relaxation, many a mission hall turned itself into a dry pub on Saturday evening, offering refreshment, games, song, and—of course—nonalcoholic libation. Billed variously as "The Saturday Entertainment" or "The Men's Club" (or more transparently as the "Gospel Temperance Tea Meeting"), these evenings became mission standards during the last decades of the century. Charteris started one called "The Holly Tree" in the rough Lawnmarket area of Edinburgh in 1876, and "a daily average" of 350 to 400 people entered this "public-house without drink."[83] At Lyndhurst Road's mission hall in the mid-1880s, the Saturday evening men's club attracted forty to sixty men who enjoyed skittles, draughts [checkers], dominoes, chess, newspapers, and vocal and instrumental music performed sometimes by a guest, but "chiefly by the men themselves." Tea, coffee, and cocoa were drunk, and "nearly all indulge[d] in smoking."[84] One enterprising London mission charged the men a penny admission and used the money to establish a loan fund for "working men."[85]

Self-reliance had its limitations, however, and church mission workers turned to mutual aid and cooperative ventures to cushion the harshness of a competitive society. Earlier in this chapter we noted that some of these projects, such as Pilrig's nonprofit housing project or various work societies, purchasing cooperatives, insurance schemes, and penny banks, were already active in the 1830s and 1840s. Mutual aid and cooperative efforts remained important mission hall characteristics throughout the Victorian period. Mission halls on both sides of the Atlantic continued to fund "work societies" that created employment for women who could knit or sew.[86] Some missions maintained employment registers of available jobs, and matched those seeking with those hiring. Mrs. King at the Litcham Street Mission listed "finding employment" as one of her responsibilities, and churches in Hartford and Philadelphia also had an "employment bureau" in operation.[87]

Banking continued to be a standard service. Berean Presbyterian Church, an African-American congregation in Philadelphia, established a "Building and Loan Association" in 1888.[88] Most banking operations were more modest "penny provident funds" or "thrift societies." One New York City mission bank gave depositors a stamp book to record their progress. Usually open for business just before or after another church event, such as the Saturday evening men's club, penny banks did a brisk business. One managed by Miss Eliza Wigham for thirty-four years in the mission district of Newington United Presbyterian Church, Edinburgh, had between four and five hundred depositors and five thousand transactions per year; the amount on deposit averaged between four and five hundred pounds. Bethany Presbyterian's banking operation in Philadelphia had ten thousand depositors.[89]

Although most deposits in these banks were intended for general purposes, a few of the savings clubs were specifically designed to help people budget for large, intermittent expenses. St. George's Free Church, as early as the 1840s, was collecting and paying bank-rate interest on the weekly deposits of those saving toward "rent and clothing" bills. Coal clubs and blanket clubs were also popular, and Fountainbridge ran a "Shoe Club" for youngsters.[90]

Missions also pooled buying power and passed wholesale prices along both to members of buying clubs and other purchasers in the mission district. The Bible women at Springbank Mission in Glasgow were among the more active wholesalers, beginning with cloth and flannel and then advancing to coal. Charteris's Tolbooth mission in Edinburgh provided wholesale wallpaper, although in this instance enthusiasm faded quickly after landlords began raising rents on the improved properties.[91]

Insurance programs were yet another example of mutual aid. "Provident Societies" or "Friendly Societies" collected dues and paid out benefits. Brick Church in New York City ran a "Burial Society" that paid out fifty dollars for funeral expenses. The Provident Society operated in Birmingham by Carr's Lane provided a death benefit but also gave medical coverage and sick pay; in London, the men's Friendly Society at the Kentish Town Mission did the same. The "Women's Sick-Benefit and Sharing Out Club" at Kentish Town collected five pence a week from its members, and in return they received medical care whenever needed and eight pence per day whenever the doctor certified them unable to work. By the early twentieth century, the sponsoring congregation, Lyndhurst Road, became concerned that men thrown out of work even temporarily were unable to keep up their medical insurance cards, and so the deacons sought donations from the congregation's middle-class members to pay insurance fees for the unemployed.[92]

Medical attention of a minimal sort—free medicine, vouchers for a doctor's visit, a ticket to the hospital, and simple nursing by the Bible woman or lady visitor—were part of mission work when the Victorian era began. But, by the end of the nineteenth century, mission hall medicine became better organized and more highly skilled. Trained nurses joined the staff at larger missions, and in some settings the Bible woman seems to have evolved toward a sick nurse, or at least an amalgamation of nursing and charitable duties. Fountainbridge in 1904 was referring to Miss Mackay as a "Nurse Biblewoman," and in Pittsburgh in 1912, a woman carrying the title of "district nurse" was still in charge of distributing free coal, clothing, and food to the "deserving poor."[93] The expectation seems to have been that medical work would complement, not replace, the religious and social services that a previous generation of workers provided. During the second half of the 1880s, Charteris's formation in Scotland of an order of deaconesses who were trained as nurses as well as religious workers was an attempt to formalize the connection.[94]

Whatever their titles, the women were busy; the "sick nurse" at Kilburn Mission in London logged 2,345 visits in one year; an energetic nurse from Christ Presbyterian Church in New York City compiled in 1914 even more impressive statistics: 843 patients totaling 2,810 home visits and 1,377 office visits; 635 persons sent to the clinic, 163 to the dispensary, and 85 to the hospital; 1,058 medicines and prescriptions given out, and 4 births and 12 deaths attended.[95] Virtually all the nurses were salaried, although occasionally one was volunteering her services, as was the case with Miss Wyld, "a Lady of independent means" who was commended for "devoting her whole life" to nursing at the Fountainbridge Mission in Edinburgh.[96]

Physicians and dentists were more likely to be volunteers donating several hours per week to mission work, although some were compensated from charitable money. By the end of the century, large missions in New York and Philadelphia added dispensaries or clinics. In 1913, Brick Presbyterian Church procured a second-hand dental chair, installed it in the Christ Church hall, and opened a clinic staffed by four volunteer dentists, each giving two afternoons or evenings per week.[97]

Missions also established more formal relationships with hospitals by the 1880s and 1890s. Some continued to work on the traditional system of providing a voucher that the hospital would accept, but other missions reserved a number of beds or even a room on a standing basis for their patients. Lyndhurst Road had worked out such an arrangement with two London hospitals in the 1890s, and Third Presbyterian Church in Chicago contracted with the Presbyterian Hospital in that city for a "room" plus two beds.[98]

Church missions provided miscellaneous medical services, too. In 1893, Bethany Presbyterian Church's "Sick Diet Kitchen" in Philadelphia sent out "three thousand kettles of beef tea, and five thousand tumblers of jelly, besides clam broth and delicacies for the sick"; Pittsburgh's First Church gave out juice, jelly, and fruit to patients.[99] Medical supplies and equipment were also provided or loaned. In London, Mrs. King had on hand "surgical appliances for crippled children and others" at the Litcham Street Mission; Central Presbyterian Church in Rochester added a "invalid wheel chair" to its list of equipment in 1895.[100] First Presbyterian in Pittsburgh had a "free dispensary for babies" in the basement of the church, and it provided either training and home visitation for nursing mothers or free "sterilized milk" for "mothers unable to buy it."[101] Fresh-air was important to the recovery of some patients, and in her 1899 report, Miss Juppe, who directed mission work for New York's Brick Church, sent ninety children and four adults to the country for a week or more.[102] Springbank Mission in Glasgow made first-aid classes a part of its educational programs for young men and women.[103]

Mothers' Meetings were the featured women's activity at mission halls. The gatherings began early in the nineteenth century as a way of serving women who could not attend ordinary worship because they could not leave their children. Led by women for women, the mid-week mothers' hour included prayer, praise, scripture reading, and a "gospel address." A nursery, or creche, was a standard accompaniment, as was a social gathering afterward. Whatever their origins, the meetings in time carried a significance beyond mere substitute worship; they became times for discussion, planning, and mutual support. The fact that churches started "Young Women's Meetings" for those who were not yet mothers confirms that the events carried a significance beyond the obvious. Bonds were established among the women themselves and those established between volunteers and mission mothers suggest that gender could sometimes be more powerful than class.[104]

One story from Scotland shows how the weekly sessions could also raise the women's feminist consciousness. Mrs. Charteris, the minister's wife of Park Church in Glasgow, led the mother's meeting at Port Dundas Mission, and she was in the habit of holding the gatherings in her own home as it was more pleasant for "tea-drinking" than the mission room. One afternoon, the minister himself passed through, and Mrs. Charteris asked him to put some coals on the fire, which he did. "There now, see to that," remarked one of the Port Dundas women, "If it had been us, we would have been told: 'I do my work, you do yours.'" To which the minister replied, "Oh, but when you go home you must tell them that plan is quite out of fashion."[105]

Women from the mothers' meeting became important supporters of temperance work, children's activities, and other programs that benefited women. One of the oldest and most common schemes was a Maternal Society, whose members passed baby linens on to the next woman who needed them. Some mission halls provided a day nursery where working women could leave their children. The creche at Lyndhurst Road's mission in the 1890s was open from 7:30 A.M. until 8:00 P.M. Monday through Friday, and from 7:30 A.M. until 2:00 P.M. on Saturday. Users paid three pence a day for infants under age two, and four pence for two to four year olds; fees covered only about 12 percent of expenses, with the rest subsidized by donations from the church.[106]

What can be said about the response of the poor and the success of the mission programs? To begin, the reader should be warned that the records on which this study is based give only indirect voice to the poor, and this only sporadically. Still, certain generalizations seem supportable. The types of programs that missions ran, based as they were on mutual aid and cooperation, were undoubtedly more effective for the upper ranks of the poor—those for whom a "helping hand" could make a difference between need and modest comfort—than for the truly destitute. It was also true that the programs did not reach all, or perhaps even a very large percentage, of the potential beneficiaries; the cities grew faster than missions and churches could be built. Indeed, many of urban industrialism's problems were beyond the scope of voluntary activity. Just as certainly, not every one who came in contact with mission halls found the activities to their liking. As among the upper ranks of society, men were less responsive to religious appeals than women. Some of both sexes found the services irrelevant, patronizing, or threatening to established modes of behavior. Cochrane, based on his years of experience in Edinburgh, said the three most common reasons given by those who turned him away were "I gang to nae kirk noo, but I think mysel' as guid as any o' them"; "better no' to promise, than to promise and no' to perform"; and "Man, I wudna be seen in company wi' yon folk."[107]

Yet having conceded the lack of total acceptance, the mission workers were almost universally optimistic about the response they received—certainly more so than would be suggested by historical accounts that allege disdain and rejection on the part of the working poor.[108] Mission visitors reported that they were, "with very few exceptions," well received during their rounds and able to enter "freely into conversation" with lodging-house residents.[109] Even if such claims are exaggerated (as is altogether likely), the numbers of children enrolled in classes, sick patients seen by nurse-Bible women, women attending a mothers' meeting, or men at a "Pleasant Sunday Afternoon" men's club are more trustworthy, and the reality is that mission halls quickly attracted overflow crowds. One Chicago church, with only a little work, had 143 children for the opening day of Sunday School at a new mission. Enrollments for well-established Sunday Schools or sewing classes ran to several hundreds in many places. By far the most common complaint among mission workers was not that they were rejected but that their facilities were "overcrowded" or "hopelessly overcrowded."[110] The veracity of the claims is supported by the significant sums of money that congregations donated to build more spacious quarters.

When mission halls and preaching stations were closed, it was not because they had failed to attract an audience. Many, in time, became independent, self-governing congregations. Others were phased out as the services were no longer needed, at least in that location. Second Church in Philadelphia closed its Beth Eden mission in 1914 because the work was "now duplicated by other agencies in the same neighborhood"; in Pittsburgh, branch operations of the Carnegie Library supplanted mission libraries. Basic educational services, in particular, came under the province of government, and congregations such as Chicago's Third Presbyterian found that even their sewing classes were now offered in the schools. In other cases, programs expanded beyond the congregation's ability to manage them and were either spun off as separate institutions or transferred elsewhere; Bethany's savings bank in Philadelphia was turned over to Wanamaker's department store and its collegiate classes became the Wanamaker Institute of Industries.[111]

A great many of the poor, as attested by their participation, found that the combination of evangelical Christianity and social service met real spiritual and practical needs. The poor, as much as anyone else, sought friendship, community and spiritual nurture; they also valued the education and benefitted from economic cooperation. Children found mission classes preferable to the streets, and so did parents who saw education as the only hope, however fragile, of a better life.

Missions may also have received a cordial welcome in poor neighborhoods because they invested more energy and money in empowerment—education, mutual aid, cooperative activity—than in direct relief. They then reinforced their credibility with a willingness, even eagerness, to turn facilities over to local control whenever they could. The fact that mission workers were not well paid also gave integrity to their work. Bible women and lady residents lived on meager wages among the poor they served. Although it might be argued that middle-class volunteers shared with their families and business partners complicity in an inequitable economic system, such an analytic view was not often appreciated; rather, the poor saw the visitors and teachers and physicians coming as volunteers, without visible gain from the assistance they offered. Neither volunteers nor mission directors could easily be accused of profiting from the plight of the people they served.

Still another element that contributed to the success of mission halls was that those attending sponsoring congregations and those attending missions held common understandings about both spiritual and worldly success. The skilled ranks of labor, if not the entire working class, craved respectability as much as the middle class. Mission programs, then, were hardly an imposition of the middle upon the bottom of society.[112] Indeed, congregations in which the working class was heavily represented were some of the most active in city missions; Bellgrove in Glasgow, Pilrig in Edinburgh, and Bethany in Philadelphia are three examples. Bethany, one of America's most vigorous city-mission churches, had just about 50 percent blue collar workers with another 27 percent clerical and sales personnel. Peter Hillis's study of nine midcentury Glasgow congregations found significant working-class representation in all.[113] Furthermore, former mission chapels, far from disdaining the mix of evangelism and temporal aid they had received, launched their own identical missions to help others as soon as they were able to do so.

Regardless of the real, if imperfect, accomplishments of urban missions, the standard mixture of evangelism and practical social services that characterized nineteenth-century urban outreach was changing considerably by the decades surrounding 1900. As we have already noted, some services were taken over by governments or independent agencies. Professional social workers were challenging the authority of the lady residents and volunteers; scientific objectivity was valued above sentiment, efficiency above benevolence and compassion.[114] Those external trends were important, but they joined two important developments within the congregations and missions themselves—an intensifying dichotomy between evangelism and social reform, and the emergence of entertainment as a primary mission function.

Nineteenth-century city missionaries had seen no contradiction between individual salvation and social betterment; they pursued both simultaneously and were convinced that these were two dimensions of the same phenomenon. But by the end of the Victorian age, congregations were less and less convinced of the essential unity between evangelism and reform. Historians—most notably George Marsden—have described the "diverging paths" that led some toward evangelical fundamentalism's rejection of Social Christianity and others toward reform-oriented liberalism's suspicion of evangelism.[115] The separation showed up at the local level, too, as one or the other half of nineteenth-century mission work was jettisoned.

Lyndhurst Road in the 1890s provides an intriguing, if atypical, example of both factions coexisting within the same congregation. The church ran two quite distinct mission stations, staffed presumably with different-minded volunteers. There was Kentish Town with its medical and mutual aid activities and, at the same time, Southampton Row with a single-minded focus on temperance, visitation, and prayer meetings.[116]

Most congregations, however, followed either one method or the other. On the one side were those who turned toward a single-dimensional focus on evangelistic work. Often, this redirection was marked by the passing of a generation of missionaries, Bible-women, and lay volunteers. Pilrig's housing project, as we noted, died with its contributors and directors. Garscube Mission's working-dress service ended in 1905 when the lay leader from Lansdowne Church had to stop due to age and ill health.[117] At Lansdowne's other Glasgow mission, Springbank, Agnew's position was now taken by Daniel Jolly, whose reports were dominated by open-air services, "special evangelistic meetings," tract distribution, and tabulations of conversions.[118] In other congregations, such as Second Presbyterian in Philadelphia, foreign mission contributions now surpassed home missions in the budget.[119] Some reminders of Central Presbyterian's earlier reformism lingered in the Rochester congregation's continuing contributions to freedmen's causes and African American education, but the church's focus by 1900 was more on open-air work and foreign missions to the exclusion of urban reform; in 1901, it turned down an appeal to help with a mission to Italian immigrants in Rochester, but funded a missionary to Puerto Rico.[120]

Those who chose social involvement came to think of evangelism as a betrayal of the objectivity and expertise they now valued. A few rejected religiously based reform altogether and sought change by other routes. Thomas's departure from the Presbyterian ministry for socialist politics was one example, and Addams's unaffiliated settlement house work, a second. In Britain, Edward Lewis resigned in 1914 from his King's Weigh House pulpit, now convinced, he said, that "the modern church as a whole, works against the free movement of the prophetic spirit."[121] A larger number stayed in the church and reorganized city mission work to match the objective model espoused by the new profession of social work. Old-fashioned Bible women were replaced by trained social workers and nurses. Brick Church by 1910 had twenty-six full-time "paid expert workers" at its Christ Church agency.[122]

A second, more subtle and perhaps more insidious development transformed the city mission at the end of the century: leisure activities—recreation, entertainment, athletics—came to absorb a larger and larger part of mission time and resources. As they did so, they both transformed and deemphasized the earlier aspects of mission work—evangelism, mutual aid, and material assistance to the poor. Recreation was not necessarily at cross purposes with the mission hall's other goals. Saturday evening entertainments were initially part of temperance work, fresh-air outings were first organized for their medical benefits, and small "treats," prizes, and games were long part of Sunday School programs. It was also true that mission districts were woefully short of wholesome, healthy athletic and recreational facilities, and providing these met a legitimate need.

To an extent, then, the explosion of leisure activities around the turn of the century was simply an augmentation of work that had a long history. But at the same time, something was different when leisure pursuits were valued for their own intrinsic qualities. Middle-class attitudes toward leisure had changed;

leisure was now seen as a necessity of life, not a luxury. If so, then leisure had to be provided for the poor as well. There was a significant danger, however, and it lay in the temptation to entertain the poor, to render them happy without materially changing their circumstances. Collecting subscriptions to subsidize cooperative buying schemes, sick insurance, or housing was one thing; raising funds for an afternoon's picnic in the country was another. When flower arranging became an equivalent to sewing classes for the girls, and wood carving to carpentry for the boys, the objective had changed.

One by one, traditional mission programs were augmented or reshaped to meet the demands of leisure culture. Visitation turned into a "Flower Mission," with lady visitors delivering bouquets of flowers with a biblical text card attached. A Christmas goose club joined the coal, rent, and blanket clubs as worthy causes for which families should save. Charteris's Blackfriars' Mission in Edinburgh organized summer garden parties for women and children, and on Sunday afternoons, small children gathered for "Sunday Home"—"innocent games," dolls for the smallest ones, and refreshment.[123] By 1909, "treats" had become the largest budget item, after salaries and utilities, at Fountainbridge Mission.[124]

Clubs, often with catchy names, became a major strategy for packaging mission activities. The girls who were taking sewing lessons at First Presbyterian Church in Pittsburgh were inducted into the "Progress Club," those doing fancy work were assembled as the "True Blue Club."[125] Clubs had their own officers and dues and social activities. In the 1890s at Shaftesbury Mission in Bristol, there was a Men's Club, Skittles Club, Young Men's Club, a Boys' Brigade, a Rugby Club, a Women's Club, and a Girls' Club.[126] Well-equipped mission halls provided "club rooms" where members could gather daily or nightly for games, reading, conversation, and refreshment; Lyndhurst Road's mission hall had a girls' club room "made comfortable with fire and lamps, the current newspapers and magazines and other books."[127] King's Weigh House in London and First Presbyterian Church in Pittsburgh each saw their major mission to young clerks and shop girls to be a noon-time club where members gathered during their lunch hour; "Thomas Binney Institute" provided "recreation and social life" for London store clerks, while First Presbyterian's "Noon Rest and Recreation Club" for store girls offered reading, painting, and games.[128]

Athletics and excursions gained prominent places in mission hall schedules. Calisthenics or "drill" were commonly on the agenda for both boys' and girls' clubs. Where facilities existed, competitive sports became typical activities for young men. Football, rugby, and cricket were popular in Britain, as baseball was in America. The Warburton Mission in Hartford organized an annual "excursion down the river"; thirty-four Springbank children took a Fair Week Trip to

Lochfyne, and on other occasions Springbank youngsters were taken to a country farm for milk and buns and a day of outdoor games; and, in 1884, 170 men and women from Kentish Town were treated to an August bank holiday picnic.[129]

The early Victorian belief that each activity had to be edifying had faded beyond recognition. Turn-of-the-century mission schedules listed "weekly hikes," "physical drill and recreation," Christmas entertainments, Halloween parties, "recreation room," stereopticon exhibitions, "soirees," and flower arranging exhibitions. The open-armed acceptance of leisure as a legitimate mission hall activity, of course, reflected changing cultural attitudes, and as we shall see in the next chapter, the new values made their mark on the habits of the churches as well as the mission halls.

# ten

## Good Friends and Companions
### Social, Recreational, and Fellowship Activities

"Next to a man's home, nothing so influences him at every part of his life as a congenial Church connection," Charles Irvine wrote in 1913 as he considered his thirty-year membership in Broughton United Free Church in Edinburgh. Irvine knew, of course, that church was to be a person's "spiritual home . . . where he receives impressions and influences which shape his soul-nature, which keep him in touch with the eternal." But this was not the whole story. The church was also a person's "fraternal home," Irvine concluded; "the companionships and friendships which he forms within this sacred circle are a constant source of strength to him, and a stand-by throughout his whole life."[1]

Irvine's words—congenial, home, companionship, friendship—reveal a dimension of church life that had always been present, but that grew immensely during the last decades of the century. By the early 1900s, fellowship was for nearly everyone an essential, if not paramount, feature of church life. "A time of happy intercourse and social reunion" was how a satisfied group of Huddersfield Congregationalists described one of their church festivals. Whatever else the church meant, it meant good friends, good times, and family-like associations. Regent Square used more theological language to make the same point: "Our Christian organization is social, and the Church of Christ is the family of God." Friendliness became the measure of a successful congregation. In Brooklyn, a member recalled with approval that after the service was over at Plymouth Church, "people gathered in knots to chat over—pretty much everything, for it was like one big family."[2]

As friendship and familiarity gained importance, affability replaced piety as the primary trait that members were expected to acquire. "Let us get better acquainted: do not be too formal about making calls; we are a family," implored the Congregationalists in Binghamton, New York.[3] "Sociability," according to a church in Indianapolis, was "a virtue which Christians should cultivate." Churchgoers there were encouraged, above all, to be cordial: "Coldness and formality is a great obstacle to Christian fellowship. The members of a Church should know one another. Do not take it for granted that others know you without some effort on your part to be known. There is a mutual obligation here; make the acquaintance of all new comers. Give a cordial welcome to strangers; take them by the hand; make them feel at home."[4] Every congregation, it seemed, wanted to be known for its friendliness. Welcome committees were organized, and genial members stationed by the entrance to greet visitors. New members were received no longer into the "privileges" of the church, but into its "fellowship." In Liverpool, a Congregational church, when explaining its rules for admission to the Lord's Supper, bypassed phrases such as "all believers" or "all the faithful" to say that all "Christian friends" were welcome at the table.[5]

The elevation of fellowship to a primary position among the church's functions gave old activities and old words a new twist, as we are beginning to see. We noted earlier that a church's "social meeting" had once meant its mid-week prayer meeting; now the same phrase signified a party with food and entertainment. For a time, as definitions were shifting, congregations had to clarify which was meant. In 1859, a Chicago Congregational church carefully explained that its monthly "Church Sociable" was "not an ordinary religious meeting for worship, but a gathering of families and individuals of the congregation for friendly social intercourse, aided by instrumental and vocal music." Only the closing of the festivities by "a hymn and prayer" separated the occasion from a secular gathering.[6]

Other events and words took on distinctly social connotations, too. In the 1880s, congregations valued house-to-house visitation as a way of "strengthening our fellowship," whereas a generation earlier they would have mentioned care and discipline.[7] To take yet another example, "church festival" came, in common usage, to imply strawberries and ice cream, however much liturgical reformers may have wished to reserve the term for Easter or Pentecost. New Year's Day, once a time for prayer and fasting in Scotland, became by the end of the 1880s an occasion for a festive "New Year's Breakfast" in one congregation.[8] Mothers' meetings, which originated as alternative worship services, now emphasized companionship more. If language can be trusted, Cowcaddens Free Church had at least inverted the priorities when it advertised its version as an "hour of fellowship and prayer." By 1901, at King's Weigh House, prayer had been dropped from the title completely: the event was now simply the "Mothers' Social Hour."[9]

The social dimensions of women's missionary groups gained prominence, too. Of course when women met to sew clothing for the poor, the pleasure of each other's company was always an implicit benefit; over time, however, socializing became an explicit and even independent event. By the beginning of the new century, the Senior and Junior Sewing Circles in Huddersfield were "frequently preceded by a Tea" that the ladies took turns hosting.[10] In Hartford, a circle that met on Saturday afternoons to make clothes for a mission in India, began in the 1880s to put away their needles every fourth time for a gathering purely of a "social character, closing with a supper."[11] The Ladies Aid Society of First Congregational Church in Cleveland evolved even more radically by the early 1900s; unlike more traditional Ladies Aid groups that focused on mission work and visitation, this one now had only two responsibilities: "to foster the spirit of sociableness in the church by means of socials, readings, entertainments of various kinds, and to raise money for furnishing and other purposes of like nature."[12]

The elevation of fellowship placed a new value not only on affability, but also on participation. Church clubs and organized activities multiplied by the dozens, and the refusal or hesitancy of a churchgoer to become involved in at least one was sure sign that he or she had not truly become part of the family. Nonparticipators made the active members anxious. Why did the person not get involved? Was recalcitrance alone the cause, or had the congregation not been welcoming and friendly enough? A church in Indianapolis, apparently believing that the fault lay with the laggards, prodded the hesitant to become active in their "personal labors" for the congregation; there was no excuse for not taking a part. "If we cannot do one thing," the congregation's manual reasoned, "we may do another."[13] In Philadelphia, however, the session of Second Church worried that the church was doing something wrong if "*all* the Young People of the Church" were not "thoroughly interested in several activities."[14] One Ladies Aid Society solved the problem of nonjoiners handily: it simply declared that all women were automatically members and, not wishing anyone to escape participation, added that all men were "honorary members."[15]

The new emphasis on fellowship created a huge increase in the sheer volume of weekly activity and a veritable explosion of organized church groups, each with its own elected officers, committees, treasury, and schedule of events. As late as the 1870s and 1880s, there would have been many more groups and events scheduled at the mission hall than at the church; in the 1890s, however, the churches caught up. They, too, became busy places as new clubs and organizations, new entertainments and meetings turned them into seven-day-a-week operations. In 1907, when Stephen Griswold analyzed the changes he had seen during his sixty years as a member of Brooklyn's Plymouth Church, he concluded, "One thing is very noticeable: the growth of church societies."[16] Boylston Congregational Church in 1882 had only a Sunday School and a Ladies Aid Society meeting in its building; by 1896, it had added a Christian Endeavor Society, Junior Christian Endeavor, King's Daughters, Young Men's Lyceum, Junior Lyceum, Boys' Brigade, and a

Young Women's Foreign Missionary Society.[17] At Chicago's Second Presbyterian Church the list of organizations and their officers filled a dozen pages in the 1906 church manual.[18] Regent Square, in 1911, offered eight separate groups or activities for women; there was an equivalent number for young men, including an "At Home" social, a Sunday afternoon "tea," and a club room for games, reading, and conversation.[19]

Although they would not become typical for another quarter century, church socials had their simple beginnings in the 1840s as ways of marking special occasions such as a congregation's anniversary or the arrival of a new pastor. Beecher, who probably held the earliest regularly scheduled church socials beginning in 1848, seems to have come to the idea as much out of expediency as anything else; as we noted in an earlier chapter, it was a more efficient use of his time to bring sections of the congregation to him rather than to visit house to house. Not one to miss an opportunity, Beecher quickly recognized a second outcome—people not only met him, they met each other. "Many who might not otherwise have been acquainted for years," one report concluded, "have been brought together as Christians and friends, and the result has been the awakening of a deep interest in each other, and the promoting of the kindest feelings throughout the congregation."[20]

It was this ability of the church social to acquaint members with each other that people found valuable. If you wanted the pastor and elders or deacons to know the people better, visitation still seemed the better plan, but if you wanted the people to know each other, then socials were indispensable. Thus, socials grew in popularity along with the view that the church was primarily a gathering of friends. The importance of getting members to know each other seemed particularly important when, as in Beecher's case, the congregation itself had just been founded and had no common memory or experience to bind it together. John Caird instituted a series of "soirees" when he was organizing Glasgow's Park Church in the early 1860s.[21] Pastors like Beecher and Caird seemed to sense intuitively that their work would go better if the people were joined together in community. This, of course, was something that village pastors could assume existed naturally, but in the cities and suburbs, it was something that had to be created.

By the 1880s and 1890s, church socials were well-established parts of congregational life. While the underlying goal was always better fellowship, church leaders came to realize that there could be other "advantages of more frequent friendly intercourse amongst the members."[22] Socials gave pastors and church officers an informal opportunity to gauge reactions to a proposed change or to build support for it, as the deacons of King's Weigh House did before switching from quarterly to weekly offerings. A Presbyterian church in Philadelphia hoped that social events would boost participation, and it planned its "regular Social gatherings . . . with a view of enlisting . . . all of the People in our different Church organizations and Activities." A number of congregations used church socials to help new members fit in more quickly. And, as in the beginning, socials remained favorite ways to enjoy anniversaries, reunions of former members, arrivals of new ministers, dedications of buildings, final mortgage payments, or whatever else was deemed worthy of celebration.[23]

Churches also learned that social activities were effective ways of thanking volunteers. Lansdowne, for instance, held an annual event for all its office-bearers and mission workers, to which the mission congregation was invited. At Cowcaddens Free Church, it was the collectors for the Sustentation Fund that were feted annually. And, end-of-the-year picnics were common rewards for volunteer choir singers and Sunday School teachers.[24]

The back side of this was that volunteers who did not feel adequately recompensed by whatever social activity was proffered could turn surly, as Govan parish found out. After showing only lukewarm enthusiasm for a teachers' picnic in the summer of 1889, the teachers—mostly young women and a much smaller number of young men—decided on their own that they wanted a "conversatione [sic] & dance." The minister, John Macleod, objected, not so much to dancing *per se* but to Sunday School teachers, as teachers, dancing—or so he tried to explain at a teachers' meeting in February 1890. Offered the alternative of a conversazione without dancing, no teacher would even make a motion to accept the substitute. The teachers' discontent apparently simmered just below a boil for the next few years as they refused to hold any social activity at all or, as they did in 1894, cancelled their conversazione because the trustees would not grant them the use of the building past midnight (the teachers said unless the party could last until two o'clock, it was not worth having). Not surprisingly, the resentment took its toll on the Sunday School work; teachers refused to accept additional assignments or submit timely reports, Sunday absenteeism became a significant problem, attendance at teachers' preparation meetings fell so low they were nearly discontinued, and quarterly teachers' meetings became occasions for grumbling and sharp words.[25] Such had become the importance of a conversazione or social meeting.

Church socials that were intended for the entire congregation took great effort to organize; food and entertainment had to be procured, finances managed, the hall decorated, and tickets distributed or sold. Most congregations appointed a standing Soiree Committee or Social Committee to take charge of arrangements during the year, but other systems were possible. At Lyndhurst Road, the deacons' wives organized the food, and the deacons saw to entertainment and tickets.

In Indianapolis, a church divided itself into four "sections," each responsible for hosting one of the congregation's quarterly church suppers.[26] When church socials were only very occasional events, committees often rented the necessary tables, china, and utensils, but it was not very long until church minutes began to record purchases such as "twelve new Tea pots" or "six hundred cups and saucers" or "sundry kitchen furniture & utensils & various etceteras."[27] Holding a party for several hundred people was not inexpensive, even if much of the work was volunteered. Prosperous congregations sometimes paid the cost out of current revenue, but it was more common to try to put the social on a break-even basis either by putting out a plate for donations or by selling tickets to those who attended.[28]

Every church social—or "sociable" or "soiree" or "conversazione," as they were sometimes called—demanded food and entertainment if nothing else. An 1874 congregational Christmas party in the Yorkshire town of Bingley produced "beef and ham sandwiches . . . , currant and plain cracknels, tea-cakes, spice bread, matrimony cake and queen cakes." For the price of a ticket (nine pence for adults, six for those under age eight), attenders were also regaled with recitations and readings in a well-decorated hall. A social meeting at Regent Square in 1899 featured abundant diversions—piano duets, comic songs, recitations, sketches, glees, and renditions from violin and bassoon. The selections were all secular, many with an American flavor—"Marching Through Georgia," "Old Folks at Home," "May Morning," and "Good Night Ladies." At Cowcaddens, where tastes were more evangelical, the annual congregational soiree heard gospel songs performed by the "Albatross Crew"; the Lansdowne congregation relied on music by its own church choir. Oratory was another favored amusement, with as many as a dozen or more speeches or toasts delivered at some events; the great majority of talks were by men, but Lyndhurst Road's deacons did note that female speakers were scheduled for its January 1893 "Quarterly Church Festival." Summertime took congregations into the outdoors for picnics, for which one Pittsburgh church ordered "two boxes or a barrel of Crackers, a box of Lemons, and a half gal. of Lemon Syrup" to supply its Fourth of July outing.[29]

Children shared in the growing emphasis on social events and organized groups. Many children's activities originated at the mission hall and then were adapted for the home congregation when some began to feel "that the children of the Church had been neglected."[30] Sunday School youngsters were gathered for Christmas parties and presents, and for Spring entertainments with music and readings. "Lime-light illustrations," stereopticon views, and phonograph demonstrations were popular modern diversions at many of these affairs. Warm weather meant a Sunday School picnic or excursion. Steamer trips were popular with churches along the Clyde in Scotland; sports and games highlighted the day for those who stayed on land. Govan's Sunday School teachers planned for weeks before an outing in 1889. The children, from both the mission and home Sunday Schools, were marched "in companies to the station" for the reserved train cars that took them to the country where games, prizes, "pastry and milk" followed. Despite their preparation, the teachers reflected afterward that before repeating the event, they needed to buy a cricket ball, bat, wickets, some swings, pails, skipping ropes, camp grate, and alphabetical cards; predictably, they also resolved to start planning earlier the next time.[31] A group of Cleveland Congregationalists withstood foul weather on their 1896 excursion and recorded their survival by a terse sentence in the church yearbook: "big rain—300 wet people; 300 jolly people."[32]

The children of the congregation were also expected to be joiners. Not even the tiniest babies were allowed to escape when congregations created "cradle rolls" that infants joined at birth. For older children, local chapters of the Band of Hope were ubiquitous across Scotland and England, first at mission halls and then at churches. The greatest number of children's groups at the end of the century were connected to home or foreign missions; nearly every congregation had its version for boys and girls—King's Sons, King's Daughters, Boys' Mission Band, Girls' Missionary Circle, Willing Workers, Seed Sowers, and so forth. Children listened to mission stories, filled their boxes with pennies, sewed clothing for orphanages, or packed cartons for India. The Mission Band at Union Park Congregational Church in Chicago studied Africa, the Sandwich Islands, and China in 1887 and collected twenty-nine dollars in their "jugs" for the congregation's city mission.[33] The children of the Juvenile Missionary Association at Regent Square were assured that their donations were appreciated: "the sick Chinese children will thank you . . . , [and] Jesus knows and approves of all you do *for Him*."[34]

The Bible classes that served teenagers and adults were converted into "organized classes" with officers, committees, meetings, social and recreational events, and annual reports. Often the classes chose distinctive names; in Hyde Park, Massachusetts, in 1913, the men's and women's groups became the Brotherhood Class and the Bethany Class, the young men chose to be called the Baraca Class, and the young women who met in the balcony corner were the "Ahkeoquoins."[35] The young men's Bible class in Chicago that selected "Fellowship Class" as its name understood perhaps better than most what had become the most powerful selling point.[36] The extent to which these classes had become highly organized is witnessed by a Young Men's Class at the Forty-first Street Presbyterian Church in Chicago: the group's thirty-six page handbook listed ten officers and eleven committees for 1903. Every Thursday was designated as this class's "social" evening, with "special musical and literary programs from time to time" in addition to the weekly availability of magazines, periodicals, and "many games."[37]

Groups and activities for youth drew particular attention during the last third of the nineteenth century. Although a few young men's groups had existed in Britain in the 1830s and early 1840s, most of these were short lived and virtually forgotten by midcentury.[38] They also differed from later youth groups by limiting their purposes to "spiritual objects"[39] and mission work. One such association at St. George's, Glasgow, had met weekly to hear one of its members "read an essay of a religious character" and had run a mission Sunday School for "poor children."[40]

But during the 1870s, a renewed interest in youth work appeared on both sides of the Atlantic. The motivation came not so much from any anxiety about disappearing youth, but from the ever greater numbers of unattached young men and women who flooded church services.[41] What leaders confronted was opportunity, not disinterest. On New Year's Day 1878, the elders of St. George's Free Church in Edinburgh made a discussion of their responsibility to "young men generally, not members of families of the congregation" their first order of business.[42] Similar conversations occurred elsewhere. H. E. C. Daniels, a youth organizer in Chicago, articulated some years later what he had been thinking in the 1870s:

> At the Sunday evening services our Church was literally packed with young people. Many of them were total strangers in the city, and most of them without church connection or church home. The problem which presented itself was how to hold this grand body of young people; how to convince them that the brightest, cheeriest and most homelike place in all the world is the Father's House; how to throw such influences around them as should neutralize the temptations of a great city, and so direct the energy and power of their young manhood and womanhood that it should stand for good and for God in the world.[43]

Church leaders searched for the best way of getting these young adults involved in the church. One route was to create separate youth organizations and functions; a second was to incorporate the young people into currently existing, cross-generational activities. Congregations encouraged youth to accept positions as ushers, collectors, teachers, and mission workers; some Lyndhurst Road deacons pointed out the advantage of having young people ready to relieve those who were growing older.[44] A brainstorming session at Philadelphia's Second Presbyterian Church came up with possibilities of each type in 1883: a Saturday afternoon Young Men's Bible Class, an evening group to study church history, a

Musical and Literary Association for Young Men and Young Ladies, participation in planning for a new chapel, a Bible class on Sunday morning, an invitation to become Sunday School teachers, or election of some young men as deacons.[45]

The creation of separate youth groups and events was by far the more accepted method. Congregational leaders soon found that the young not only sought a separate identity but preferred to organize themselves, rather than be organized. The Philadelphia elders wisely decided to lay aside their own list and ask the youth what they wanted, although there is no record of how their consultation with only young men was received by the young women.[46] A few years later, the elders of St. George's Free Church decided they should establish a guild to get young people who only attended worship to become more involved; after they consulted the youth (both men and women in this case), they backed off, having learned that the young people intended to form their own committee.[47]

Youth group organizers seem to have understood—whether consciously or not is hard to guess—that giving people a job, or better yet a title, secured loyalty. Consequently, the lists of officers and committees or sub-sections of work could be long. The society at the Congregational church in Hyde Park, Massachusetts, operated with ten committees, and Lyndhurst Road's guild had twelve "branches" of work in 1895.[48] When both young men and women were enrolled in the same association, care was usually taken to include both sexes among the officers, although men were more likely to be presidents and treasurers, and women to be vice-presidents and secretaries.[49]

Elaborate self-government was not the only characteristic that distinguished late nineteenth-century youth organizations from earlier ones; predictably, these groups also gave greater prominence to fellowship, entertainment, and recreation. Even the choice of a name could suggest the new emphasis: there was a Young Men's Fraternal Society at Bristol's Redland Park Congregational Church, which had a Ramblers Guild and a Literary Guild to go along with its Bible study, temperance programs, and volunteer mission work. The Young Women's Christian Fellowship Association at Regent Square alternated weekly between Bible study and a program of music and readings. A group of young Chicago Congregationalists included "Ye Pink Tea," an "Apron Social" and a "Strangers' Social" in their 1887 schedule. A Sunday evening society at First Presbyterian Church, Pittsburgh, advertised six suppers and four picnics to complement its devotional meetings and missionary lectures for 1912. Leisure and entertainment exerted a powerful pull even on the reluctant; a new Young People's Guild was founded in 1890 at Lyndhurst Road with the determination to be "an entirely Spiritual Guild and not a Recreative Guild," but in two years it had a standing committee in charge of recreation.[50]

Groups for young men and young women—defined in most places as those over age eighteen, though in some places those as young as fourteen or fifteen could join—were organized according to one of two patterns: there was the cultural or literary model typified by discussions of literature, art, music, and science, and there was a more evangelical model established by the Christian Endeavor Society.[51]

The Christian Endeavor movement was founded in 1881 by a Congregational minister, Francis E. Clark of Portland, Maine; it spread across America in the 1880s and into Britain during the following decade.[52] Most churches quickly added a Junior Christian Endeavor Society for those under age fourteen. Conventions rallied youth from different congregations to create a sense of belonging to something very grand. Clark's model prescribed a weekly Bible study and devotional meeting, most often scheduled on Sunday evening before the congregational service. Each society elected officers and appointed a prescribed set of committees for Prayer Meeting, Look-Out (recruiting), Social, and Mission tasks. The format called for the application of evangelical energy and enthusiasm to each task; being systematic was important, too. A Chicago group's handbook specified exactly how the Look-Out Committee was to station people at each door of the church and in each section of pews to "look-out" for new faces; names were taken down in notebooks, introductions made, a member assigned to be the newcomer's "friend," and visits made until success was achieved.[53]

Wherever Christian Endeavor caught on, it was described in superlatives. A young people's group in Chicago remained independent until 1897 when the majority felt "that the time had come to get into line with . . . 'the greatest movement of the century.'" Once affiliated, the Chicago congregation was enthused about the result of its association.

> [Christian Endeavor] represents the maintenance of a prayer meeting
> every Monday night . . . ; the purchasing of a carefully selected library
> of over three thousand volumes; a reading table supplied with the best
> religious and secular periodicals of the day; the social life, directed and
> influenced, of hundreds of young people . . . ; a large part of the teach-
> ing force of three Sabbath Schools; . . . gifts, in the last ten years only,
> of $7,072.40 to home missions, $1,452.91 to foreign missions . . . ;
> numbers of men and women all over this land . . . engaged in the
> Master's work; and last and best of all, it represents the love, patience
> and directing Spirit of our Lord and Master Jesus Christ.[54]

The second model—the cultural or literary association—was actually the older of the two, and at least some of these societies were later converted to the Christian Endeavor pattern. Cultural or literary associations, less evangelical in tone than Christian Endeavor, drew inspiration and method from the mutual improvement societies earlier in the century and even more so from the educational practices popularized by the Chautauqua Movement and from the intellectual habits prized by various collegiate or secular literary and philosophical clubs, quarterly magazines, and subscription lecture series. They also reflected the determination of late Victorian churchgoers to connect religion and culture in a mutually affirmative way: religious values vitalized the arts, and cultural enlightenment extended and reinforced morality.[55]

The agendas of the societies were ambitious. At Philadelphia's Second Presbyterian Church the desire was to see "the study of Music cultivated and Essays on Scientific and religious Subjects read." A young men and women's Reading Society at Lansdowne Church in Glasgow wrote and discussed "short papers" on Shakespeare, Milton, Goldsmith, Carlyle, and Macaulay in 1899. In Manchester, the Withington Church's fortnightly "Literary and Discussion Society" (which seems to have been open to older members of the congregation, too) tackled current issues such as Irish home rule, vegetarianism, and evolution, plus literary giants such as Eliot and Emerson, and historical debates such as whether Queen Elizabeth was really "Good Queen Bess." Like all of these groups, this one paused in its intellectual pursuits occasionally for a "soiree" or lime-light display.[56]

A set of minutes kept by the woman who was secretary of the Young People's Guild at the Lyndhurst Road Church in London provides a glimpse inside one of these literary groups, although a somewhat atypical one. The Lyndhurst Road Guild was founded about 1890 and grew quickly to one hundred members within its first year; average attendance was about sixty-five. With its standing committees for Mission, Work, Look-Out, Choir, Temperance, and Recreation, this guild obviously borrowed as much from the Christian Endeavor model as from the literary pattern, and in 1899 it changed its name to Christian Endeavor. Its topics, then, were as much evangelical as cultural, and some meetings were spent praying, singing, or reading and discussing the Bible. The group set its own syllabus and chose topics such as "Happiness," "Duty," "The Uses of Suffering," "The Opium Trade," "Peace," "The Lesson of Job," "Shakespeare," "Luther," "New Guinea and the South Sea Islands," "Matthew 25:40," and "The Secret of Overcoming Sin." About the meeting on sin, the secretary remarked wistfully, "Good attendance & useful speeches, but it was generally felt to be a rather difficult subject to deal with."[57]

The Guild's young women shared in the work of chairing meetings, making speeches, and participating in discussion, but the secretary, perhaps with an eye toward equity, counted whether as many women had spoken up as had men; there seldom were.[58] The secretary's own preferences were transparent; she did not like long pauses in the discussion, or "rather long" speeches, or people who came unprepared ("This might have been a very interesting meeting had members come prepared to speak but few appear to have done so"). Fellowship was important; one well-attended meeting was given over entirely to "talking to one another, and trying to get to know one another better." There were garden meetings in the Spring, as well as outings and visits to museums.

One of the most active, and enduring, literary groups was the Govan Young Men's Association founded in 1876 and still active on the eve of World War I. From the beginning the group was as much interested in fellowship and recreation as in culture; in fact, its constitution may have implied an edge to sociability when it listed the goals as "the promotion of Christian fellowship, and the Religious and Intellectual Improvement of the Young Men of the Parish." The group met Thursday evenings from November through March, alternating between members' meetings at which they discussed their own essays or held debates, and large public meetings at which guest speakers and musicians performed and admission was charged to defray the cost. An annual supper dance was begun in 1877, for which "double tickets" were sold and members arrived with young ladies on their arms for "a pleasant evening in listening to a selection of high class music skillfully rendered by a party of friends, interspersed with an occasional indulgence in dancing."[59]

Surprisingly, this group of young Scots stayed together as they aged, rather than dropping out to make way for the next generation. By the 1890s, there were attempts to change the name to the Govan Literary Association, as "young men" did not seem to describe gentlemen who held the rank of colonel or were congratulated for their silver wedding anniversaries. There were also proposals to admit women as equal members, which seemed sensible enough to many men whose wives accompanied them to all the public events only to be barred on alternate weeks from the debates and discussions. Both changes eventually occurred, but not until 1905 and 1913 respectively, which reveals how important the identifications with youth and with masculinity still were to the majority. And, it suggests how self-defining the fellowship must have been to them in their youth when they had not only cultivated their minds but had freely engaged in such male activities as whistling contests and smoking on those Thursday evenings when they were alone.

Spurred on by the "muscular Christianity" movement, many youth activities at the end of the nineteenth century were designed especially to appeal to boys' and young men's sense of rugged masculinity. In 1881, Charteris convinced the Church of Scotland to start Young Men's Guilds as a "rally-point round which young men in the Church may be united, and toward which others as yet outside may be attracted." The guilds highlighted three things—"Friendship," "Enlightened Spirituality," and "Service." The language was vigorous, even military. Young men, Charteris said, were "battling with actual difficulties, intellectual problems, moral questions, and still more fiercely with temptations of the heart." A young man wanted "a real religion, something practical he can take with him into the fight and scramble." He did not want to be thought "pious" or have Christianity "rob him of his reputation of manliness." What Charteris hoped was that the guilds would convince young men that "the ideal Christian life and the ideal manly life are one and the same thing."[60]

Another Scot, William Alexander Smith, initiated the Boys' Brigade movement in 1883 on a more explicitly military basis. He, too, hoped to promote "a true Christian Manliness." Boys' Brigades spread through the churches of Britain in the 1880s and 1890s, and to a lesser extent in America after 1887. The lads were organized into military companies, assigned a rank, equipped with uniforms and rifles, and turned out for Bible study, drill, first-aid instruction, gymnastics, and athletic competitions. At the Free College Church in Glasgow, boys who had "served their time in the Brigade" were then taken into the Young Men's Fellowship by the "usual draft."[61]

Sports had become an important dimension of church youth work by the 1890s. In part, this was because football, cricket, swimming, and baseball were better draws than prayer meetings. But churches also believed that physical activity, competition, and sportsmanship built character. A Glasgow congregation argued that "if we are to maintain our influence over the boys, we must organise and regulate their out-door sports, and use these as a means not only of developing their bodies but of training their characters."[62] As a result, beginning in the 1880s, church schedules filled with football (soccer), cricket, baseball, basketball, swimming, rambling, bowling, gymnastics, and cycling. Young women were not excluded entirely from these activities; Regent Square's cycling club was open to both sexes, and girls took their part in gymnastics, bowling, and swimming. A 1909 newsletter from Lyndhurst Road shows the young ladies of the congregation engaged in "tape drill" and "musical skipping."[63] But athletics were considered especially appropriate ways of engaging boys in church work. It was not enough, of course, just to get a young man into an athletic club; there was a reciprocity between religion and athletic competition, as each enhanced the other. "What we want to show," Regent Square's 1909 manual explained, "is that [athletics] flourish better with, and because of, membership with the Church. We wish to express our belief that Christ was so eminently the ideal man as to be very much more than that."[64]

The priority given to fellowship activities made churches different places by 1900. The change came rapidly in the late 1880s and especially the 1890s, as churchgoers were systematically organized into clubs and associations, and the number of weekly events mushroomed. Early in the Victorian period, Reformed congregations kept a distance between religion and leisure entertainments; now social events and diversions were routine aspects of congregational life. The difference was most apparent in the area of youth work, but there were also more organized adult Bible classes, more men's leagues and brotherhoods, and more women's missionary circles. Indeed, it would be hard to imagine a type of cultural or leisure activity that could not have been found in at least one congregation—handicraft and hobby clubs, choral societies, orchestras, athletic unions, book groups, dramatic readings, and even dancing classes.

The changes did not occur without causing some tension and voicing of concern. Near the turn of the century, one elderly London Congregationalist complained tartly about what he considered "auxiliaries" to the main work of the church: "You may get people to church, but not by these means will they be made Christians."[65] In Pittsburgh, a group of United Presbyterian trustees—who belonged to the denomination most reluctant to embrace the new style—grumbled as late as 1915 that none of them "was in favour of holding so many entertainments in [the] church building." But such voices never amounted to more than a small minority, and even the Pittsburgh trustees were complaining only about the amount, not the virtue of leisure. By the early 1900s no church board would any longer have behaved as Pilrig's did near midcentury when it charged that a Saturday evening men's temperance social was no more than a "play-place for the frivolous" and closed the group down.[66]

Whatever they thought of the theological implications, congregations found that they faced more difficult financial and administrative challenges as a result of the increased activity. One approach, represented by the guild movements in both Britain and America, was to consolidate previously separate groups under a single umbrella making them easier to keep track of, and theoretically easier to administer. A single women's missionary society might have a number of "circles" within it, or a women's guild might have several sub-sections, such as a Bible class, mothers' meeting, Dorcas Society, lady visitors, committee for congregational socials, Zenana mission society, and so forth. An executive committee and general officers provided coordination to the work.

Even with consolidation, greater activity forced a larger central administration. More office staff and more full-time professionals were required to keep up with the heavier schedule. Church manuals and annual reports had to be enlarged simply to list all the activity. Auditors inherited the task of verifying dozens of individual accounts. And, in what would certainly have been the adjustment most visible to those outside the congregation, a church that gave priority to fellowship needed not only a larger building, but a different assortment of physical spaces in which to carry out ministry.

# eleven

## Church Buildings
*Setting and Symbol*

In 1909, a Regent Square member reminisced about an ambitious renovation project that the London congregation had undertaken nearly a half century earlier. Back in 1860, the sanctuary had been fitted out with new pews—"more roomy" ones with "sloping backs and all comfortably cushioned." The "pitch of the galleries was altered to allow the sitters comfortably to see and hear the minister," and new lighting, heating, and ventilation were installed. Into the once blank wall behind the pulpit, carpenters cut "a large window . . . which, fitted with stained glass, added brightness to the interior and formed a graceful ornament." "So great were the alterations," the old member thought, "that, as respects the interior of the Church, it might have been said that the Old Regent Square had disappeared."[1] It was, of course, not the renovation that had caused the transformation of Regent Square's character, but the other way round. The building was but setting and symbol for what had already occurred and was occurring in liturgical practice, aesthetic taste, and expectations of comfort.

Ease and elegance—two achievements of those Regent Square remodelers—became measures by which congregations judged their church buildings. Far to the north along the wild Grampian coast where the village of MacDuff faced the North Sea, a parishioner wrote a blunt assessment in 1904 of the local edifice's shortcomings: "the building itself labours under two great deficiencies—the want of artistic decoration to relieve the somewhat uninspiring expanse of plainness, and the want of heating apparatus."[2]

If late Victorian congregations sought anything more diligently than luxury and comfort, it was additional room. To be more precise, what they desired was not just *more* building space, but *different* space, tailored to the flurry of activity in which congregations were now engaged. They needed Sunday School rooms, fellowship halls, kitchens, meeting rooms, and recreational areas. A Congregational minister in Manchester, assessing his church's needs in 1887, put "more adequate buildings . . . for educational and social purposes" high on his list.³ One of his colleagues in London, put it more tersely: "One want, *more room.*"⁴

Thus, Victorian congregations proved to be eager renovators and ambitious builders. Greater physical comfort, aesthetic refinement, and new forms of space were their goals. They took great pride in what they constructed; jubilee histories and annual reports were replete with self-satisfied descriptions; probably three-quarters of the local church news submitted to the weekly *American Presbyterian* at the end of the 1860s told of new furnaces, paint, carpet, and pews. Trustees and deacons guarded the investments with insurance policies and attention to safety and security. Custodians were hired to take care of the structures throughout the year; spring or summer occasioned a rigorous cleaning when carpets were turned out, walls brushed down, and wood polished to remove the winter's soot and grime.

The facilities that congregations required at the beginning of the Victorian period were minimal and straightforward. There had to be a main sanctuary, of course, and a smaller "lecture hall" or chapel for prayer meetings. It was common to have a "session room" or deacons' room where board meetings could be held, and perhaps a pastor's study unless this was provided in the manse. Occasionally, a congregation had a "waiting room" where those who had travelled great distances could remain and refresh themselves between services, but it was more likely that other space would double for that need. A corner for the women's sewing circle was required in some churches, although such meetings more often occurred in homes. (Whatever space the congregation owned or rented as an off-site mission station was of course additional, but it is not the subject of discussion here.)⁵

The advent of congregational, as opposed to mission, Sunday Schools created the first significant demand for additional space. When Plymouth Church opened its doors in Brooklyn in 1848, it managed with only four rooms—a sanctuary, lecture room, one classroom, and a pastor's study. When a fire leveled that first structure (actually an 1831 building purchased from another congregation), Plymouth built a larger church in 1850 that better reflected its midcentury needs and ambitions. It included eleven rooms—the "main audience room" seating two thousand, a "lecture room" about one-third as large, a Sunday School room (24' by 64') plus four smaller 10' by 16' classrooms for Bible and infant classes, two social parlors (24' by 32'), a reception room, and a pastor's study.⁶

Plymouth Church, as we noted earlier, was among the first to hold regular church socials and hence to include such space in its building plans. But over the next decades, social rooms became increasingly common. By 1870, Park Congregational Church in Brooklyn had fitted out its building with a large "social room" under the rear gallery; two additional parlors and a kitchen went along with a committee room, pastor's study, large Sunday School room, infant class room, library, and "work room" for ladies' sewing.[7]

By the beginning of the twentieth century, churchgoers craved even more ambitious facilities. Educational methods had rendered the old single, open Sunday School room obsolete, and Pittsburgh's First Presbyterian Church bragged in 1912 that it possessed enough individual rooms to allow each of thirty classes to have "a room of its own, where it can enjoy the lesson away from noise and interruption." When Acocks Green counted up its new Birmingham facilities in 1896, it had four Sunday School rooms, a young men's club room, a young ladies' club room, a minister's study, deacons' room, two cloak rooms with lavatories, a library, a room for "tea or cutting up, with a tea boiler," a woodcarving room, and a sizeable "recreation hall." And, as a sign both of affluence and appreciation of ease, Acocks Green announced that the two levels of its building were connected by an elevator.[8]

Acquiring the space to expand church programs from worship alone to education and fellowship was not always an easy task. Congregations often inherited buildings planned and constructed in a day when a church kitchen or social hall—let alone a gymnasium—was unimaginable. Now, when they considered adding proper facilities, they could easily find themselves surrounded on all sides by commercial construction.[9] Thus, congregations needed more than a little ingenuity to retrofit existing space or expand into new. Of course, as long as the use was only occasional, it made sense to rent temporary quarters; for instance, for their earliest socials King's Weigh House contracted for rooms in a London tavern and Second Presbyterian in Philadelphia was given the use of Heseltine's Galleries.[10] This option, however, made little sense if the church was going to need the space continuously or frequently.

Congregations tried when possible, or in emergencies, to use their current space for more than one purpose. In Scotland, the parish day school could double as a site for church activities both on evenings and weekends. Many a missionary society meeting or Bible class convened in a far corner of the balcony or in the choir seats; Sunday schools could overflow into kitchens, and parlors could serve as temporary sewing rooms. The recreational rooms and social halls at the mission station could be borrowed for congregational use. One kirk session, lacking any better location, held its meetings in the cleaning woman's sitting room, and paid her an extra £4.4 for the trouble.[11]

Victorians, however, preferred in their churches as well as in their homes to separate rooms by function; at minimum, the "private" space where the congregation acted as family needed to be separated from the "public" space where it worshipped.[12] There was, then, an urge to reconfigure and partition existing space to meet changing needs. One possibility was to convert the unfinished cellars beneath the church. St. George's parish in Edinburgh was studying in 1888 whether it could, by putting in a stove, banish the cold and damp successfully enough to use the cellars for more than storage. Some years earlier, Park Congregational Church in Brooklyn had walled off and floored 30 percent of its cellar to gain two parlors, a sewing room, and a kitchen. Other congregations, however, faced more difficult choices, and at times they ended up stealing space from one use for a more pressing priority. For instance, to get a kitchen in 1872, Rochester's Central Presbyterian Church was forced to convert space currently being used as the pastor's study.[13]

When space inside the building filled up, congregations looked for more. The most common strategy was to lease or build a separate "church hall" for the necessary meeting rooms. If adjacent land was still available, it was the preferred location. Second Presbyterian Church in Philadelphia was able in 1885 to attach a significant addition to its 1868–72 edifice; St. George's Free Church in Edinburgh, had enough land at the rear for "a suitable vestry for the Minister and better accommodation for the Church Officer." But other urban congregations, such as St. George's parish in central Glasgow, found themselves hemmed in and had to go around the corner or down the street to find a building site or set of rooms for rent. In 1862, St. George's parish in Edinburgh considered itself fortunate to find a suitable three-story hall only a couple of blocks away in Randolph Place where it housed its prayer meeting, Sunday School, and "Ladies Work Society."[14]

The addition of space and the multiplication of church events forced trustees or deacons to rethink their management and stewardship of church property. Greater assets called for increased insurance coverage and attention to security.[15] Busy buildings that were unlocked every evening rather than once or twice a week raised concerns. Lyndhurst Road lost four communion chalices and a pulpit clock in 1913 to thieves who were assumed to have "secreted themselves in the Church" and then done their work after the evening's meetings had ended. Trustees at Third Presbyterian Church in Chicago declared that all church events had to be over by 10:30 P.M. and instructed the sextons to begin shutting out the lights if members did not leave promptly; the building, the trustees explained, "is on a prominent corner and becomes an attractive place for passers-by if the doors are open at an unseemly hour."[16]

With increased activity, most congregations thought it wise to develop rules about how and when the building could be used. A nightly curfew, for instance, protected the custodian from an extended day even where security was of little concern. St. Kenneth's Church in Glasgow posted a list of building rules in 1904: there would be no smoking or alcohol and no meetings on Saturday (which was cleaning day); each event had to be approved by the session or minister; and only the custodian could move furniture, light the gas lamps, or adjust the heating and ventilation.[17] Not every group of trustees, and not every custodian, adjusted gracefully to having the building put in steady service, and there were occasional complaints about extra cleaning or fears of damaged floors or charges that young boys from the Sunday School had been allowed out of their area and were "abusing the church."[18]

Separate rules governed the use of the building by outside groups. Congregations regularly opened their space to a wide variety of voluntary societies and community groups; one church or another hosted the Sabbath Observance Committee, the Salvation Army, the Women's Christian Temperance Union, the Seaman's Friend Society, university baccalaureates and commencements, tract societies, or Sunday School conventions. In addition to enforcing restrictions on the manner in which the building could be used, congregations charged outside groups a standard fee to cover overtime for the custodian and the cost of light and heat. (In some places, where trustees determined to place building use on a self-supporting basis, even groups within the congregation were assessed for special events, although at a lesser rate.)[19]

Staffing and cleaning a more highly used building also called for certain adjustments. All except the very smallest churches hired a full-time custodian, variously referred to as the sexton, chapelkeeper, janitor, caretaker, or church officer. Usually the position was filled by a man, but an occasional congregation, in London and Pittsburgh at least, employed a woman.[20] Compensation typically entailed a small salary plus housing. Depending on the size of the building to be tended, one or two women might be hired to assist with cleaning and, where there were still pews with gates, to serve as pew-openers in the galleries on Sunday. If the church hall was at another location, there was a separate hallkeeper, usually a widow who was permitted to live upstairs rent free in exchange for custodial services.

The sextons were responsible for normal custodial services—maintaining and cleaning the building, tending to heat and light, setting up tables and chairs for meetings, and unlocking and locking the building on time. Many of the job descriptions, however, added other responsibilities such as maintaining the list of pewholders, collecting pew rents, taking messages and running errands for the pastor, guarding the Sunday collection until it could be deposited, or checking out library books. With the increase in traffic during weekdays, congregations found it necessary to increase the compensation for their custodians, and in large churches to hire more help. As the staff grew larger and the work increased, trustees reorganized responsibilities in search of greater efficiency. Near the end of the century, Central Presbyterian Church in Rochester expected its "building manager" to supervise other cleaners, identify needed repairs, schedule rooms, maintain account books, take tickets at events, "wait on ladies at socials," and generally "see that everything was in order and properly cared for."[21]

Finding space for new activities was only one of several considerations that churches had in mind as they renovated and enlarged their facilities; they also sought to display the comfort and good taste that signified middle-class respectability. The public spaces especially had to be beautified to meet heightened aesthetic demands, and their level of comfort and convenience raised to the standards expected by greater affluence and new technology. Early nineteenth-century Reformed churches had been plain and unadorned inside. Any of Scotland's ancient churches that still stood had been shorn of their embellishments at the Reformation, and Congregationalists and Presbyterians had built and appointed their structures with puritan restraint. As late as 1850, Old South's deacons were obliged to assure members that a recent redecoration had been carried out in a "chaste manner."[22] Beauty could acceptably be sought and found in simplicity, but never in unabashed luxury.

Yet by the early 1900s, luxury was an altogether appropriate word for the Gothic spires, stained glass, plush pew cushions, and dark, ornately carved wood that graced Reformed houses of worship. Every church body wanted to be able to say of itself as did St. Andrew's parish, Edinburgh, in the mid-1880s: "The comfort and appearance of the interior of the Church, are creditable to the liberality and good taste of the Congregation."[23]

What was happening in design and architecture was, of course, not isolated from the comfort expected in Victorian homes; the same affluence and cultivation of taste motivated each.[24] Nor was the appearance of the sanctuary disconnected from the liturgical and musical reforms discussed in Part 1. Robed choirs, chanted psalms, festival days, and printed service books were matched by stained glass and grained wood. Marks of elegance could be seen in all aspects of the congregation's life. Silver communionware replaced any remaining pewter pieces. Church manuals began to show the hand of a designer, not just a printer, as art nouveau lettering and illustrations ornamented the pages of the most style-conscious congregations. In a clear presentation of its self-image, Cleveland's First Congregational Church filled the cover of its 1894 yearbook with a sketch of two fashionable ladies attired in the latest of coats, hats, and fur handmuffs—and carrying Bibles. In London, the members of Kensington Presbyterian Church chose a new, more elegant-sounding name, St. John's, in 1887.[25]

A first wave of interior renovations began about 1860 as congregations determined to be more comfortable while they worshipped. A second wave occurred a generation later at the end of the century and was often initiated by the installation or repositioning of an organ, or by the decision to upgrade a heating system or introduce electric lighting. Renovation projects could also be generated by a change in liturgical practice such as an end to table service for communion. It was very easy for one change to spur several more. For instance, in the 1850s, Broughton Place installed a "choir pew" and took out its "old-fashioned precentor's desk." Since the desk had been affixed to the pulpit, its removal suggested some alterations to the pulpit, and in turn, the new pulpit and choir seats prompted a repositioning and improvement of the gas lighting.[26] Among the churches of Turriff presbytery in northern Scotland, the renovations of the 1890s, in which kirk after kirk placed a single ornate oak communion table at the front of the church, signaled the end of the old-style table sacraments.

The rationale for what were often quite lavish expenditures on the "church fabric" (as Victorians often referred to their buildings and grounds) was plainly stated. King's Weigh House in 1875 explained that it had "expended this large amount for the advantage and Comfort of all connected with this church & congregation." In Edinburgh, St. George's kirk session, with a keen sense of what the market for sittings demanded in the 1860s, justified a renovation project by saying it was needed "for the comfort of the Worshippers and the sake of Revenue from seat letting."[27]

The choices that decorating committees made were remarkably similar. Dark, rich palettes of color were applied, carpets laid, stained glass installed, and old straight-backed pews replaced. Broughton Place in 1870 wanted pews "of modern design, uniformly fitted with hair cushions covered with crimson cloth." At the same time, it added a larger pulpit graced by an "ornamental front." "Enriched capitals" now sat atop the pillars under the gallery, and pilasters adorned the front wall. Woodwork was "stained dark," and the walls painted "a brown hue." Over head, decorations were stencilled on the ceiling.[28] That same year in Rochester, Central Presbyterian Church adopted a similar decorating scheme. The new pews were to be of black walnut with crimson seat cushions, and footstools were ordered to match; the existing pulpit was grained black walnut, too. Carpet was laid. The ceiling was painted in two shades of pearl with gilt around the dome, the walls were done in a "delicate shade of French grey," and the interior columns were "bronzed."[29] A "new colour scheme" at Edinburgh's Greenside parish saw "deep red" paint applied to the previously cream-colored walls and "dark brown varnish" brushed over the old "pews of natural pine."[30]

The women of the church, not surprisingly, were called upon for leadership in many of these undertakings. When Philadelphia's Second Presbyterian Church finished a major project in 1860, the session thanked "Mrs. Doctor Patterson" for "the commendable zeal which she displayed in effecting a renovation of our Church edifice in a manner so tasteful and fitting."[31] Women came to the task not only with experience in the selection of carpets and paints, but with considerable financial strength. When a special subscription was taken to raise the funds (and this was the typical choice), women were prominent among the collectors; at Moseley Road, Birmingham, in the 1890s, women made all the solicitations.[32] More significantly, however, the women usually had significant cash already in hand as a result of their own subscriptions, sales of work, bazaars, suppers, and socials. In Hyde Park, Massachusetts, it was the Young Ladies Aid Society that paid for a "large illuminated window" at the front of the sanctuary in 1884. At Fourth United Presbyterian in Pittsburgh, the Ladies Aid Society in 1883 paid for new carpet, stained glass, paint, frescoes, and masonry repairs. In this instance, the trustees had approached the women and asked them to take charge of the work, but women did not always wait to be asked. In Glasgow in 1911, the Ladies Association approached the managers of Lansdowne Church and proposed that "certain matters connected with what might be termed the Domestic Affairs of the congregation might be more beneficially dealt with by the Ladies." Such a delegation of responsibility would, the women suggested coyly, save the managers' time. The women's offer was hardly abstract; they had money in their account and had already drawn up a detailed list of projects. They proposed new upholstery, carpet and table covers for the vestry; more reupholstering and new blinds were slated for the ladies' parlor.[33]

Beautiful surroundings and comfortable seating were prized, but churchgoers also wanted to be able to see and hear well. These were not characteristics that church buildings automatically had. For one thing, major churches in cities and towns— even towns of modest size—had become quite large, seating as many as twenty-five hundred people. For a second thing, there was more to see and hear—organs, choirs, a central communion table, clerical robes, pulpit scarfs, flowers, stained glass, and the performance of a star preacher. The more worship was considered a form of entertainment and compared to the stage, the more churchgoers insisted on being able to see and hear well. The demand for prime seating along the center aisle did not grow entirely from a desire to be seen; people also wanted to see. Old square box pews, which turned family members toward each other, may have served another age, but now people wanted to face forward as they did in the theater. Huge amphitheaters, such as Plymouth Church in Brooklyn or City Temple in London, were built with stellar preachers in mind and boasted clear lines of sight and good acoustics. But, older structures were simply lucky if they could provide as much, and even many new structures sacrificed function for Gothic beauty.

The ability to see well was an important consideration to those who were installing new pews; if for no other reason, they knew that pews behind pillars could not be rented for a very high price, if at all. As noted earlier, while Regent Square was reseating its main floor in 1860 with more comfortable pews, it also altered the "pitch of the galleries . . . to allow the sitters comfortably to see and hear the minister."[34] Where old-fashioned high pulpits were still in place, midcentury remodelers lowered them so that worshippers could watch the preacher without tilting their heads uncomfortably. This reduction of "the altitude of the pulpit," as Old South's pew proprietors called it, undoubtedly did allow for more comfortable posture, but it can also be interpreted as an symbol that clergy no longer enjoyed the deference they once did: preachers were now located actually as well as conceptually on the level of a friend, not a patriarch.[35]

Stained glass also served more than one purpose. It could be prized for its splendor alone, or for the worshipful aura its light cast, or for the prestige it brought to a congregation. At the same time, however, it was touted for its purely practical benefits. One congregation claimed its colored glass was "to prevent the Glare of light so much complained of by many members." Thus, the decision to start with the window behind the pulpit was not entirely because this was the most visible location; sun streaming through an east window on a bright Sunday morning came directly into the upraised eyes of the worshippers.[36]

Too little light was as troubling as too much. Most Victorian renovation projects included plans for improved artificial lighting. Gas lamps were installed in city and town churches between 1825 and 1860 and remained the standard lighting source until electricity became available sometime after 1880. Gaslight was an improvement over candlelight, both in terms of power and safety, and its presence allowed Sunday evening worship services to become the rule, leaving afternoons for leisure and family. But, more light was continually sought, particularly as the use of service books and printed orders of worship made poorly lit sanctuaries greater obstacles than they had once been.

The ability to hear well was important, too. Most churches allotted a few seats near the front for those with hearing loss, and a few installed innovations such as "Gutta percha hearing tubes" running from the pulpit to designated pews close by.[37] A congregation unfortunate enough to have unsatisfactory acoustics struggled. Lyndhurst Road's new building opened in 1884 with great expectations, but was plagued with irritating reverberations. The deacons tried raising the platform, hanging curtains around the gallery facade, and placing a sounding board above the pulpit and organ case. With the building into its second year, they were still tinkering.[38] Street noise was another hazard for a city church, and St. George's Free Church installed double windows in 1881 "to prevent noise and drafts."[39]

Increasingly, churchgoers demanded—and expected—comfortable heating and ventilation. Indeed, cold drafts, troublesome "heating apparatus" and poor ventilation were ever present topics on committee agendas, especially in Scotland. St. George's Free Church, at the beginning of the twentieth century, actually had a separate "Heating and Ventilation Committee" that fielded complaints about "low temperature & cold draughts."[40] The installation of double windows, "India rubber tubing" around doors or "glass frames" around the entries were methods of protection against "the ingress of cold draughts of air to the church"; St. George's parish in Edinburgh erected "an elegant porch . . . to protect the worshippers in the middle area from those drafts which have always been with them a ground of complaint." One London congregation tried, as "an experiment for a few Sundays," lighting the gas lamps to see whether the heat they threw off would counteract the "drafts."[41] Where success was achieved, church leaders took satisfaction that the warmth had "greatly conduce[d] to the comfort of the Congregation."[42]

Heating the parlors and other small rooms of the church posed no greater challenge than heating most homes—a small grate or gas fire would do. Warming the sanctuary, however, was a more difficult task. Most large churches placed one or more coal furnaces in the cellar and allowed the warm air to rise naturally through vents in the floor. That much was fairly straightforward; getting the air to circulate properly through the pews and both under and in the galleries was another matter. In 1879, Greenside parish gave its system a test; discouragingly, "six hours full power of the stoves only raised the heat a very few degrees" because of poor circulation. Old-style enclosed pews were a serious impediment to proper air flow, a point that might have contributed as much to their removal as did the straight, uncomfortable backs. "Reseating the church" was one of Greenside's responses to its system's poor showing.[43]

Improvements in heating technology in the years around 1900 brought high hopes and much renovation. The hot air furnaces that were "recommended by hygienic experts" during the early 1800s fell somewhat out of favor as many concluded that the "sunless cellar air" pulled up into the sanctuary was "heavy and headachy." Consequently, hot-water systems were welcomed as improvements.[44] Those who retained hot-air furnaces received a boost from electricity which made it possible for blowers to force air where it was needed. St. George's Free Church, with great optimism, installed a new system of blowers that exchanged "used air" for fresh, and promised to leave the worshippers comfortably "warmed in winter and cool in summer."[45]

Proper ventilation—an adequate supply of fresh air—was considered critical. Plymouth Church took satisfaction in 1850 that its new building had succeeded "in providing warmth; and, what is more important in crowded audiences, pure air without currents."[46] In truth, the combination of a packed church and poor ventilation could be suffocating even in cool weather, let alone in American summers. A London churchgoer, writing in 1896, argued that, according to current standards, if a thousand people were enclosed for an hour and a half, the air needed to be changed four or five times.[47] Churches were equipped with "ventilators" in their domes or ceilings or high on their walls, but the results were as likely to be disappointing as not. Trustees were perpetually inspecting their ventilators, seeking to have the mechanisms "put right," looking for ways to improve, or arguing whether it was more effective to apply their energies to pulling in fresh air or "withdrawing the vitiated air."[48]

Gas lamps gave even greater urgency to the matter of proper ventilation. Not only did flames use oxygen, they emitted heat and noxious fumes. The great appeal of electric lighting at Lansdowne Church was that it would "remove complaints about heat and gas fumes."[49] Ten years earlier, churchgoers at Philadelphia's Second Presbyterian Church had been anxious about the "ancient and antiquated method of lighting the church"—all the gas was turned on with one valve, and then the sexton hurriedly made his rounds lighting each lamp. Meanwhile, various heating "burners" and a gas motor powering the organ added their effusions to the mixture. It was Second Church's choir that complained most vehemently; all the fumes ended up, they said, in the rear loft where they were stationed. According to the Music Committee, "The escape of gas from the engine and from the lights and burners in the Church is a most serious matter. It seems to find its way directly into the organ loft to the great discomfort of the singers and possibly to the injury of their voices. Members of the choir have complained that they would be in good voice upon their arrival at the church, but after breathing the atmosphere of the organ loft for a short time would be unable to sing."[50]

Electricity provided not only fume-free lighting, but numerous other small conveniences as well, and congregations were easily captivated by what technology made possible. Central Presbyterian Church in Rochester installed a set of signals "to call the sexton, notify the organist, etc." St. George's Free Church was able to hook up an automatic timer that silenced the tower chime clock between ten o'clock at night and seven in the morning, and Old South members could avoid the stairs by using an elevator. St. George's parish church in Edinburgh spent twenty-three pounds to become the proud owner of a "magic lantern" machine and its accompanying screen.[51]

Church organists may have been among those who benefitted most from the installation of electricity. Compared to the older mechanical action instruments, modern electro-pneumatic action allowed the huge organs that Victorians loved to be played, even at full organ, without as much "bodily exertion of the organist," as one London deacon explained.[52] By the 1900s, the days of hiring an "organ boy" to pump up air pressure manually were gone in all but smaller congregations. But until electricity came along, the gas-powered hydraulic motors that replaced human strength were noisy and unreliable. At Second Presbyterian Church in Philadelphia, "the continual pumping and throbbing of the engine [was] distinctly audible in all parts of the Church." "It is exceedingly annoying," the Music Committee concluded, "not only to our own members, but to strangers." At King's Weigh House, members at a church meeting who "complained of the disturbing influence of the organ motor" were told that if *they* were bothered where they sat, they should just imagine "how distracting it is for Dr. Hunter [the pastor] to have the machinery working directly behind him."[53]

Compared to renovating an existing church, the chance to start from the ground up with a brand new building provided greater scope to congregations seeking comfort, taste, and technological convenience, and Victorians were prolific builders as well as remodelers. Leaving aside reconstruction after a disastrous fire, several factors led congregations to erect new buildings. In Scotland, the Disruption initiated a great rush of construction as the Free Church put down roots in towns and cities across the land. Second, all denominations organized additional congregations in response to the growth of urban population or the settlement of new suburbs; indeed, about half of the congregations considered here did not exist in 1830. Denominational boards, such as the Presbyterian Board of Church Erection in the United States, lent financial support. Some new congregations emerged from mission stations, others were started by the planned departure—or 'hiving off' as it was known—of a portion of a well-established congregation to start a satellite, and still others were spontaneous efforts of residents who wanted a church in their neighborhood. Not a few of these new church developments were built on speculation—that is, planners erected buildings large enough to anticipate the projected growth of a community.

Third, some congregations decided for a new building because their old location was being overrun by urban development. They found themselves in a deteriorating neighborhood, or in danger of being left behind by the removal of their members to the suburbs, or surrounded by commerce rather than any people at all. These churches faced a choice, as we shall see momentarily, either to stay and adapt to their new circumstances or to sell and build elsewhere. There were, it should be added, a few congregations that were given no option in the matter. King's Weigh House, for example, was twice obliged to relocate because its property was in the way of London transportation projects.

A fourth, and more common, reason that congregations erected new churches was that they had outgrown their present quarters. If additional educational or fellowship space was the only problem, this might be added; however, a congregation that overflowed its sanctuary usually found an expansion architecturally impractical. There were exceptions: the Congregational church in Hyde Park, Massachusetts, added eleven feet to each side of its sanctuary to hold forty-two more pews in 1883.[54] But usually a church that had outgrown its sanctuary found the structure inadequate in other ways as well. Auxiliary space was likely to be in short supply, and when matters of modern comfort, taste, and convenience were added to the calculation, it made sense to have a whole new building, either by relocating or by tearing down and rebuilding on the same spot.

Particularly in robust towns too small to make "hiving off" a practical solution to overcrowding, congregations went through the process more than once. The Presbyterian church in Indiana, Pennsylvania, for instance, followed a typical course. It worshipped in a small, plain 1827 structure until 1857 when it put up a larger, classically adorned building with steeple and columns. Between 1904 and 1906 the congregation erected a third building on the same site; this time it was a 1000-seat Victorian Gothic structure with art glass windows and dome, ample classrooms, parlors, kitchen and dining room, and the most modern comforts and conveniences.[55] New sanctuaries such as this one, in whatever town or city they happened to be built, were highly visible witnesses not only to the faith, but to the success and social position of the congregations and their members. As the Indiana elders wrote after examining their partially constructed building, "[We are] building a house to the glory of His Name for years to come, in which Presbyterians may quietly take pride."[56]

Gothic was the Victorian architectural style of choice. For a time, early in the period, the classical style was a powerful rival, as exemplified by churches such as Liverpool's Great George Street Congregational Church (1841) or Glasgow's St. Vincent Street United Presbyterian Church (1857–58), or Philadelphia's Third Presbyterian Church, which was remodeled to accord with classical tastes in 1837.

There was also a brief flirtation around midcentury with an ornate Italianate style as used for Arch Street Presbyterian Church (1853–55) in Philadelphia.[57]

But for a century that produced both Sir Walter Scott's romances and William Morris's dedication to the medieval craft ideal, it was Gothic that was favored. In addition to its aesthetic appeal, architects promised congregations that Gothic construction was less expensive than the competing classical style. Gothic also had the advantage of appearing discretely "religious" in an age when many civic and commercial buildings adopted classical forms; its distinctiveness not only satisfied the Victorian need for separation between the personal and the public, but also drew attention to itself more easily (a trait that was not lost on church boards as they began to adopt commercial advertising methods).[58]

At times the Gothic was rendered with historic authenticity. More often it pulsed with Ruskinian energy and color or, in keeping with the era's eclectic spirit, coalesced with elements of other styles—perhaps a tall, solid corner tower borrowed from the Romanesque or a central dome reminiscent of Renaissance classicism. Where high-church worship was admired—St. Peter's Presbyterian Church (1852–53) in Rochester, Govan parish church (1883–88) in Glasgow, or Redland Park Congregational Church (1860) in Bristol—the Gothic interior was characterized by a long nave and a communion table at the far end of the chancel. More commonly, Reformed architects reshaped the Gothic cross to make a T-shaped, chancel-less sanctuary, with the front wall dominated by pulpit and organ case.[59]

Victorian architects, responding to churchgoers' desires to see and hear more successfully than a long, narrow nave permitted, created an innovative variation on the Gothic theme. The late-Victorian sanctuary drew inspiration from the huge nineteenth-century preaching amphitheaters built for Beecher or Parker, and perhaps from the oval-shaped sanctuaries of certain seventeenth-century Protestant houses of worship such as the Huguenot Temple at Charendon, France. They also shared many features with secular theaters. Rather than being rectangular, the sanctuaries were round, or approximately so. Lyndhurst Road (1883–84) in London was hexagonal; the First Presbyterian Church (1904–6) in Indiana, Pennsylvania, octagonal; King's Weigh House (1891), elliptical; and Barclay Memorial Free Church (1862–64) in Edinburgh, what historian Gavin Stamp aptly characterized as a "squashed pear."[60]

The secret of this roundish, auditorium-style sanctuary was that the pews could be arranged in a semi-circle around a central pulpit, backed by organ and choir. Configured in this way, a large congregation could be accommodated without anyone's being very far from the front. A floor that sloped from rear to front as in a theater and an absence of supporting pillars meant lines of sight were unobstructed; the balconies around the rear each faced forward as well, a distinct advantage over the side-galleries of a rectangular plan. A rounded plan also promised better acoustics than a rectangle since the elimination of a single, flat rear wall opposite the pulpit minimized annoying echoes. Overall, the oval format gave a much greater feeling of intimacy than the hierarchical long-nave plan. Quite beyond comfort and convenience, it was a design that celebrated fellowship and family quite as much as did the congregations that worshipped there.[61]

Architects were also finding ways to incorporate educational, social and administrative space into one coherent, integrated building that obviated the make-shift practice of having a nearby hall. One ingenious and frequently copied scheme was the "Akron Plan," so-called for its origin in 1867–72 at the First Methodist Church in Akron, Ohio. The plan stacked two or more levels of classrooms, each opening onto balconies surrounding a large, high, semi-circular assembly room that could be used for lectures, prayer meetings, Sunday School devotional exercises, or social gatherings. As an added advantage, the straight wall of the assembly room was connected to the sanctuary by moveable partitions that, when open, provided additional seating for worship.[62]

The manner in which space was arranged in the building erected by the First Congregational Church of Cleveland in 1891 provides an interesting study in the way congregations and their architects understood the nature of the church. The building was oriented so that the social and education rooms fronted on the street and the worship space sat to the rear. An early nineteenth-century churchgoer would have considered that an odd reversal of importance, but to many turn-of-the-century Christians it must have seemed an altogether natural metaphor for the way they had approached the church. They began with fellowship and proceeded to worship.[63]

Location was perhaps the most critical decision facing a congregation that planned a new edifice. When committees came to select this parcel of land or that, they studied the alternatives inside their targeted sector of the city with all the diligence of retailers planting a new store. Naturally, they wanted a highly visible, centrally located corner near public transportation—and all at a good price. Parker, it was said, chose Holborn Viaduct as a site for his City Temple because amid London's confusing maze of streets and alleys, it was one place everyone recognized and knew how to find.[64]

Selecting the best available building lot was, of course, important, but the more vexing question for a city congregation was whether to stay in the same general area or to relocate in an entirely new neighborhood farther out. For the Church of Scotland, radical relocation was a moot point; a parish was a geographical as well as an ecclesiastical entity, and there was simply no process of thought that could have imagined the separation of a church from its place. The Free Church, too, thought in the parish model. For the other groups we are considering, the church was a body of believers. If the believers moved to the West End or to the suburbs, it was quite easy to think that their fellowship should naturally go with them.

This was a distinction that could affect the way those outside a congregation interpreted a decision to relocate. In Scotland, where church was associated more with place than with people, a congregation such as Wellington Street United Presbyterian which moved to University Avenue in Glasgow's fashionable West End in 1884 was likely to come in for sharp criticism for abandoning its territory and pursuing middle-class affluence. When Dr. Eadie's members left Cambridge Street in central Glasgow for Lansdowne Avenue in 1863, someone pinned to the door of the imposing Gothic building: "This church is not for the poor and needy/But for the rich and Dr. Eadie./The rich step in and take their seat,/But the poor walk down to Cambridge Street."[65] In Boston, however, the conceptual framework was different; when Old South left the central commercial district and moved out among the elegant residences of the Back Bay, whatever criticism the deacons received came from inside the congregation, merely from a minority of pewholders sentimentally attached to the old building.[66]

Old South's decision to move makes a good starting point for understanding what was a common phenomenon among the free floating congregations that did not think of themselves as a geographical parish. As early as 1852 in Boston, there were indications that many families were moving farther out, and the pastor said he was aware of "young families who already feel the inconvenience of coming to worship from a distance." The solution in the 1850s was to establish a second center for worship in the outlying section and eventually to organize a new congregation there. By the mid-1860s, however, it was clear that everyone was moving, and the streets around the old meetinghouse and chapel were almost entirely commercial. Coming to the meetinghouse on Sunday morning was not so bad, but at night when the stores and businesses had closed, the empty streets were "hardly a suitable place for females to walk." So, in 1866, the congregation acquired a new site for prayer meetings on Freeman Place only "a few steps" from a horse car stop. Some were sorry to leave the old chapel, but they said they recognized that God was not confined to place; the Israelites had, after all, moved their tabernacle along with them as migrated. By the time another decade had passed, the congregation had moved all of its activities to the Back Bay. It built a splendid new church on Boylston Street opposite Copley Plaza; the total cost of the land, church, chapel, classrooms, parlors, and parsonage was just under a half million dollars.[67] Because for Old South the word "church" meant the members, it seemed quite natural that the congregation's new building should be situated where its people now lived.

Stories similar to the migration of Wellington, Lansdowne, and Old South were found in all large cities—for example, in New York, Philadelphia, and Pittsburgh. Fifth Avenue Presbyterian Church moved successively up Manhattan Island, dedicating new buildings in 1835, 1852, and 1875. Philadelphia's Second Church moved westward to the Rittenhouse Square neighborhood, where it put up a Gothic structure in 1868–72. In Pittsburgh, Fourth United Presbyterian Church moved out to Friendship Avenue in the 1890s, citing as its reasons that it would once again be located where its members actually lived and that it was leaving behind a building that lacked the expected modern conveniences.[68]

Not every congregation made the same choice; some chose to stay in the central city. There was certainly plenty of mission work to keep a church busy if it could attract enough contributing members to remain financially solvent. With better transportation, it was at least theoretically possible for middle-class residents to commute to church on Sunday as they did to work on week-days if the church's worship or activities were sufficient magnets. Such a plan was not, however, particularly compatible with the all-week-long, family-oriented fellowship model toward which most churches were moving at the end of the century. But there were congregations that did not live together in a neighborhood. Regent Square stayed where its name indicated and although no more than a third of its members came from the immediate area, it survived with an emphasis on ministry to young adults. Brick Church in New York City made splendid worship and liberal preaching reason enough for people to travel to where it was. City Temple made a decision in 1874 to rebuild in the City of London rather than to move outward; it flourished with the evangelical preaching of Parker and later with the liberal, social gospel emphasis of R. J. Campbell.[69]

But the story of King's Weigh House illustrates how tricky it was to find a successful niche. In 1883, the construction of a subway station forced the congregation from its Fish Hill Street meetinghouse in the City of London. The preference was to stay in the City, but a search could not turn up any property that could be purchased with the compensation they had received from the underground railroad. Thus, the church became a migrant, but an unwilling one. For the next eight years, it met in the Cannon Street Hotel while it sought property, ultimately found what seemed a suitable plot on Duke Street near Grosvenor Square, and completed a new building in 1891. King's Weigh House had now moved into a fashionable neighborhood, but it had not come there because its members already lived there. It chose Mayfair because a lot was available and affordable, and it went in the hope that it could attract members from the district.

When the Duke Street sanctuary was dedicated in 1891, the members trusted that its beauty and comfort would make them competitive.

The members were disappointed. Between 1891 and World War I, they tried, despite their dwindling numbers, to find a new definition of an urban church that would work for them. They had little success and considerable bad luck, but their struggle encapsulated the possibilities that lay before urban congregations at the end of the Victorian era. They tried, through the Thomas Binney Institute which operated from the basement, to become a noontime gathering place for young men and women clerks and office workers; it was a viable mission project, but it did not help generate the income that was needed to pay the bills. For a time, the congregation touted itself as the denomination's voice in the nation's capital, and it imagined Congregational preachers from across the land using its pulpit to address the nation, and the country's leaders gathering to listen. At one point in the early twentieth century, it started a men and boys choir, hoping to develop a reputation for music and liturgy that would draw Mayfair's affluent residents from their Anglican pews. In another effort, it hired a spell-binding Scot named John Hunter to fill its pulpit; fine preaching would be the inducement that would bring in the crowds. Hunter was good, and he did attract attention and people who paid pew rent. Unfortunately for King's Weigh House, he spent most of the congregation's endowment renovating the sanctuary to his high-church taste, and then—with ill grace, one would think—abruptly returned to Scotland. He left behind a beautiful house of worship, but without people it was an empty shell. His successor Russell came and went quickly; he wanted the now-standard fellowship-church model, but soon concluded that a church without a neighborhood base was an improbable likeness of a family. One more effort aimed to make King's Weigh House a center for Social Christianity under the leadership of Campbell and Edward Lewis, but this too came to a premature end when Campbell left for the Anglican Church and Labour politics, and Lewis withdrew from organized religion altogether.[70]

Buildings could embody, but they could not create, clarity of vision. Certainly King's Weigh House's glorious 1891 building could not. Conversely, strong congregations did express their aspirations and their faith in stone, glass, metal, and wood. Ease and elegance were the manifestation of social expectations. Central pulpits and auditorium-style sanctuaries captured the Reformed emphasis on preaching. And, as faith came to be associated more with fellowship than with piety, members renovated and built in ways that embodied the transformed congregation.

# Epilogue
## From Piety to Fellowship

From three until four o'clock each week, the men of Paddock Congregational Church in Huddersfield assembled for a service billed as a "Pleasant Sunday Afternoon." There was a brief gospel talk, but this was hardly what ensured a good attendance either in Huddersfield or anywhere else where a "P.S.A." became popular.[1] Two things drew crowds: fellowship and entertainment. Local P.S.A. chapters were called "brotherhoods" to emphasize the fraternity and goodwill that were expected. One Birmingham meeting had a picnic every July, two socials, cycling and rambling clubs, a P.S.A. magazine, and book prizes for perfect attendance.[2] If companionship was one attraction, a second was entertainment. Every successful P.S.A. offered a mix of songs, instrumental music, and recitations, and each performance was applauded heartily by the audience just as in the theater. A London series promised "bright singing, which is led by a special choir, the organ, and a band of stringed and wind instruments" plus an assortment of "sacred solos."[3] Half men's club, half music hall, the P.S.A. delivered a show that was "Brief, Bright, and Brotherly."[4]

The P.S.A. was merely illustrative of the extent to which social activities and entertainment characterized church life by 1900: piety had given way to fellowship. So thorough was the transformation that Booth, after his survey of church life in turn-of-the-century London, now *defined* "congregationalist" as "a peculiar use of social life in connection with religious work and congregational unity."[5] He might have said the same about "presbyterian."

There was little discussion about whether the new style was cause for celebration or concern. Occasionally someone complained that congregations seemed overrun with activity, much of it only tangentially religious. Booth recorded one parent's lament that "there are too many societies and meetings, so that many of the young people spend all their spare time in attending them, and see nothing of their homes."[6] Those old enough to remember a day when

Calvinists shunned all that was not edifying worried about the loss of seriousness and virtue. "Are we mastering the world by the power of God and making it what God meant it to be," Dale once asked, "or is the world mastering us?"[7] It was a question that could not always have been answered confidently. In the case of one "Cyclists' Gospel Band" that pedalled out from London to rural villages where "the cycles were stacked, the banner raised, and the members stood round and proclaimed the Gospel and sang hymns," it is doubtful that even the cyclists themselves could have distinguished means from ends with certainty.[8]

But success was a powerful argument in favor of the friendly, entertaining church; crowds of smiling faces were difficult to gainsay. Of course, more discretely theological justifications could be given. Christ's admonition to love one another was mentioned, as was the character of the first-century Christian community— "a veritable family circle," according to one New Englander. Others reasoned that church-sponsored social events and entertainments protected believers from "worldly and evil amusements." "The church," it was argued, "ought to provide, within the circle of Christian propriety and consistency, all the recreation its adherents need." Mostly, however, the changes were justified by their popularity— and by the fear of what a failure to be convivial and diverting might portend. If churches had to compete for members not only with each other but also with a dizzying array of commercial enticements for leisure and consumption, then a "chilly" church seemed unlikely to survive in the marketplace.[9]

By the early twentieth century, the transformation of the congregation from a "devotional" to a "social" model (to use Holifield's categories) was complete.[10] Activities and practices that would have startled the churchgoer of 1830 flourished everywhere: springtime excursions and summer picnics, athletic teams and hand-icraft clubs, bazaars and suppers, dances and literary institutes, women's guilds, men's clubs, Christian Endeavor societies for the youth, and organized Sunday School classes ranging from adult Bible studies all the way down to a cradle roll for newborns. Worship now featured organs, choirs, and individual communion cups. Public discipline had been discontinued in favor of confidential pastor counseling, and money was contributed in sealed envelopes. Buildings were comfortable, fashionable, and equipped with up-to-date kitchens, social halls, and recreational space. Hearty participation, not piety, was the standard by which churchgoing was judged.

Considered in retrospect, the transformation occurred with surprisingly minimal disruption or discord at the local level. These were for the most part peaceable kingdoms, assiduously avoiding confrontation. Reformed churchgoers embraced modern consumer culture with no more awareness or forethought than other citizens. Historian William Leach has remarked that "the culture of consumer capitalism may have been among the most nonconsensual public cultures ever created"; its "vision of the good life" dominated daily activity so completely that "other ways of organizing and conceiving life" were simply not considered.[11]

Congregations were no exception; they stepped eagerly into the commercialized world of fashion and comfort, entertainment and leisure. Wanamaker's Sunday School Christmas extravaganzas at Bethany Church were of one piece with the quasi-religious, quasi-commercial holiday displays at his Philadelphia department store.[12] One stereotype that needs to be laid aside is that of the stiff-backed church leader doggedly holding back change. Of course there were such people, but most avidly adopted the fruits of the modern age, especially if there was a promise of greater efficiency and convenience.

Congregations were confident, perhaps overly so. There were occasional admissions of discouragement or dismay at the social and cultural changes swirling around them, but these lapses were rare. The sentiments of the King's Weigh House deacons were more usual. "Thus while we look back with thankfulness to the progress already made," they reflected, "we also look forward with equal confidence to the future."[13]

These deacons and others like them sought to reinvent the congregation, to refashion it for a new century. Taken together, congregations experimented with numerous—and often conflicting—models: the church as efficient business operation, as refuge for the weary, as agent of empowerment for the poor, as prophetic pulpit, as social center, as source of entertainment and recreation, as family, as circle of friends, as place of worship and prayer, as spiritual home. One conclusion of this study is that nineteenth-century congregations had a more complex, rich, and resilient history than we have sometimes supposed.

Yet, I believe it is possible to admire the resilience and creativity of Victorian congregations without suggesting that each of their strategies came free of short term difficulties and was equally capable or worthy of longevity. For instance, their very considerable efforts to deal with urban poverty were never able to match the city's need. Nor perhaps could they have been; their greater legacy may be that they show us the limits of what purely voluntary activity—whether religious or secular—can achieve in a complex industrial society.

City missions are not the only aspects of the late Victorian church that seem quaint or insufficient today. The turn-of-the-century social congregation was unimaginable apart from its heavy reliance on female volunteers. Those arrangements were accepted as welcome opportunities by women at the time, but they would fit badly with current gender roles. Women are not the only ones for whom contemporary culture holds out other demands and other attractions. For today's overscheduled middle-class family, the requirements that the social congregation made upon its members' time must seem exhausting if not impossible. Ironically, the social congregation is still a powerful enough model to impose its measure of guilt on present-day ministers and congregations who cannot match the past frenzy of organized activity without becoming weary.

In the end, it is the ironies that abound. Proponents presumed that frequent opportunities for fellowship would naturally make all comers feel welcome: the social church was the inclusive church. Yet after Booth finished observing the new social congregations of London at the end of the 1890s, he remarked that they were "a very efficient religious system, applicable where there are no insurmountable differences in class or education."[14] In practice, the more a congregation relied on sociability and taste to bind members together, the more it set inevitable limits to its fellowship.

As cities grew larger and more impersonal, congregations pursued community ever more assiduously. Yet it might be argued that the very meaning of community and fellowship—mediated as they now were by market relationships—had been inadvertently transformed along the way. When camaraderie was so brazenly orchestrated and marketed, friendship risked becoming one more commodity offered for consumption. Handiwork and sweets were not the only goods advertised and sold at church bazaars; so too was the pleasure of good company.

Booth again, in another passage, reported—to his surprise, one suspects—that by the end of the century he found "no trace of sourness or severity . . . ; pleasure is not tabooed."[15] It would be hard not to concur that this was a welcome advance over the austere religion of 1830. The freedom to enjoy the arts and nature, and to heighten worship with richer colors and more magnificent sounds can only seem—to this writer at least—an improvement. Choral or instrumental music was no more intrinsically 'performance' than a pastoral prayer or sermon. Yet when it came to be applauded and cheered on a pleasant Sunday afternoon, it very likely was so.

Congregations could not ignore the emerging entertainment industry, and for a time many church leaders believed they could complete on an equal footing. But the rise of national markets and mass media with vast budgets and commercialized glamour made such a hope shortlived for small and even for most large congregations. As a final irony, contemporary televised entertainment (including televised religion) is capable of being consumed individualistically; it can separate rather than unite, and thus undermine the very sense of fellowship that the social congregation prized.

None of this mandates an unduly harsh judgment on leaders and members of late Victorian congregations. They were forced to navigate uncommonly turbulent social and cultural waters, and they were no more blind than most in their generation as they sailed forth. Historians and other scholars are just now beginning to understand the blandishments of modern consumer culture, and here we have seen only religion's very earliest engagement with it. However instructive or troubling these first encounters are, a great deal more research and thought is needed to understand the routes that were taken by congregations during the rest of the twentieth century.

# Notes

## Preface

1. Elizabeth Fox-Genovese, "Female Experience in American Religion," *Religion and American Culture* 5 (winter 1995): 17.

2. Martin E. Marty, *A Nation of Behavers* (Chicago: University of Chicago Press, 1976).

3. For examples of the recent interest in congregational studies, see James P. Wind and James W. Lewis, eds., *American Congregations*, 2 vols. (Chicago: University of Chicago Press, 1994); Carl Dudley, ed., *Building Effective Ministry: Theory and Practice in the Local Church* (San Francisco: Harper and Row, 1983); David Roozen, William McKinney, and Jackson Carroll, *Varieties of Religious Presence: Mission in Public Life* (New York: Pilgrim Press, 1984); James F. Hopewell, *Congregation: Stories and Structures* (Philadelphia: Fortress, 1987); James P. Wind, *Places of Worship: Exploring Their History* (Nashville: American Association for State and Local History, 1990); Carl Dudley, Jackson Carroll, and James P. Wind, eds., *Carriers of Faith: Lessons of Congregational Studies* (Louisville: Westminster/John Knox Press, 1991); and Barbara Wheeler and Edward Farley, eds., *Shifting Boundaries: Contextual Approaches to the Structure of Theological Education* (Louisville: Westminster/John Knox Press, 1991). On the history of the field, see Barbara Wheeler, "Uncharted Territory: Congregational Identity and Mainline Protestantism," in Milton J. Coalter, John M. Mulder, and Louis B. Weeks, eds., *The Presbyterian Predicament: Six Perspectives* (Louisville: Westminster/John Knox Press, 1990), 67–89; James P. Wind and James W. Lewis, "Introduction," in Wind and Lewis, eds., *American Congregations*, 2:1–20; Allison Stokes and David A. Roozen, "The Unfolding Story of Congregational Studies," in Dudley, Carroll, and Wind, eds., *Carriers of Faith*, 183–92; and Charles D. Cashdollar, "The Recent Turn to Congregational Studies Among Church Historians: A Review Essay," *Journal of Presbyterian History* 77 (summer 1999): 107–18.

4. Wheeler, "Uncharted Territory," in Coalter, Mulder, and Weeks, eds., *Presbyterian Predicament*, 67.

5. E. Brooks Holifield, "Toward a History of American Congregations," in Wind and Lewis, eds., *American Congregations*, 2:23–53. Holifield proposes four stages in the development of congregations: "comprehensive congregations, 1607–1789," "devotional congregations, 1789–1870," "social congregations, 1870–1950," and "participatory congregations, 1950–1990."

6. The body of literature that has grown up around the 1851 census is very large and more complicated than can be summarized here. Readers interested in the subject are referred to Hugh McLeod, *Religion and Society in England, 1850–1914* (New York: St. Martin's Press, 1996), and especially to Robin Gill, *The Myth of the Empty Church* (London: SPCK, 1993), which challenges the more traditional emphasis on secularization as a cause of the decline in churchgoing. Gill finds that free church attendance in Britain continued to climb until the 1880s and 1890s and then began a steady decline. Denominational competition and Victorian optimism led to excess building, and Gill sees the consequent overcapacity as a significant structural factor in the demise; empty churches led to the accumulation of debt, shared clergy, lessened vitality, and the perception that religion was outdated. Some recent historical work has cast a more positive light on the Victorian churches' performance. For instance, D. W. Bebbington, in *Evangelicalism in Modern Britain: A History from the 1730s to the 1980s* (London: Unwin Hyman, 1989), notes rightly that participation was lower in both the eighteenth and twentieth centuries; therefore, he concludes, "the churches had managed to

recruit more effectively despite the immense growth in population of the early nineteenth century, despite industrialisation and urbanisation" (108). Jeffrey Cox, in his extremely perceptive *The English Churches in a Secular Society: Lambeth, 1870–1930*, makes the same point when he notes that "compared to the last third of the twentieth century, the mid-Victorian period appears to swarm with religious activity" (4).

7. Don S. Browning, "Congregational Studies as Practical Theology," in Wind and Lewis, eds., *American Congregations*, 2:192.

## *Chapter 1*

1. Regent Square Pres. Ch., London, "Testimony of Some Who Tried It [1915]," *Regent Square Misc. Papers*, United Reformed Ch. Hist. Soc., London.

2. Quoted by Charlotte Erickson, *Invisible Immigrants: The Adaptation of English and Scottish Immigrants in Nineteenth-Century America* (Ithaca, N.Y.: Cornell University Press, 1972), 258.

3. For standard background, see R. Tudur Jones, *Congregationalism in England, 1662–1962* (London: Independent Press, 1962); various aspects are also developed in Michael Watts, *The Dissenters*, vol. 2, *The Expansion of Evangelical Nonconformity* (Oxford: Clarendon Press, 1995); John W. Grant, *Free Churchmanship in England, 1870–1940* (London: Independent Press, 1955); and Clyde Binfield, *So Down to Prayers: Studies in English Nonconformity, 1780–1920* (Totowa, N.J.: Rowman and Littlefield, 1977). The general English context is provided by Owen Chadwick, *The Victorian Church*, 2 vols. (London: Adam and Charles Black, 1971–1972).

4. For standard background, see John Von Rohr, *The Shaping of American Congregationalism, 1620–1957* (Cleveland: Pilgrim Press, 1992).

5. For standard background on Scotland's denominations, see two volumes by Andrew L. Drummond and James Bulloch, *The Church in Victorian Scotland* and *The Church in Late Victorian Scotland, 1874–1900* (Edinburgh: St. Andrew Press, 1975, 1978); and J. H. S. Burleigh, *A Church History of Scotland* (London: Oxford University Press, 1960).

6. For standard background, see A. H. Drysdale, *The English Presbyterians: A Historical Handbook of their Rise, Decline, and Revival* (London: Publishing Office of the Presbyterian Church of England, 1891); see also Chadwick, *Victorian Church*, 1:398–99.

7. For standard background, see James H. Smylie, *A Brief History of the Presbyterians* (Louisville: Geneva Press, 1996); Randall Balmer and John R. Fitzmier, *The Presbyterians* (Westport, Conn.: Greenwood Press, 1993); and Lefferts A. Loetscher, *A Brief History of the Presbyterians*, 4th ed. (Philadelphia: Westminster Press, 1983).

8. A 1782 merger had united most, but not all, Reformed and Associate Presbyterians into the Associate-Reformed Presbyterian Church; the 1858 merger united the Associate-Reformed group with the majority of the Associate Presbyterians who had remained outside the 1782 merger. For standard background, see Wallace N. Jamison, *The United Presbyterian Story: A Centennial Study, 1858–1958* (Pittsburgh: Geneva Press, 1958). A merger in 1958 joined these United Presbyterians with the main Presbyterian body.

9. Frank Thistlethwaite, *The Anglo-American Connection in the Early Nineteenth Century* (Philadelphia: University of Pennsylvania Press, 1959); David D. Hall, "The Victorian Connection," in Daniel Walker Howe, ed., *Victorian America* (Philadelphia: University of Pennsylvania Press, 1976), 81ff. Three recent titles applying the adjective "Victorian" to American culture are Thomas J. Schlereth, *Victorian America: Transformations of Everyday Life, 1876–1915* (New York: Harper, 1991); Anne C. Rose, *Victorian America and the Civil War* (New York: Cambridge University Press, 1992); and Louise L. Stevenson, *The Victorian Homefront: American Thought and Culture, 1860–1880* (New York: Twayne, 1991).

10. Smiley, *Brief History of the Presbyterians*, 92, 136–37; Von Rohr, *Shaping of American Congregationalism*, 405–6; Jones, *Congregationalism in England*, 328–29; Philip D. Jordan, "Cooperation Without Incorporation: America and the Presbyterian Alliance, 1870–1880," *Journal of Presbyterian History* 55 (spring 1977): 13–35. Though it was still in the future so far as our study extends, these two bodies would unite

in 1970 to form the "World Alliance of Reformed Churches (Presbyterian and Congregational)," thereby testifying to the common Reformed heritage that transcended variations in polity.

11. See Thistlethwaite, *Anglo-American Connection,* esp. 76–102, and Betty Fladeland, *Men and Brothers: Anglo-American Antislavery Cooperation* (Urbana: University of Illinois Press, 1972).

12. St. George's Free Church, Edinburgh, *Deacons' Court Minutes,* 9 March 1857, 7 November 1859; see also W. Harrison Daniel, "English Presbyterians, Slavery, and the American Crisis of 1860," *Journal of Presbyterian History* 58 (spring 1980): 50–63.

13. Richard Carwardine, *Transatlantic Revivalism: Popular Evangelicalism in Britain and America, 1790–1865* (Westport, Conn.: Greenwood Press, 1978).

14. Central Pres. Ch., Rochester, *Session Minutes,* 6 September 1899. Morgan was minister of New Court Congregational Chapel in north London, where he preached regularly to an "overflow crowd." Charles Booth, *Life and Labour of the People in London. Third Series: Religious Influences,* 7 vols. (1902–4; reprint, New York: AMS Press, 1970), 1:231.

15. Paul T. Phillips, *A Kingdom on Earth: Anglo-American Social Christianity, 1880–1940* (University Park: The Pennsylvania State University Press, 1996).

16. Ebenezer Minshall, *Fifty Years Reminiscences of a Free Church Musician* (London: James Clarke, 1910), 50, 53.

17. *Carr's Lane Church, Birmingham: Bicentenary Celebration, 1748–1948,* 4.

18. St. George's Free Ch., Edinburgh, *Session Minutes,* 13 May 1906. See also Robert T. Handy, *A History of Union Theological Seminary in New York* (New York: Columbia University Press, 1987).

19. Carr's Lane Cong. Ch., Birmingham, *Manual 1835,* 55–58.

20. Huron Cong. Ch., Huron, SD, *Manual 1908.*

21. Quoted in Charles Booth, *Life and Labour of the People in London,* 7:113.

22. This transformation, characterized here as a change in emphasis from piety to fellowship, is close to what E. Brooks Holifield means by "devotional congregations, 1789–1870" and "social congregations, 1870–1950"; there will be more to say about these categories in the Epilogue. E. Brooks Holifield, "Toward a History of American Congregations," in Wind and Lewis, eds., *American Congregations,* 2:23–53.

## *Chapter 2*

1. Second Pres. Ch., Philadelphia, *Session Minutes,* 8 April 1850.

2. St. George's Free Ch., Edinburgh, *Session Minutes,* 10 October 1870, 7 November 1870, 6 November 1876, 21 December 1881, 7 May 1883, 2 July 1883, 2 April 1888; Central Pres. Ch., Rochester, NY, *Session Minutes,* 22 July, 1890, 15 February 1891, 4 August 1893, 1 September 1903; Free College Ch., Glasgow, *Annual Report, 1878,* 17; Second Pres. Ch., Philadelphia, *Session Minutes,* 22 June 1881, 25 January 1888, 27 November 1889, 28 January 1891; Withington Cong. Ch., Manchester, *Manual 1890,* 58–59.

3. Although the small Cumberland Presbyterian Church permitted the ordination of women as elders in 1892, the main American Presbyterian body did not do so until 1930, and the American United Presbyterians not until their merger with the Presbyterians in 1958. Lois A. Boyd and R. Douglas Brackenridge, *Presbyterian Women in America: Two Centuries of a Quest for Status* (Westport, Conn.: Greenwood Press, 1983), 113–14, 138, 152–53. Although none of the Congregational churches examined in this study had female deacons, there was usually nothing in the written by-laws to prevent this. Women did not gain admission to the eldership in Scotland until 1966. Nigel Cameron, ed., *Dictionary of Scottish Church History and Theology* (Edinburgh: T. and T. Clark; Downers Grove, Ill.: Intervarsity Press, 1993), 886–87. In 1921, the Presbyterian Church of England authorized women elders and deacons. James Barr, *The United Free Church of Scotland* (London: Allenson, 1934), 260–61.

4. Occasionally a congregation referred to this as the Examining Committee because of its responsibility for meeting with and exploring the Christian experience of prospective church members. Old South Congregational Church, Boston, *Church Records,* 25 January 1858, 14 January 1861. Second Congregational

Church, Hartford, had a "Standing Committee" in 1838 that included the pastor, deacons and three annually chosen members; their responsibilities included applications for membership, disciplinary cases, and "whatever business may be referred to them by the church." *Confession of Faith and Covenant 1838*, 23. In 1897 the "Prudential Committee" of First Congregational Church, Hartford, included the pastor, clerk, treasurer, Sabbath School superintendent, the six deacons, and six additional members in three-year terms. *Manual 1897*, 59–64.

    5. As an example of Scottish practice, St. George's Free Church in Edinburgh, with about 1,200 members in 1901, had forty-eight active elders, a ratio of one elder for every 25 members; Regent Square Presbyterian Church in London, with a membership of 750 in 1911, counted twenty-eight elders, or one for every 27 members. In contrast, American Presbyterians selected proportionally fewer elders. Just before the turn of the century, the 815-member Brick Presbyterian Church in New York City had only twelve elders (one to 68 members), and by 1912 the large, active First Presbyterian Church in Pittsburgh, with 1,540 members, operated with twenty-four elders on its session (one to 64 members).

    As an example of Congregational practice, in 1899 Lozells Congregational Church in Birmingham had seven deacons for 395 members, or one for every 56 members; in Bristol in 1890, Redland Park Congregational Church had ten deacons for 354 members, or one for every 35. In the United States, even large city churches managed with very few deacons. The Congregational Church in Hyde Park, Massachusetts, in 1895 had only six deacons for 688 members (one to 115); First Congregational Church in Chicago named eight deacons to care for its 799 members in 1884 (one to 100), and the 579-member First Congregational Church in Hartford was served in 1888 by six deacons (one to 97). There were exceptions to these general patterns. For instance, some American churches implemented ambitious visitation plans and required more church officers (see Chap. 7); new church developments often established large boards in anticipation of growth; or, a board could appear larger than it functionally was if some of its members were slowed by age; the method of communion distribution, even the number of aisles in the sanctuary, could suggest a necessary number of servers. St. George's Free Church, Edinburgh, *Deacons' Court Minutes*, 1 June 1903; Regent Square Pres. Ch., London, *Hand Book 1911*, 10; Brick Pres. Ch., New York City, *Annual Report 1899*, 13; First Pres. Ch., Pittsburgh, *Manual 1912*, 7; Lozells Cong. Ch., Birmingham, *Manual 1899*, 3; Redland Park Cong. Ch., Bristol, *Manual 1890*, 6; Cong. Ch., Hyde Park, MA, *Manual 1895*, 17; First Cong. Ch., Chicago, *Manual 1884*, 3; First Cong. Ch., Hartford, *Manual 1888*, 3.

    6. Old South Cong. Ch., Boston, *Church Records*, 8 January 1866.

    7. Ibid., 29 January 1866.

    8. I found no instance where an objection was raised, which suggests only that sessions selected men whom they knew well and considered certain to pass scrutiny; it is also probable that a man who knew himself vulnerable would have found some excuse to decline the position prior to the issuing of an edict.

    9. Greenside Parish, Edinburgh, *Session Minutes*: compare the appointment of new elders recorded 2 December 1872 and 3 February 1873 with the election described 8 March 1875 and 12 April 1875. Also, Greyfriars Parish, Edinburgh, *Session Minutes*, 27 January 1879; St. George's Parish, Edinburgh, *Session Minutes*, 1 January 1881.

    10. St. George's Free Ch., Edinburgh, *Session Minutes*, 3 November 1843, 16 April 1913.

    11. King's Weigh House Cong. Ch., London, *Church Minutes*, 21 April 1846.

    12. Ibid., 18 December 1860.

    13. Ibid., May 1860; Cowcaddens Free Ch., Glasgow, *Session Minutes*, 21 October 1867, 26 November 1873; Old South Cong. Ch., Boston, *Church Records*, 8 March 1875.

    14. See the report of such a discussion in Old South Congregational Church, Boston, *Church Records*, 8 March 1875. The congregation, although admitting that the system worked well elsewhere did not think it right for Old South; instead, for a brief time, the congregation experimented with a recall system, whereby members could, with cause, petition the Church Committee for a vote on any incumbent deacon. At the same time the congregation decided to retire deacons at age seventy to "emeritus" status, allowing them to keep the title and assist in serving communion, but no longer to participate in the regular business of the board. The experiment was repealed, however, after several months (10 January 1876).

15. J. Aspinwall Hodge, *What is Presbyterian Law?* (Philadelphia: Presbyterian Board of Publication, 1882), 294–96. The question had been under debate within the church since 1849 when it had been placed before the New School General Assembly, and 1857 when the Old School Assembly had debated it. Two impatient congregations instituted the practice without denominational authorization and found themselves subject to judicial proceedings in 1869 and 1872.

16. Central Pres. Ch., Rochester, *Session Minutes*, 3 April 1875, 12 April 1875.

17. Old South Cong. Ch., Boston, *Church Records*, 25 January 1858; First Cong. Ch., Hartford, *Confession of Faith and Covenant 1838*, 23; Second Cong. Ch., Hartford, *Manual 1897*, 59–64; Carr's Lane Cong. Ch., Birmingham, *Manual 1871*, 63.

18. Second Pres. Ch., Philadelphia, *Session Minutes*, 4 February 1885; King's Weigh House Cong. Ch., London, *Church Minutes*, 23 June 1846; St. George's Free Ch., Edinburgh, *Session Minutes*, 1 October 1843; Greenside Parish, Edinburgh, *Session Minutes*, 23 March 1873.

19. St. George's Parish, Edinburgh, *Session Minutes*, 17 January 1868; [James Thin], *Memorials of Bristo United Presbyterian Church* (Edinburgh: Morrison and Gibbs, 1888), 202–3.

20. J. W. D. Carruthers, ed. *The Ter-Jubilee Book of the North Church of Perth, 1747–1897* (Perth: George Miller, 1898), 113–16.

21. This characterization of elders and deacons is based on descriptions in St. George's Free Ch., Edinburgh, *Session Minutes*, 10 October 1870, 7 November 1870, 6 November 1876, 21 December 1881, 7 May 1883, 2 July 1883, 2 April 1888; Central Pres. Ch., Rochester, *Session Minutes*, 22 July, 1890, 15 February 1891, 4 August 1893, 1 September 1903; Free College Ch., Glasgow, *Annual Report 1878*, 17; Second Pres. Ch., Philadelphia, *Session Minutes*, 22 June 1881, 25 January 1888, 27 November 1889, 28 January 1891; Withington Cong. Ch., Manchester, *Manual 1890*, 58–59.

22. The trustees were males, but Boylston Cong. Ch., Boston, had a female treasurer, Miss Mary Reed, from its temporary organization as a preaching station in 1869 until her death in 1878; using an adjective usually reserved for male business leaders, the congregation remembered her as "one of its most efficient laborers." *Manual 1879*, 28. Religious bodies could avail themselves of incorporation in all of the states except Virginia and West Virginia, which allowed church property to be held by trustees nominated by the churches and appointed by the courts. William Henry Roberts, *Manual for Ruling Elders and Church Sessions* (Philadelphia: Presbyterian Board of Publication, 1897), 374. The speed with which local congregations availed themselves of the added protection of incorporation depended on the state laws for religious bodies and on the aggressiveness and sophistication of the local officers. Philadelphia's First Presbyterian Church, founded in 1698, had been incorporated since 1796 but it was unusual; across the state, Fourth United Presbyterian Church in Pittsburgh, founded in 1849, did not incorporate until 1865. Rochester's Central Presbyterian Church was founded in 1836 and incorporated in 1858. Congregationalists followed a similar pattern: Cleveland's First Congregational Church was incorporated within a year of its organization in 1834, and Plymouth Congregational Church in Rochester, New York, was also prompt in 1853–54; however, Union Park Congregational Church in Chicago was founded in 1860 and not incorporated until 1878; First Congregational Church in Rochester, Massachusetts, which traced its history back to 1683, did not incorporate until 1902. First Cong. Ch., Rochester, MA, *Manual 1909*, 4–9; First Cong. Ch., Cleveland, *Manual 1881*, 22; Fourth U.P. Ch., Pittsburgh, *Trustees' Minutes*, 2 January 1865; Central Pres. Ch., Rochester, NY, *Trustees' Minutes*, 1:5; Union Park Cong. Ch., Chicago, *Manual 1887*, 32.

23. See, for instance, Old South Cong. Ch., Boston, *Standing Committee Records*, 4 April 1843.

24. Von Rohr, *Shaping of American Congregationalism*, 155, 292–93; Henry Martyn Dexter, *A Hand-Book of Congregationalism* (Boston: Congregational Publishing Society, 1880), 111.

25. Roberts, *Manual for Ruling Elders and Church Sessions*, 378.

26. Ibid., 382.

27. Drummond and Bulloch, *Church in Victorian Scotland*, 82, 98–99.

28. For an example of a *Quoad Sacra* church constitution, see Park Parish, Glasgow, *Session Minutes*, 20 July 1864. Also, Drummond and Bulloch, *Church in Victorian Scotland*, 115, 120.

29. Greenside Parish, Edinburgh, *Session Minutes*, 4 November 1872. For other examples, see 6 May

1879 and 17 April 1879; St. George's Parish, Edinburgh, *Session Minutes*, 8 July 1896; Greyfriars Parish, Edinburgh, *Session Minutes*, 22 December 1839, 13 February 1873.

30. James Reid, *The Book of Greyfriars' Church Dumfries: A Bicentenary Sketch, 1727–1927* (Dumfries: Standard Press, 1927), 41. Reid calculates that the town income exceeded expenditures except when undertaking the construction of a new building.

31. For examples of the shift of responsibility for repairs to the kirk session, see Greenside Parish, Edinburgh, *Session Minutes*, 17 April 1879; St. George's Parish, Edinburgh, *Session Minutes*, 1 March 1880; Greyfriars Parish, Edinburgh, *Session Minutes*, 13 February 1873, 16 December 1892, 5 April 1896. By 1896, Greyfriars had reluctantly conceded that it was going to have to pay the cost of collecting seat rents, "all ordinary repairs," and fire insurance.

32. Second Pres. Ch., Philadelphia, *Session Minutes*, 25 March 1837, 3 April 1850; *American Presbyterian*, 20 May 1869.

33. Old South Cong. Ch., Boston, *Church Records*, 16 November 1853.

34. See, for example, First Cong. Ch. Chicago, *Manual 1859*, 34; or Cong. Ch., Binghamton, NY, *Manual 1875*, 17.

35. See St. George's Free Ch., Edinburgh, *Deacons' Court Minutes*, vol. 6; Cowcaddens Free Ch., Glasgow, *Congregational Minute Book*, 3 February 1868.

36. Quoted by Von Rohr, *Shaping of American Congregationalism*, 293.

37. The fifty-eight-member First Congregational Church in Rochester, NH, is one example. Its Standing Committee of three deacons, three at-large members, and the pastor attended to finances, property, membership, and discipline, but even here the three at-large members formed a subcommittee with special responsibility for temporal affairs. *Manual 1909*, 20.

38. Antoinette Brown was ordained pastor of the First Congregational Church of Butler and Savannah, New York, in 1853, but soon left for social work, marriage, and a subsequent career as a Unitarian minister. By 1919, sixty-eight of 5,695 American Congregationalist ministers were women, including at least eighteen serving as sole pastors, and fourteen in joint pastorates. Von Rohr, *Shaping of American Congregationalism*, 198, 343. The Presbyterian Church, USA, first ordained female ministers in 1956, and ordination for United Presbyterian women became possible when the denomination merged with the Presbyterians two years later; Presbyterians in the American South, still separated from their northern cousins until 1983, first permitted the ordination of women in 1963. Boyd and Brackenridge, *Presbyterian Women in America*, 152–53; Loetscher, *Brief History of Presbyterians*, 117. Women were eligible for ordination in the Church of Scotland in 1968. Cameron, ed., *Dictionary of Scottish Church History and Theology*, 886–87. English Presbyterians declared in 1921 that there was "no barrier in principle" to the ordination of women, but were not quick to act upon their resolve. Barr, *United Free Church of Scotland*, 260–61. The English Congregational Union said in 1892 that women meeting the educational requirements for ministry might be ordained, and the first such ordination took place in 1917. Elaine Kaye, "A Turning-Point in the Ministry of Women: The Ordination of the First Woman to the Christian Ministry in England in September 1917," in W. J. Sheils and Diana Wood, eds., *Women in the Church* (Oxford: Basil Blackwell, 1990), 507–9.

39. See Burleigh, *Church History of Scotland*, 101, 277. In *Quoad Sacra* churches, the patronage rights were lodged in all male heads of family over age twenty-one who were both communicants and seatholders. See Park Parish, Glasgow, *Session Minutes*, 20 July 1864.

40. Drummond and Bulloch, *Church in Victorian Scotland*, 329, 337. Male communicants of Edinburgh parishes apparently gained the right to choose a minister a few years earlier. When the Greenside pulpit became vacant in 1871, elders scurried to verify the communion roll so that the "new" law on city ministers could be implemented. As the law was interpreted here, any parishioner who had communed at least once during the preceding three years was considered to be on the list of eligible voters; very recent enrollees with less than a year in the parish were excluded. See Greenside Parish, Edinburgh, *Session Minutes*, 13 February, 6 March, 3 April, 20 June, 2 October 1871.

41. Roberts, *Manual for Ruling Elders and Church Sessions*, 321, 333–35. Presbyterian law gave

congregations the option of including adult financial supporters, but recommended limiting the vote to communicant members.

42. For examples, see Plymouth Cong. Ch., Rochester, *Manual 1856,* 14; First Cong. Ch., Chicago, *Manual 1859,* 33. Both by-laws required a simple majority at each meeting, but the Chicago by-laws stipulated there also had to be a majority of church members present at the society meeting. George Punchard, *A View of Congregationalism* (Salem, Mass.: John Jewett, 1840), 120.

43. Old South Cong. Ch., Boston, *Church Records,* 29 December 1856, 9 January 1882; Second Pres. Ch. Philadelphia, *Session Minutes,* 28 September 1895, 1 January 1911; Central Pres. Ch., Rochester, *Session Minutes,* 1 February 1914; also Canning Street Pres. Ch., Liverpool, *Jubilee Memorial, 1846–1896,* 15; St. George's Free Ch., Edinburgh, *Session Minutes,* 12 November 1866.

44. Second Pres. Ch., Philadelphia, *Session Minutes,* 13 February 1833, 4 April 1833.

45. Old South Cong. Ch., Boston, *Church Records,* 7 January 1834. Stearns served only two or three weeks before resigning due to poor health; he died in 1837 at age thirty-six. Emerson Davis, *Biographical Sketches of the Congregational Pastors of New England,* 1:153 (five-volume typescript of pre-1869 manuscript, Congregational Library, Boston, 1930).

46. Old South Cong. Ch., Boston, *Church Records,* 29 December 1856, 6 January 1857. For later examples of "nearly unanimous" votes, see the 228–9 results for the Rev. Mr. Pagan at St. George's Parish, Edinburgh (*Session Minutes,* 27 July 1909); or the 159–9 decision for the Rev. Theodore Hopkins at Central Presbyterian Church, Rochester (*Session Minutes,* 5 September 1881); the same congregation elected the Rev. Henry Stebbins by a unanimous vote of 280 members in 1887 (25 December 1887); the Rev. Archibald Scott was elected "without a dissentient voice" to the pulpit of Greenside Parish, Edinburgh, in 1871 (*Session Minutes,* 2 October 1871). The case of the Rev. Roger S. Kirkpatrick's narrow margin, 632–532, at Govan Parish Church, Glasgow, was exceptional; there was apparently widespread opinion that he was not an appropriate choice, possibly because his younger brother James was currently serving the parish as the minister of St. Bride's, one of its mission chapels; yet in this instance the call went ahead despite the division. (*Session Minutes,* 17 December 1898, 6 July 1899).

47. Old South Cong. Ch., Boston, *Church Records,* 2 February 1857; King's Weigh House Cong. Ch., London, *Church Meeting Minutes,* 20 January 1870, 17 March 1870, 26 September 1879; St. George's Free Ch., Edinburgh, *Session Minutes,* 4 February 1867, 24 January 1870; Stephen M. Griswold, *Sixty Years with Plymouth Church* (New York: Revell, 1907), 109–10.

48. St. George's Free Ch., Edinburgh, *Session Minutes,* 13 May 1892, 15 November 1895; Old South Cong. Ch., Boston, *Church Records,* 18 December 1882, 12 January 1883, 26 January 1883, 11 January 1884, 7 March 1884.

49. The by-laws of Carr's Lane Cong. Ch., Birmingham, specified with unusual frankness that in church meetings, "it is also proper, that nothing be introduced by any member without previous conference with the Pastor." *Manual 1835,* 47.

50. Alan C. Brown, *The Maxwell Story: Maxwell Parish Church, 1865–1965* (Glasgow, 1965), 15; Kaye, *King's Weigh House,* 97; E. D. Fingland, *St. John's Presbyterian Church, Kensington* (London, 1912), 16.

51. Griswold, *Sixty Years with Plymouth Church,* 129; Plymouth Cong. Ch., Brooklyn, *Manual 1874,* 15.

52. For examples of elders or deacons leading mid-week prayer meeting, see Second Pres. Ch., Philadelphia, *Session Minutes,* 8 June 1854, 30 December 1869; Old South Cong. Ch., Boston, *Church Records,* 9 January 1860; Plymouth Cong. Ch., Brooklyn, *Manual 1850,* 17; Regent Square Pres. Ch., London, *Annual Report 1847,* 39; St. George's Free Ch., Edinburgh, *Deacons' Court Minutes,* 15 November 1847; St. George's Free Ch., Edinburgh, *Session Minutes,* 23 October 1893, 18 June 1906; *Jubilee Memorial of Saint Andrew's Parish and Congregation, Greenock* (Greenock: MacKelvie, 1889), 51; The *Session Minutes* of Fourth United Presbyterian Church, Pittsburgh, recorded on 14 July 1907, "The pastor appointed [Elders] Mr. Thomas Lees and D. M. Corbett to attend the spiritual wants of the church during his absence while on his vacation." An unsigned letter in the Lyndhurst Road Congregational Church newsletter for April 1912, was glad to see lay preaching at outdoor mission services and commented, "We have very much over-

professionalised the office of preacher in our denomination." Handling of the interim between pastors varied depending on local circumstances. Congregations with "colleague pastors" (co-pastors) continued under the leadership of the remaining pastor, shifting responsibilities internally to manage as best they could while searching for a replacement. To a lesser extent, the presence of an assistant pastor provided continuity and stability. Pulpits left completely empty were supplied by a rotation of visiting preachers, by a regularly assigned "stated supply," or by an acting or interim pastor, often a locally available academic or retiree. The more irregular the arrangement, the greater the burden that fell on the lay officers for the ongoing administration of the congregation. For examples of alternate arrangements see *Historical Sketch of Wellington United Presbyterian Congregation, Glasgow, 1792–1892* (Glasgow: Maclure, 1893), 26–27 [colleague pastor]; Brick Pres. Ch., New York, *Annual Report 1910*, 1, 3 [interim]; Second Pres. Ch., Philadelphia, *Session Minutes*, 17 September 1979 [weekly supplies plus an interim for pastoral care]; ibid., 6 May 1908 [assistant]; Park Parish, Glasgow, *Session Minutes*, 27 February 1910 [interim pastor]; Central Pres. Ch., Rochester, *Session Minutes*, 8 March 1888 ["acting pastor"].

53. See Boyd and Brackenridge, *Presbyterian Women in America*, 14.

54. The 1892 action allowed sessions to appoint women to serve, but unlike men, they were not ordained; ordination did not accompany the work until 1923; American United Presbyterians opened the office fully to women in 1906. Boyd and Brackenridge, *Presbyterian Women in America*, 109–12.

55. Drummond and Bulloch, *Church in Late Victorian Scotland*, 169.

56. *Manual 1867*, 23–24. The copy now in the Congregational Library, Boston, was owned by the congregation's clerk, and his inked emendations indicate that the first three deaconesses were appointed on 11 December 1868.

57. *Manual 1879*, 22–23. See also Von Rohr, *Shaping of American Congregationalism*, 342–43.

58. This was the case at Plymouth Church, Brooklyn, where deaconesses joined the Board of Deacons in 1869 with the authority to "assist in discharging all the duties of Deacons, except serving at the Communion season," but five years later, there were still no women on the Music, Church Work, or Sabbath School Committees. Inked amendment to clerk's copy of *Manual 1867*, 23, now in Congregational Library, Boston; *Manual 1874*, 48–49. Deaconesses were members of the Church Committee in Boylston Cong. Ch., Boston, but not the Prudential [financial] Committee. *Manual 1879*, 22–23.

59. These salaried parish workers are treated more fully in Chapter 9. A job description for an assistant minister in Cowcaddens Free Church, Glasgow, in 1890 included preaching at one Sunday service, addressing the "fellowship meeting" during the week, youth work, "systematic family visitation," and other work as assigned by the minister. *Deacon's Court Minutes*, 24 June 1890. Boston's Old South made its assistant minister responsible for its city mission work and its Sabbath School; at Second Presbyterian Church, Philadelphia, the assistant was traditionally left in charge for summer months while the minister (and much of the congregation) sought cooler accommodations. *Session Minutes*, 10 May 1905. In Pilrig Free Church, Edinburgh, the assistant was given the Sunday afternoon service. Ebenezer Turner, *The Story of Pilrig Church* (Edinburgh: Blackwood, 1913), 40.

60. See Old South Cong. Ch., Boston, *Church Records*, vol. 5. Congregational meetings were not well attended among Presbyterians either. In a typical notation, the trustees at Fourth United Presbyterian Church, Pittsburgh, recorded, "Like congregational meetings of preceding years, this one was slimly attended." *Trustees' Minutes*, 8 January 1877.

61. The intent of the time restrictions was to prevent a flood of new members or renters after the announcement of a upcoming controversial decision; one congregation required that voters for a new pastor had to be on the roll before the vacancy had occurred. Park Parish, Glasgow, *Session Minutes*, 20 July 1864.

62. The Congregational Church in Ridgefield, Connecticut, permitted voting at age fifteen. *Manual 1904*, 28.

63. Benjamin F. Bittinger, *Manual of Law and Usage* (Philadelphia: Presbyterian Board of Publication, 1888), 137. Roberts, *Manual for Ruling Elders and Church Sessions*, 334, 375–76, 382. Similar disparities existed in Britain; at least before 1885 in Wellington U. P. Ch., Glasgow, women could vote only on church,

not on temporal, matters. *Historical Sketch of Wellington United Presbyterian Congregation, Glasgow,* 31.

64. Drummond and Bulloch, *Church in Victorian Scotland,* 114–15.

65. Bittinger, *Manual of Law and Usage,* 137, 153; Hodge, *What is Presbyterian Law?,* 56.

66. Punchard, *View of Congregationalism,* 126. Punchard did acknowledge some variation in practice: "I shall not be understood to say, that no Congregational church pursues a different course. I have had occasion to know of one, at least, which followed a different practice to its cost." Also, John Mitchell, *The Practical Church Member, Being a Guide to the Principles and Practice of the Congregational Churches of New England* (New Haven: Nathan Whiting, 1835), 37, 45.

67. Dexter, *Hand-Book of Congregationalism,* 111. New York State provided a special case for both Congregationalists and Presbyterians because the 1813 New York State Law for Ecclesiastical Organizations limited church suffrage to males of legal age; not until the repeal of this law in 1874 did women vote in New York congregations. Congregational church manuals in that state routinely carried a digest of the law. See Plymouth Cong. Ch., Brooklyn, *Manual 1850,* 37, or Plymouth Cong. Ch., Rochester, *Manual 1856,* 13. The preparers of the Rochester manual, unlike those elsewhere, italicized the word *male* to give it greater emphasis in the digest of the law; it is easy to wonder whether Elizabeth Cady Stanton's membership in this congregation contributed to the editorial decision.

68. Watts, *Dissenters,* 2:195.

69. *A Concise History of First Congregational Church, Ridgefield, Connecticut* (1843), 22; the congregational rules also required a two-thirds vote of male members for suspension or excommunication. This language still existed in the 1868 *Concise History and Manual,* but the owner of the copy now in the Congregational Library, Boston, inked out the word "male," indicating that the rule had been altered (22, 25).

70. In Old South's *Church Records,* vol. 5, the language shifts from "meeting of the brethren" to "meeting of the members" in 1896. The 1879 *Manual* for Boylston Church reported that "all adult members of this church are entitled to the right of voting" (26).

71. Central Cong. Ch., Jamaica Plain, MA, *Manual 1898,* 9; First Cong. Ch., Hyde Park, MA, *Manual 1870,* 12. Lyndhurst Road Cong. Ch, London, *Deacons' Minutes,* 26 February 1883.

72. Fourth U.P. Ch., Pittsburgh, *Trustees' Minutes,* 4 January 1869.

73. Turner, *Story of Pilrig Church,* 26.

74. Old South Cong. Ch., Boston, *Church Records,* 7 January 1834.

75. Regent Square Pres. Ch., London, *Spring Visitation Magazine* (June 1912): 6. For an insightful examination of how women were "familiar with and adept at political maneuvering" in the world of secular politics, see Lori D. Ginzberg, *Women and the Work of Benevolence: Morality, Politics, and Class in the 19th-Century United States* (New Haven: Yale University Press, 1990), chap. 3, esp. p. 77.

76. Greyfriars Parish, Edinburgh, *Session Minutes,* 6 July 1875. For examples of successful petition campaigns, see St. George's Parish, Edinburgh, *Session Minutes,* 27 April 1882; Old South Cong. Ch., Boston, *Church Records,* 11 May 1836; or George Logan, *Park [Free] Church, Helensburgh: The First Hundred Years* (Glasgow, 1964), 32.

77. Fourth U. P. Ch., Pittsburgh, *Session Minutes,* 28 November 1857.

78. King's Weigh House Cong. Ch., London, *Deacons' Minutes,* 26 February 1863; Lyndhurst Road Cong. Ch., London, *Deacons' Minutes,* 1 August 1905.

## *Chapter 3*

1. Minshall, *Fifty Years' Reminiscences,* 53.

2. Greenside Parish, Edinburgh, *Session Minutes,* 5 December 1870.

3. Griswold, *Sixty Years with Plymouth Church,* 40.

4. William Adamson, *The Life of Joseph Parker, Pastor of City Temple, London* (New York: Revell, 1902), 127.

5. Griswold, *Sixty Years with Plymouth Church*, 39–40, 53.

6. Standard works include James Hastings Nichols, *Corporate Worship in the Reformed Tradition* (Philadelphia: Westminster Press, 1968); Julius Melton, *Presbyterian Worship in America: Changing Patterns Since 1787* (Richmond, Va.: John Knox Press, 1967); Duncan Forrester and Douglas Murray, eds., *Studies in the History of Worship in Scotland*, 2d ed. (Edinburgh: T. and T. Clark, 1996); William D. Maxwell, *A History of Worship in the Church of Scotland* (New York: Oxford University Press, 1955); Charles Greig M'Crie, *The Public Worship of Presbyterian Scotland* (Edinburgh: Blackwood, 1892); Horton Davies, *Worship and Theology in England*, vol. 3, *From Watts and Wesley to Maurice, 1690–1850* and vol. 4, *From Newman to Martineau, 1850–1900* (Princeton: Princeton University Press, 1961–1962); also, David Frew, *The Parish of Urr, Civil and Ecclesiastical: A History* (Dalbeattie: Thomas Fraser, 1909), 281.

7. Only a rare congregation published attendance numbers in its annual report or manual (although financial data was almost universally included), and they were even less likely to record such data in their official minutes. But there is reason to believe that attendance was high, and that if it slipped at all over the century, it did not do so dramatically. Impressionistic reports described Sunday morning attendance as robust or "uniformly large," and numerous congregations found the need to build larger sanctuaries. Particularly with urban populations continuing to climb, churches were more likely to complain about a shortage of space than a shortage of people. It may be that because pews were visibly full, counting seemed unnecessary. The few scattered instances of data adequate for calculation suggest morning attendance equal to about 70 or 80 percent of the membership total. In small towns, it might be as high as the upper 80s, and in popular urban churches there were enough visitors and non-member pewholders to push attendance to as much as double the official membership. Charles Booth's survey of London churches just prior to the end of the century, noted some variation in attendance, with low attendance often associated with a church whose constituency had moved away. Some of Booth's reporters found that "the congregation was small for the size of the church" or that "only about half of a full congregation" was present, but the more common notation for churches in middle-class neighborhoods was "well-filled, and in some cases crowded, both morning and evening on Sunday." Booth, *Life and Labour of the People in London*, 1:119, 1:224–33, 3:62–63. See also a study by D. R. Pugh, "The Strength of English Religion in the Nineties: Some Evidence from the North West," *Journal of Religious History* 12 (June 1983): 260.

8. Based on a survey of church manuals listed in the bibliography. In Britain only a few Congregational churches in northern cities of Manchester, Liverpool, and Birmingham broke ranks by an earlier 10:30 or 10:45 starting time. American practice, although clustered at 10:30, was more uneven, with worship hours of 10:00 or 10:15 being the norm in Cleveland; by the turn of the century, some large, central churches in New York, Philadelphia, and Chicago had adopted an 11:00 opening hour.

9. Reprinted in *American Presbyterian*, 4 December 1856.

10. Carr's Lane Cong. Ch., Birmingham, *Manual 1835*, 43.

11. Ibid.

12. Quoted by Melton, *Presbyterian Worship in America*, 33.

13. Regent Square Pres. Ch., London, "Sabbath When We Were Boys," *Spring Visitation Magazine* (May 1910): 7. Also, Von Rohr, *Shaping of American Congregationalism*, 230, and Melton, *Presbyterian Worship in America*, 22. Von Rohr suggests that at least among some eighteenth-century American Congregationalists, the opposition to scripture reading had more to do with the length of a service in an unheated sanctuary than with any continued animus toward Anglican practice.

14. *Jubilee Memorial of Saint Andrew's Parish and Congregation, Greenock*, 47, describing an 1835 order of worship; Regent Square Pres. Ch., London, *Spring Visitation Magazine* (May 1910): 6–7; First Pres. Ch., St. Louis, *Manual 1861*, 39; Carr's Lane Cong. Ch., Birmingham, *Manual 1835*, 42–44; Joel Parker and T. Ralston Smith, *The Presbyterian's Hand-Book of the Church for the Use of Members, Deacons, Elders, and Ministers* (New York: Harper, 1861), 19–21, 167–69; Davies, *Worship and Theology in England*, 4:74–78; Melton, *Presbyterian Worship in America*, 21–22; Von Rohr, *Shaping of American Congregationalism*, 229–30.

15. Melton, *Presbyterian Worship in America*, 22–24, 36–39; Chadwick, *Victorian Church*, 1:409.

16. Chadwick, *Victorian Church*, 1:409, reports a range among English Congregationalists of forty-

five minutes to two hours.

17. Kaye, *King's Weigh House,* 76–77; Jones, *Congregationalism in England,* 218–22; Davies, *Worship and Theology in England,* 4:287.

18. Adamson, *Life of Joseph Parker,* 127.

19. Quoted in Von Rohr, *Shaping of American Congregationalism,* 302; Griswold, *Sixty Years with Plymouth Church,* 57; Melton, *Presbyterian Worship in America,* 38–39, 50; Clifford E. Clark, Jr., *Henry Ward Beecher: Spokesman for a Middle-Class America* (Urbana: University of Illinois Press, 1978), 31–32, 122–23.

20. Von Rohr, *Shaping of American Congregationalism,* 301–2; Melton, *Presbyterian Worship in America,* 38–39, 50. Drummond and Bulloch, *Church in Victorian Scotland,* 48; Maxwell, *Worship in the Church of Scotland,* 170–71. Forrester and Murray, eds., *Studies in the History of Worship in Scotland,* 88; Cameron, ed., *Dictionary of Scottish Church History and Theology,* 670–71; Davies, *Worship and Theology in England,* 4:332.

21. Kenneth D. M'Laren, *Memoir of the Very Reverend Professor Charteris* (London: A. and C. Black, 1914), 8.

22. Second Pres. Ch., Philadelphia, *Session Minutes,* 18 February 1881; George W. Sprott, *Worship and Offices of the Church of Scotland* (Edinburgh: Blackwood, 1882), 246–47; Andrew Duncan, *The Scottish Sanctuary As It Was And As It Is* (Edinburgh: Andrew Elliot, 1880), 106–7; *The Late Rev. William Barras: Memorial Volume* (Glasgow: Aird and Coghill, 1893), 54; Minshall, *Fifty Years' Reminiscences,* 55; Melton, *Presbyterian Worship in America,* 18, 52–53, 95, 142; Jones, *Congregationalism in England,* 221.

23. Griswold, *Sixty Years with Plymouth Church,* 52–53.

24. Central Pres. Ch., Rochester, *Trustees' Minutes,* 24 August 1891; Cong. Ch., Hyde Park, MA, *Manual 1895,* 6; Fourth U.P. Ch., Pittsburgh, *Trustees' Minutes,* 28 January 1903; King's Weigh House Cong. Ch., London, *Church Minutes,* 2 January 1896; Lansdowne U.P. Ch., Glasgow, *Annual Report 1906,* 41.

25. A petition from members spurred the inclusion of responsive readings at Central Presbyterian Church, Rochester (*Session Minutes,* 1 October 1883); a unison Lord's Prayer was included in Second Presbyterian Church, Philadelphia, in 1881 (*Session Minutes,* 28 September 1881) and in Clinton Congregational Church, Brooklyn by 1882 (*Manual 1875,* 3); also, Kaye, *King's Weigh House,* 73–74. A correspondent for the *Congregationalist* reported having heard for the first time the Lord's Prayer "audibly repeated by the whole congregation" in the fall of 1872 in Nottingham (quoted by Grant, *Free Churchmanship,* 36). Central Presbyterian Church, Rochester, added a unison Lord's Prayer in 1897 (*Session Minutes,* 12 January 1897); St. George's Free Church, Edinburgh, did so in 1889 (*Session Minutes,* 4 February 1889); and First Congregational Church, Hartford, initiated a unison prayer in 1890 (*Manual 1897,* 108); but St. Andrew's and St. Stephen's parishes in Edinburgh did not do so until 1917 and 1923. George Christie, *The Story of St. Andrew's, Edinburgh* (Edinburgh, 1934), 42; Christopher Nicholson Johnston, Lord Sands, *The Story of St. Stephen's, Edinburgh, 1828–1928* (Edinburgh: William Blackwood, 1927), 80.

26. [Thin], *Memorials of Bristo United Presbyterian Church,* 69, says the congregation "voluntarily fell into the habit" of kneeling for prayer in 1872; in Clinton Congregational Church, Brooklyn, the congregation was instructed to "bow or kneel" for the Lord's Prayer (*Manual 1875,* 3); See Second Pres. Ch., Philadelphia, *Music Committee Minutes,* 24 Sept. 1895; Brick Pres. Ch., New York, *Annual Report 1902,* 33–34.

27. See, for instance, First Cong. Ch., Hartford, which set communions for December, February, April, June, August, and October (*Manual 1858,* 8–10).

28. Charles D. Cashdollar, "The Pursuit of Piety: Charles Hodge's Diary, 1819–1820," *Journal of Presbyterian History* 55 (fall 1977): 269.

29. *American Presbyterian,* 30 December 1869.

30. Quoted in Leigh Eric Schmidt, *Consumer Rites: The Buying and Selling of American Holidays* (Princeton: Princeton University Press, 1995), 180.

31. On the emergence and commercialization of Christmas and Easter, see Schmidt, *Consumer Rites,* chaps. 3 and 4; Stephen Nissenbaum, *The Battle for Christmas* (New York: Knopf, 1996); R. Lawrence Moore, *Selling God: American Religion in the Marketplace of Culture* (New York: Oxford University Press, 1994),

205–6; and William Leach, *Land of Desire: Merchants, Power, and the Rise of a New American Culture, 1880–1920* (New York: Vintage, 1993), 84, 213, 332–38. Central Presbyterian Church, Rochester, began Lenten services in 1896 (*Session Minutes*, 7 January 1896); First Congregational Church, Cleveland, had services by 1895 (*Yearbook 1896*, 15); the Congregational Church in Hyde Park, Massachusetts, was conducting Good Friday Services by 1892 (*Manual 1895*, 9), and Lyndhurst Road Congregational Church, London, was doing the same by the mid-1890s (*Deacon's Minutes*, 28 January 1895).

32. Kaye, *King's Weigh House*, 71, 73–74.

33. Clinton Avenue Cong. Ch., Brooklyn, *Manual 1875*, 3–4.

34. Julius Melton, "A View from the Pew," *American Presbyterians* 71 (fall 1993): 163–64.

35. Melton, *Presbyterian Worship in America*, 83–84; in 1867 after he left Philadelphia for a teaching post at Princeton, Shields brought out *The Presbyterian Book of Common Prayer*, a version of the Anglican service book adjusted as he believed the Westminster divines intended (85–86); see also Second Pres. Ch., Philadelphia, *Session Minutes*, January—December 1861, 28 December 1864.

36. MacIntosh instituted a unison Lord's Prayer and a reading of the Decalogue immediately, and by the end of his pastorate in 1896, the Apostles' Creed was added. Second Pres. Ch., Philadelphia, *Session Minutes*, 18 February 1881; *Music Committee Minutes*, 24 September 1895. In 1886, McIntosh increased the number of communions to five, essentially bimonthly except for the omission of August. *Session Minutes*, 17 February 1886, 14 April 1886, 25 June 1886.

37. John Kerr, *The Renascence* [sic] *of Worship: The Origin, Aims, and Achievements of the Church Service Society* (Edinburgh: Hitt, 1909), 3.

38. Ibid., 12, 21, 33–34, 38–45; Johnston, *Story of St. Stephen's*, 80.

39. Melton, "A View from the Pew," 161, connects the use of set forms in family worship to the desire for forms in public worship.

40. Ibid., 167–72. Comegys was the author of *An Order of Worship with Forms of Prayer for Divine Service* (1885) and *A Presbyterian Prayer Book for Public Worship* (1895); he edited an American edition of the Scottish *Book of Common Order* and was a founder of the American Church Service Society in 1897.

41. Govan Parish, Glasgow, *Leaflets . . . ,* 6 April 1884.

42. Ibid., 18 May 1884, 25 May 1884, 20 December 1884; Macleod's church-year letters continued until the eve of World War I, by which time the emphasis had gradually shifted from explanation to promotion.

43. Govan Parish, Glasgow, *Session Minutes*, 17 June 1884.

44. Govan Parish, Glasgow, *Leaflets . . . ,* 25 May 1884, 21 March 1885, Easter 1890, 23 March 1893, Christmas 1904.

45. Two communions continued to be common in remote areas of the Highlands. Duncan, *Scottish Sanctuary*, 117. Govan went from two to four communions in 1875 (*Session Minutes*, 14 October 1875), to monthly in 1882 (9 January 1882); with five additional holiday celebrations (New Year's Day, Palm Sunday, Easter, Pentecost, and Christmas) the total reached seventeen (22 November 1898).

46. Lansdowne United Presbyterian Church in Glasgow went from four to six communions in 1874 (*Annual Report 1873*, 43; *Annual Report 1874*, 42); Newington United Presbyterian Church, Edinburgh, observed six also. *Newington United Presbyterian Church, Jubilee Memorial, 1848–1898* (Edinburgh: Hunter, 1898), 93.

47. Because it was common for Congregationalists and Presbyterians in Boston, New York, and Philadelphia to suspend services for one or two months during the hot summer season, bimonthly communion might mean only five, not six, celebrations per year. (This paragraph is based on church manuals and other materials listed in the bibliography.)

48. Govan Parish, Glasgow, *Session Minutes*, 23 October 1856; see also Johnston, *Story of St. Stephen's*, 82n.

49. *Jubilee Memorial of St. Andrew's Parish and Congregation, Greenock*, 48–49; Reid, *Book of Greyfriars' Church, Dumfries*, 16; William C. Hay, *The High Church, Airdrie: A Short History Commemorating the Centenary of the Church, March, 1938* (Airdrie, 1938), 18; Johnston, *Story of St. Stephen's*, 82–85. On the pre-

nineteenth-century communion season, see Forrester and Murray, eds., *Studies in the History of Worship in Scotland,* 77–79; Leigh Eric Schmidt, *Holy Fairs: Scottish Communions and American Revivals in the Early Modern Period* (Princeton: Princeton University Press, 1989); Marilyn J. Westerkamp, *The Triumph of the Laity: Scots-Irish Piety and the Great Awakening, 1625–1760* (New York: Oxford University Press, 1988); and James G. Leyburn, *The Scotch-Irish: A Social History* (Chapel Hill: University of North Carolina Press, 1962), 288–89.

50. D. MacNichol, *Chapter from the Religious Life of a Highland Parish* (Paisley: Parlane, 1903), 49.

51. Frew, *The Parish of Urr,* 282–83; John Firth also recalled a time when men went off to the ale house "and with unsteady gait returned to witness the second or third table." *Reminiscences of an Orkney Parish,* 2d ed. (Stromness: John Rae, 1922), 140.

52. Park Parish, Glasgow, *Session Minutes,* 26 November 1867.

53. St. George's Parish, Edinburgh, *Session Minutes,* 11 June 1861; Greenside Parish, Edinburgh, *Session Minutes,* 10 June 1872; Govan Parish, Glasgow, *Session Minutes,* 14 October 1875.

54. Duncan, *The Scottish Sanctuary,* 133; Reid, *Book of Greyfriars' Church, Dumfries,* 36.

55. Greyfriars Parish, Edinburgh, *Session Minutes,* 18 October 1885.

56. Govan Parish, Glasgow, *Session Minutes,* 9 July 1884.

57. St. George's Free Ch., Edinburgh, *Session Minutes,* 21 June 1886. See also, Johnston, *Story of St. Stephen's,* 82–83; *Newington United Presbyterian Church, Jubilee Memorial,* 93. Fast days were abolished in smaller towns during the mid-1880s, too. Helensburgh's ended in 1885 (Logan, *Helensburgh,* 35), Greenock's stopped after the Spring Fast Day, 1886 (*Jubilee Memorial of St. Andrew's Parish and Congregation, Greenock,* 35), and Dumfries's ceased in 1889 because they were "being observed more as holidays" (Reid, *Greyfriars' Church, Dumfries,* 36). Stirling's fast days ended in 1887, Anstruther's in 1888, and Banff's in 1889. G. D. Henderson, *The Scottish Ruling Elder* (London: James Clarke, 1935), 258.

58. Duncan, *The Scottish Sanctuary,* 133; examples of consolidations with weekly prayer meeting (*Gilcomston* [Aberdeen] *Free Church Quarterly Record,* vol. 15 (October 1898); Logan *Helensburgh,* 35), with Sunday evening service (Greenside Parish, Edinburgh, *Session Minutes,* 8 April 1872, 10 June 1872; Park Parish, Glasgow, *Session Minutes,* 16 October 1910), with youth services (St. George's Free Church, Edinburgh, *Session Minutes,* 22 June 1891, 24 June 1901, 20 June 1904; *Jubilee Memorial of St. Andrew's Church and Congregation, Greenock,* 49–50); for a church experimenting with the convenience of Friday rather than Saturday service, see Cowcaddens Free Church, Glasgow, *Session Minutes,* 4 June 1871.

59. St. George's Free Ch., Edinburgh, *Deacons' Court Minutes,* 3 March 1862.

60. [Charles Irvine], *Thirty Years of Broughton United Free Church, Edinburgh* (Edinburgh: Howie and Seath, 1914), 78.

61. Drummond and Bulloch, *Church in Victorian Scotland,* 189–90; Forrester and Murray, eds., *Studies in the History of Worship in Scotland,* 166; Maxwell, *Worship in the Church of Scotland,* 171–72 (although Maxwell gives a date after the end of Chalmers's ministry at St. John's).

62. For examples, see Christie, *Story of St. Andrew's, Edinburgh,* 32; St. George's Parish, Edinburgh, *Session Minutes,* 14 June 1866.

63. St. George's Free Ch., Edinburgh, *Session Minutes,* 6 November 1883, 9 January, 1884, 3 May 1886.

64. St. George's Parish, Edinburgh, *Session Minutes,* 3 December 1866; Frew, *The Parish of Urr,* 283.

65. Schmidt, *Holy Fairs,* chap. 4; long communion tables were also customary for English Congregationalists during the Georgian period (Davies, *Worship and Theology in England,* 3:45–46).

66. Fourth U. P. Ch., Pittsburgh, *Session Minutes,* 23 June 1893.

67. Second Pres. Ch., Philadelphia, *Session Minutes,* 28 September 1881.

68. One London congregation provided communion after morning worship every first Sunday of the month and after evening on the third which gave its members twenty-four opportunities per year (Falcon Square Cong. Ch., London, *Manual 1872,* 5). Handsworth Church, Birmingham, was alternating morning and evening communion every other month, allowing six occasions each (*Manual 1900,* 4), but Carr's Lane and Edgbaston churches in the same city celebrated the sacrament every first Sunday morning and third

Sunday evening (Carr's Lane, *Manual 1871*, 6; Edgbaston, *Manual 1894*, 6). Moseley Road, Birmingham, offered twelve morning and four evening communions (*Manual 1890–91*, 7–8).

69. Lyndhurst Road Cong. Ch., London, *News Sheet*, January 1905.

70. Second Pres. Ch., Philadelphia, *Session Minutes*, 21 December 1881.

71. See R. Milton Winter, "Presbyterians and Prayers for the Sick," *American Presbyterians* 64 (fall 1986): 141–55; Hodge, *What is Presbyterian Law?*, 93.

72. Central Pres. Ch., Rochester, *Session Minutes*, 1 February 1882; Second Pres. Ch., Philadelphia, *Session Minutes*, 25 November 1894.

73. St. George's Free Ch., Edinburgh, *Session Minutes*, 30 March 1909, 24 June 1912.

74. St. George's Parish, Edinburgh, *Session Minutes*, 6 April 1907; Logan, *Helensburgh*, 36.

75. King's Weigh House Cong. Ch., London, *Church Minutes*, 2 December 1834; *Deacons' Minutes*, 29 November 1853; Kaye, *King's Weigh House*, 78.

76. Withington Cong. Ch., Manchester, *Manual 1886*, 7–8; also Great George St. Cong. Ch., Liverpool, *Regulations 1869*, Rule #5. In 1884, Lyndhurst Road deacons asked the minister to appeal to the congregation for better compliance (*Deacons' Minutes*, 2 January 1884). In Edinburgh, a Church of Scotland parish had the opposite problem: some members were putting in more than one card (perhaps trying to make up for a previous absence?). Greenside Parish, Edinburgh, *Session Minutes*, 6 December 1875.

77. St. George's Free Ch., Edinburgh, *Session Minutes*, 9 November 1846.

78. Because St. George's Free Church elders passed out the cards during home visits and the cards were exchanged at the preparatory service for tokens which were turned in at the table service, the system was still not very tight. In 1877, the congregation stopped using tokens entirely, arguing quite rightly that "to use the Cards alone would secure an accuracy in recording the attendance of members at the Lord's table hitherto impossible" (*Session Minutes*, 19 March 1877). Govan Parish, Glasgow, was using "tickets" at least as early as 1870 (*Session Minutes*, 5 April 1870). Pilrig Free Church, Edinburgh, used both tokens and cards from 1852 to 1872, then cards alone (Turner, *Story of Pilrig Church*, 53); Wellington United Presbyterian Church, Glasgow, shifted to cards in 1853 (*Historical Sketch of Wellington United Presbyterian Congregation, Glasgow*, 22). Central Presbyterian Church, Rochester, did not use cards until 1913 (*Session Minutes*, 13 May 1913).

79. Griswold, *Sixty Years with Plymouth Church*, 53.

80. Second Pres. Ch., Philadelphia, *Session Minutes*, 28 September 1881; Moseley Road Cong. Ch., Birmingham, *Manual 1892–93*, 7.

81. Billerica, MA, *Manual 1884*, 7; St. George's Free Ch., Edinburgh, *Session Minutes*, 23 October 1893; Hay, *High Church, Airdrie*, 18; Park Church in Helensburgh (1907) and Pilrig in Edinburgh (1912) were other Free churches that changed (Logan, *Helensburgh*, 36; Turner, *Story of Pilrig Church*, 54).

82. Central Pres. Ch., Rochester, *Session Minutes*, 6 January 1882, 20 January 1882.

83. Lyndhurst Road Cong. Ch., London, *Deacons' Minutes*, 25 June 1883.

84. *Newington United Presbyterian Church, Jubilee Memorial*, 87.

85. Clipping File, "Individual Communion Service," Presbyterian Historical Society, Philadelphia. Thomas claimed to have experimented with individual cups at a service in Vaughnsville, Ohio, in 1893; his multiple cup filler was first used at the Market Square Presbyterian Church in Lima in 1894. The device, available in brass or aluminum, consisted of a raised container with twenty-four nozzles beneath; by sliding under a tray of cups, positioning it carefully, and opening the tap, each miniature cup was properly filled.

86. Central Pres. Ch., Rochester, *Session Minutes*, 13 May 1894.

87. Central Pres. Ch., Rochester, *Trustees' Minutes*, 1903 newspaper clipping announcing Stebbins's retirement, attached 2:181.

88. Both advertisements appeared in the June 1903 *Assembly Herald*. Clipping file, "Individual Communion Service," Presbyterian Historical Society, Philadelphia.

89. Second Pres. Ch., Philadelphia, *Session Minutes*, 7 November 1899, 9 January 1900, 6 March 1900, 9 November 1901, 8 January 1902, 5 March 1902, 7 May 1902.

90. Logan, *Helensburgh*, 36. In central Scotland, it had been common to use a whole loaf of bread, cut partway through with deep slices to allow pieces to be gripped and torn off easily; in the northeast, cutting the bread into "dice" was apparently an older tradition, and in Dumfriesshire and Galloway, shortbread was the common choice because it was unleavened (Sprott, *Worship and Offices of the Church of Scotland*, 240). Elsewhere in Britain, congregations moved only deliberately toward individual cups; the Airdrie Free Church waited until 1911 (Hay, *Airdrie*, 19); Lyndhurst Road Congregational Church, London, was still debating without decision in 1913 (*Deacons' Minutes*, 25 February 1913). The opposition commonly tried to minimize any danger of contagion. Church of Scotland pastor James Cooper wrote in his diary, "All that is needed is that, as with us, the Chalice should be wiped at the end of each pew, and all *invalids* communicated at home." And, he added sharply, "How can we be discerning the Lord's Body and be so much afraid of germs?" (H. J. Wotherspoon, *James Cooper: A Memoir* [London: Longmans, 1926], 224–25). But people *were* concerned about germs, and individual cups in time spread widely among the United Frees, and to Cooper's regret, the established church authorized local option for individual cups in 1907 (243).

91. Old South Cong. Ch., Boston, *Church Records*, 28 January 1896.

92. Ibid., 27 November 1896. Old South's annual inventory of silver in 1910 listed forty-seven cups, three tankards, six flagons, twelve dishes or plates, and one baptismal basin (6 April 1910); some of the silver is now displayed by the Boston Museum of Fine Art.

93. Ibid., 30 November 1896. The vote was seventy-five for change, ninety-five against.

94. Ibid., 28 January 1896.

95. St. George's Free Church, Edinburgh, managed to maintain three services into the 1890s, but it was a prominent congregation with an ability to tap a large urban population; it also had two ministers, and during the few periods when it did not, elders ran the afternoon service (*Session Minutes*, 27 January 1896, 29 June 1896). The highly evangelical members at Cowcaddens Free Church, Glasgow, also sustained three services (*Deacons' Court Minutes*, 4 May 1891). Brooklyn's Plymouth Congregational Church had three, although a deacon rather than Beecher led in the afternoon; even this was abandoned sometime before 1867 (*Manual 1850*, 27; *Manual 1867*, 30).

96. Clinton Cong. Ch., Brooklyn, *Manual 1875*, 4–5.

97. Second Pres. Ch., Philadelphia, *Session Minutes*, 30 October 1889.

98. Carr's Lane Cong. Ch., Birmingham, *Manual 1835*, 42 [lack of capitalization is in original]. The writer was not entirely willing to accept distance as an excuse: "in fixing a place of abode . . . every church member *should*, and every one that loves the house of God *does*, taken into consideration its convenience for attending public worship."

99. St. Paul's Cong. Ch. (Hawley Road), London, *List of Members 1869*, 12–13 [emphasis added].

100. Lyndhurst Road polled its members to see if starting a half hour earlier would help. What the deacons learned was that of those available to come at either 6:30 or 7:00, 6:30 was the two-to-one preference, but 6:30 precluded attendance by workers, and so 7:00 was retained. Lyndhurst Road Cong. Ch., London, *Deacons' Minutes*, 1 August 1905.

101. Free College Ch., Glasgow, *Annual Report 1889*, 13.

102. Lyndhurst Road Cong. Ch., London, *Deacons' Minutes*, 26 January 1891, 28 October 1913.

103. Central Pres. Ch., Rochester, *Session Minutes*, 2 November 1885, 29 November 1885.

104. First Cong. Ch., Hartford, *Manual 1897*, 108. Hartford's vesper series began in 1891; "while largely musical they include exercises essentially instructive and devotional." The Philadelphia church returned one Sunday a month to an evening hour; the suggestion for the late afternoon services came from the Music Committee of the Trustees (*Session Minutes*, 20 November 1887, 13 December 1888, 30 January 1889); Brick Presbyterian Church, after a few years, moved vespers to Friday at five o'clock and advertised a "Choral Service and Sermon" for Sunday evening; the Friday vespers was preceded by a half-hour organ recital (*Year Book 1890*, 5; *Annual Report 1903*, 19; *Annual Report 1904*, 20).

## Chapter 4

1. Carr's Lane Cong. Ch., Birmingham, *Manual 1835*, 44.

2. Second Pres. Ch., Philadelphia, *Session Minutes*, 4 February 1887; Edgbaston Cong. Ch., Birmingham, *Manual 1894*, 6; Brick Pres. Ch., New York, *Annual Report 1899*, 16; Cowcaddens Free Ch., Glasgow, *Deacons' Court Minutes*, 21 March 1895; Cong. Ch., Rochester, NH, *Manual 1876*, 21; Union Park Cong. Ch., Chicago, *Manual 1887*, 4; Central Pres. Ch., Rochester, *Session Minutes*, 28 May 1890; First Pres. Ch., Pittsburgh, *Manual 1912*, 10; Falcon Square Cong. Ch., London, *Manual 1872*, 5.

3. Bowdoin Street Cong. Ch., Boston, *Articles of Faith and Covenant 1837*, 13.

4. Carr's Lane Cong. Ch., Birmingham, *Manual 1835*, 46.

5. Second Pres. Ch., Chicago, *Manual 1856*, 7.

6. Minshall, *Fifty Years' Reminiscences*, 11–12.

7. Carr's Lane Cong. Ch., Birmingham, *Manual 1835*, 45–46.

8. Watts, *Dissenters*, 2:195; Mitchell, *Practical Church Member*, 156–66.

9. Hodge, *What is Presbyterian Law?*, 80–81, 325. See Boyd and Brackenridge, *Presbyterian Women in America*, chap. 6.

10. Second Pres. Ch., Chicago, *Manual 1856*, 7.

11. Redland Park Cong. Ch., Bristol, *Manual 1890*, 5.

12. Third Pres. Ch., Chicago, *Manual 1899*, 58.

13. St. George's Free Ch., Edinburgh, *Session Minutes*, 1 January 1846; a "voluntary circle of Brethren for their own mutual and spiritual improvement and edification" had sprung up at Old South Church in Boston during the 1830s (*Church Records*, 21 December 1832).

14. Cowcaddens Free Ch., Glasgow, *Session Minutes*, 14 February 1889. One rural American congregation substituted district prayer meetings instead of a general midweek prayer meeting as a way of reducing the number of trips members had to make to a central location (Pres. Ch., Binghamton, NY, *Manual 1833*).

15. Second Pres. Ch., Philadelphia, *Session Minutes*, 13 February 1833.

16. Old South Cong. Ch., Boston, *Church Records*, 28 October 1834.

17. Ibid., 24 June 1832; St. George's Free Ch., Glasgow, *Session Minutes*, 14 November 1854. See also, Charles E. Rosenberg, *The Cholera Years: The United States in 1832, 1849, and 1866* (Chicago: University of Chicago Press, 1962).

18. See, for example, Old South Cong. Ch., Boston, *Church Records*, 22 February 1833, 28 October 1834, 27 December 1850; First Cong. Ch., Hartford, *Manual 1897*, 107.

19. See Charles D. Cashdollar, "The Social Implications of the Doctrine of Divine Providence: A Nineteenth-Century Debate," *Harvard Theological Review* 71 (July–October 1978): 265–84. Also, McLeod, *Religion and Society in England*, 215–16.

20. Park Parish, Glasgow, *Session Minutes*, 13 September 1914.

21. Park Street Cong. Ch., Boston, *Articles of Faith and Covenant 1850*, 7; Union Park Cong. Ch., Chicago, *Manual 1887*, 93. The phrase "concert of prayer" itself was older and apparently originated in the midst of Anglo-American millennial hopes in the eighteenth century. William R. Hutchison, *Errand to the World: American Protestant Thought and Foreign Missions* (Chicago: University of Chicago Press, 1987), 38.

22. See, for example, references to planning such services in Lyndhurst Road Cong. Ch., London, *Deacons' Minutes*, 28 November 1892; Central Pres. Ch., Rochester, *Session Minutes*, 22 November 1898.

23. Lyndhurst Road Cong. Ch., London, *Deacons' Minutes*, 3 January 1900; Central Pres. Ch., Rochester, *Session Minutes*, 3 January 1866, 1 December 1899.

24. *Late Rev. William Barras*, 19–20.

25. Second Pres. Ch., Chicago, *Manual 1856*, 7.

26. Second Pres. Ch., St. Louis, *Manual 1844*, 7.

27. Central Pres. Ch., Rochester, *Session Minutes*, 14 November 1894; the second congregation was

Brick Presbyterian Church; they contacted J. Wilbur Chapman, but found that they were already too late to book him for March; they changed the dates to April 2–12, recognizing that having a star evangelist was more important than the date (2 April 1895).

28. Canning Street Pres. Ch., *Jubilee Memorial, 1846–1896* (Liverpool: George Reed, 1896), 10–11.

29. First Cong. Ch., Chicago, *Manual 1859*, 38–39.

30. Carr's Lane Cong. Ch., Birmingham, *Manual 1835*, 44.

31. St. George's Free Ch., Edinburgh, *Session Minutes*, 1 January 1846.

32. Second Pres. Ch., Philadelphia, *Session Minutes*, 11 October 1882; Withington Cong. Ch., Manchester, *Manual 1886*, 10.

33. Central Pres. Ch., Rochester, *Session Minutes*, 1 February 1888; Old South Cong. Ch., Boston, *Church Records*, 8 January 1835; Second Pres. Ch., Philadelphia, *Session Minutes*, 8 November 1914; St. George's Free Ch., Edinburgh, *Session Minutes*, 22 January 1894.

34. Brick Pres. Ch., New York, *Manual 1914*, 9.

35. Plymouth Cong. Ch., Brooklyn, *Manual 1850*, 17; elders led prayer meeting in St. Andrew's Free Church, Greenock (*Jubilee Memorial of St. Andrew's Parish and Congregation*, 51) and at Regent Square Presbyterian Church, London (*Annual Report 1847*, 39); in Philadelphia, elders rotated alphabetically month by month (Second Pres. Ch., *Session Minutes*, 8 June 1854, 30 December 1869); at St. George's Free Church in Edinburgh, it was Elder Ferrier who was for many years in charge of prayer meeting (*Session Minutes*, 22 October 1906).

36. St. George's Free Ch., Edinburgh, *Session Minutes*, 23 October 1893.

37. Adamson, *Life of Joseph Parker*, 138–40; Joseph Parker, *A Preacher's Life: An Autobiography and an Album* (Boston: Crowell, 1899), xv; Booth, *Life and Labour of the People in London*, 3:48.

38. Brick Pres. Ch., New York, *Manual 1914*, 9; Withington Cong. Ch., Manchester, *Manual 1886*, 10.

39. Withington Cong, Ch., Manchester, *Manual 1886*, 10.

40. Lyndhurst Road Cong. Ch., London, *Manual 1914*. 23.

41. Anne M. Boylan, *Sunday School: The Formation of an American Institution, 1790–1880* (New Haven: Yale University Press, 1988), 14–17, 142–49; also, Bernard Wishy, *The Child and the Republic: The Dawn of Modern American Child Nuture* (Philadelphia: University of Pennsylvania Press, 1968).

42. *American Presbyterian*, 9 September 1869; Congregational minister James Merrill of Davenport, Iowa, noted slyly that "an incidental advantage gained by this method is that it enables the minister to reach a large number in his congregation who, although men in years, are but children in spiritual attainments" (*New Englander* 40 [March 1881]: 254).

43. Paddock Cong. Ch., Huddersfield, *Yearbook 1903*, 17; Central Pres. Ch., Rochester, *Session Minutes*, 7 June 1909; Second Pres. Ch., Philadelphia, *Session Minutes*, 30 October 1889; Regent Square Pres. Ch., London, *Annual Report 1884*, 8.

44. Duncan, *The Scottish Sanctuary*, 104.

45. See, for example, *Historical Sketch of Wellington United Presbyterian Congregation, Glasgow*, 22; Third Pres. Ch., Chicago, *Manual 1889*, 24; King's Weigh House Cong. Ch., London, *Church Minutes*, 10 September 1850; Carr's Lane Cong. Ch., Birmingham, *Manual 1903*, 12–13. Carr's Lane planned its service for children aged fourteen and under.

46. M'Laren, *Charteris*, 11, 40; Lozells Cong. Ch., Birmingham, *Manual 1899*, 23; Free College Ch., Glasgow, *Annual Report 1887*, 13; Fourth U. P. Ch., Pittsburgh, *Session Minutes*, 19 February 1869; James Hood Wilson, *The King's Message and Other Addresses* (London: Nisbet, 1887), iv.

47. Third Pres. Ch., Chicago, *Manual 1889*, 24; Macleod prepared five slightly different services, which he rotated monthly. The "First Sunday of the Month" service was: hymn, prayer of confession and Lord's Prayer, hymn, lessons, creed, intercessions and thanksgivings, hymn, sermon, Beatitudes or Commandments, hymn, offering, Nunc Dimittis or hymn, benediction. Macleod's well-worn, hand-written copy of all five services, *Liturgy for Use in Children's Service*, is among the Govan parish papers in the Strathclyde Regional Archives, Glasgow.

48. Wilson, *The King's Message*, iv. Also, J. H. Wilson, *The Gospel and its Fruits: A Book for the Young* (London: Nisbet, 1874); James Wells, *Bible Echoes: Addresses to the Young*, 3d ed. (London: Nisbet, 1878); James Wells, *Bible Children: Studies for the Young* (London: Nisbet, 1885). In 1874, Wilson's *The Gospel and its Fruits* was in its "third thousand," and Wells's *Bible Children* had reached its "fifth thousand" by 1885. Newton's books, which carried titles such as *The Safe Compass* (1863), *Bible Jewels* (1867), *Leaves from the Tree of Life* (1873), and *Rays from the Sun of Righteousness* (1876), were issued by Robert Carter, publisher of numerous works by Scottish and American Reformed writers; volumes could be purchased individually for $1.25 or in boxed sets of six for $7.50. *Congregationalist* 8 (January—December 1879): 66ff., 152ff., 246ff., 318ff., 426ff., 509ff., 593ff., 681ff., 768ff., 854ff., 950ff., 1032ff.

49. Wells, *Bible Children*, 79–92.

50. Wilson, *King's Message*, iv–v.

51. Wilson, *Gospel and its Fruits*, 179–202, esp. 186.

52. Redland Park Cong. Ch., Bristol, *Manual 1890*, 4.

53. Bittinger, *Manual of Law and Usage*, 30; Lansdowne U.P. Ch., Glasgow, *Annual Report 1899*, 6; Lansdowne held its Children's Day on the first Sunday of November (*Annual Report 1896*, 37); see also Central Pres. Ch., Rochester, *Session Minutes*, 18 May 1898; First Cong. Ch., Cleveland, *Yearbook 1896*, 15, and *Yearbook 1903*, 32.

54. *American Presbyterian*, 25 December 1856; by the 1870s and 1880s, churches were collecting special offerings at Christmas; Old South designated its collection for Boston city missions (*Church Records*, 12 January 1885), and Lyndhurst Road in London raised money for a Christmas dinner for the destitute (*Deacons' Minutes*, 18 December 1882).

55. New Broad Street Cong. Ch., London, *Year Book 1857*, 40; *Late Rev. William Barras*, 79–80; Old South Cong. Ch., Boston, *Church Records*, 19 December 1873.

56. Bethany Pres. Ch., Philadelphia, "The Christmas Sabbath at Bethany Sabbath School," 25 December 1887.

57. *American Presbyterian*, 27 November 1856; for examples of church services, see Plymouth Cong. Ch., Brooklyn, *Manual 1854*, 18, or Central Pres. Ch., Rochester, *Session Minutes*, 7 November 1895; it was not uncommon for neighboring churches to unite for a joint service on Thanksgiving. Second Presbyterian Church in Philadelphia met with Calvary Presbyterian Church in 1869 and with West Arch Street Presbyterian Church in 1872 (Second Pres., Ch., *Session Minutes*, 8 November 1869, 3 November 1872); in Boston, Old South, Central, and Mt. Vernon Congregational churches united with First Baptist and First Unitarian churches for an 1885 service (Old South Cong. Ch., *Church Records*, 30 October 1885).

58. Kenneth L. Ames, *Death in the Dining Room and Other Tales of Victorian Culture* (Philadelphia: Temple University Press, 1992), 85–92.

59. For an example of such a service, see Central Pres. Ch., Rochester, *Session Minutes*, 30 May 1890, 1 February 1895. Central Church began its Memorial Day services in 1890.

60. Govan Parish, Glasgow, *Session Minutes*, 19 June 1897; St. George's Free Ch., Edinburgh, *Session Minutes*, 5 June 1911.

61. Plymouth Cong. Ch., Rochester, *Manual 1856*, 4–5.

62. *Newington United Presbyterian Church, Jubilee Memorial*, 7–9; the publication of commemorative albums or histories was another common feature of anniversary activity.

63. The Westminster Shorter Catechism (1647) stipulated baptism for "infants of such as are members of the visible Church" (Hodge, *What is Presbyterian Law?*, 85). Beecher, at least, was an exception here; beginning in 1868, Plymouth Church declared its willingness to baptize children "of believing parents," whether one was a member of the congregation or not. The Congregational Library, Boston, holds the clerk's copy of *Manual 1867*, which includes an inked amendment to the rules, effective 18 December 1868 (21).

64. Johnston, *Story of St. Stephen's*, 92; Duncan, *The Scottish Sanctuary*, 110–11. Hodge, *What is Presbyterian Law?*, 90; also Dexter, *Hand-Book of Congregationalism*, 85. An 1885 questionnaire circulated among Presbyterian churches in England revealed private baptism to be customary in most places (Davies,

*Worship and Theology in England,* 4:109).

65. Carr's Lane, Birmingham, *Manual 1835,* 47; Pres. Ch., Binghamton, NY, *Manual 1833,* 30; Second Cong. Ch., Hartford, *Manual 1860,* 21; Johnston, *Story of St. Stephen's,* 92.

66. Second Pres. Ch., Philadelphia, *Session Minutes,* 6 May 1885; Central Pres. Ch., Rochester, *Session Minutes,* 1 February 1876, 6 December 1863. Pastors were required to have the consent of their church officers (or church meetings) before performing a baptism, but exceptions were recognized; Pittsburgh pastor H. H. Marlin, in 1893, was called to St. Francis Hospital where he administered baptism to a dying young man shot through the bowels; Marlin's session, upon hearing his report, concurred that there had been no time for regular approval. Fourth U. P. Ch., Pittsburgh, *Session Minutes,* 25 May 1893.

67. There were congregations that did not follow this pattern. Children's Day became a popular time for baptisms at the end of the century. Central Presbyterian Church, Rochester, baptized infants at preparatory service until 1897, when it shifted to the Sunday after communion (*Session Minutes,* 2 June 1865; 12 October 1897), and Old South, Boston, included baptism in its Easter Sunday afternoon children's worship (*Church Records,* 18 April 1897).

68. Plymouth Cong. Ch., Brooklyn, *Manual 1854,* 17; also First Cong. Ch., Chicago, *Manual 1884,* 23.

69. Central Pres. Ch., Rochester, *Session Minutes,* 8 June 1879.

70. Second Pres. Ch., Chicago, *Manual 1856,* 18–19.

71. Prior to the publication of denominational service books, the words of the baptismal covenant would have been particular to each congregation, although there was a lot of borrowing and copying that occurred. Copies of services, or at least of the parental covenants, were found in many congregational manuals. See, for example, Clinton Avenue Cong. Ch., Brooklyn, *Manual 1882,* 12; Central Cong. Ch., Jamaica Plain, MA, *Manual 1898,* 22; Ch. of the Pilgrims [Cong.], Brooklyn, *Confession of Faith and Covenant 1855,* 16; Ch. of the Mediator [Cong.], Brooklyn, *Covenant and Confession of Faith 1868,* 10; Brick Pres. Ch., New York, *Manual 1869,* 10; Sixth Pres. Ch., Chicago, *Manual 1883,* 15.

72. Edmund S. Morgan, *The Puritan Family: Religion and Domestic Relations in Seventeenth-Century New England* (New York: Harper and Row, 1966), 31–32; John Demos, *A Little Commonwealth: Family Life in Plymouth Colony* (New York: Oxford University Press, 1970), 162–63. Between Lord Hardwicke's Marriage Act (1754) and its repeal in 1836, no Nonconformist chapel wedding was recognized as legal (Davies, *Worship and Theology in England,* 3:137).

73. Handsworth Cong. Ch., Birmingham, *Manual 1900,* 23–24; New Broad Street Cong. Ch., London, *Year Book 1857,* 21.

74. Park Parish, Glasgow, *Session Minutes,* 13 November 1910; St. George's Free Ch., Edinburgh, *Session Minutes,* 10 May 1899, 6 March 1911.

75. Old South Cong. Ch., Boston, *Church Records,* 3 June 1890.

76. Clinton Avenue Cong. Ch., Brooklyn, *Manual 1882,* 13–14. Also, Davies, *Worship and Theology in England,* 4:105–6, 108.

77. Park Parish, Glasgow, *Session Minutes,* 13 November 1910. The choir of St. George's Free Church, Edinburgh, was paid £6.5.0 for a funeral in May 1910. *Session Minutes,* 6 June 1910. According to the Westminster Directory (1644), "praying, reading, and singing, going to and at the grave, have been grossly abused, are in no way beneficial to the dead, and have proved many ways hurtful to the living; therefore let all such things be laid aside" (quoted by Davies, *Worship and Theology in England,* 4:108).

78. *American Presbyterian,* 19 March 1857; for a similar description of a Baltimore funeral a few years later, see *American Presbyterian,* 21 January 1869.

79. Bethany Pres. Ch., Philadelphia, *Annual Report 1894,* 12; Cong. Ch., Ridgefield, CT, *Church History and Manual 1868,* 10; First Cong. Ch.. Chicago, *Manual 1859,* 37.

*Chapter 5*

1. Second Pres. Ch., Philadelphia, *Music Committee Minutes*, 29 March 1893, 10 May 1893.

2. Ibid., 26 February 1895, 26 March 1895, 13 May 1895.

3. When tunes as well as psalm words were printed, some publishers cut the pages so that the top half carrying the tune and bottom with the words could be turned separately, allowing users to mix and match.

4. The main American Presbyterian body's 1788 directory permitted both psalms and hymns, but the smaller United Presbyterian denomination banned hymns until 1925 (James Rawlings Sydnor, "American Presbyterian Hymnals," *American Presbyterians* 68 [spring 1990]: 3; Wallace Jamison, *United Presbyterian Story*, 140–42). American Congregationalists made a gradual transition to hymns during the latter half of the eighteenth century (Von Rohr, *Shaping of American Congregationalism*, 231). Most English Congregationalists also adopted hymn singing during the eighteenth century, but, aside from various unofficial collections, there was no denominational hymnal until 1859 (Jones, *Congregationalism in England*, 298–99; Louis F. Benson, *The English Hymn: Its Develpment and Use in Worship* [London: Hodder and Stoughton, 1915], 454). A commitment to psalm singing persisted in the Scottish Free Church, many of whose congregations did not sing hymns until after the publication of a *Free Church Hymnal* in 1882. In contrast, the Relief Church, one of the forebears of the United Presbyterian Church, published a hymnal at the end of the eighteenth century. Some Church of Scotland parishes were singing hymns from their own editions at the beginning of the Victorian period; the Church published its first official hymnal in 1870 (Millar Patrick, *Four Centuries of Scottish Psalmody* [London: Oxford University Press, 1949], 218–19; Johnston, *Story of St. Stephen's*, 118–19). In many congregations, hymns were adopted in Sunday School and occasional services before they were accepted for the formal Sunday worship.

5. Second Pres. Ch., Philadelphia, *Session Minutes*, 9 November 1836. For a similar job description in Britain, see Govan Parish, *Session Minutes*, 10 July 1856. As long as the old system remained in place, the job description did not change. Cowcaddens Free Church in Glasgow, still organless in 1890, required its precentor to "conduct praise at all diets of worship" and provide a "class for instruction in Psalmody." *Session Minutes*, 1 May 1890.

6. Second Pres. Ch., Philadelphia, *Session Minutes*, 9 November, 1836. McAlister earned £25 for his work at Govan (*Session Minutes*, 10 July 1856); St George's parish in Edinburgh paid £35 (*Session Minutes*, 11 February 1862); in Glasgow, salaries ranged from £20 at Cowcaddens Free to £50 at the Free College Church (Cowcaddens Free Ch., *Session Minutes*, 11 September 1871; Free College Ch., *Annual Report 1878*, 18). In London, Regent Square Presbyterian paid £50 (*Annual Report 1869*, 31), but during the same decade King's Weigh House offered Mr. Franklin only £25 as a starting salary, "it being dependant [sic] upon your exertions and the satisfaction you give, how soon they increase the same." (*Deacons' Minutes*, 28 October 1862). Few American congregations used precentors after the 1830s, but Pittsburgh's Fourth United Presbyterian, which did, paid $150 (*Trustees' Minutes*, 10 May 1870).

7. King's Weigh House Cong. Ch., London, *Church Minutes*, 23 September 1862; Cowcaddens Free Ch., Glasgow, *Session Minutes*, 30 October 1871; St. George's Free Ch., Edinburgh, *Deacons' Court Minutes*, 2 March 1885. Also, Govan Parish, *Session Minutes*, 10 July 1856; St. George's Parish, Edinburgh, *Session Minutes*, 11 February 1862; Second Pres. Ch., Philadelphia, *Session Minutes*, 21 March 1844.

8. Minshall, *Fifty Years' Reminiscences*, 12–13. Minshall said that "ultimately it was found necessary to replace [the precentor]. A kindly message was sent to him that as he had lost his voice, Mr. —— would in future 'pitch the tune.' This rather irritated the old man, who sent a message back, 'If I've lost my voice, Mr. —— hasn't found it.' "

9. Greenside Parish, Edinburgh, *Session Minutes*, 8 July 1872, 6 July 1874.

10. St. George's Free Ch., Edinburgh, *Deacons' Court Minutes*, 10 December 1848; *Session Minutes*, 13 March 1907.

11. Patrick, *Four Centuries of Scottish Psalmody*, 196.

12. Fingland, *St. John's Presbyterian Church, Kensington*, 7; Fourth U. P. Ch., Pittsburgh, *Trustees'*

*Minutes,* "1885 Annual Report," also 3 February 1913.

    13. King's Weigh House Cong. Ch., London, *Deacons' Minutes,* 19 July 1869.

    14. Patrick, *Four Centuries of Scottish Psalmody,* 135.

    15. Eighteenth-century singing schools, both in Britain and America, were Enlightenment efforts to improve psalmody; the leaders set out to eliminate the irregular or folk style of singing that then commonly decorated the tunes according to the precentor's tastes with grace notes or other embellishments; the singing schools taught a regular style of singing that was faithful to the printed score. Patrick, *Four Centuries of Scottish Psalmody,* 135–46; Gilbert Chase, *America's Music,* 2d ed. (New York: McGraw-Hill, 1966), 22–25.

    16. First Cong. Ch., Hartford, *Manual 1897,* 71–74.

    17. Ibid., *Manual 1897,* 71–74.

    18. St. George's Free Ch., Edinburgh, *Deacons' Court Minutes,* 8 January 1844. Also, Duncan, *The Scottish Sanctuary,* 14.

    19. Christie, *Story of St. Andrew's, Edinburgh,* 37; Greyfriars Parish, Edinburgh, *Session Minutes,* 24 September 1837.

    20. St. George's Free Ch., Edinburgh, *Deacons' Court Minutes,* 11 April 1845.

    21. Govan Parish, Glasgow, *Session Minutes,* 5 December 1872.

    22. Johnston, *Story of St. Stephen's,* 173–74.

    23. Patrick, *Four Centuries of Scottish Psalmody,* 193; A. R. Howell, *Paisley Abbey: Its History, Architecture, and Art* (Paisley: Gardner, 1929), 39.

    24. Hay, *High Church, Airdrie,* 12; Canning Street Pres. Ch., Liverpool, *Jubilee Memorial,* 10. Talmadge, employing his usual sarcasm, wrote in the *New York Independent* that the best way "to destroy congregational singing" (aside from selecting only unfamiliar tunes) was to "get an irreligious choir and put them in a high balcony back of the congregation." He predicted the method would be as cheap as it was effective: "the theatrical troupe are not busy elsewhere on Sabbaths, and you can get them at half price" (reprinted in *Congregationalist* 2 [January 1873]: 37–40).

    25. Quoted by Kaye, *King's Weigh House,* 74.

    26. First Cong. Ch., Chicago, *Manual 1859,* 39.

    27. Second Pres. Ch., Philadelphia, *Session Minutes,* 21 March 1844.

    28. St. George's Free Ch., Edinburgh, *Session Minutes,* 2 March 1868.

    29. St. George's Free Ch., Edinburgh, *Deacons' Court Minutes,* 7 December 1863. In a preface to the congregation's local tune book, Binney chided the members, "Many persons would appear to have no idea that there is anything like obligation or duty connected with [singing]; while some, who can sing in private, and are well acquainted with secular music, seem to think it beneath them to open their lips in the public solemnities of the Church" (quoted by Kaye, *King's Weigh House,* 72). Beecher was known to stop his congregation in the middle of a hymn and urge, "Sing it with more spirit, and let everybody sing" (Griswold, *Sixty Years with Plymouth Church,* 54). Lyndhurst Road's manual listed among the obligations of membership, "obtaining a Tune Book (Bristol) and making use of it to sing correctly the tunes in common use" (*Manual 1883,* 20).

    30. See, for example, Christie, *The Story of St. Andrew's, Edinburgh,* 41, when Mr. Ramage was "allowed to resign in 1861."

    31. St. George's Free Ch., Edinburgh, *Deacons' Court Minutes,* 21 October 1850. Perhaps such a notice board did help; there is at least the tale of a late-comer in Berwickshire who slipped into a pew during the opening psalm and asked the man next to him what tune had been called, and heard in response, "I no ken; I'm at the AULD HUNDERT" (related in Patrick, *Four Centuries of Scottish Psalmody,* 146).

    32. St. George's Parish, Edinburgh, *Session Minutes,* 23 February 1866, 6 April 1868, 14 December 1868, 1 March 1869, 5 April 1869.

    33. St. George's Free Ch., Edinburgh, *Deacons' Court Minutes,* 8 June 1885.

    34. Greenside Parish, Edinburgh, *Session Minutes,* 3 December 1877, 7 January 1878, 14 January 1879.

    35. Second Pres. Ch., Philadelphia, *Session Minutes,* 9 March 1837.

36. Old South Cong. Ch., Boston, *Standing Committee Records*, 8 April 1845; St. George's Free Ch., Edinburgh, *Deacons' Court Minutes*, 12 March 1849.

37. Plymouth Cong. Ch., Brooklyn, *Manual 1854*, 19. Beecher's administrative structure was copied by other American Congregationalists. See, for instance, the identical charge to the music committee in Plymouth Church, Rochester (*Manual 1856*, 11).

38. Hay, *High Church, Airdrie*, 17.

39. J. S. Curwen, "Hymn-Singing," *Congregationalist* 3 (April 1874): 209–17; Patrick, *Four Centuries of Scottish Psalmody*, 198–99; Erik Routley, *The Music of Christian Hymns* (Chicago: G.I.A. Publications, 1981), 88.

40. Lozells Cong. Ch., Birmingham, *Manual 1899*, 28.

41. St. George's Free Ch., Edinburgh, *Session Minutes*, 23 November 1881, 2 July 1883.

42. Chase, *America's Music*, 151–53, 158–61; Routley, *Christian Hymns*, 87.

43. Sydnor, "American Presbyterian Hymnals," 3–4. Prior to that, tune books, as distinct from word books, were largely confined to the choir (5). Benson, *English Hymn*, 477–78, 534–35.

44. For example, Edinburgh's St. Stephen's published its own hymnal in 1834–35 at the price of 4s.6d. (Johnston, *Story of St. Stephen's*, 118–19) and Greyfriars' hymnal came out in a new edition in 1877 for a cost of one shilling (*Session Minutes*, 23 July 1877). Brick Presbyterian Church, New York, put out *The Sacrifice of Praise* in 1869 with a music edition in 1872 (Sydnor, "American Presbyterian Hymnals," 8) and Elder W. A. Hubbard edited an 1891 volume that Central Presbyterian Church, Rochester, adopted and sold to members for seventy-five cents (*Session Minutes*, 30 January 1891, 25 March 1891). Second Church in Philadelphia adopted the Presbyterian *Hymnal* in 1911 "with a supplement of 8 or 16 pages containing such extra hymns as may be selected by our Pastor" (*Session Minutes*, 25 October 1911).

45. *American Presbyterian*, 29 January 1857.

46. *Church of Scotland Psalm and Hymn Tune Book* (Edinburgh: Thomas Nelson, 1869), iii.

47. Old South Cong. Ch., Boston, *Church Records*, 14 January 1895.

48. Cowcaddens Free Ch., Glasgow, *Session Minutes*, 30 November 1887.

49. Von Rohr, *Shaping of American Congregationalism*, 300.

50. *Bible Songs: A Collection of Psalms Set to Music for Use in Church and Evangelistic Services, Prayer Meetings, Sabbath Schools, Young People's Societies, and Family Worship* (Pittsburgh: United Presbyterian Board of Publication, 1901), 3.

51. Old South Cong. Ch., Boston, *Church Records*, 7 February 1859.

52. Johnston, *Story of St. Stephen's*, 118–19.

53. Kaye, *King's Weigh House*, 75.

54. Sydnor, "American Presbyterian Hymnals," 7.

55. Second Pres. Ch., Philadelphia, *Session Minutes*, 6 October 1874.

56. Lyndhurst Road Cong. Ch., London, *Deacons' Minutes*, 20 December 1885.

57. Greenside Parish, Edinburgh, *Session Minutes*, 8 February, 1869, 8 March 1869, 11 March 1869, 2 April 1869, 3 May 1869, 10 June 1869. For other examples, see Christie, *Story of St. Andrew's, Edinburgh*, 37, 41; Second Pres. Ch., Philadelphia, *Session Minutes*, 13 December 1888; *Historical Sketch of Wellington United Presbyterian Congregation*, 18; Turner, *Story of Pilrig Church*, 53. Not every congregation had such difficulty; Session Clerk James Thin recalled that in Bristo United Presbyterian Church, Edinburgh, the members in 1872 "voluntarily fell into the habit" ([Thin], *Memorials of Bristo United Presbyterian Church*, 69). St George's Free Church Session voted 16–5 for standing in 1882, and "correctly judged the general feeling" of its members when it did so (*Session Minutes*, 1 March 1882).

58. Robert S. Candlish, ed., *The Organ Question: Statements by Dr. Ritchie and Dr. Porteous for and against the Use of the Organ in Public Worship in the Proceedings of the Presbytery of Glasgow, 1807–8* (Edinburgh: Johnstone, 1856), 185–86.

59. Reid, *The Book of Greyfriars' Church Dumfries*, 26; Second Pres. Ch., Philadelphia, *Session Minutes*, 23 June 1836, 4 November 1836, 9 November 1836; John H. Taylor, ed., "Letters to a Pastor (1869) [of Bethnal Green Chapel]," *Journal of the United Reformed Church History Society* 1 (April 1976): 204.

60. For instance, Mark Smith, *Religion in Industrial Society: Oldham and Saddleworth, 1740–1865* (Oxford: Clarendon Press, 1994), 151–52, reports the presence of "fiddles, flute, bassoon, and trumpet" at Uppermill Congregational Church, and a "pipe and string band" at Springhead Congregational Church.

61. *Carr's Lane Meeting House, A Retrospect* (Birmingham: Hudson, 1898), 24; Handsworth Cong. Ch., Birmingham, *Manual 1900*, 23–24; King's Weigh House Cong. Ch., London, *Church Minutes*, 1 December 1872; Binney quoted by Kaye, *King's Weigh House*, 76; also, Smith, *Religion in Industrial Society*, 152, and Watts, *Dissenters*, 2:185–86. Minshall, who became organist at London's City Temple in 1876, recalled that there was already an organ at Friar Lane, Nottingham, when he arrived as a twelve-year-old student in 1857; there was also an organ available at Leatherhead where he continued his schooling; and there was a one-manual organ at the Old Chapel, Oswestry, where he took his first job as organist in 1862 (Minshall, *Fifty Years' Reminiscences*, 15, 18, 24).

62. "Introduction of Organs in Congregational Churches," *New-England Magazine* 9 (August 1835): 123–28; "Biographical Memoir of William M. Goodrich, Organ-Builder," *New-England Magazine* 6 (January 1834): 25–44; "Organ-Building in New England," *New-England Magazine* 6 (March 1834): 205–15. Von Rohr, *Shaping of American Congregationalism*, 232; Old South Cong. Ch., Boston, *Standing Committee Records*, 2 April 1849 [the organ was noted as being twenty-two years old in 1849 while under repair]; Bowdoin Street Cong. Ch. [after the fire, Hanover Street Ch. rebuilt on Bowdoin Street], *Articles of Faith and Covenant 1837*, 5; First Cong. Ch., Hartford, *Manual 1897*, 71–74; Plymouth Cong. Ch., Brooklyn, *Manual 1867*, 10.

63. Melton, *Presbyterian Worship in America*, 35–36.

64. Quoted by George P. Hays, *Presbyterians* (New York: J. A. Hill, 1892), 438.

65. Old Union U. P. Ch., Mars, Pennsylvania, *Session Minutes*, 11 May 1895, 19 November 1895, 25 October 1897, 26 December 1897.

66. Merle Rife, *A History of Graystone United Presbyterian Church, 1808–1978* (Indiana, Pennsylvania, 1978), 7–8.

67. William Andrews, ed., *Bygone Church Life in Scotland* (London: Andrews, 1899), 98, 101–2.

68. The Scottish Episcopal Church did construct a splendid cathedral in the West End of Edinburgh during the 1870s, and its Father Willis organ was ready in 1879; it is conceivable, though undocumented, that its presence spurred decisions to build organs in three of Edinburgh's fashionable Church of Scotland parishes, St. Stephen's (1878–80), St. Andrew's (1880), and St. George's (1882).

69. Candlish, ed., *The Organ Question*, 66–67; James Thomson, *History of St. Andrew's Parish Church, Glasgow* (Glasgow: Robert Anderson, 1905), 25–28.

70. M'Crie, *Public Worship of Presbyterian Scotland*, 326–27. Andrews, ed., *Bygone Church Life*, 106–7.

71. Thomson, *St. Andrew's Parish Church, Glasgow*, 87; Park Parish, Glasgow, *Session Minutes*, 2 October 1865, 1 May 1866; John Railton, *The Old High Kirk of Kilmarnock* (Kilmarnock, 1940), 70; Reid, *Book of Greyfriars' Church Dumfries*, 26; T. M. M'William, ed., *The Kirks of the Turriff Presbytery* (Banff, 1904), 34; Howell, *Paisley Abbey*, 41; Duncan, *The Scottish Sanctuary*, 38; Andrews, ed., *Bygone Church Life*, 107; Forrester and Murray, eds., *Studies in the History of Worship in Scotland*, 99–100; A. K. H. Boyd, "The Organ in Scotland," *Frasers Magazine* 72 (October 1865): 520–24.

72. Canning Street Pres. Ch., Liverpool, *Jubilee Memorial*, 9; St. John's Wood Pres. Ch., London, *One Hundred Years* (London, 1970), 3; Regent Square Pres. Ch., London, *A Centenary of Regent Square* (London, 1927), 40.

73. Canning Street Pres. Ch., Liverpool, *Jubilee Memorial*, 14, 17, 19.

74. Ames, *Death in the Dining Room*, chap. 4.

75. *Late Rev. William Barras*, 70–71.

76. Taylor, ed., "Letters to a Pastor (1869)," 205–6.

77. Christie, *Story of St. Andrew's, Edinburgh*, 41; St. John's Wood Pres. Ch., London, *One Hundred Years*, 3; *Gilcomston Free Church Quarterly Record*, vol. 15 (October 1898); Reid, *Book of Greyfriars' Church Dumfries*, 26; Park Parish, Glasgow, *Session Minutes*, 3 February 1865.

78. Johnston, *Story of St. Stephen's*, 126; Logan, *Helensburgh*, 32; St. George's Parish, Edinburgh, *Session Minutes*, 27 April 1882; Second Pres. Ch., Philadelphia, *Session Minutes*, 23 June 1836; Hay, *High Church, Airdrie*, 17; [Thin], *Memorials of Bristo United Presbyterian Church*, 212.

79. Lansdowne U. P. Ch., Glasgow, *Annual Report 1880*, 10.

80. Reed organs were the popular parlor instruments of the nineteenth century, and larger models were produced for churches. Although local congregations tended to use terms imprecisely and often interchangeably, there were two kinds of reed organs: the French-designed harmonium (1842) and the Boston-produced cabinet organ (or American organ as it was known in Britain). Powered by the player's feet, a bellows forced air through metal reeds to produce sound. The harmonium worked by compressed air, and the American organ by suction of air. Both approximated the sound of a pipe organ, although the American organ reputedly did so more accurately and came in larger models with two manuals and, if electrified, with a pedal keyboard. Percy Sholes, *Oxford Companion to Music*, 10th ed. (London: Oxford University Press, 1970), 865–67.

81. St. George's Free Ch., Edinburgh, *Deacons' Court Minutes*, 5 June 1899; [Irvine], *Thirty Years of Broughton United Free Church, Edinburgh*, 73; Lyndhurst Road, London, *Manual 1886*, 13. Also Redland Park Cong. Ch., Bristol, *One Hundred Years* (Bristol, 1961), 21; Lansdowne United Presbyterian Church, Glasgow, *Annual Report 1881*, 12.

82. Griswold, *Sixty Years with Plymouth Church*, 55–56; Minshall, *Fifty Years' Reminiscences*, 39.

83. Certain urban churches did employ women organists; Cowcaddens Free Church in Glasgow, Lyndhurst Road Congregational Church in London, and Fourth United Presbyterian Church in Pittsburgh had women organists; Cowcaddens and Lyndhurst Road paid £20 to £30 per year in the 1880s; Fourth Church paid Miss Willa Cunningham $300 per year in 1908. Cowcaddens Free Ch., *Deacons' Court Minutes*, 7 September 1897; Lyndhurst Road, *Deacons' Minutes*, 30 June 1884; Fourth U. P. Ch., *Trustees' Minutes*, 12 October 1908. In Turriff Presbytery in the north of Scotland, about 45 percent of the organists whose sex can be identified were female in 1904. M'William, ed., *Kirks of the Turriff Presbytery*, passim.

84. See, for example, Cowcaddens Free Ch., Glasgow, *Session Minutes*, 5 May 1913.

85. Minshall, *Fifty Years' Reminiscences*, 33.

86. Greyfriars Parish, Edinburgh, *Session Minutes*, 1 July 1888. Greyfriars found itself hiring organists frequently because its salary was only a quarter to a third of the professional rate in Edinburgh, and consequently it tended to hire young organists who quickly moved on. The successful candidate in this 1888 audition was eighteen years old; his salary was to be £25.

87. Johnston, *Story of St. Stephen's*, 127. Another Scottish clergyman, upon receiving a complaint that the organ voluntary was not "worship," replied bluntly, "I don't say it is, but neither is the shuffling of feet and slamming of pew doors as people are coming in and going out: and don't you think the organ, which drowns these noises, is the pleasantest sound of the two?" Quoted in Boyd, "The Organ in Scotland," 524.

88. Park Parish, Glasgow, *Session Minutes*, 16 December 1866, 2 May 1870.

89. Ibid., September 1866; Central Pres. Ch., Rochester, *Trustees' Minutes*, 25 April 1864, 6 January 1866, 1 September 1875; St. George's Free Ch., Edinburgh, *Deacons' Court Minutes*, 6 December 1897, 6 November 1905; Lyndhurst Road Cong. Ch., London, *Deacons' Minutes*, 30 November 1885, 31 October 1887; Govan Parish, Glasgow, *Session Minutes*, 21 November 1898.

90. Lyndhurst Road Cong. Ch., London, *News Sheet*, January 1898.

91. Peoples' Cong. Ch., Brooklyn, Promotional Leaflet, [1885]. The leaflet also included an advertisement for voice lessons taught by Soper ("*Voice examination free*"). Soper's *Vocalist's Guide*, "a new valuable pamphlet, devoted exclusively to the true system of managing the voice in singing," was also touted for purchase.

92. Second Pres. Ch., Philadelphia, *Music Committee Minutes*, 24 September 1895. See also, Park Parish, Glasgow, *Session Minutes*, 2 February 1911, for an appeal to the congregation for increased choir funding on the grounds that it would be "a matter of lasting regret" if "this distinctive feature of Park Church" were allowed to lose its excellent reputation.

93. Second Pres. Ch., Philadelphia, *Session Minutes*, 3 February 1872.

94. In Philadelphia, Second Pres. Ch. waged a long battle with St. Stephen's Episcopal Church, which regularly lured away its best singers and even two of its organists (*Music Committee Minutes*, 27 October 1899; *Session Minutes*, 9 June 1912). In Edinburgh, St. George's parish raised a bass singer's salary to £25 but still was unable to keep him (*Session Minutes*, 3 October 1870, 5 December 1870).

95. Second Pres. Ch., Philadelphia, *Music Committee Minutes*, 23 November 1896; Cong. Ch., Ithaca, NY, *Manual 1895*, 25, 38–62.

96. Second Pres. Ch., Philadelphia, *Music Committee Minutes*, 24 September 1895, 29 November 1898. Nearly a half century earlier, the prominent New York City Presbyterian choirmaster and hymn writer Thomas Hastings made the same point: "Quartette choirs . . . will of necessity reveal every excellence and defect in such a manner, as to invite commendation or censure from the *amateurs* below. Larger choirs are not liable to the same objection; for the commingling of many voices offers less inducements to individual criticism." Thomas Hastings, "Church Music," *New Englander* 6 (July 1848): 430.

97. Brick Pres. Ch., New York, *Annual Report 1914*, 15; Carr's Lane Cong. Ch., Birmingham, *Manual 1903*, 11.

98. Lyndhurst Road Cong. Ch., London, *News Sheet*, 1893–1913 passim; *Deacons' Minutes*, 27 October 1903; *Manual 1887*, 17; Redland Park Cong. Ch., Bristol, *One Hundred Years*, 21; Edgbaston Cong. Ch., Birmingham, *Manual 1894*, 53; Lansdowne U. P. Ch., Glasgow, *Annual Report 1876*, 22.

99. First Cong. Ch., Cleveland, *Yearbook 1896*, 20–21; Govan Parish, Glasgow, *Session Minutes*, 28 May 1874, 12 May 1879.

100. Lansdowne U. P. Ch., *Annual Report 1885*, 9; *Annual Report 1905*, 15; First Cong. Ch., Cleveland, *Society Records*, 1 January 1857; *Trustees' Minutes*, "Annual Report," 1914; First Cong. Ch., Hartford, *Manual 1888*, 22; *Manual 1896*, 25.

101. Central Pres. Ch., Rochester, *Trustees' Minutes*, 1 September 1875; Third Pres. Ch., Indianapolis, *Hand Book 1874*, 26; Lansdowne U.P. Ch., Glasgow, *Annual Report 1875*, 10; *Annual Report 1889*, 11, *Annual Report 1893*, 17. Meanwhile the old-fashioned congregational singing practices disappeared. More people read notation, modern hymnals printed tunes as well as words, and organs steadied the insecure, thus making the earlier rote instruction redundant. Regent Square Presbyterian Church in London, however, did devise the helpful system of announcing hymn tunes several weeks ahead so that "families of the Congregation, especially those where there are young people, can effectively assist our Congregational Praise by practising these Hymns at home." *Spring Visitation Magazine* (May 1910); *Hand Book 1911*, 18.

102. Johnston, *Story of St. Stephen's*, 78–79. Worshippers did not stay seated for anthems at St. George's Free Ch. until 1911 (*Session Minutes*, 23 January 1911); see also Elwyn A. Wienandt and Robert H. Young, *The Anthem in England and America* (New York: Free Press, 1970).

103. *Anthem Book of the United Free Church of Scotland* (London: Novello, 1905).

104. Brick Pres. Ch., New York, *Annual Report 1914*, 3:18–19 [Ch. of the Covenant was a mission church associated with Brick].

105. Brick Pres. Ch., New York, *Annual Report 1914*, 15.

106. First Pres. Ch., Chicago, "Orders of Worship," 22 December 1901, 3 April 1904, also "Special Music," [November-December] 1911. Foote and Parker were currently active American organists and composers, Foster and West were respected English Victorian organists and composers.

107. First Cong. Ch., Hartford, *Manual 1897*, 71–74; St. George's Parish, Edinburgh, *Session Minutes*, 4 November 1912; *Historical Sketch of Wellington United Presbyterian Congregation, Glasgow*, 40; Second Pres. Ch., Philadelphia, *Music Committee Minutes*, 11 November 1896.

108. Cowcaddens Free Ch., Glasgow, *Session Minutes*, vol. 2, undated advertising poster, c. 1885–94; Howell, *Paisley Abbey*, 41; King's Weigh House Cong. Ch., London, *Church Minutes*, 20 January 1904; Second Pres. Ch., Philadelphia, *Music Committee Minutes*, 27 November 1900.

109. Minshall, *Fifty Years' Reminiscences*, 131, 136.

110. Ibid., 135.

111. Ibid., 132–33.

112. St. George's Parish, Edinburgh, *Session Minutes*, 9 April 1888, 26 February 1889, 6 November 1906, 14 January 1908, 6 June 1910, 7 November 1910.

113. Lyndhurst Road Cong. Ch., London, *News Sheet*, April 1897.

## Chapter 6

1. King's Weigh House Cong. Ch., London, *Church Minutes*, 30 March 1830; for the most recent revision of rules and procedures for admitting members, see 27 October 1829. King's Weigh House's practice of involving two deacons in the interviews was not universally followed. At Carr's Lane in Birmingham and New Broad Street in London, the church appointed two members (who might or might not be deacons) to interview and report on incoming members (Carr's Lane, *Manual 1835*, 19–20; New Broad Street, *Year Book 1857*, 14–15). Other Congregational churches, especially in the United States, assigned the interviews to a permanent "examining committee" made up of deacons and at-large members (Dexter, *Hand-Book of Congregationalism*, 101–2; Punchard, *View of Congregationalism*, 127–29).

2. New Broad Street Cong. Ch., London, *Year Book 1857*, 14–15.

3. Great George Street Cong. Ch., Liverpool, *Regulations 1869*, Rule # 1.

4. King's Weigh House Cong. Ch., London, *Church Minutes*, 31 January 1843. Judging by descriptions in manuals, lay interviews with prospective members seem to have been discontinued in other London congregations. For example, Bedford New Town Cong. Ch., *Manual 1854*, 2; Haverstock Cong. Ch., *Year Book 1862*, 52.

5. King's Weigh House Cong. Ch., London, *Church Minutes*, 2 July 1861; also 1 October 1874 ("the following were proposed for admissions") and 5 November 1874 ("the following were admitted to membership").

6. Ibid., 22 January 1904 [emphasis added]. Hunter's new procedures were adopted 24 January 1902.

7. Similarly, Lyndhurst Road Cong. Ch., London, stopped taking votes on individual candidates in 1888. If no objections were raised during the month, then the applicants were either automatically declared members or elected "en bloc" without comment (*Deacons' Minutes*, 23 January 1888).

8. First Cong. Ch., Hartford, *Confession of Faith and Covenant 1835*, 5–7; Second Cong. Ch., Hartford, *Confession of Faith and Covenant 1838*, 24–25.

9. First Cong. Ch., Hartford, *Confession of Faith and Covenant 1835*, 16–18; Second Cong. Ch., Hartford, *Manual 1860*, 17–18. As early as 1840, George Punchard, a Congregational minister from New Hampshire, sensed public examinations were falling out of favor and felt obliged to defend the traditional practice, though even he admitted it could be "considered a fiery ordeal for a timid person" (Punchard, *View of Congregationalism*, 127n).

10. Second Cong. Ch., Hartford, *Manual 1902*, 15.

11. First Cong. Ch., Chicago, *Manual 1859*, 27.

12. Sixth Pres. Ch., Chicago, *Manual 1877*, 9.

13. Central Pres. Ch., Rochester, *Session Minutes*, 27 March 1860, 3 April, 1864. The use of church covenants was found in the Presbyterian churches of upstate New York and the Midwest, which had been influenced by their contact with Congregationalism during the Plan of Union.

14. Ibid., 20 September 1832, 19 March 1853, 10 December 1853, 15 December 1853, 7 September 1854, 14 June 1855, 18 February 1881, 9 November 1904.

15. New Broad Street Cong. Ch., London, *Year Book 1857*, 14 [emphasis added].

16. First Pres. Ch., Philadelphia, *Church Manual 1841*, 45.

17. First Pres. Ch., Philadelphia, *Manual 1905*, 9.

18. Greyfriars Parish, Edinburgh, *Session Minutes*, 9 May 1839, 4 October 1880. In St. George's Parish, Edinburgh, members in the 1880s were admitted "on the recommendation of the Moderator [i.e., the minister]" (*Session Minutes*, 29 October 1887).

19. Johnston, *Story of St. Stephen's*, 87.

20. Greenside Parish, Edinburgh, *Session Minutes*, 6 November 1971; Greyfriars Parish, Edinburgh, *Session Minutes*, 21 April 1876.

21. St. George's Free Ch., Edinburgh, *Session Minutes*, 24 October 1850. Old habits of thought were hard to break. The traditional phrase for new communicants was "admitted for the first time to the Lord's Table"; the clerk's new language in 1850—"admitted for the first time as members of this church"—retained the now redundant "for the first time" even though joining a church was not repeatable in the sense that taking communion was. As late as 1895, there was a reference to a candidate "for admission to the Lord's Table for the first time" (*Session Minutes*, 24 June 1895).

22. Cowcaddens Free Ch., Glasgow, *Session Minutes*, 28 April 1865, 9 April 1868, 26 October 1871, 19 February 1891.

23. Sixth Pres. Ch., Chicago, *Manual 1877*, 9; also see King's Weigh House Cong. Ch., London, *Church Minutes*, 5 September 1830; Second Cong. Ch., Hartford, *Confession of Faith and Covenant 1838*, 24–25; Cong. Ch., Rochester, NH, *Manual 1891*, 18–19; Second Pres. Ch., Philadelphia, *Session Minutes*, 10 December 1853, 15 December 1853. First Cong. Ch., Hartford, *Confession of Faith and Covenant 1835*, 5–7; Bowdoin Street Church, Boston, *Articles of Faith and Covenant 1837*, 12.

24. King's Weigh House Cong. Ch., London, *Church Minutes*, 22 January 1904; Gilcomston Free Ch., Aberdeen, *Quarterly Record*, vol. 16 (January 1899).

25. Holloway Cong. Ch., London, *Year Book 1851*, 4.

26. For example, the Congregational Church in Rochester, NH, included a by-law that after a year, visitors from other congregations "are not included in the usual invitation to our communion, unless they give satisfactory reasons for not removing their relation" (*Articles of Faith and Covenant 1859*, 11–12).

27. Central Pres. Ch., Rochester, *Session Minutes*, 8 July 1863, 2 June 1867, 11 June 1882, 20 December 1910; Lyndhurst Road Cong. Ch., London, *Deacons' Minutes*, 31 May 1897.

28. Central Pres. Ch., Rochester, *Session Minutes*, 20 December 1910.

29. Ibid., 31 May 1892; Lyndhurst Road Cong. Ch., London, *Deacons' Minutes*, 3 June 1889; St. George's Free Ch., Edinburgh, *Session Minutes*, 23 January 1899, 20 March 1899. By the latter part of the century, some large urban congregations were holding formal classes for incoming adult members, too. See Cowcaddens Free Ch., Glasgow, *Session Minutes*, 26 October 1871; Regent Square Pres. Ch., London, *Hand Book 1911*, 18.

30. Lyndhurst Road Cong. Ch., London, *Deacons' Minutes*, 6 April 1882.

31. Barnes, in the ensuing passages, assured his hearers that God through Christ gave "strength to fulfil your engagements." First Pres. Ch., Philadelphia, *Church Manual 1841*, 45–46. Abbreviated though very similar phrases are found in Lyman Beecher's manual (Bowdoin Street Cong. Ch., Boston, *Articles of Faith and Covenant 1837*, 15–19).

32. Old South Cong. Ch., Boston, *Form of Covenant 1826*, 9; Second Cong. Ch., Hartford, *Confession of Faith and Covenant 1838*, 21, *Manual 1860*, 18–19. Old South noted that the inclusion of Doddridge's hymn was "in compliance with a request from some of the members of the church" (9). Also, Bowdoin Street Cong. Ch., Boston, *Articles of Faith and Covenant*, 12.

33. Sprott, *Worship and Offices of the Church of Scotland*, 94.

34. Cowcaddens Free Ch., Glasgow, *Session Minutes*, 9 April 1868.

35. Based on "forms of admission" from Second Pres. Ch., Chicago, *Manual 1856*, 13–17, *Manual 1870*, 4–7; Second Pres. Ch., St Louis, *Manual 1857*, 10–11; Central Pres. Ch., Rochester, *Session Minutes*, 1:161–62 [insert, 1860s]; First Pres. Ch., Philadelphia, *Church Manual 1841*, 45–52; First Pres. Ch., Indianapolis, *Manual 1878*, 42–44; Bowdoin Street Cong. Ch., Boston, *Articles of Faith and Covenant 1856*, 17–21; North Cong. Ch., Hartford, *Catalogue 1839*, 8–12; Plymouth Cong. Ch., Brooklyn, *Manual 1854*, 14–16; Cong. Ch., Harlem, NY, *Manual 1866*, 11. Despite these common local rituals, the national Presbyterian bodies took pains to clarify that for Presbyterians the actual point of admission was the Session's vote, not the congregational ceremony (Hodge, *What is Presbyterian Law?*, 142–43).

36. First Pres. Ch., Chicago, *Manual 1870*, 6; Central Cong. Ch., Jamaica Plain, MA, *Church Manual 1898*, 20.

37. Old South Cong. Ch., Boston, *Church Records,* 7 April 1899, 28 April 1899.

38. For examples of revised creeds or local adoptions of the 1883 Congregational creed, see Park Street Cong. Ch., Boston, *Articles of Faith and Covenant 1916,* 3–4; Cong. Ch., Billerica, MA, *Manual 1884,* 11–13; First Cong. Ch., Rochester, MA, *Manual 1909,* 9; First Cong. Ch., Rochester, NH, *Manual 1891,* 10–11; Cong. Ch., Hyde Park, MA, *Manual 1895,* 37–40, *Manual 1913,* 16; Boylston Cong. Ch., Boston, *Manual 1896,* 13–16; Union Park Cong. Ch., Chicago, *Manual 1887,* 18–19; Cong. Ch., Ridgefield, CT, *Manual 1904,* 15–16; Cong. Ch., East Hartwick, VT, *Manual 1891,* 10–11; Cong. Ch., Binghamton, NY, *Manual 1894,* 21–22; Central Cong. Ch., Jamaica Plain, MA, *Manual 1898,* 15–17; First Cong. Ch., Hartford, *Manual 1897,* 47–49.

39. First Cong. Ch., Binghamton, NY, *Manual 1894,* 13.

40. In the copy of Plymouth Cong. Ch., Brooklyn, *Manual 1867,* that is deposited in the Congregational Library, Boston, the question is inked out with a marginal notation, "Jan^y 7/70 Amendment" (18).

41. First Cong. Ch., Hartford, *Manual 1897,* 46 [emphasis added].

42. First Cong. Ch., Rochester, MA, *History and Manual 1909,* 14–15, 17; Second Cong. Ch., Hartford, *Manual 1902,* 12.

43. New Broad Street Cong. Ch., London, *Year Book 1857,* 24; on this general point, see Grant, *Free Churchmanship,* 15.

44. Roberts, *Manual for Ruling Elders and Church Sessions,* 46–47.

45. Second Pres. Ch., St. Louis, *Manual 1857,* 10.

46. First Pres. Ch., Philadelphia, *Church Manual 1841,* 46.

47. First Pres. Ch., Indianapolis, *Manual 1878,* 41. Also, First Pres. Ch., Pittsburgh, *Communicants' Manual 1912,* 12: "The Presbyterian Church does not require from its members any subscription to a confessional statement. This is required only of its ministry." On Scotland, see Cameron, ed., *Dictionary of Scottish Church History and Theology,* 805–6.

48. Griswold, *Sixty Years with Plymouth Church,* 121.

49. The following description is based on lists of duties and church covenants in the church manuals listed in the bibliography. Where such statements did not exist, as in Scotland, the church's expectations remained implicit. While tacit precepts can often be deduced (by examining disciplinary cases, for instance), these paragraphs reflect the overt statements and promises made at entry into a congregation; more subtle behavioral standards will be taken up in Chapter 7.

50. Second Cong. Ch., Hartford, *Confession of Faith and Covenant 1838,* 17; First Pres. Ch., Philadelphia, *Manual 1841,* 50.

51. Central Cong. Ch., Jamaica Plain, MA, *Manual 1898,* 19; First Cong. Ch., Rochester, NH, *Manual 1891,* 13; First Pres. Ch., Philadelphia, *Manual 1905,* 12.

52. Carr's Lane Cong. Ch., Birmingham, *Manual 1835,* 40. [A *rout* was an evening social gathering, a soiree.]

53. New Broad Street Cong. Ch., London, *Year Book 1857,* 33.

54. First Pres. Ch., Philadelphia, *Manual 1905,* 10.

55. Second Cong. Ch., Hartford, *Confession of Faith and Covenant 1838,* 16; also Second Pres. Ch., Chicago, *Manual 1856,* 16; First Pres. Ch., Chicago, *Manual 1870,* 6.

56. Great George Street Cong. Ch., Liverpool, *Manual 1870,* 3.

57. Ibid., 3.

58. Lyndhurst Road Cong. Ch., London, *Deacons' Minutes,* 30 November 1909.

59. Central Cong. Ch., Jamaica Plain, MA, *Manual 1898,* 20–21; First Pres. Ch., Philadelphia, *Manual 1905,* 10.

60. Great George Street Cong. Ch., Liverpool, *Manual 1870,* 3.

61. First Pres. Ch., Pittsburgh, *Communicants' Manual 1912,* 13.

62. Regent Square Pres. Ch., London, *Manual 1909,* 1–2.

63. Second Pres. Ch., Philadelphia, *Session Minutes,* 21 April 1897, 25 April 1897, 26 May 1897; St. George's Parish, Edinburgh, *Session Minutes,* 1 November 1880.

64. Griswold, *Sixty Years with Plymouth Church,* 73–74.

65. Regent Square Pres. Ch., London, *Spring Visitation Magazine* (June 1912): 6, 4–5.

66. Regent Square Pres. Ch., London, *News Sheet,* April 1894. An enterprising Cleveland congregation included a directory of its members' shops and businesses in the church handbook, a service that undoubtedly encouraged members to patronize each others' establishments (First Cong. Ch., Cleveland, *Yearbook 1894*).

67. *Regent Square Misc. Papers,* United Reformed Church History Society, London.

68. Alan C. Brown, *The Maxwell Story* (Glasgow, 1965), 34.

69. Minshall, *Fifty Years' Reminiscences,* 84; Cong. Ch., Hyde Park, MA, *Manual 1895,* 22; Second Pres. Ch., Philadelphia, *Session Minutes,* 20 October 1885; Lozells Cong. Ch., Birmingham, *Manual 1899,* 5.

70. The story in this and in the following paragraphs is related in Griswold, *Sixty Years with Plymouth Church,* 12, 17–21.

71. Ibid., p. 28.

72. Based on a tabulation of 167 available annual or cumulative percentages for fifty-three congregations from 1809 through 1917; 141 of the 167 reports are clustered plus or minus 6 points from 66 percent. This coincides with the figures compiled by Clive Field, "Adam and Eve: Gender in the English Church Constituency," *Journal of Ecclesiastical History* 44 (January 1993): 63–79, which reported the percentages of women among Baptist and Congregational nonconformist members as 65.2 percent (1826–50), 67.2 percent (1851–75), 67.6 percent (1876–1900), and 68.6 percent (1901–25). Bebbington's study of nineteenth-century Cumbrian Congregationalism found females comprising 58 to 68 percent of the membership (*Evangelicalism in Modern Britain,* 128–29).

73. Paddock Cong. Ch., Huddersfield, *Yearbook 1903,* 10–13; Ch. of the Covenant, Chicago, *Manual 1886–87,* 28–35, 36–40; Cong. Ch., Hyde Park, MA, *Directory 1895,* 31–38.

74. Carr's Lane Cong. Ch., Birmingham, *Manual 1871,* 12–13. In contrast to women's predominance in membership, Bebbington found attendance "much nearer equality" among Cumbrian nonconformists; women, especially female domestic servants, were more in evidence at evening services after household chores were ended (*Evangelicalism in Modern Britain,* 128–29). The London religious census of 1881, the first to attempt a reporting of attendance by gender, concluded that 46.7 percent of nonconformist attenders were women (Field, "Adam and Eve: Gender in the English Free Church," 72).

75. Walton Park Cong. Ch., Liverpool, *Report and Statement of Accounts 1872–73,* 3; *Report and Statement of Accounts 1875,* 3; Bowdoin St. Cong. Ch., Boston, *Articles of Faith and Covenant 1837,* 5, 9–10. On this point, see also Curtis D. Johnson, *Islands of Holiness: Rural Religion in Upstate New York, 1790–1860* (Ithaca: Cornell University Press, 1989), 62–63.

76. Johnson, *Islands of Holiness,* 57. See also, Richard D. Shiels, "The Feminization of American Congregationalism, 1730–1835," *American Quarterly* 33 (spring 1981): 46–62, and Moore, *Selling God,* 84. Ann Douglas, in *The Feminization of American Culture* (New York: Knopf, 1978), 98–99, is among those who have noticed that the predominance of women seems to have characterized the colonial period as well. The study of Center Congregational Church, New Haven, by Harry S. Stout and Catherine Brekus found a significant gender gap beginning in the mid-seventeenth century ("A New England Congregation: Center Church, New Haven, 1638–1989" in Wind and Lewis, eds., *American Congregations,* 1:41–45, 63–67). Stout and Brekus suggest that perhaps women's experiences with the dangers of childbearing and childrearing made them "more thoughtful about their spiritual condition" and that women relished the "public identity" afforded to them by religious participation. Once women became a majority, the pattern was "self-perpetuating": people "expected women to be godly" and the churches were defined as feminine territory. For another excellent discussion of the gender gap in eighteenth-century and nineteenth-century American churches, and a summary of the relevant literature, see Leonard I. Sweet, *The Minister's Wife: Her Role in Nineteenth-Century American Evangelicalism* (Philadelphia: Temple University Press, 1983),

35–43. Sweet argues that although the most common explanation for the phenomenon is "the consistency between conversion's demand for a 'melting' into submissiveness and women's socialized role of submission," a more important factor was the churches' ability to give women "something of universal significance to do with their lives at a time when economic and social forces were sabotaging their traditional roles" (88). On England, see Field, "Adam and Eve: Gender in the English Church Constituency," cited above; Bebbington, *Evangelicalism in Modern Britain,* 128–29; and McLeod, *Religion and Society in England.* 66–70, 157–58.

77. This argument is made most strongly and convincingly by Johnson, *Islands of Holiness.*

78. Cong. Ch., Jamaica Plain, MA, *Manual 1898,* 35.

79. Fifty-six percent of the pupils at the Carr's Lane congregational school were girls in 1871. At Glasgow's Lansdowne U. P. Ch. in 1866, there were fifty-two girls and twenty-nine boys. Girls made up 54 percent of the Sunday School children at St. George's Free Ch., Edinburgh, in 1858. Carr's Lane Cong. Ch., Birmingham, *Manual 1871,* 12–13; Lansdowne U. P. Ch., Glasgow, *Annual Report 1866,* 15; St. George's Free Ch., Edinburgh, *Deacons' Court Minutes,* 5 July 1858.

80. Mark C. Carnes, *Secret Ritual and Manhood in Victorian America* (New Haven: Yale University Press, 1989).

81. Old South's women comprised 84 percent of the membership in 1841, 79 percent in 1855, and 75 percent in 1863. *Form of Covenant 1841,* 73–88; *Form of Covenant 1855,* 109–19; *Members 1863,* 5–21.

82. Seventy-six percent of new converts in an 1863 revival were women; the average age of converts, which Elder William Alling also calculated, was 20.5 in 1863. Central Pres. Ch., Rochester, *Session Minutes,* 7 June, 1863; also 8 July 1863, 2 June 1867.

83. Sweet, *The Minister's Wife,* 232–35; Moore, *Selling God,* 211–12; Gail Bederman, " 'Women Have Had Charge of the Church Work Long Enough': The Men and Religion Forward Movement of 1911–12 and the Masculinization of American Protestantism," *American Quarterly* 41 (September 1989): 432–65. For an exploration of the literary manifestations of this movement, see Donald Hall, ed., *Muscular Christianity: Embodying the Victorian Age* (Cambridge: Cambridge University Press, 1994).

84. *Mayfield United Free Church, 1875–1925* (Edinburgh, 1925), 10, 13; P. K. Livingstone, *The Boys' Brigade in Kirkcaldy* (Kirkcaldy, 1953), 2–3; Daniel Martin, "The United Presbyterian Church Policy on the Men's Movement: An Historical Overview," *Journal of Presbyterian History* 59 (fall 1981): 408–39; Regent Square Pres. Ch., London, *Spring Visitation Magazine* (June 1912): 4–5.

85. First Cong. Ch., Ridgefield, CT, *Concise History and Manual 1868,* 25. A two-thirds majority of males was needed; the word *male* has been inked out in the copy now held by the Cong. Library, Boston; the amendment is, however, undated.

86. Ibid., 6.

87. This practice may have had its origins in the desire for a separate male voting list at a time when women did not yet hold suffrage rights in the church. If so, it lasted well beyond its reason for existence; Old South still printed separate membership rolls at the beginning of the twentieth century (*Service of Admission and Catalogue 1899,* 15–72).

88. Cong. Ch., Hyde Park, Massachusetts, *List of Members 1915.* The layout and indentations looked like this:

> Crighton, Andrew W. 7 Highland St.
> > Annette [Goodwin] (A. W.) 7 Highland St.
> > Eleanor G. 7 Highland St.

89. The minutes for a session meeting in Pittsburgh read: "The following persons were received to the communion of this congregation. The list of names was lost. Adjourned, with closing prayer" (Fourth U. P. Ch., *Session Minutes,* 30 November 1861).

90. Redland Park Cong. Ch., Bristol, *One Hundred Years* (Bristol, 1961), 8–9; Central Pres. Ch., Rochester, *Session Minutes,* 17 December 1862.

91. First Pres. Ch., Chicago, *Manual 1884,* 24.

92. Central Pres. Ch., Rochester, *Session Minutes,* 30 November 1894.

93. Second Pres. Ch., St. Louis, *Manual 1857*, 13–20; St. George's Free Ch., Edinburgh, *Deacons' Court Minutes*, 2 March 1863; Moseley Road Cong. Ch., Birmingham, *Manual 1893–94*, 13.

## Chapter 7

1. Third Pres. Ch., Indianapolis, *Hand Book 1874*, 25; Second Pres. Ch., St. Louis, *Manual 1844*, 8–9; Carr's Lane Cong. Ch., Birmingham, *Manual 1835*, 16–18.

2. Plymouth Cong. Ch., Brooklyn, *Manual 1854*, 30–41; Carr's Lane Cong. Ch., Birmingham, *Manual 1835*, 42–49. For other examples of manuals providing instruction about the nature of congregationalism or presbyterianism, see First Cong. Ch., Chicago, *Manual 1859*, 3–15; Third Pres. Ch., Chicago, *Manual 1892*, 3–6; Redland Park Cong. Ch., Bristol, *Manual 1890*, 2; Withington Cong. Ch., Manchester, *Manual 1887*, 12–13. Horton's pastoral letter near the front of Lyndhurst Road's 1883 manual helped members to understand a church, not as a building, but as a "local assembly of those that believe" and a "spiritual community"—that is, as both a "visible" and "invisible" body (9–14).

3. This paragraph and the following ones are based on lists found in First Cong. Ch., Hartford, *Confession of Faith and Covenant 1835*, 14–18; Carr's Lane Cong. Ch., Birmingham, *Manual 1835*, 55–58; Fifth Pres. Ch., Baltimore, *Manual 1845*, 11–13; Second Pres. Ch., Chicago, *Manual 1856*, 21–22; First Cong. Ch., Chicago, *Manual 1859*, 25; First Cong. Ch., Rochester, NH, *Articles of Faith and Covenant 1859*, 18–19; Cong. Ch., Binghamton, NY, *Manual 1875*, 6–7; Sixth Pres. Ch., Chicago, *Manual 1877*, 13–15; *Manual 1883*, 19–21; Ch. of the Covenant (Pres.), Chicago, *Manual 1885–86*, 20; Cong. Ch., East Hardwick, VT, *Manual 1891*, 16–19; Third Pres. Ch., Chicago, *Manual 1892*, 10–11.

4. Mark A. Noll, "Presbyterian Devotional Literature," *American Presbyterians* 68 (fall 1990): 207–19. See also James H. Smylie, "Of Secret and Family Worship," *Journal of Presbyterian History* 58 (summer 1980): 95–115.

5. Donald Macleod, *The Sunday Home Service* (London: Isbister, 1885).

6. Church Service Society, *Home Prayers* (Edinburgh: William Blackwood, 1879).

7. For an insightful discussion of the role of family bibles in Victorian homes, see Colleen McDannell's chapter "The Bible in the Victorian Home" in Colleen McDannell, *Material Christianity: Religion and Popular Culture in America* (New Haven: Yale University Press, 1995), 67–102.

8. Church Service Society, *Home Prayers*, 5.

9. Smylie, "Of Secret and Family Worship," 99; Louise Stevenson, *The Victorian Homefront*, 8–10, notes that the model of patriarchal family devotions "looked to the past" when fathers labored at home.

10. McDannell, *Material Christianity*, 100–101.

11. Smylie, "Of Secret and Family Worship," 100–102.

12. Boylan's *Sunday School* is an excellent study of United States schools; Thomas W. Laqueur, *Religion and Respectability: Sunday Schools and Working Class Culture, 1780–1850* (New Haven: Yale University Press, 1976) is more interested in mission schools, but provides some information on British congregational schools as well.

13. Paul W. Koper, "The United Presbyterian Church and Christian Education: An Historical Overview," *Journal of Presbyterian History* 59 (fall 1981): 288–92.

14. Johnston, *Story of St. Stephen's*, 150–51.

15. Boylan, *Sunday School*, 17. Even mission Sunday Schools were cautious to seek out parental consent before enrolling a child off the streets. Among Old School Presbyterians in the United States, there was a short-lived movement in the 1840s advocating a return to catechizing by elders and clergy and a "revival" of "family instruction" (Koper, "United Presbyterian Church and Christian Education," 294).

16. St. George's Free Ch., Edinburgh, *Session Minutes*, 21 June 1886, 14 July 1886, 25 October 1886.

17. Boylan, *Sunday School*, 16–17.

18. Lansdowne U. P. Ch., Glasgow, *Annual Report 1902*, 40; Free College Ch., Glasgow, *Annual Report*

1886, 13–14; St. George's Free Ch., Edinburgh, *Deacons' Court Minutes*, 8 February 1847, 12 December 1859.

19. Handsworth Cong. Ch., Birmingham, *Manual 1900*, 6; Acocks Green Cong. Ch., Birmingham, *Manual 1896*, 26–27; Govan Parish, Glasgow, *Sunday School Minutes*, 24 December 1889, 9 June 1892, 18 June 1894; St. George's Free Ch., Edinburgh, *Session Minutes*, 10 January 1892; Lansdowne U. P. Ch., Glasgow, *Annual Report 1885*, 40, *Annual Report 1892*, 39; First Cong. Ch., Hartford, *Manual 1885*, 43–44; Boylston Cong. Ch., Boston, *Manual 1896*, 25–26; Cong. Ch., Hyde Park, MA, *Directory 1895–96*, 42; Third Pres. Ch., Chicago, *Manual 1892*, 19; Central Pres. Ch., Rochester, *Session Minutes*, 2 (1886):274; Second Pres. Ch., Philadelphia, *Session Minutes*, 23 April 1881.

20. Koper, United Presbyterian Church and Christian Education," 298; Lyndhurst Road Cong. Ch., London, *News Sheet*, October 1910.

21. Boylan, *Sunday School*, 109, 114.

22. Ibid., 108.

23. For example, there was "Mr. Wilbur's Bible Class" at Plymouth Church, Brooklyn (Griswold, *Sixty Years with Plymouth Church*, 127–28).

24. The offices most commonly held by women were the superintendencies of the primary or intermediate departments; women also were harmonium players, song leaders, librarians, secretaries, and, in at least one instance in Philadelphia, treasurer (First Pres. Ch., *Manual 1905*, 2–3).

25. For examples, see St. George's Free Ch., Edinburgh, *Deacons' Court Minutes*, 10 October 1859.

26. Govan Parish, Glasgow, *Sabbath School Minutes*, 9 June 1892, 12 December 1895.

27. Carruthers, ed., *The Ter-Jubilee Book of the North Church of Perth*, 118; St. George's Free Ch., Edinburgh, *Session Minutes*, 10 January 1892.

28. Boylan, *Sunday School*, 48, 135, calculated the same ratio, although in reference to American congregations of several denominations. In my sample, the range extended from 1:6 to 1:15 with a large concentration of cases showing one teacher for every 9, 10, or 11 pupils. Boylan's indication of average class attendances of six to ten also matches my findings for Britain and American Reformed congregations. As one example, Plymouth Church, Brooklyn, had thirty-two classes in its "main room" in 1854, and with an average attendance of two hundred pupils, this came out to 6.3 per class. Plymouth also had an "infant department" for the youngest children, and it ran three Bible classes, two of which averaged six to ten students per Sunday and one which averaged twenty-five to thirty-five students. Plymouth Cong. Ch., Brooklyn, *Manual 1854*, 13.

29. Boylan, *Sunday School*, 137, reproduces an American floor plan showing the small classes "gathered in semicircles around their teachers."

30. The system of prizes and rewards, though popular with both teachers and parents, was not without controversy. Some believed it fomented envy or overemphasized competition (Boylan, *Sunday School*, 44). Prize schemes flourished however, particularly in Britain. A Scottish plan called "The Higher Instruction of Youth," which gave "awards for correct repetition of the *Shorter Catechism*," spread to the Presbyterian Church of England (Canning St. Pres. Ch, Liverpool, *Jubilee Memorial*, 18). The Free Church's General Assembly ran "Welfare of Youth" competitive examinations for scholars age twelve and above. Many of the schemes were actually competency-based rather than competitive, although this too could lead to misunderstanding. The Govan parish Sunday School Committee received a complaint in 1894 that so many prizes were being given that "it was no longer a prize scheme"; the teachers defended their system and argued that "if they had all come up to the required standard of proficiency that they should get a prize" (*Sunday School Minute Book*, 18 January 1894).

31. See Boylan's excellent chapter, "Conversion and Christian Nurture," *Sunday School*, 133–65.

32. *Jubilee Memorial of Saint Andrew's Parish and Congregation, Greenock*, 73; see also Boylan, *Sunday School*, 98–99; an article "The Religious Life of Children" in the *Congregationalist* 3 (June 1874): 341–45, made the case for "systematic and continued teaching" in graded classes.

33. Boylan, *Sunday School*, 46–49. Most schools maintained collections both for teachers and for students; the number of volumes ranged from a hundred or so to well over a thousand; Central Presbyterian

Church, Rochester, had fifteen hundred volumes in 1889 and was still growing (*Session Minutes*, 2 [1889]:376); Union Park Church in Chicago had 1,321 volumes with an average circulation of 170 per week in 1886 (*Manual 1887*, 110); in Huddersfield, the readers averaged a little better than a book every two weeks (Paddock Cong. Ch., *Year Book 1903*, 25).

34. Govan Parish, Glasgow, *Sunday School Minute Book*, 7 September 1893; Lyndhurst Road Cong. Ch., London, *Manual 1886*, 18; St. George's Free Ch., Edinburgh, *Deacons' Court Minutes*, 17 October 1853; Boylan, *Sunday School*, 215; James Smylie, "American Sunday School Union Papers," *Journal of Presbyterian History* 58 (winter 1980): 372.

35. See Raymond J. Cunningham, "From Preachers of the Word to Physicians of the Soul: The Protestant Pastor in Nineteenth-Century America," *Journal of Religious History* 3 (December 1965): 327–46, and Belden C. Lane, "Presbyterian Republicanism: Miller and the Eldership as an Answer to Lay-Clerical Tensions," *Journal of Presbyterian History* 56 (winter 1978): 311–25. Although it is based on Church of England clergy, Alan Haig's *The Victorian Clergy: An Ancient Profession Under Strain* (London: Croom Helm, 1984) is instructive, especially the chapter "Clergy Growth and Professionalization," 1–19.

36. King's Weigh House Cong. Ch., London, *Church Minutes*, 8 November 1859, 1 January 1863.

37. Ibid., 26 May 1909.

38. Second Pres. Ch., Philadelphia, *Session Minutes*, 8 January 1879, 15 January 1879; St. George's Parish, Edinburgh, *Session Minutes*, 25 April 1909; Griswold, *Sixty Years with Plymouth Church*, 101–2. Congregations found various ways of paying tribute to deceased pastors—lengthy obituaries in city or religious newspapers, remarks entered into the church's minute books, commissioned portraits or publications, and memorial renovations to the church building.

39. Founded in 1847, the congregation exceeded 500 members during its sixth year, passed 1,000 during 1858, 1,500 during 1864 and 2,000 in 1871 (Plymouth Cong. Ch., Brooklyn, *Manual 1867*, 14; *Manual 1874*, 15).

40. Plymouth Cong. Ch., Brooklyn, *Manual 1850*, 17; see also, *Manual 1867*, 8.

41. Crescent Cong. Ch., Liverpool, *Annual Report 1873*, 5; First Orthodox Cong. Ch., Cincinnati, *Manual 1874*, 41.

42. New Broad Street Cong. Ch., London, *Year Book 1857*, 16; also Redland Park Cong. Ch., Bristol, *Manual 1890*, 8.

43. Withington Congregational Church, Manchester (*Manual 1886*, 6) and Paddock Congregational Church, Huddersfield (*Yearbook 1903*, 8) both announced the district from the pulpit the preceding Sunday. St. George's Free Ch., Edinburgh, *Session Minutes*, 1 January 1846; *American Presbyterian*, 4 September 1856.

44. Sixth Pres. Ch., Chicago, *Manual 1883*, 18–19.

45. First Cong. Ch., Chicago, *Manual 1859*, 35; see also, Cunningham, "From Preacher of the Word to Physician of the Soul," 339–41.

46. Griswold, *Sixty Years with Plymouth Church*, 129. Beecher did not hire an assistant pastor until the congregation had nearly two thousand members in 1870, and then partly because he was so often away on speaking tours. "For a long time," according to Griswold, "Mr. Beecher and Plymouth Church followed the prevailing custom, relying upon volunteer service for such extra work in the line of parish visitation as was beyond the pastor's power."

47. See R. Milton Winter, "Presbyterians and Prayers for the Sick," *American Presbyterians* 64 (fall 1986): 141–55.

48. Cong. Ch., Binghamton, NY, *Manual 1875*, 6.

49. First Pres. Ch., Chicago, *Catalogue of Members 1869;* see also Second Presbyterian Church, Chicago, *Year Book 1906*, 10, which hired a woman as church "missionary" to help with visitation. As we will see in Chapter 9, women employed as missionaries and Bible women carried out many of the administrative and pastoral responsibilities associated with city mission work.

50. David E. H. Mole, "The Victorian Town Parish: Rural Vision and Urban Mission," in Derek Baker, ed., *The Church in Town and Countryside* (Oxford: Basil Blackwell, 1979), 366.

51. Second Pres. Ch., Philadelphia, *Session Minutes*, April 1881; St. George's Free Ch., Edinburgh,

*Session Minutes*, 3 November 1843.

52. *Jubilee Memorial of Saint Andrew's Parish and Congregation, Greenock,* 146; also, *History of Broughton Place United Presbyterian Church* (Edinburgh: Oliphant, 1872), 145; St. George's Parish, Edinburgh, *Session Minutes*, 9 October 1911.

53. St. George's Free Ch., Edinburgh, *Session Minutes*, 24 October 1910.

54. Withington Cong. Ch., Manchester, *Manual 1887*, 24.

55. For examples of gender-related arrangements for visitation of servants, see Edgbaston Cong. Ch., Birmingham, *Manual 1894*, 34; Lyndhurst Road Cong. Ch., London, *Deacons' Minutes*, 6 July 1884; St. George's Free Ch., Edinburgh, *Deacons' Court Minutes*, 9 December 1850. A. Allan MacLaren, *Religion and Social Class: The Disruption Years in Aberdeen* (London: Routledge and Kegan Paul, 1974), 136, implies that the unwillingness of elders to visit servants or shop girls was evidence of class prejudice; but since the women who easily made the visits came from the same middle-class situations, it is likely that the hesitancy had nothing at all to do with class and everything to do with gender.

56. *History of Broughton Place United Presbyterian Church*, 149; First Cong. Ch., Hyde Park, MA, *Manual 1913*, 10; Moseley Road Cong. Ch., Birmingham, *Manual 1893–94*, 13; King's Weigh House Cong. Ch., London, *Church Minutes*, 28 March 1901; Acocks Green Cong. Ch., Birmingham, *Manual 1896*, 42; St. George's Free Ch., Edinburgh, *Session Minutes*, 1 January 1846. St. Andrew's Parish, Greenock, started a "Female Association for Promoting the Interests of Religion and Education in the Parish and Congregation of St. Andrew" in 1837 at the "instigation of Miss Janet G. Dunlap, to aid the Minister and the Session"; the congregation's Jubilee historian noted that the minutes from the time carried "an admirable defence of woman's right to undertake Christian work" (*Jubilee Memorial of St. Andrew's Parish and Congregation, Greenock*, 27, 79–80).

57. Drummond and Bulloch, *Church in Victorian Scotland*, 82.

58. In 1912, St. George's Parish, Edinburgh, sought legal advice as to whether the obligation to set aside one-half of the door collection was still in force. Finding that it was not, they closed their separate poor fund in 1913 and determined to spend out of general receipts whatever "experience from time to time show to be desirable" for poor relief (*Session Minutes*, 13 May 1912, 10 January 1913).

59. Greenside Parish, Edinburgh, *Session Minutes*, 8 July 1872; St. George's Free Ch., Edinburgh, *Session Minutes*, 1 October 1878, 19 October 1896.

60. Second Cong. Ch., Hartford, *Confession of Faith and Covenant 1838*, 25–26; *Manual 1860*, 25.

61. Central Pres. Ch., Rochester, *Session Minutes*, 6 March 1876; St. George's Free Ch., Edinburgh, *Deacons' Court Minutes*, 3 February 1879.

62. King's Weigh House Cong. Ch., London, *Deacons' Minutes*, 29 June 1852.

63. Second Pres. Ch., Philadelphia, *Session Minutes*, 15 February 1839, 5 December 1839.

64. Greenside Parish, Edinburgh, *Session Minutes*, 7 February 1870; King's Weigh House Cong. Ch., London, *Deacons' Minutes*, 2 August 1853.

65. St. George's Free Ch., Edinburgh, *Session Minutes*, 7 December 1885.

66. Central Pres. Ch., Rochester, *Session Minutes*, 30 January 1891; for what it was worth, the session did exact a promise that the records be "treated as confidential."

67. Illegitimacy rates were approximately half again as high in nineteenth-century Scotland as in England or Wales, which may partially account for the prevalence of such cases in Scotland. Paul Thompson, *The Edwardians: The Remaking of British Society* (Bloomington: University of Indiana Press, 1975), 303. Smith's study of nonconformity in Oldham and Saddleworth, England, confirms that nonattendance was the most frequently cited transgression (*Religion in Industrial Society*, 144).

68. See Watts, *Dissenters*, 2:205; Boyd Hilton, *The Age of Atonement: The Influence of Evangelicalism on Social and Economic Thought, 1795–1865* (Oxford: Oxford University Press, 1988), 136–47; also V. Markham Lester, *Victorian Insolvency: Bankruptcy, Imprisonment for Debt, and Company Winding-Up in Nineteenth-Century England* (Oxford: Clarendon Press, 1995), 68.

69. First Cong. Ch., Rochester, NH, *Manual 1876*, 20; Cowcaddens Free Ch., Glasgow, *Session Minutes*, 26 November 1868; Old South Cong. Ch., Boston, *Church Records*, 9 March 1860; Central Pres.

Ch., Rochester, *Session Minutes*, 8 June 1870.

70. Second Pres. Ch., Philadelphia, *Session Minutes*, 14 June 1836, 6 September 1838.

71. First Cong. Ch., Ridgefield, CT, *Manual 1904*, 32–33.

72. See, among many examples, Second Cong. Ch., Hartford, *Confession of Faith and Covenant 1838*, 26; First Cong. Ch., Ridgefield, CT, *Concise History 1843*, 24–25; Union Park Cong. Ch., Chicago, *Manual 1887*, 25.

73. Plymouth Cong. Ch., Rochester, NY, *Manual 1856*, 11.

74. Old South Cong. Ch., Boston, *Church Records*, 11 January 1830.

75. Ibid., 11 January 1830, 9 February 1832, 16 February 1832.

76. St. George's Free Ch., Edinburgh, *Session Minutes*, 6 December 1881, 23 January 1882, 24 April 1882, 11 July 1882, 22 January 1883.

77. Great George Street Cong. Ch., Liverpool, *Regulations 1869*, Number 7.

78. Cowcaddens Free Ch., Glasgow, *Session Minutes*, 16 March 1868, 30 April 1868.

79. Fourth U. P. Ch., Pittsburgh, *Session Minutes*, 17 June 1869, 5 September 1869.

80. First Pres. Ch., Indiana, Pennsylvania, *Session Minutes*, 23 September 1859, 10 November 1859.

81. King's Weigh House Cong. Ch., London, *Deacons' Minutes*, 29 June 1852, 27 July 1852, 28 September 1852.

82. Greyfriars Parish, Edinburgh, *Session Minutes*, 5 August 1838, 19 August 1838, 9 September 1838.

83. For examples of sessions or diaconates sharing information, see Old South Cong. Ch., Boston, *Church Records*, 22 June 1840; Govan Parish, Glasgow, *Session Minutes*, 14 October 1858; St. George's Free Ch., Edinburgh, *Session Minutes*, 3 May 1852, 3 December 1855, et seq.

84. Second Pres. Ch., Philadelphia, *Session Minutes*, 8 December 1838; St. George's Free Ch., Edinburgh, *Session Minutes*, 11 July 1862, 19 October 1896.

85. Greyfriars Parish, Edinburgh, *Session Minutes*, 8 December 1844, 27 April 1845.

86. Central Pres. Ch., Rochester, *Session Minutes*, 12 July 1858, 1 September 1858, 8 September 1858, 3 October 1858.

87. Cong. Ch., Jamaica Plain, MA, *Manual 1898*, 13.

88. Old South Cong. Ch., Boston, *Church Records*, 14 July 1830, 9 February 1832.

89. Second Pres. Ch., Philadelphia, *Session Minutes*, 19 September 1843. It should be noted that this was the second time the session had arbitrated between the same two women; an earlier outbreak of animosity in 1836 had been settled, or so the session thought (17 June 1836). Its reemergence two or three years later testifies to the precariousness of many such reconciliations.

90. Central Pres. Ch., Rochester, *Session Minutes*, 29 March 1892.

91. On the use of church discipline to mark a community's ethical boundaries, see Kai Erikson's *Wayward Puritans: A Study in the Sociology of Deviance* (New York: Wiley, 1966).

92. Fourth U. P. Ch., Pittsburgh, *Session Minutes*, 2 February 1857.

93. Old Union U. P. Ch., Mars, PA, *Session Minutes*, Summer 1863 through January 1864 passim.

94. Central Pres. Ch., Rochester, *Session Minutes*, 30 April 1873.

95. St. Paul's Cong. Chapel (Hawley Road), London, *List of Names and Residences 1869*, 13–14.

96. St. George's Free Ch., Edinburgh, *Session Minutes*, 13 January 1853. The contrast between two cases makes the point. One woman, separated from her husband, had become the focus of neighborhood gossip and brought "scandal . . . on the congregation." She was suspended, and the district elder was told to keep a sharp eye on the situation. In another instance, however, where a couple was living apart and there was "no public scandal" and their conduct was "unexceptional," the two were simply admonished to remain circumspect (20 October 1851, 21 October 1844).

97. Fourth U. P. Ch., Pittsburgh, *Session Minutes*, 2 February 1880; Old South Cong. Ch., Boston, *Church Records*, 9 February 1832.

98. Central Pres. Ch., Rochester, *Session Minutes*, 21 April 1879; Old South Cong. Ch., Boston, *Church Records*, 9 February 1832.

99. King's Weigh House Cong. Ch., London, *Deacons' Minutes*, 2 November 1854; Central Pres. Ch.,

Rochester, *Session Minutes*, 19 February 1866; Cowcaddens Free Ch., Glasgow, *Session Minutes*, 4 September 1872; St. George's Free Ch., Edinburgh, *Session Minutes*, 20 June 1881.

100. King's Weigh House Cong. Ch., London, *Deacons' Minutes*, 27 November 1860.

101. Park Parish, Glasgow, *Session Minutes*, 29 December 1861.

102. Cowcaddens Free Ch., Glasgow, *Session Minutes*, 1 June 1898.

103. Greenside Parish, Edinburgh, *Session Minutes*, 12 May 1872.

104. For a particularly effective examination of the evangelicals' generosity toward unwed mothers, see Regina Kunzel, *Fallen Women, Problem Girls: Unwed Mothers and the Professionalization of Social Work, 1890–1945* (New Haven: Yale University Press, 1993). Also, Carroll Smith-Rosenberg, "Beauty, the Beast, and the Militant Woman: A Case Study in Sex Roles and Social Stress in Jacksonian America," 109–28 in Carroll Smith-Rosenberg, *Disorderly Conduct: Visions of Gender in Victorian America* (New York: Oxford University Press, 1985).

105. St. George's Free Ch., Edinburgh, *Session Minutes*, 21 April 1853, 22 August 1853, 22 April 1858.

106. Lyndhurst Road Cong. Ch., London, *Deacons' Minutes*, 29 June 1885, 30 September 1886, 1 November 1886, 5 February 1888; St. George's Free Ch., Edinburgh, *Session Minutes*, 6 June 1910; Govan Parish, Glasgow, *Session Minutes*, 9 October 1856.

107. Second Pres. Ch., Philadelphia, *Music Committee Minutes*, 4 April 1902; Cowcaddens Free Ch., Glasgow, *Session Minutes*, 18 December 1901, 13 November 1901; after 1899 Cowcaddens tried no disciplinary cases that did not involve a church official or someone sentenced to prison.

108. First Cong. Ch., Ridgefield, CT, *Manual 1904*, 35–52; Plymouth Cong. Ch., Brooklyn, *Manual 1874*, 23; Union Park Cong. Ch., Chicago, *Manual 1887*, 26.

109. Cowcaddens Free Ch., Glasgow, *Session Minutes*, 15 November 1891, 18 February 1892; Central Pres. Ch., Rochester, *Session Minutes*, 16 March 1892, 4 February 1896, 6 May 1896; Park Street Cong. Ch., Boston, *Articles of Faith and Covenant 1916*, 7; Old South Cong. Ch., Boston, *Church Records*, 22 January 1875.

110. Govan Parish, Glasgow, *Session Minutes*, 27 January 1875. Henderson, *Scottish Elder*, 246, notes that cases of antenuptial fornication were handled privately by the minister beginning in 1884 at Gilcomston and in 1897 at Oxnam.

## Chapter 8

1. Brown, *Maxwell Story*, 21.

2. Greenside Parish, Edinburgh, *Session Minutes*, 6 November 1871, 4 December 1871, 8 January 1872, 8 July 1872, 5 January 1874, 2 February 1874, 8 February 1874, 7 December 1874, 6 December 1875, 14 February 1876, 13 March 1876.

3. Sidney Pollard, *The Genesis of Modern Management: A Study of the Industrial Revolution in Great Britain* (Cambridge: Harvard University Press, 1965); Alfred Chandler, *The Visible Hand: The Managerial Revolution in American Business* (Cambridge, Mass.: Belknap Press, 1977). Ben Primer, *Protestants and American Business Methods* (Ann Arbor: UMI Research Press, 1979), finds similar borrowing of business methods and language among American Methodists, Episcopalians, Southern Baptists, and Disciples of Christ in the 1890s and early twentieth century; this might suggest that Presbyterians and Congregationalists, with a high proportion of middle-class business leaders among their officers, were among the quickest to adapt business practices to the church.

4. Paul H. Heidebrecht, "Chicago Presbyterians and the Businessman's Religion, 1900–1920," *American Presbyterians* 64 (spring 1986): 38–48. Heidebrecht's study deals with the first two decades of the twentieth century and emphasizes church agencies and associations; his interpretation appears equally valid at an earlier date and in local churches.

5. See, for example, T. W. Aveling's "Church Administration," a five-part series that ran in the *Congregationalist* 6 (March–July 1877): 168–73, 226–32, 271–77, 345–49, 433–39. Aveling encouraged dea-

cons to see that meetings were "conducted in a business-like manner." Among his other recommendations were fire-proof safes, specified delegation of tasks, printed forms, specially printed ledger books, improved communication of financial needs to members, and annual reports.

6. Plymouth Cong. Ch., Brooklyn, *Manual 1867*, 10; St. George's Free Ch., Edinburgh, *Session Minutes*, 2 June 1843; First Cong. Ch., Binghamton, NY, *Manual 1875*, 5.

7. Second Pres. Ch., Philadelphia, *Session Minutes*, 7 November 1854.

8. Central Pres. Ch., Rochester, *Session Minutes*, 16 February 1897.

9. St. George's Free Ch., Edinburgh, *Deacons' Court Minutes*, 6 October 1902. Four typical examples, representing different segments of the Reformed community, show local churches supporting a mixture of denominational and nondenominational causes, together with their own local projects. Park Parish in Glasgow accepted contributions for foreign missions in January, home missions in February, colonial churches in March, its own city mission project in April, and the army and navy chaplains in May. Like some other city congregations, Park skipped over the vacation months of summer and resumed in November with a collection for the conversion of the Jews, and in December with two collections, for the Royal Infirmary and for the Church of Scotland's Education Committee (*Session Minutes*, 6 November 1866). In London, Lyndhurst Road had a schedule that included Hackney College, the denominational fund in aid of weaker churches, two local mission projects at Cricklewood and Kentish Town, the London Missionary Society, a hospital, Sunday School work, the Evangelical Continental Society, the Missionary Daughters' School, the London City Mission, and the London Congregational Union (*Deacons' Minutes*, 6 January 1890). Second Presbyterian Church in Chicago conducted appeals for foreign missions (twice), home missions, education of young men, Bible and tract societies, Bethel Society, Aid for Norwegian Churches, campaign to build a church in Egypt, denominational Board of Church Erection, Sunday School agent for the city, colleges and seminaries abroad, Armenian churches, and their own mission Sunday School (*Manual 1856*, 10). In Boston, Park Street Church collected for foreign missions, the denomination's Education Society, American and Foreign Christian Union, city missions, Bible Society, Western College Society, Sunday School work, home missions, Seaman's Friend Society, tract distribution, and the poor of the congregation (*Articles of Faith and Covenant 1850*, 10).

10. Plymouth Cong. Ch., Brooklyn, *Manual 1850*, 33.

11. Regent Square Pres. Ch., London, *Annual Report 1847*, 36–37.

12. For instance, Govan's elders in 1857 directed the minister and session clerk to "prepare a statement of the different purposes to which the Church Collections are applied with the view to its being read to the congregation for the purpose of leading them to increase their collections" (Govan Parish, Glasgow, *Session Minutes*, 11 June 1857). See also Sixth Pres. Ch., Chicago, *Manual 1883*, 17; Regent Square Pres. Ch., London, *Circular*, 1 January 1845, *Regent Square Misc. Papers*, United Reformed Church History Society, London.

13. *American Presbyterian*, 4 December 1856.

14. Regent Square Pres. Ch., London, *Annual Report 1848*, 1; King's Weigh House, London, *Deacons' Minutes*, 10 November 1862; Park Parish, Glasgow, *Session Minutes*, 22 October 1911; Greyfriars Parish, Edinburgh, *Session Minutes*, 5 December 1897; Central Pres. Ch., Rochester, *Session Minutes*, 3 November 1886, 9 March 1897; Fourth U. P. Ch., Pittsburgh, *Session Minutes*, 10 February 1912. For an example of a sample form touted in a religious newspaper, see *American Presbyterian*, 4 December 1856.

15. An example of an 1848 form used for home solicitation is preserved in *Regent Square Misc. Papers*, United Reformed Church History Society, London; Turner, *Story of Pilrig Church*, 10–11; St. George's Free Ch., Edinburgh, *Deacons' Court Minutes*, 11 December 1843, 9 June 1845; Fourth U. P. Ch., Pittsburgh, *Session Minutes*, 7 April 1879; Lansdowne U. P. Ch., Glasgow, *Annual Report 1865*, 5–6; St. George's Parish, Edinburgh, *Session Minutes*, "1854–55 Report" [2:126], also 29 December 1858; Brown, *Maxwell Story*, 34; Old South Cong. Ch., Boston, *Church Records*, 6 December 1842, 20 November 1848, 20 January 1851, 12 January 1874, 8 January 1877.

16. *American Presbyterian*, 18 December 1856.

17. *Carr's Lane Meeting House, A Retrospect: 1898*, 51.

18. First Cong. Ch., Hartford, *Manual 1858*, 8–10; *Manual 1867*, 9.

19. Duncan, *Scottish Sanctuary*, 149.

20. Central Pres. Ch., Rochester, *Session Minutes*, 23 April 1888.

21. St. George's Free Ch., Edinburgh, *Deacons' Minutes*, 11 December 1843, 4 November 1872; Govan Parish, Glasgow, *Session Minutes*, 4 January 1883.

22. Greenside Parish, Edinburgh, *Session Minutes*, 8 July 1872; Greyfriars Parish, Edinburgh, *Session Minutes*, 13 February 1873; St. George's Parish, Edinburgh, *Session Minutes*, 2 February 1873; Johnston, *Story of St. Stephen's*, 107n. Bellgrove United Presbyterian Church in Glasgow had a similar experience; mission boxes in the vestibule had "never proved a success" and pew collections "proved a means of increasing revenue" (*Late Rev. William Barras*, 60, 75). Glasgow's Park parish did not start pew collections until 1911 (*Session Minutes*, 17 February 1911), and the Prospect Street Presbyterians in Hull did not change until 1917 (*"Where Our Fathers Praised Thee": History of Prospect Street Church* [Hull: Presbyterian Church of England, 1923], 34). There was one other disadvantage to church door collections, as an occasional congregation found out to its dismay: a plate left unguarded by the door could disappear. The deacons' court at St. George's Free Church, Edinburgh, became concerned in 1892 about the "proper Officering of the Church Vestibule when Collections are being made . . . in view of what has recently taken place in several Churches of the City, and as to how the Plates could be best protected." A month later, the deacons wondered if they could put a cover on the plates "so as to prevent the Church Door Collections lying exposed" (*Deacons' Court Minutes*, 3 October 1892, 7 November 1892). In December 1890, Cowcaddens Free Church in Glasgow lost a Sunday morning door collection with "no clue" as to the "perpetrator or perpetrators of the dishonest act." In this case, the bag had been put in a closet during the service; henceforth, they concluded, the bag would go into the office safe (*Deacons' Court Minutes*, 3 October 1892).

23. See, for instance, Lyndhurst Road Cong. Ch., London, *Deacons' Minutes*, 28 April 1884; Lansdowne U. P. Ch., Glasgow, *Managers' Minutes*, 13 December 1871; St. George's Free Ch., Edinburgh, *Deacons' Court Minutes*, 10 March 1845, 8 January 1883, 5 December 1893.

24. A sampling of available rates of benevolent giving: Great George Street Cong. Ch., Liverpool: benevolences were 76 percent of total giving (*Manual 1872*, 45); St. George's Free Ch. Edinburgh: 79 percent [cumulative 1843–74] (David MacLagan, *St. George's Edinburgh: A History of St. George's Church 1814 to 1843 and of St. George's Free Church 1843 to 1873* [London: Nelson, 1876], 195–97); Free College Ch., Glasgow: 70–77 percent (*Annual Reports 1877*, 12–13, *Annual Report 1878*, 7–17, *Annual Report 1890*, 11–13, *Annual Report 1892*, 13–14); Lyndhurst Road Cong. Ch., London: 70 percent (*Manual 1914*, 71); Regent Square Pres. Ch., London: 66 percent (*Annual Report 1884*, 29–32); Carr's Lane Cong. Ch., Birmingham: 56 percent (*Manual 1871*, 9, 34); First Pres. Ch., Pittsburgh: 56 percent (*Manual 1912*, 22–24); Second Pres. Ch., Philadelphia: 52 percent (*Session Minutes*, 1 April 1900); Third Pres. Ch., Chicago: 51 percent (*Manual 1892*, 50); Central Pres. Ch., Rochester: 50 percent (*Session Minutes*, 1 April 1870); Plymouth Cong. Ch., Brooklyn: 48 percent [cumulative 1869–73] (*Manual 1874*, 10); Cowcaddens Free Ch., Glasgow: 41 percent (*Deacons' Court Minutes*, 15 March 1894); Wellington U. P. Ch., Glasgow: 40 percent [1891–92] (*Historical Sketch of Wellington United Presbyterian Congregation, Glasgow*, 80–89); First Cong. Ch., Cleveland: 21 and 29 percent (*Society Records*, 22 June 1880, 9 May 1887); Paddock Cong. Ch., Huddersfield [165 members]: 12 percent (*Year Book 1903*, 19); Handsworth Cong. Ch., Birmingham [70 members]: 5 percent (*Manual 1900*, 12–13); Mayfield Free Ch., Edinburgh in the first year of its existence gave only 1 percent, but after four years it reached a more normal 45 percent, and after twelve years it gave 57 percent (*Mayfield Free Church, 1875–96* [Edinburgh, 1896], 21–24).

25. Old South Cong. Ch., Boston, *Standing Committee Records*, 9 April 1860.

26. King's Weigh House Cong. Ch., London, *Church Records*, 2 October 1860, 29 January 1861, 26 February 1861, 15 April 1862.

27. St. George's Parish, Edinburgh, *Session Minutes*, 27 February 1879; Fourth U. P. Ch., Pittsburgh, *Session Minutes*, 16 September 1878.

28. Cowcaddens Free Ch., Glasgow, *Session Minutes*, 31 December 1913; St. George's Free Ch., Edinburgh, *Session Minutes*, 1 January 1846.

29. St. George's Free Church did both in 1847 when a meeting was called to elect a new pastor (*Session Minutes*, 22 September 1847).

30. Central Pres. Ch., Rochester, *Session Minutes*, 2 April 1913.

31. *A Centenary of Regent Square, 1827–1927* (London, [1927]), 32; *Life and Work*, February 1879; *Free Church Monthly Record*, 1882, passim.

32. Lyndhurst Road Cong. Ch., London, *Deacons' Minutes*, 26 September 1887, 27 June 1887; Forty-first Street Pres. Ch., Chicago, *Church News*, vol. 13 (February 1906).

33. Regent Square Pres. Ch., London, undated posters [based on names of ministers; the first comes from 1869–88 and the second from 1907–25], *Regent Square Misc. Papers*, United Reformed Church History Society, London. First Pres. Ch., Chicago, poster, 16 November 1890, "Orders of Service" file, Presbyterian Historical Society, Philadelphia.

34. Lyndhurst Road, *Deacons' Minutes*, 2 October 1882, 25 July 1911; Govan Parish, Glasgow, *Session Minutes*, 28 February 1899; Cowcaddens Free Ch., Glasgow, *Deacons' Court Minutes*, 7 June 1893; Central Presbyterian Church in Rochester decided in 1912 on a ten-week trial of five dailies, with instructions to one trustee that he should "take charge and . . . report to the Board the apparent results" (*Trustees' Minutes*, 3 April 1912).

35. Lyndhurst Road Cong. Ch., London, *Deacons' Minutes*, 16 December 1884; St. George's Parish, Edinburgh, *Session Minutes*, 8 January 1907; Cowcaddens Free Ch., Glasgow, *Deacons' Court Minutes*, 2 September 1896; Central Pres. Ch., Rochester, *Session Minutes*, 3 January 1889; *Trustees' Minutes*, 7 October 1908, 7 February 1910, 3 January 1915. The Rochester trustees may have been independently creative, but it is just as likely that they had read fellow Presbyterian Charles Stelzle's *Principles of Successful Church Advertising* (1908) or heard about the electric sign with two-foot letters that Stelzle put up on the facade of New York's Labor Temple (Moore, *Selling God*, 214).

36. Central Pres. Ch., Rochester, *Session Minutes*, 11 May 1897; Fifty-second Avenue Pres. Ch., Chicago, *Year Book 1903*, passim. Choosing a church motto was a popular activity in both Britain and America; Booth, *Life and Labour of the People in London*, 2:156–57, lists five children's as well as over a dozen adult "motto texts" in his section of Congregational documents.

37. Greenside Parish, Edinburgh, *Session Minutes*, 8 February 1874; Redland Park Cong. Ch., Bristol, *Manual 1890*, cover page; Lyndhurst Road Cong. Ch., London, *Deacon's Minutes*, 2 April 1891, 28 January 1884.

38. Acocks Green Cong. Ch., Birmingham, *Manual 1896*, 18. See also F. K. Prochaska, *Women and Philanthropy in Nineteenth-Century England* (Oxford: Clarendon Press, 1980), 47–72, which finds the idea for fund-raising bazaars to be derived from commercial urban marketplaces such as the Soho Bazaar, which opened its stalls in London in 1815; by the 1820s, charity bazaars for hospitals and asylums were held in public halls or hotels, and subsequently the idea spread to North America. As churches became more comfortable with the worlds of commerce and popular entertainment, they too learned to capitalize on the bazaar's potential as a fund-raiser.

39. Cavendish Cong. Ch., Manchester, *Grand Bazaar 1909* [program].

40. Paddock Cong. Ch., Huddersfield, *Yearbook 1903*, 5, 31.

41. *Late Rev. William Barras*, 75; Moseley Road Cong. Ch., Birmingham, *Manual 1892–93*, 22; Bethany Pres. Ch., Philadelphia, *Annual Report 1896*, 17.

42. Withington Cong. Ch., Manchester, *Manual 1890*, 57.

43. See Walter Licht, *Industrializing America* (Baltimore: Johns Hopkins University Press, 1995), 151–56, for a discussion of "the divisional, line, and staff-differentiated system of management developed by the railroads."

44. Cowcaddens Free Ch., Glasgow, *Session Minutes*, 4 April 1892, *Deacons' Court Minutes*, 23 March 1891; Boylston Cong. Ch., Boston, *Manual 1896*, 7.

45. Griswold, *Sixty Years with Plymouth Church*, 129.

46. Central Pres. Ch., Rochester, *Trustees' Minutes*, 4 November 1896.

47. First Cong. Ch., Hartford, *Manual 1858*, 22, *Manual 1888*, 3–5; Second Pres. Ch., Chicago,

*Manual 1856,* 3, *Year Book 1906,* 5.

48. Central Pres. Ch., Rochester, *Session Minutes,* 13 May 1913.

49. Brick Pres. Ch., New York, *Annual Report 1991,* following p. 84.

50. Plymouth Cong. Ch., Brooklyn, *Manual 1874,* 26–27.

51. First Cong. Ch., Cleveland, *Manual 1869,* 10, 18; the committees were Visitation of the Sick (three male and four female), General Social Visitation and Ministry to Necessities of the Poor (four and two), Visiting Strangers (three and four), Religious Visitation (four and three), Benevolent Contributions (one and six), and Prayer Meetings (four and three).

52. Plymouth Cong. Ch., Rochester, *Manual 1877,* 23.

53. Central Pres. Ch., Rochester, *Session Minutes,* 16 November 1897; King's Weigh House Cong. Ch., London, *Church Minutes,* 18 June 1903; Second Cong. Ch., Hartford, *Manual 1917,* 5–6.

54. St. George's Free Ch., Edinburgh, *Deacons' Court Minutes,* 8 December 1844; Moseley Road Cong. Ch., Birmingham, *Manual 1897–98,* 15, 19.

55. Free College Ch., Glasgow, *Annual Report 1892,* 13–14; Cowcaddens Free Ch., Glasgow, *Deacons' Court Minutes,* 15 March 1894; Central Pres. Ch., Rochester, *Trustees' Minutes,* 9 April 1900; First Cong. Ch., Cleveland, *Yearbook 1896,* 8–9; Second Pres. Ch., Philadelphia, *Session Minutes,* 1 April 1900; Brick Pres. Ch., New York, *Annual Report 1899,* 20. As a point of reference, on the eve of World War I the English pound was being exchanged for $4.87 (*World Almanac and Encyclopedia 1914* [New York: New York World, 1913], 294.

56. Old South Cong. Ch., Boston, *Standing Committee Records,* 9 April 1860 (and each succeeding April), *Church Records,* 14 January 1861. The $40 raised from current churchgoers suggests its own degree of affluence; those attending Plymouth Church in Brooklyn averaged about $32 over the 1860s (*Manual 1867,* 11, 14; *Manual 1874,* 10, 15).

57. Great George Street Cong. Ch., Liverpool, *Manual 1872,* 45; Carr's Lane Cong. Ch., Birmingham, *Manual 1871,* 9, 34.

58. Plymouth Cong. Ch., Brooklyn, *Manual 1874,* 10.

59. Handsworth Cong. Ch., Birmingham, *Manual 1900,* 12–13.

60. Carr's Lane Cong. Ch., Birmingham, *Manual 1871,* 17.

61. Old South Cong. Ch., Boston, *Society Records,* 20 January 1891, 19 January 1892, 16 January 1900, 17 January 1905, 18 January 1910, 19 January 1915, and index to volume 13 (1897–1910).

62. Brick Presbyterian Church, New York, *Annual Report 1914* includes reports from two such satellite congregations, Christ Church and the Church of the Covenant.

63. Bulloch and Drummond, *Church in Victorian Scotland,* 15. Among the initial motivations for the fund was the Free Church's intention to have a presence in every Scottish parish; it was thus vital to redistribute resources from areas where they were strong immediately after the Disruption to those where they were weak; see also Donald C. Smith, *Passive Obedience and Prophetic Protest: Social Criticism in the Scottish Church, 1830–1945* (New York: Peter Lang, 1987), 52–53, 58.

64. Scottish United Presbyterians had a Fund for Augmentation of Stipends, American Presbyterians and English Presbyterians each had Sustentation Funds, English Congregationalists ran a Fund in Aid of Weaker Churches, and the Church of Scotland had a Fund for Endowments for Chapels of Ease and a Small Livings Fund. Jones, *Congregationalism in England,* 312; Drysdale, *English Presbyterians,* 118; Clifford Merril Drury, *Presbyteran Panorama: One Hundred and Fifty Years of National Missions History* (Philadelphia: Presbyterian Board of Christian Education, 1952), 178.

65. Boston's Old South Church was one congregation that sold pews. Pews could be passed down to heirs or sold, or auctioned for nonpayment of taxes. In 1853, 87 of the church's 133 pews (84 of 93 on the main floor) were "owned"; the rest were in the hands of the society and were rented. There were complications with this system. After several generations, ownership was often unclear, and consequently so was the responsibility for taxes and privilege of voting. When Old South wanted to sell its old house of worship in 1875, the necessity of gaining consent from each pew proprietor had to be settled in the civil court, at last in the church's favor. Pew valuations in 1861 were set at $100 to $800 on the floor, $50 to $75 in the gallery; tax was assessed at 3.5 percent (*Standing Committee Records,* 1 April 1853, 9 April 1855, 8

April 1861, 14 April 1874, 13 April 1875, 11 April 1876). In First Congregational Church, Cleveland, where ownership of "slips" (as pews were called here) was also possible, proprietors who owned more sittings than they needed were entitled to the profits if the extra seats could be let for more than the tax, although the church said it hoped the profits would be returned to the church as a "donation" (*Society Records*, 18 January 1858).

66. The Committee blamed the women of the congregation for this vanity. The "mothers and sisters of bygone generations" could worship God from any seat, but now "even the serving maid whose unrefined taste prompts her to enter the House of God oppressed with the weight of Silk, Brocade and glittering toggery must have a conspicuous place to display herself" (Old South Cong. Ch., Boston, *Standing Committee Records*, 8 April 1861).

67. Sittings in Paddock Congregational Church, Huddersfield, went for one to three shillings per quarter (*Yearbook 1903*, 16); Regent Square Presbyterian Church, London, offered seats at prices from two to eight shillings per quarter (*Manual 1909*, 16); when Wellington Church moved to a location on the west of Glasgow in 1884, its pews rents went from twenty-two to fifteen shillings per half year (*Historical Sketch*, 30); Union Park's rates went from $8 to $160 (*Manual 1887*, 142–48); Old South's pew taxes, though generally low because of the church's large investment income, ranged from $1.75 to $28 (*Standing Committee Records*, 8 April 1861); it is worth noting that Old South's rate differential had been only about two to one in the 1840s (*Standing Committee Records*, 10 April 1846), but had risen along with the contrasts in wealth in the city.

68. Central Pres. Ch., Rochester, *Trustees' Minutes*, 11 March 1884; Park Parish, Glasgow, *Session Minutes*, 24 October 1865.

69. Kaye, *King's Weigh House*, 92.

70. Callum G. Brown, "The Costs of Pew-Renting: Church Management, Church-going and Social Class in Nineteenth-Century Glasgow," *Journal of Ecclesiastical History* 38 (July 1987): 347–61. Brown goes on to note that after the Disruption, demand for seats in the established kirks declined, causing falling seat prices. By the 1860s, the town council had come to see the churches as a drain on revenues and a "constant financial headache."

71. Greyfriars Parish, Edinburgh, *Session Minutes*, 29 November 1840, 17 November 1879.

72. St. George's Parish, Edinburgh, *Session Minutes*, 5 December 1848, 7 October 1861, 1 April 1862.

73. Griswold, *Sixty Years with Plymouth Church*, 107.

74. See Fourth U. P. Ch., Pittsburgh, *Trustees' Minutes*, 23 February 1876, 9 March 1876.

75. Ibid., 8 January 1872.

76. Central Pres. Ch., Rochester, *Trustees' Minutes*, 22 February 1893. The death had apparently left the widow without means, as the trustees also conveyed their sorrow at "the unfortunate financial conditions" that the family faced.

77. First Cong. Ch., Binghamton, NY, *Manual 1875*, 5. Also, Lansdowne U. P. Ch., Glasgow, *Managers' Minutes*, 14 June 1915; Fourth U. P. Ch., Pittsburgh, *Trustees' Minutes*, 13 January 1876.

78. Smith, *Religion in Industrial Society*, 159, makes essentially this same point: "Historians have tended to concentrate on the propensity of differential pew rents to reinforce social differentiation within the chapels, while ignoring its corollary that the richer attenders were effectively persuaded to subsidize the sittings of the poor."

79. For instance, evangelicals in upstate New York built "Bethel" churches in towns along the Erie Canal. Intended to serve the needs of boatmen, they were "free" churches—that is, free of pew rents. As the canal era ended, these churches—one of which became Rochester's Central Pres. Ch.—began to rent pews according to prevailing custom. Clipping from *Democrat and American*, 10 April 1858, in Central Pres. Ch., Rochester, *Session Minutes*, 1:1. See also, Paul E. Johnson, *A Shopkeeper's Millennium: Society and Revival in Rochester, New York, 1815–1837* (New York: Hill and Wang, 1978), 153–54. Among non-Reformed groups, the Methodists had a longstanding aversion to pew-renting, but during the 1850s, their upwardly mobile, urban congregations also began to charge pew rent, which simply attests to the pervasiveness of the system in middle-class communities. Paul Conkin, *The Uneasy Center: Reformed Christianity in Antebellum America* (Chapel Hill: University of North Carolina Press, 1995), 251–52.

80. First Cong. Ch., Cleveland, *Society Records*, 6 January 1890.

81. Lyndhurst Road Cong. Ch., London, *Manual 1883*, 20.

82. Withington Cong. Ch., Manchester, *Manual 1887*, 10.

83. St. George's Parish in Edinburgh recognized the simple lesson of supply and demand. Because the Free Church schism drew off a substantial part of its congregation in the 1840s, seats were in plentiful supply for a generation. The kirk session warned the town council against trying to recoup its lost revenue by raising seat rates. If the price of rentals went up, people would simply stop paying and take their pick of the unrented seats, the elders concluded (*Session Minutes*, 2 December 1867, 7 November 1870). After the Disruption, the Glasgow town council marked down its now-surplus pews to half-price—a typically "commercial" response, according to Brown, "Costs of Pew-Renting," 357.

84. Pilgrim Cong. Ch., Clayville, NY, *Manual 1890*, 12.

85. First Cong. Ch., Binghamton, NY, *Manual 1894*, 11.

86. Central Pres. Ch., Rochester, *Trustees' Minutes*, 22 June 1891, 27 January 1892.

87. King's Weigh House Cong. Ch., London, *Church Minutes*, 26 April 1912.

88. First Cong. Ch., Cleveland, *Society Records*, 6 January 1890.

89. Ibid.

90. Fourth U. P. Ch., Pittsburgh, *Trustees' Minutes*, 26 January 1887.

91. Lyndhurst Road Cong. Ch., London, *Deacons' Minutes*, 24 February 1896; Central Pres. Ch., Rochester, *Session Minutes*, 14 March 1914. Also, Fourth U. P. Church, Pittsburgh, *Trustees' Minutes*, 11 September 1893; St. George's Free Ch., Edinburgh, *Deacons' Court Minutes*, 17 July 1848.

92. Regent Square Pres. Ch., London, *Juvenile Missionary Association Annual Report 1872*.

93. Bedford New Town Cong. Ch., London, *Manual 1854*, 3.

94. Fourth U. P. Ch., Pittsburgh, *Trustees' Minutes*, 17 January 1910.

95. Handsworth Cong. Ch., Birmingham, *Manual 1900*, 4; Withington Cong. Ch., Manchester, *Manual 1886*, 15; Regent Square Pres. Ch., London, *Hand Book 1911*, 19–21.

96. Greenside Parish, Edinburgh, *Session Minutes*, 8 November 1875.

97. First Cong. Ch., Cleveland, *Society Records*, 7 May 1860. This was not the first time that this society's trustees had exposed their personal credit. At the end of December 1858, the congregation's old furnace stopped working; the trustees quickly bought a new one "on four months time"—a decision permitted only by their confidence that "the generosity of this church and society would come promptly to our aid and not allow us to suffer." Ibid., 30 December 1858.

98. See, for instance, King's Weigh House Cong. Ch., London, *Deacons' Minutes*, 29 October 1861, 26 November 1861.

99. Fourth U. P. Ch., Pittsburgh, *Trustees' Minutes*, 17 January 1865, 25 November 1867, 8 November 1869, 13 December 1869.

100. Ibid., November 1869. The total of money owed to pastors could be substantial. S. H. Lee's salary at First Congregational Church in Cleveland was supposed to be $3,000 per year, but in 1876 he received only a little over half that amount. By 1878, the congregation was indebted to him for $2,210, and Lee, cutting his losses, left for another church (*Society Records*, 18 February 1878, 27 May 1878). A year later in Glasgow, William Barras's congregation owed him £109 in back salary (*Late Rev. William Barras*, 62).

101. First Cong. Ch., Cleveland, *Society Records*, 28 December 1857; Greenside Parish, Edinburgh, *Session Minutes*, 6 March 1876, 5 June 1876; King's Weigh House Cong. Ch., London, *Church Minutes*, 18 June 1874.

102. St. George's Free Ch., Edinburgh, *Deacons' Court Minutes*, 4 July 1904.

103. Although salary reductions were generally not considered appropriate ways of closing a budget deficit, extreme distress during a national depression was an exception. Fourth United Presbyterian Church in Pittsburgh was suffering badly in 1877; it had already borrowed fifteen hundred dollars and lost income normally raised by a church festival. In the circumstances, both the minister and the choir leader agreed to 33 percent cuts (*Trustees' Minutes*, 22 January 1877, 7 May 1877, 9 July 1877). That same year, in Rochester,

New York, the minister volunteered to take a 17 percent reduction because, he said, "in these hard times all of us ought to be willing to accept our portion of the great depression." His offer, however, was declined by the trustees who were confident the church could weather the storm (Central Pres. Ch., Rochester, *Trustees' Minutes*, 23 April 1877).

104. St. George's Parish, Edinburgh, *Session Minutes*, 14 January 1908.

105. Ibid., letter to congregation (November 1871), 2 February 1873, 3 November 1873, 14 January 1908; First Cong. Ch., Cleveland, *Society Records*, 21 January 1861; King's Weigh House Cong. Ch., London, *Church Minutes*, 30 April 1896; Fourth U. P. Ch., Pittsburgh, *Trustees' Minutes*, 18 August 1869, 28 June 1872, 29 December 1873; Greenside Parish, Edinburgh, *Session Minutes*, 5 March 1877, 8 April 1878.

106. Greyfriars Parish, Edinburgh, *Session Minutes*, 16 November 1877; Central Pres. Ch., Rochester, *Trustees' Minutes*, 24 June 1861.

107. Frew, *Parish of Urr*, 302; Moseley Road Cong. Ch., Birmingham, *Manual 1893–94*, 28; *Manual 1894–95*, 21; *Manual 1896*, 14–15.

108. Fourth U. P. Ch., Pittsburgh, *Trustees' Minutes*, 9 January 1871, 6 March 1871.

109. Ibid., 30 January 1872, 17 December 1877, 26 January 1887; October 1908 [congregational meeting].

110. Johnston, *Story of St. Stephen's*, 176–79. See also, Greenside Parish, Edinburgh, *Session Minutes*, 10 June 1872, 6 December 1875, 2 January 1876; St. George's Free Ch., Edinburgh, *Deacons' Court Minutes*, 4 December 1876, 2 July 1877, 25 March 1889; [Thin], *Memorials of Bristo United Presbyterian Church*, 207.

111. Plymouth Cong. Ch., Brooklyn, *Manual 1874*, 14; Griswold, *Sixty Years with Plymouth Church*, 185–86.

112. Old South Cong. Ch., Boston, *Society Records*, 19 January 1904. First Congregational Church in Cleveland received $8,500 when its Harbor Street Mission was razed by the railroad in 1881; First Church did not, however, use the money for endowment, but instead constructed a new $11,000 sanctuary that was sufficiently large and well sited to make the congregation financially viable (*Society Records*, 26 October 1881). The construction of an underground station in 1883 displaced King's Weigh House from its Fish Street Hill Meetinghouse. This congregation's experience was less happy; it received an arbiter's award of £37,450, less than half the valuation the congregation put on its property. Homeless for eight years, it finally found property and rebuilt in 1891 just off Grosvenor Square in London's expensive West End (Kaye, *King's Weigh House*, 96–97, 100; King's Weigh House, *Church Minutes*, 1 March 1883, 27 March 1883).

113. Ibid., 19 January 1915; First Cong. Ch., Hartford, *Manual 1888*, 22; Fourth U. P. Ch., Pittsburgh, *Trustees' Minutes*, 21 January 1863; 12 January 1867; 18 May 1885; St. George's Free Ch., Edinburgh, *Deacons' Court Minutes*, 1 January 1894. The Hartford church owned stores, the Pittsburgh congregation owned five single-family "tenement" houses, and St. George's Free held "bonds and dispositions" for lands near Inverness.

114. St. George's Parish, Edinburgh, *Session Minutes*, 9 January 1882, 9 October 1899; Fourth U. P. Ch., Pittsburgh, *Trustees' Minutes*, 2 July 1870; St. George's Free Ch., Edinburgh, *Deacons' Court Minutes*, 1 February 1892, 1 January 1894, 17 February 1905; Govan Parish, *Session Minutes*, 14 April 1870; King's Weigh House Cong. Ch., London, *Church Minutes*, 6 July 1899.

115. Central Pres. Ch., Rochester, *Trustees' Minutes*, 8 January 1859; St. George's Free Ch., Edinburgh, *Deacons' Court Minutes*, 1844, passim; Fourth U. P. Ch., Pittsburgh, *Trustees' Minutes*, February 1860.

116. Carr's Lane Cong. Ch., Birmingham, *Manual 1835, Manual 1871, Manual 1903*.

117. Cowcaddens Free Ch., Glasgow, *Session Minutes*, 23 November 1891.

118. Falcon Square Cong. Ch., London, *Manual 1872*, 8–9.

# Chapter 9

1. Turner, *Story of Pilrig Church*, 10–12, 15, 28, 22–23. On Blaikie's advocacy, see D. Smith, *Passive Obedience and Prophetic Protest*, 193n.

2. *Social Christianity* seems a more appropriate phrase than *Social Gospel* for what is intended in this chapter. Both in the nineteenth century and among historians, the former term has been allowed to stand for various Christian efforts to alleviate social and economic suffering. Although usage has varied, the latter term has more often been used to describe not the benevolent activity alone but the articulation of a theological rationale for it; it has also been placed at the very end of the nineteenth century, where it is understood as a corollary to Theological Liberalism. However, at the local level, theological clarity seldom rose to the foreground; rather, congregations tried as best they could to meet needs as and when encountered. Additionally, one of the arguments here is that local concern for urban poverty was evident much earlier in the century than is usually inferred from the phrase Social Gospel. The literature on Social Christianity (and the Social Gospel) is voluminous. For the best recent discussion linking British and American movements, see Paul T. Phillips, *A Kingdom on Earth: Anglo-American Social Christianity, 1880–1940* (University Park: The Pennsylvania State University Press, 1996).

3. Highgate Pres. Ch., London, *Jubilee, 1887–1937* [London, 1937], 13.

4. Norwood Cong. Ch., Liverpool, *Manual 1870–71*, 3–4; *Manual 1872–73*, 13.

5. Third Pres. Ch., Chicago, *Manual 1899*, 74.

6. Lansdowne U. P. Ch., Glasgow, *Annual Report 1875*, 36.

7. Lyndhurst Road Cong. Ch., London, *Manual 1887*, 38.

8. Brick Pres. Ch., New York, *Annual Report 1914*, 30–32.

9. Central Presbyterian Church in Rochester denied a request for a "temperance meeting . . . on the question of the Constitutional Prohibiting Amendment" because it was "not expedient to interrupt the regular services." Later, a satisfactory time was found and the meeting held, although clearly the elders considered this a building rental not an official congregational function (*Session Minutes*, 21 January 1891, 28 January 1891). Later, in 1899, they agreed to allow the Anti-Saloon League "to be heard" in the church (*Session Minutes*, 27 December 1899). Some church boards made a clear distinction between temperance and prohibition and were noticeably less hospitable to the prohibitionists. Second Presbyterian Church in Philadelphia deemed a request from the Anti-Saloon League "inadvisable" and turned it down (*Session Minutes*, 7 January 1914). St. George's Free Church refused to let a "Total Abstinence Society" be formed in the congregation unless it would "widen the basis of its constitution" to temperance (*Session Minutes*, 1 October 1878).

10. See, for example, Old South Cong. Ch., Boston, *Society Records*, 19 January 1886; Central Pres. Ch., Rochester, *Trustees' Minutes*, 4 May 1904; Greyfriars Parish, Edinburgh, *Session Minutes*, 9 May 1841; St. George's Free Ch., Edinburgh, *Deacons' Court Minutes*, 5 April 1858; Cowcaddens Free Ch., Glasgow, *Deacons' Court Minutes*, 5 April 1903. Churches in the United States, wary of church-state boundaries, did seem to draw a line between petitioning and political organizing. For instance, Rochester's Central Church refused to allow a local option meeting in the church "on the ground that it might possibly lead to political complications" (*Session Minutes*, 2 February 1894).

11. Brick Pres. Ch., New York, *Manual 1914*, 72–73.

12. Lyndhurst Road Cong. Ch., London, *Manual 1892*, 121.

13. Gary S. Smith, "The Spirit of Capitalism Revisited: Calvinists and the Industrial Revolution," *Journal of Presbyterian History* 59 (winter 1981): 489.

14. Old South Cong. Ch., Boston, *Church Records*, 15 March 1852.

15. Thomas Cochrane, *Fifty-One Years in the Home Mission Field and Reminiscences, 1826–1898* (Edinburgh: James Thin, 1989), 87. On Chalmers, see John F. McCaffrey, "Thomas Chalmers and Social Change," *Scottish Historical Review* 60 (April 1981): 32–60.

16. St. George's Free Ch., Edinburgh, *Session Minutes*, 20 June 1904.

17. Lansdowne U. P. Ch., Glasgow, *Annual Report 1906*, 54; *Annual Report 1908*, 54; St. George's Free Ch., Edinburgh, *Deacons' Court Minutes*, 15 June 1868.

18. Mayfield Free Ch., Edinburgh, *Mayfield United Free Church, 1875–1925*, 23.

19. Old South Cong. Ch., Boston, "Report of Lowell Street Mission," *Standing Committee Records*, 9 April 1859. Also, Boylan, *Sunday School*, 14–16.

20. Lansdowne U. P. Ch., Glasgow, *Annual Report 1879*, 31.

21. Booth's survey of London Congregationalists noted this same inclination to make missions "more independent and more responsible." *Life and Labour of the People in London*, 7:118.

22. St. George's Free Ch., Edinburgh, *Deacons' Court Minutes*, 3 July 1865.

23. *Carr's Lane Meeting House: A Retrospect: 1898* (Birmingham, Hudson, 1898), 45; St. John's Wood Pres. Ch., *One Hundred Years, 1870–1970*, 6; Govan Parish, Glasgow, [undated history of building the parish church], *Session Minutes*, 8:13; Brick Pres. Ch., New York, *Annual Report 1899*, 65–94.

24. Old South Cong. Ch., Boston, *Society Records*, 14 April 1863. Andrew Wallace, speaking to the Young Men's Association of Govan Parish in 1877, marked the fruits of pauperism as "lunacy," "drinking," and "wife and child desertion" (Wallace, *The Parish of Govan as It Was and Is* [Glasgow: Cossar, 1877], 15).

25. *Newington United Presbyterian Church, Jubilee Memorial*, 72–73.

26. Cochrane, *Fifty-One Years*, 72.

27. Booth, *Life and Labour of the People in London*, 1:177–78.

28. Third Pres. Ch., Chicago, *Manual 1899*, 73–74; William G. Glass, "Liberal Means to Conservative Ends: Bethany Presbyterian Church, John Wanamaker, and the Institutional Church Movement," *American Presbyterians* 68 (fall 1990): 181–92; Lansdowne U. P. Ch., Glasgow, *Annual Report 1891*, 16; *Annual Report 1892*, 16; *Annual Report 1907*, 79.

29. For examples of congregationally conducted census tallies, see Lansdowne U.P. Ch., Glasgow, *Annual Report 1875*, 20; Cowcaddens Free Ch., Glasgow, *Session Minutes*, 15 September 1891; Brick Pres. Ch., New York, *Annual Report 1900*, 123–25. Cleveland churches organized an interdenominational "House-to-House Visitations" in 1901 and 1902, with workers fanning out across the city with census cards to record name, address, number of people, number of people under age eighteen, number in church at least once a month, number attending Sunday School, and denominational preference (First Cong. Ch., Cleveland, *Trustees' Minutes*, 10 May 1902).

30. Quoted by Cochrane, *Fifty-One Years*, 74.

31. Third Pres. Ch., Chicago, *Manual 1899*, 75; Second Pres. Ch., Philadelphia, *Session Minutes*, 20 October 1885, 1 December 1886; *Mayfield United Free Church*, 20.

32. Fifth Pres. Ch., Chicago, *Manual 1876*, 14.

33. Plymouth Cong. Ch., Brooklyn, *Manual 1874*, 12.

34. Second Pres. Ch., Philadelphia, *Session Minutes*, 12 April 1905.

35. Old South Cong. Ch., Boston, *Standing Committee Records*, 5 April 1862. Plans were already underway to construct a mission chapel; a site had been procured for $11,700, and the building costs, including furnishing, were projected at $26,000 (*Standing Committee Records*, 8 April 1861).

36. St. George's Free Ch., Edinburgh, "Fountainbridge Mission Report 1909," 11.

37. Lansdowne U. P. Ch., Glasgow, *Annual Report 1905*, 36–37.

38. Second Pres. Ch., Philadelphia, *Session Minutes*, 15 April 1908.

39. James B. Hunt, "Jane Addams: The Presbyterian Connection," *American Presbyterians* 68 (winter 1990): 241. See also Kenneth McDonald, "The Presbyterian Church and the Social Gospel in California, 1890–1910," *American Presbyterians* 72 (winter 1994): 249, which argues that with the "growing importance of women in church social work" there was also a "growing uncertainty of the male-dominated power elite, who did not know how to deal with these changes in gender relationships."

40. Lyndhurst Road Cong. Ch., London, *Manual 1895*, 26–27. Booth's *Life and Labour of the People in London* asserted that the Kentish Town Mission was "the best example of its kind" (1:177).

41. Cochrane, *Fifty-One Years*, 76–77, 107, 127.

42. Lyndhurst Road Cong. Ch., London, *Manual 1892*, 79.

43. Lansdowne U. P. Ch., Glasgow, *Annual Report 1874*, 32; King's Weigh House Cong. Ch., London, *Church Minutes* [program for the Darby Street Mission pasted in following 9 April 1885].

44. Old South Cong. Ch., Boston, *Standing Committee Records*, 9 April 1860.

45. Third Pres. Ch., Chicago, *Manual 1885–86*, 26.

46. Quoted by Wotherspoon, *James Cooper*, 85; Cooper, an Aberdeen minister, was struck by the

low status this implied for the male missionary, but one might just as easily be struck by the esteem in which the female director was held or at least by the gender equity reflected in the public's views. The men were paid more, although the fact that the women also received room and board at the mission does narrow the gap. In 1872, Springbank Mission was paying William Agnew £80 while Miss Lang received £31 and lodging. By 1905, however, the gap between their successors was wider—£140 to £36 plus housing, a difference that perhaps reflected the growing professional distinction between a seminary-trained missionary and a self-taught Bible woman (Lansdowne U. P. Church, Glasgow, *Annual Report 1872*, 17; *Annual Report 1905*, 22). Neither of the Springbank salaries, by the way, was very high. The missionary's was well below the minimum for parish clergy while £50 plus lodging was more typical for Bible women; one Edinburgh woman received £75 in 1903 (St. George's Free Ch., Edinburgh, *Session Minutes*, 1 December 1903). United States salaries for women mission workers ranged between $400 and $500 during the last third of the century. The origins of the salaried Bible woman have been traced to 1857, with the establishment of Anglican Ellen Ranyard's London Bible and Domestic Female Mission. See Prochaska, *Women and Philanthropy*, 126–30, 137, and Donald M. Lewis, "'Light in Dark Places': Women Evangelists in Early Victorian Britain, 1838–1857," in Sheils and Wood, eds., *Women in the Church*, 415–18.

47. Norwood Cong. Ch., Liverpool, *Manual 1871–72*, 11.

48. Lansdowne U. P. Church, Glasgow, *Annual Report 1889*, 15; Brick Pres. Ch., New York, *Annual Report 1914*, 3:14.

49. First Cong. Ch., Hartford, *Manual 1885*, 45–46.

50. Lansdowne U. P. Ch., Glasgow, *Annual Report 1873*, 37–39.

51. Brick Pres. Ch., New York, *Annual Report 1914*, 57–58.

52. Johnston, *Story of St. Stephen's*, 152–154. In 1840, according to the parish minister's report, there were 250 enrolled in the Yearly Society, and about 100 had received employment from the Work Society. The pastor was convinced that the association with the parish cultivated spiritual growth as well, and so the needy were helped from a "temporal and religious and moral view."

53. St. George's Free Ch., Edinburgh, *Session Minutes*, 12 October 1846, 9 November 1846; *Deacons' Court Minutes*, 4 November 1844. The Rose Street project, which also operated a day school, originated in 1837 before the Disruption separated St. George's Free from St. George's Church of Scotland parish.

54. First Pres. Ch., St. Louis, *Manual 1861*, 33–34.

55. Old South Cong. Ch., Boston, *Society Records*, 14 April 1863.

56. King's Weigh House Cong. Ch., London, *Church Minutes* [program for the Darby Street Mission pasted in following 9 April 1885]; First Cong. Ch., Hartford, *Manual 1888*, 17–19.

57. Kaye, *King's Weigh House*, 93; Brick Pres. Ch., New York, *Annual Report 1899*, 80.

58. Free College Ch., Glasgow, *Annual Report 1878*, 16.

59. Lansdowne U. P. Ch., Glasgow, *Annual Report 1875*, 20.

60. Prospect Street Pres. Ch., Hull, *Report 1880*, 4–5; *Thirty Years Work, 1868–1898* (Hull, 1898), 18–19.

61. Hay, *High Church, Airdrie*, 18; Lansdowne U. P. Ch., *Annual Report 1889*, 44.

62. Prospect Street Pres. Ch., Hull, *Report 1880*, 4–5; Regent Square Pres. Ch., London, *Annual Report 1881*, 29; Lyndhurst Road Cong. Ch., London, *Manual 1892*, 67; [Irvine], *Thirty Years of Broughton United Free Church, Edinburgh*, 54.

63. Acocks Green Cong. Ch., Birmingham, *Manual 1896*, 2; Redland Park Cong. Ch., Bristol, *Manual 1890*, 5; First Pres. Ch., Pittsburgh, *Manual 1912*, 34.

64. Mayfield Free Ch., Edinburgh, *Mayfield United Free Church, 1875–1925*, 43.

65. Cochrane, *Fifty-One Years*, 94.

66. Lansdowne U. P. Ch., Glasgow, *Annual Report 1878*, 50; *Annual Report 1879*, 34, *Annual Report 1889*, 29.

67. Lansdowne U. P. Ch., Glasgow, *Annual Report 1871*, 20; *Annual Report 1872*, 21; *Annual Report 1878*, 34; *Annual Report 1887*, 44; *Annual Report 1889*, 43; *Annual Report 1898*, 46.

68. Lansdowne U. P. Ch., Glasgow, *Annual Report 1867*, 22; *Annual 1869*, 22.

69. Glass, "Liberal Means to Conservative Ends: Bethany Presbyterian Church," 186; Bethany Pres. Ch., Philadelphia, *Annual Report 1894*, 9. Lyndhurst Road Cong. Ch., London, *News Sheet*, April 1899.

70. *American Presbyterian*, 4 March 1869.

71. Second Pres. Ch., Philadelphia, *Session Minutes*, 4 March 1834. Boylan, *Sunday School*, 24, comments that church schools "assumed special importance" to groups shut out of other opportunities— "girls, adults, blacks, factory children, frontier residents."

72. John B. Macnab, "Bethlehem Chapel: Presbyterian and Italian Americans in New York City," *Journal of Presbyterian History* 55 (summer 1977): 145–60; Elizabeth Lee Abbott and Kenneth A. Abbott, "Chinese Pilgrims and Presbyterians in the United States, 1851–1977," *Journal of Presbyterian History* 55 (summer 1977): 125–77; Third Presbyterian Church, Chicago, began a mission school for Chinese immigrants in 1885 (*Manual 1899*, 76–77).

73. Regent Square Pres. Ch., London, *Annual Report 1869*, 14–15.

74. Old South Cong. Ch., Boston, *Society Records*, 14 April 1863.

75. Ibid., 14 April 1863, 4 April 1870; Regent Square Pres. Ch., London, "Circular," 1 January 1845, *Regent Square Misc. Papers*, United Reformed Church History Society, London; Lansdowne U. P. Ch., Glasgow, *Annual Report 1869*, 20–21.

76. Macnab, "Bethlehem Chapel," 151; Brick Pres. Ch., New York, *Annual Report 1900*, 92. Mayfield Free Church in Edinburgh was one that understood its mission classes as training girls "for going to service" (*Mayfield United Free Church*, 47).

77. Lansdowne U. P. Ch., Glasgow, *Annual Report 1876*, 43.

78. Third Pres, Ch., Chicago, *Manual 1899*, 71; Lansdowne U. P. Ch., Glasgow, *Annual Report 1881*, 41, 45; *Annual Report 1888*, 42; Plymouth Cong. Ch., Brooklyn, *Manual 1874*, 13.

79. First Pres. Ch., Pittsburgh, *Manual 1912*, 37.

80. Third Pres. Ch., Chicago, *Manual 1899*, 74.

81. On the relation of women to temperance, see Barbara Leslie Epstein, *The Politics of Domesticity: Women, Evangelicalism, and Temperance in Nineteenth-Century America* (Middletown, Conn.: Wesleyan University Press, 1981), 107; Ruth Bordin, *Women and Temperance: The Quest for Power and Liberty, 1873–1900* (Philadelphia: Temple University Press, 1981), 7.

82. The Band of Hope movement for children under age sixteen was founded by Anne Jane Carlile, widow of an Irish Presbyterian minister, in 1847 in Leeds. Lilian Lewis Shiman, " 'Changes Are Dangerous': Women and Temperance in Victorian England," in Gail Malmgreen, ed., *Religion in the Lives of English Women* (Bloomington: Indiana University Press, 1986), 196.

83. M'Laren, *Charteris*, 55; Magnusson, *Out of Silence*, 46. On the general relationship between the saloon and working-class recreation, see Roy Rosenzweig, *Eight Hours for What We Will: Workers and Leisure in an Industrial City, 1870–1920* (Cambridge: Cambridge University Press, 1983), 53; Brian Harrison, *Drink and the Victorians: The Temperance Question in England, 1815–1872* (Pittsburgh: University of Pittsburgh Press, 1971), 319–33.

84. Lansdowne U. P. Ch., Glasgow, *Annual Report 1875*, 44; *Annual Report 1885*, 56; Lyndhurst Road Cong. Ch., London, *Manual 1886*, 28–29; *Manual 1914*, 116; *Mayfield United Free Church*, 44; Regent Square Pres. Ch., London, *Annual Report 1869*, 14–15.

85. Haverstock Cong. Ch., London, *Year Book 1862*, 19.

86. In 1890, the Women's Employment Society of Brick Church, New York City, gave the following accounting of its year's work: 607 "permits to receive work" were given to needy women; income was $671 from sales of garments and $369 from subscriptions; expenses included $507 in pay to the women and $337 for materials (*Yearbook 1890*, 32, 35).

87. Lyndhurst Road Cong. Ch., London, *Manual 1883*, 27; *Manual 1885*, 33; First Cong. Ch., Hartford, *Manual 1885*, 45–46; Bethany Pres. Ch., Philadelphia, *Annual Report 1894*, 5; also, Great George Street Cong. Ch., Liverpool, *Manual 1870*, 28–29.

88. Frank T. Wilson, ed., "Living Witnesses: Black Presbyterians in Ministry, III," *Journal of Presbyterian History* 55 (summer 1977): 181–85.

89. Brick Pres. Ch., New York, *Yearbook 1890*, 22; *Newington United Presbyterian Church, Jubilee Memorial*, 64; Glass, "Liberal Means to Conservative Ends: Bethany Presbyterian Church," 183.

90. St. George's Free Ch., Edinburgh, *Deacons' Court Minutes*, 8 December 1844; "Fountainbridge Mission Report, 1909," ibid., 7:400. See also Brick Pres. Ch., New York, *Annual Report 1899*, 80; Lyndhurst Road Cong. Ch., London, *Manual 1894*, 86; *Manual 1885*, 25–33.

91. Lansdowne U. P. Ch., Glasgow, *Annual Report 1873*, 37–39; *Annual Report 1905*, 36–37; Magnusson, *Out of Silence*, 46; also Glass, "Liberal Means to Conservative Ends: Bethany Presbyterian Church," 186. Jones, in his *Congregationalism in England*, 193–94, notes one scheme as early as 1813 for the wholesaling of fresh fish.

92. Carr's Lane Cong. Ch., Birmingham, *Manual 1871*, 29; Lyndhurst Road Cong. Ch., *Manual 1892*, 117; *Manual 1893*, 82; *Deacons' Minutes*, 1 April 1913.

93. St. George's Free Ch., *Deacons' Court Minutes*, 4 April 1904; First Pres. Ch., Pittsburgh, *Manual 1912*, 46–47.

94. Drummond and Bulloch, *Church in Late Victorian Scotland*, 169.

95. St. John's Wood Pres. Ch., London, *One Hundred Years*, 5; Brick Pres. Ch., New York, *Annual Report 1914*, 2:95.

96. Central Pres. Ch., Rochester, *Session Minutes*, 17 November 1896; St. George's Free Ch., Edinburgh, *Session Minutes*, 22 October 1906. A nurse in London in 1899 was paid £55 (Lyndhurst Road Cong. Ch., *News Sheet*, January 1899) and one in New York City in 1914 earned $1,200 (Brick Pres. Ch., *Annual Report 1914*, 54).

97. Glass, "Liberal Means to Conservative Ends: Bethany Presbyterian Church," 188–89; Brick Pres. Ch., New York, *Manual 1914*, 1:54, 2:96. Historian C. Peter Williams suggests that missions placed more emphasis on medical work after 1850 because improved, more effective medical treatment was available and because shifting theology was less likely to attribute disease to providential action. See his "Healing and Evangelism: The Place of Medicine in Later Victorian Protestant Missionary Thinking," in W. J. Sheils, ed., *The Church and Healing* (Oxford: Basil Blackwell, 1982).

98. Lyndhurst Road Cong. Ch., London, *Manual 1891*, 39–40; *Manual 1894*, 86; Third Pres. Ch., Chicago, *Manual 1892*, 17–18. Third Presbyterian Church reported that treatment for "one-third of [Presbyterian Hospital's patients] is absolutely free and fully two-thirds of the remainder pay less than the cost of maintenance due to donations (47).

99. Bethany Pres. Ch., Philadelphia, *Annual Report 1894*, 5; First Pres. Ch., Philadelphia, *Manual 1912*, 47.

100. Lyndhurst Road Cong. Ch., London, *Manual 1883*, 27; Central Pres. Ch., Rochester, *Session Minutes*, 1 October 1895.

101. First Pres. Ch., Pittsburgh, *Manual 1912*, 46.

102. Brick Pres. Ch., New York, *Annual Report 1899*, 42–43; *Annual Report 1890*, 24.

103. Lansdowne U. P. Ch., Glasgow, *Annual Report 1889*, 43, 52; *Annual Report 1894*, 42.

104. Miss Lang at Springbank Mission led a "Married Men's Class" (for literacy) as well as the Mothers' Meeting, which at least raises a certain curiosity about her possible role as an intermediary between the two groups (Lansdowne U. P. Ch., Glasgow, *Annual Report 1878*, 44).

105. M'Laren, *Charteris*, 37.

106. Lyndhurst Road Cong. Ch., London, *Manual 1891*, 51; *Manual 1890*, 44.

107. Cochrane, *Fifty-One Years*, 103.

108. There is a voluminous literature relating to the historical debate about the social role of religion in Victorian Britain and America. Some have argued that religious benevolence was motivated by a desire to impose social order or, more pointedly in the case of E. P. Thompson's *The Making of the English Working Class* (1963), to impose a middle-class order upon the working-class. More recently, historians have emphasized the complexity of benevolent motives and the transformative qualities of religion. Those wishing to enter into this debate might profitably begin with the following discussions: Watts, "Paternalism and Philanthropy: Social Control or Social Harmony?," *Dissenters*, 2: 625–56; F. M. L. Thompson, *The Rise*

*of Respectable Society: A Social History of Victorian Britain, 1830–1900* (Cambridge: Harvard University Press, 1988), chap. 8; Gerald Parsons, "Social Control to Social Gospel: Victorian Christian Social Attitudes," in Gerald Parsons, ed., *Religion in Victorian Britain*, vol. 2, *Controversies* (Manchester: Manchester University Press, 1988), 39–62; McLeod, *Religion and Society In England, 1850–1914*, 109–33; Lawrence Frederick Kohl, "The Concept of Social Control and Jacksonian America," *Journal of the Early Republic* 5 (1985): 21–34; and Ken Fones-Wolf, *Trade Union Gospel: Christianity and Labor in Industrial Philadelphia, 1865–1915* (Philadelphia: Temple University Press, 1989).

109. St. George's Free Ch., Edinburgh, *Session Minutes*, 9 November 1846; Lyndhurst Road Cong. Ch., London, *Manual 1884*, 22.

110. Fifth Pres. Ch., Chicago, *Manual 1876*, 14; Cochrane, *Fifty-One Years*, 73; St. George's Free Ch., Edinburgh, "Fountainbridge Mission Report, 1909," 5.

111. Second Pres. Ch., Philadelphia, *Session Minutes*, 22 November 1914; First Pres. Ch., Pittsburgh, *Manual 1912*, 45; Third Pres. Ch., Chicago, *Manual 1899*, 72; Glass, "Liberal Means to Conservative Ends: Bethany Presbyterian Church," 190. The congregations, struggling under the weight of urban problems, were often quite relieved to see the work pass to someone else. When Springbank's day school was turned over to the government board, the church was thankful to be "relieved of a considerable charge" (Lansdowne U. P. Ch., Glasgow, *Annual Report 1874*, 18).

112. Shared values between the classes have been noted in the case of Sunday Schools by Boylan, *Sunday School*, 37–40, and Laqueur, *Religion and Respectability*, chap. 7; and in the case of British temperance by Harrison, *Drink and the Victorians*.

113. Peter Hillis, "Presbyterianism and Social Class in Mid-Nineteenth-Century Glasgow: A Study of Nine Churches," *Journal of Ecclesiastical History* 32 (January 1981): 47–67; also Peter Hillis, "Education and Evangelisation: Presbyterian Missions in Mid-Nineteenth-Century Glasgow," *Scottish Historical Review* 66 (April 1987): 50; Glass, "Liberal Means to Conservative Ends: Bethany Presbyterian Church," 188, lists the occupations of Bethany heads of households as 39.4 percent white collar (2.3 percent professional, 3.9 major proprietors, 27 clerical and sales, 0.8 semi-professional, and 5.4 petty proprietors); 49.8 percent blue collar (31.7 percent skilled, 13.9 semi-skilled, and 4.2 unskilled); and others (housewives, students, retired) 10.8 percent.

114. On the transition from evangelical women to professional social workers, see Kunzel, *Fallen Women, Problem Girls*.

115. George Marsden, *Fundamentalism and American Culture: The Shaping of Twentieth-Century Evangelicalism, 1870–1925* (New York: Oxford University Press, 1980), 6, 21–32.

116. The congregation as a whole seems to have moved to the right during the 1890s; there were more disciplinary cases, greater emphasis on temperance and Sabbath observance, more evangelistic services and revivals in the church itself. On Southampton Road Mission, see *Manual 1889*, 49; *Manual 1891*, 79–81. Southampton Row opened an evening "reading room" for working men, but found few interested laborers; indeed, Southampton Road had a much more difficult time gathering interest than did Kentish Town, presumably because it lacked the social services that the working poor found useful. Shiman's study of women and temperance identifies the emergence of a different version of temperance in the last quarter of the century, a version based not on inclusive social and moral concerns, but on the exclusive goal of "saving souls" ("'Changes Are Dangerous,'" in Malmgreen, ed., *Religion in the Lives of English Women*, 201).

117. Lansdowne U. P. Ch., Glasgow, *Annual Report 1905*, 9.

118. Ibid., 19–21.

119. Second Pres. Ch., Philadelphia, *Session Minutes*, 1 April 1915.

120. Central Pres. Ch., Rochester, *Session Minutes*, 3 April 1901, 20 June 1901; Central's interest in freedmen's causes grew from Frederick Douglass's residence in the city. In 1912, it was still sending modest contributions to support "colored" mission work through the Rochester presbytery (*Session Minutes*, 31 July 1912).

121. King's Weigh House, London, *Church Minutes*, 8 May 1914; Lewis became a journalist (Kaye, *King's Weigh House*, 117).

122. Brick Pres. Ch., New York, *Annual Report 1911*, 84.

123. M'Laren, *Charteris*, 58.

124. St. George's Free Ch., Edinburgh, "Fountainbridge Mission Report, 1909," 11.

125. First Pres. Ch., Pittsburgh, *Manual 1912*, 37.

126. Redland Park Cong. Ch., Bristol, *One Hundred Years, 1861–1961* [Bristol, 1961], 25.

127. Lyndhurst Road Cong. Ch., London, *Manual 1884*, 22–23.

128. Kaye, *King's Weigh House*, 104; First Pres. Ch., Pittsburgh, *Manual 1912*, 37.

129. First Cong. Ch., Hartford, *Manual 1897*, 114; Lansdowne U. P. Ch., Glasgow, *Annual Report 1874*, 32; *Annual Report 1879*, 33; Lyndhurst Road Cong. Ch., London, *Manual 1884*, 22–23.

## *Chapter 10*

1. [Irvine], *Thirty Years of Broughton United Free Church, Edinburgh*, 9.

2. Paddock Cong. Ch., Huddersfield, *Yearbook 1903*, 5; Regent Square Pres. Ch., London, *Annual Report 1869*, 3; Griswold, *Sixty Years with Plymouth Church*, 44.

3. First Cong. Ch., Binghamton, NY, *Manual 1875*, 20.

4. Third Pres. Ch., Indianapolis, *Hand Book 1874*, 25.

5. Great George Street Cong. Ch., Liverpool, *Regulations 1869*, Number 11.

6. First Cong. Ch., Chicago, *Manual 1859*, 37.

7. Lyndhurst Road Cong. Ch., London, *Manual 1884*, 15.

8. Cowcaddens Free Ch., Glasgow, *Deacons' Court Minutes*, 5 December 1888.

9. Ibid., 15 March 1898; King's Weigh House Cong. Ch., London, *Church Minutes*, 28 March 1901.

10. Paddock Cong. Ch., Huddersfield, *Yearbook 1903*, 30.

11. First Cong. Ch., Hartford, *Manual 1888*, 10–12.

12. First Cong. Ch., Cleveland, *Yearbook 1903*, 10.

13. Third Pres. Ch., Indianapolis, *Hand Book 1874*, 29.

14. Second Pres. Ch., Philadelphia, *Session Minutes*, 30 November 1881.

15. First Cong. Ch., Cleveland, *Yearbook 1903*, 10.

16. Griswold, *Sixty Years with Plymouth Church*, 188.

17. Boylston Cong. Ch., Boston, *Manual 1896*, 26–31.

18. Second Pres. Ch., Chicago, *Year Book 1906*, 10–21.

19. Regent Square Pres. Ch., London, *Hand Book 1911*, 32–34; the other five young men's activities were special Sunday evening worship, a Bible class, a mission study circle, organizing open air services, and editing their monthly club magazine, *Thistle.*

20. Plymouth Cong. Ch., Brooklyn, *Manual 1850*, 12, 17.

21. Park Parish, Glasgow, *Session Minutes*, 14 April 1862, 1 February 1864, 5 December 1864.

22. Lansdowne U. P. Ch., Glasgow, *Annual Report 1897*, 5.

23. King's Weigh House Cong. Ch., London, *Deacons' Minutes*, 26 February 1863; Second Pres. Ch., Philadelphia, *Session Minutes*, 28 September 1881; Lyndhurst Road Cong. Ch., London, *Deacons' Minutes*, 29 May 1893, 30 November 1909; Old South Cong. Ch., Boston, *Church Records*, 5 June 1868; First Cong. Ch., Hyde Park, MA, *Manual 1895*, 7–8; Lozells Cong. Ch., Birmingham, *Manual 1899*, 31; *Historical Sketch of the Wellington United Presbyterian Congregation, Glasgow*, 24; Gilcomston Free Ch., Aberdeen, *Quarterly Record*, vol. 15 (October 1898); *Late Rev. William Barras*, 67.

24. Lansdowne U. P. Ch., Glasgow, *Annual Report 1889*, 15; Cowcaddens Free Ch., Glasgow, *Deacons' Court Minutes*, 9 March 1888, 2 September 1891. Also, Govan Parish, Glasgow, *Session Minutes*, 12 May 1879; Neil Taverner, *"The Church on the Hill": Greenside Parish Church, Edinburgh, 1839–1989* (Edinburgh, 1989), 35.

25. Govan Parish, Glasgow, *Sunday School Minute Book*, 6 June 1889, 24 December 1889, 11 February 1890, 5 June 1890, 4 September 1890, 17 March 1892, 9 June 1892, 9 June 1892, 9 June 1892, 8 December

1892, 8 February 1893, 9 March 1893, 7 September 1893, 18 January 1894. Macleod was not dissembling when he denied any opposition to dancing *per se;* the Govan Young Men's Association, a literary club, had held dances regularly since the mid-1870s. But the fact that the church allowed young men to organize dances under the auspices of a literary club may not have worked to Macleod's advantage as he hoped. It more likely made the teachers (over three-quarters of whom were young women) feel more rather than less cheated—especially when the young men were permitted to have the hall until two o'clock in the morning for their dances (*Young Men's Association Minutes,* 15 February 1877, 22 March 1892).

26. Lyndhurst Road Cong. Ch., London, *Deacons' Minutes,* 8 January 1883, 4 March 1884; Third Pres. Ch., Indianapolis, *Hand Book 1874,* 26.

27. St. George's Free Ch., Edinburgh, *Deacons' Court Minutes,* 4 November 1889; Cowcaddens Free Ch., Glasgow, *Deacons' Court Minutes,* 6 September 1886, 14 September 1896; Turner, *Story of Pilrig Church,* 59; Govan Parish, Glasgow, *Session Minutes,* 25 February 1902. Cowcaddens, with typical Victorian concern for good order and responsibility, charged 1s. 6d. per hundred for use of its cups and saucers outside the church building with the money to go toward "renewal and upkeep" of its stock of china.

28. Old South Cong. Ch., Boston, *Standing Committee Records,* 3 October 1861; Second Pres. Ch., Philadelphia, *Session Minutes,* 19 April 1882; Moseley Road Cong. Ch., Birmingham, *Manual 1892–93,* 15; Central Pres. Ch., Rochester, *Session Minutes,* 8 September 1896; Lyndhurst Road Cong. Ch., London, *Deacons' Minutes,* 8 January 1883; Gilcomston Free Ch., Aberdeen, *Quarterly Record,* vol. 15 (October 1898); Cowcaddens Free Ch., Glasgow, *Deacons' Court Minutes,* 14 January 1902.

29. Alison Kuhne, *Three Hundred Years of History, 1695–1995, of Bingley United Reformed Church* (Bingley, 1995), 25; Regent Square Pres. Ch., "Cottage Mission Social Meeting," 11 April 1899, *Regent Square Misc. Papers,* United Reformed Church History Society, London; Cowcaddens Free Ch., Glasgow, *Session Minutes,* 9 February 1914; Lansdowne U. P. Ch., *Annual Report 1907,* 9; Lyndhurst Road Cong. Ch., *Deacons' Minutes,* 27 September 1892, 3 January 1893; Fourth U. P. Ch., Pittsburgh, *Trustees' Minutes,* 2 July 1877, also 4 June 1878, 12 May 1890.

30. Third Pres. Ch., Chicago, *Manual 1899,* 62.

31. Govan Parish, Glasgow, *Sunday School Minute Book,* 6 June 1889, 18 June 1889, 14 August 1889, 5 September 1889. Later, in 1895, the leader of a similar excursion grumbled, "the school had no football, cricket ball nor rounder ball, and had to be indebted to others for a loan of football, the games of cricket and rounders being impossible for want of material. The swings were also on loan and I find the skipping ropes were not taken back to Govan." The 1895 picnic, combining home and mission schools, was attended by 519 children accompanied by ninety-two adults (12 June 1895).

32. First Cong. Ch., Cleveland, *Yearbook 1896,* 15.

33. Union Park Cong. Ch., Chicago, *Manual 1887,* 98.

34. Regent Square Pres. Ch., London, *Juvenile Missionary Association Annual Report 1872.*

35. First Cong. Ch., Hyde Park, MA, *Manual 1913,* 24.

36. Second Pres. Ch., Chicago, *Year Book 1906,* 9.

37. Forty-first Street Pres. Ch., Chicago, *Young Men's Bible Class Manual 1903,* 10–11.

38. A Young Men's Association was formed in 1838 in St. Andrew's parish, Greenock (*Jubilee Memorial of St. Andrew's Parish and Church, Greenock,* 78). Wellington's "Young Men's Mutual Improvement Association" was formed in Glasgow in 1839, but "existed only a very few years" (*Historical Sketch of Wellington United Presbyterian Congregation, Glasgow,* 21). St. George's Free Church, Edinburgh, had a Young Men's Association founded in 1845, but by the time a second wave of youth work was being promoted in the 1880s, its existence had long been forgotten until the elders were surprised by the return of the group's minute book discovered among the papers of a deceased member (*Deacons' Court Minutes,* 17 March 1845; *Session Minutes,* 18 June 1888). A Young Men's Society existed from 1836 to 1837 at Regent Square in London; its reorganization and survival from 1841 allowed the congregation to claim in 1927 that its group was "the oldest of its kind in the country" (*Centenary of Regent Square,* 17).

39. St. George's Free Ch., Edinburgh, *Deacons' Court Minutes,* 17 March 1845.

40. T. W. Cuthbertson, *Historical Sketch of St. George's Parish Church, Glasgow* (Glasgow: Aird and

Coghill, 1894), 37.

41. Franklin B. Gillespie, "Youth Programs of the United Presbyterian Church: An Historical Overview," *Journal of Presbyterian History* 59 (fall 1981), reports a concern expressed in 1872 by Presbyterian denominational leaders in the United States about the "disappearance of children and young people from congregational worship" (315), but this concern does not seem to have been felt locally; to the extent youth were not present at regular Sunday forenoon services it was because those unattached to families attended separate youth services instead, a habit encouraged by local leaders who designed the alternate worship to cater to different tastes.

42. St. George's Free Ch., Edinburgh, *Session Minutes*, 1 January 1878.

43. Third Pres. Ch., Chicago, *Manual 1899*, 63.

44. Lyndhurst Road Cong. Ch., London, *Deacons' Minutes*, 27 June 1911.

45. Second Pres. Ch., Philadelphia, *Session Minutes*, 18 February 1883.

46. Ibid., 18 February 1883.

47. St. George's Free Ch., Edinburgh, *Session Minutes*, 10 January 1887, 4 April 1887.

48. First Cong. Ch., Hyde Park, MA, *Manual 1895*, 43; Lyndhurst Road Cong. Ch., London, *Manual 1895*, vi.

49. The society at First Presbyterian Church in Pittsburgh had eight officers in 1912—five of whom were female: three of four vice-presidents and both secretaries (the president, the second vice-president, and the treasurer were male). Four of six officers were male at Huddersfield's Paddock Ch., while in Ithaca, New York, the president was the only one of five officers who was a young man. First Pres. Ch., Pittsburgh, *Manual 1912*, 58; Paddock Cong. Ch., Huddersfield, *Yearbook 1903*, 27; First Cong. Ch., Ithaca, NY, *Manual 1895*, 34.

50. Redland Park Cong. Ch., Bristol, *Manual 1890*, 17; Regent Square Pres. Ch., "Young Women's Fellowship Association Programme, 1891–92," *Regent Square Misc. Papers*, United Reformed Church History Society, London; Union Park Cong. Ch., Chicago, *Manual 1887*, 96; First Pres. Ch., Pittsburgh, *Manual 1912*, 58; Lyndhurst Road Cong. Ch., London, *Young People's Guild Minutes*, 22 September 1890, 9 October 1892.

51. There was a rare church with a society affiliated with the Young Men's Christian Association or the equivalent women's organization, but such connections were more common at mission halls than churches.

52. Gillespie, "Youth Programs," 318; Francis E. Clark, *Memories of Many Men in Many Lands: An Autobiography* (Boston: United Society of Christian Endeavor, 1922).

53. Forty-first Street Pres. Ch., Chicago, *Manual, Young Men's Bible Class 1903*, [unpaginated] "Regulations for the Lookout Committee."

54. Third Pres. Ch., Chicago, *Manual 1899*, 67.

55. See Helen Elizabeth Meller, *Leisure and the Changing City, 1870–1914* (London: Routledge and Kegan Paul, 1976).

56. Second Pres. Ch., Philadelphia, *Session Minutes*, 18 February 1883; Lansdowne U. P. Ch., Glasgow, *Annual Report 1885*, 48–49; *Annual Report 1898*, 31; *Annual Report 1899*, 29; Withington Cong. Ch., Manchester, *Manual 1886*, 28; *Manual 1890*, 46; Third Pres. Ch., Chicago, *Manual 1885–86*, 33; *Manual 1889*, 44–45; *Manual 1894*, 40–41; *Manual 1899*, 69–70. See also, Redland Park Cong. Ch., Bristol, *Manual 1890*, 16; Cowcaddens Free Ch., *Deacons' Court Minutes*, 15 March 1898; Cavendish Road Pres. Ch., Leeds, *Centenary* (Leeds, 1964), 8–9.

57. This paragraph and the following one are based on Lyndhurst Road Congregational Church, London, *Young People's Guild Minutes*, 1890–1898, as well as the congregation's *News Sheet* and annual reports for those years.

58. About 45 percent of those who spoke were women, but without knowing the total number of each sex attending, it is impossible to be sure whether this is a proportionate showing or not.

59. This paragraph and the following one are based on Govan Parish, Glasgow, *Young Men's Association Minutes*, 1876–1905, and *Govan Literary Association Minutes*, 1905–1914.

60. Quoted in M'Laren, *Charteris*, 79–82; also 73–78.

61. Cameron, ed., *Dictionary of Scottish Church History and Theology*, 92–93; Free College Ch., Glasgow, *Annual Report 1890*, 28–29; also Livingstone, *The Boys' Brigade in Kirkcaldy*, 2; Turner, *Story of Pilrig Church*, 51; *Historical Sketch of Wellington United Presbyterian Congregation, Glasgow*, 32. The boys of Edinburgh's Greenside parish marched with "dummy guns," but in Rochester, New York, the trustees reluctantly approved actual rifles after being assured that rubber caps would cover the butts to protect the floor. Taverner, *"The Church on the Hill,"* 56; Central Pres. Ch., Rochester, *Trustees' Minutes*, 14 November 1908, 21 November 1908.

62. Free College Ch., Glasgow, *Annual Report 1890*, 29.

63. Lyndhurst Road Cong. Ch., London, *News Sheet*, April 1909, 16.

64. Regent Square Pres. Ch., London, *Manual 1909*, 8–9.

65. Booth, *Life and Labour of the People in London*, 1:129.

66. Fourth U. P. Ch., Pittsburgh, *Trustees' Minutes*, 5 April 1915; Turner, *Story of Pilrig Church*, 48.

## *Chapter 11*

1. Regent Square Pres. Ch., London, *Manual 1909*, 4–5.

2. M'William, ed., *Kirks of the Turriff Presbytery*, 60.

3. Withington Cong. Ch., Manchester, *Manual 1887*, 6–7.

4. Haverstock Cong. Ch., London, *Year Book 1862*, 10.

5. Plymouth Cong. Ch., Brooklyn, *Manual 1850*, 3; Kaye, *King's Weigh House*, 65–66; [Thin], *Memorials of Bristo United Presbyterian Church*, 70; St. George's Free Ch., Edinburgh, *Session Minutes*, 1 January 1846.

6. Plymouth Cong. Ch., Brooklyn, *Manual 1850*, 13.

7. Park Cong. Ch., Brooklyn, *Manual 1850*, 56.

8. First Pres. Ch., Pittsburgh, *Manual 1912*, 26; Acocks Green Cong. Ch., Birmingham, *Manual 1896*, 17.

9. Cuthbertson, *St. George's Parish Church, Glasgow*, 55.

10. King's Weigh House Cong. Ch., London, *Church Minutes*, 25 September 1845, 8 November 1859; Second Pres. Ch., Philadelphia, *Session Minutes*, 8 November 1869, 30 December 1869.

11. Greyfriars Parish, Edinburgh, *Session Minutes*, 10 October 1880; King's Weigh House Cong. Ch., London, *Deacons' Minutes*, 29 January 1863; Plymouth Cong. Ch., Brooklyn, *Manual 1867*, 12; Fourth Pres. Ch., Pittsburgh, *Trustees' Minutes*, 13 November 1873; Greenside Parish, Edinburgh, *Session Minutes*, 4 December 1871.

12. On the separation of public from private space, and separation of rooms by function in Victorian homes, see Ames, *Death in the Dining Room*, chap. 1. Although the amount of seating required was a natural reason for a separate 'lecture hall' for mid-week "social" prayer meetings, it was also true that the mid-week services were intended for members rather than the public; they were, in this sense, the private gatherings of the church family and, as such, they warranted space apart from that used for public worship.

13. St. George's Parish, Edinburgh, *Session Minutes*, 15 October 1888; Park Cong. Ch., Brooklyn, *Manual 1870*, 56; Central Pres. Ch., Rochester, *Trustees' Minutes*, 8 February 1872.

14. Second Pres. Ch., Philadelphia, *Session Minutes*, 23 March 1884; 3 December 1884; St. George's Free Ch., Edinburgh, *Deacons' Court Minutes*, 31 July 1876; St. George's Parish, Edinburgh, *Session Minutes*, 27 February 1879. For similar arrangements, see Johnston, *Story of St. Stephen's*, 97; Old South Cong. Ch., Boston, *Church Records*, 30 April 1866; Greenside Parish, Edinburgh, *Session Minutes*, 5 March 1877; Frew, *Parish of Urr*, 299; Henderson, *Scottish Ruling Elder*, 259.

15. It is difficult to judge how well insured congregations were. Business-minded church officers, such as those Old South Congregational Church in Boston or St. George's Parish in Edinburgh, reviewed their needs regularly and raised coverage, but the size of the increases suggests that buildings were at least

temporarily underinsured. For instance, in 1883 St. George's elders recommended a 50 percent increase from £10,000 to £15,000 and agreed to pay the extra premium from church funds when the Ecclesiastical Commission pleaded inability to do so. One of the elders' concerns was that the Commission, in a practice that was common in both Britain and the United States, had rented out the cellars for commercial storage— in this case "for the storing of Wine, Spirits, or other inflammable material" (*Session Minutes*, 8 January 1883, 25 January 1883). Central Presbyterian Church in Rochester, however, carried only $5,000 of insurance in 1860 on a building that had cost over $30,000 to construct (*Trustees' Minutes*, 22 October 1860; *Session Minutes*, undated entry, 1:325). Other expressions of concern about fire came in the installation of lightning rods, purchase of fire extinguishers, or inspection of furnaces (St. George's Free Ch., *Deacons' Minutes*, 5 December 1881, 6 April 1908; Greenside Parish, Edinburgh, *Session Minutes*, 7 December 1874).

16. Lyndhurst Road Cong. Ch., London, *Deacons' Minutes*, 2 December 1913; Third Pres. Ch., Chicago, *Manual 1892*, 15.

17. Govan Parish, Glasgow, *Session Minutes*, 3 February 1904.

18. Fourth U. P. Ch., Pittsburgh, *Trustees' Minutes*, 6 September 1880; *Session Minutes*, 22 February 1881.

19. Central Presbyterian Church in Rochester set the following fees in 1897: "new auditorium"—$75 for nonaffiliated groups and $50 for affiliated groups if they were charging an admission; weddings—$30 ($20 from 1 June through 15 September); old auditorium—$20 unaffiliated and $15 affiliated; funeral—no charge to members (*Trustees' Minutes*, 7 April 1897). St. George's Free Church in Edinburgh set up an itemized fee schedule: for the church auditorium with services of the church officer—7s. 6d.; doorkeepers, each—2s. 6d.; gas, when used—7s. 6d.; stoves, when used—7s. 6d.; precentor, when used—5s. The fees for the classroom were 5s. and an extra 2s. 6d. if gas and fire were required (*Deacons' Court Minutes*, 6 April 1863). Cowcaddens Free Church did not seem to have a formal fee schedule, but when annual cleaning or painting projects came around, the deacons sent letters to groups like the Young Men's Christian Association and the Gospel Temperance Association asking for donations (*Deacons' Court Minutes*, 4 November 1891).

20. King's Weigh House Cong. Ch., *Deacons' Minutes*, 23 August 1853; Fourth U. P. Ch., Pittsburgh, *Trustees' Minutes*, 19 March 1872.

21. Central Pres. Ch., Rochester, *Trustees' Minutes*, 1 November 1896. For examples of job descriptions, see Govan Parish, Glasgow, *Session Minutes*, 5 December 1872; St. George's Free Church, *Deacons' Court Minutes*, 10 November 1862; St. George's Parish, Edinburgh, *Session Minutes*, 13 October 1885; King's Weigh House Cong. Ch., *Deacons' Minutes*, 23 August 1853.

22. Old South Cong. Ch., Boston, *Standing Committee Records*, 5 April 1850.

23. *Notes on the History of St. Andrew's Church, Edinburgh* (Edinburgh: Lorimer and Gillies, 1884), 37; see also Andrew Landale Drummond, *The Church Architecture of Protestantism: An Historical and Constructive Study* (Edinburgh: T. and T. Clark, 1934), 81.

24. On domestic interiors, see Katherine C. Grier, *Culture and Comfort: Parlor Making and Middle-Class Identity, 1850–1930* (Washington, D.C.: Smithsonian Institution Press, 1988).

25. First Cong. Ch., Cleveland, *Yearbook 1894*, cover; Fingland, *St. John's Presbyterian Church, Kensington*, 20.

26. *History of Broughton Place United Presbyterian Church*, 152–53; M'William, ed., *Kirks of the Turriff Presbytery*, 27, 45, 65–66, 70, 74.

27. King's Weigh House Cong. Ch., London, *Church Minutes*, 1 April 1875; St. George's Parish, Edinburgh, *Session Minutes*, 20 April 1864.

28. *History of Broughton Place United Presbyterian Church*, 155.

29. Central Pres. Ch., Rochester, *Trustees' Minutes*, 11 July 1870.

30. Taverner, *"The Church on the Hill,"* 36, 38.

31. Second Pres. Ch., Philadelphia, *Session Minutes*, 14 March 1860.

32. Moseley Road Cong. Ch., Birmingham, *Manual 1892–93*, 22–25.

33. First Cong. Ch., Hyde Park, MA, *Manual 1905*, 3–6; Fourth U. P. Ch., Pittsburgh, *Trustees' Minutes*, 30 August 1879, 24 January 1883. The Lansdowne women also purchased one hundred teaspoons,

six pairs of sugar tongs, twelve small hand trays, one hundred tea cups and saucers, twenty-four bread plates, twelve bowls, twelve cream jugs, six flower glasses, and three table cloths (*Managers' Minutes*, 21 March 1911).

34. Regent Square Pres. Ch., London, *Manual 1909*, 4–5.

35. Old South Cong. Ch., Boston, *Standing Committee Records*, 14 April 1857. See also, Cuthbertson, *St. George's Parish Church, Glasgow*, 38; [Thin], *Memorials of Bristo United Presbyterian Church*, 69; *History of Broughton Place United Presbyterian Church*, 152–53.

36. St. George's Free Ch., Edinburgh, *Deacons' Minutes*, 10 November 1845; also, *History of Broughton Place United Presbyterian Church*, 155.

37. St. George's Free Ch., Edinburgh, *Deacons' Court Minutes*, 18 July 1852, 9 January 1870; Johnston, *Story of St. Stephen's*, 121; Lyndhurst Road Cong. Ch., London, *Deacons' Minutes*, 31 May 1887, 25 March 1887.

38. Lyndhurst Road Cong. Ch., London, *Deacons' Minutes*, 1 September 1884, 4 February 1886, 18 February 1886, 1 March 1886, 25 March 1887, 31 May 1887. The success of the acousticians is unrecorded, although the complaints seem to have diminished. Still, in 1913, the deacons were excited about the possibility of "electrophones" for the church (1 July 1913).

39. St. George's Free Ch., Edinburgh, *Deacons' Court Minutes*, 2 May 1881, 6 June 1881, 22 June 1881, 25 June 1881, 6 July 1881. In 1893, a donor paid for double windows in the church hall to reduce "noise in the Street" (5 June 1893).

40. Ibid., 13 January 1902.

41. St. George's Parish, Edinburgh, *Session Minutes*, 2 November 1852, 14 June 1866. See also Park Parish, Glasgow, *Session Minutes*, 9 January 1870; St. George's Free Ch., Edinburgh, *Deacons' Court Minutes*, 8 February 1875; Greenside Parish, Edinburgh, *Session Minutes*, 7 March 1870; Lyndhurst Road Cong. Ch., London, *Deacons' Minutes*, 30 March 1885.

42. King's Weigh House Cong. Ch., London, *Church Minutes*, 25 July 1843. As one further indication of the significance accorded to warmth, churches of Turriff Presbytery in the Grampians proudly included information about their heating systems in a collection of parish histories published in 1904 (M'William, ed., *Kirks of the Turriff Presbytery*).

43. Greenside Parish, Edinburgh, *Session Minutes*, 6 January 1879, 4 February 1879, 3 March 1879. St. George's Free Church in Edinburgh tried three times to improve the system in the building it occupied during the 1840s and 1850s. The furnaces originally vented into two centrally located pews where the warm air was trapped, much to the discomfort of both those in the select pews and those elsewhere. A second system emitted air through "two flues" on the front wall beneath the galleries, but it, too, was found "ill adapted for circulating the heated air through the body of the church, besides it was complained of as a nuisance to those parties sitting under the gallery in front of the flues." A third try discharged the heat into the aisles, which was the method typical elsewhere (*Deacons' Court Minutes*, 17 October 1852).

44. Johnston, *Story of St. Stephen's*, 33–34.

45. St. George's Free Ch., Edinburgh, *Deacons' Court Minutes*, 1 July 1901. By 1901, St. George's Free Church occupied its permanent site in Shandwick Place.

46. Plymouth Cong. Ch., Brooklyn, *Manual 1850*, 14.

47. Lyndhurst Road Cong. Ch., London, *News Sheet*, July 1896.

48. Johnston, *Story of St. Stephen's*, 127–28; Lansdowne U. P. Ch., Glasgow, *Managers' Minutes*, 20 June 1865; Lyndhurst Road Cong. Ch., London, *Deacons' Minutes*, 22 November 1886; Lozells Cong. Ch., Birmingham, *Manual 1899*, 30.

49. Lansdowne U. P. Ch., Glasgow, *Managers' Minutes*, 20 October 1909.

50. Second Pres. Ch., Philadelphia, *Music Committee Minutes*, 15 January 1896.

51. Central Pres. Ch., Rochester, *Trustees' Minutes*, 7 March 1892; St. George's Free Ch., Edinburgh, *Deacons' Court Minutes*, 6 June 1892; Old South Cong. Ch., Boston, *Society Records*, 16 May 1905; St. George's Parish, Edinburgh, *Session Minutes*, 2 December 1912, 10 January 1913, 3 March 1913.

52. Lyndhurst Road Cong. Ch., London, *Deacons' Minutes*, 29 October 1919. On changes in organ

technology, see William Harrison Barnes, *The Contemporary American Organ: Its Evolution, Design, and Construction* (Glen Rock, N.J.: Fischer, 1959), 129–34.

53. King's Weigh House Cong. Ch., London, *Church Minutes*, 22 January 1903.

54. First Cong. Ch., Hyde Park, MA, *Manual 1895*, 3–6.

55. Charles D. Cashdollar, *The Heritage of Calvary Church* (Indiana, Pa., 1976), 2, 4, 9.

56. First Pres. Ch., Indiana, PA, *Session Minutes*, 29 March 1905.

57. Chris Brooks and Andrew Saint, eds., *The Victorian Church: Architecture and Society* (Manchester: Manchester University Press, 1995), esp. chap. 3, "The Nonconformist Traditions: Chapels, Change and Continuity" by Chris Wakeling, and chap. 4, "The Victorian Kirk: Presbyterian Architecture in Nineteenth-Century Scotland" by Gavin Stamp. Also, Peter W. Williams, *Houses of God: Region, Religion, and Architecture in the United States* (Urbana: University of Illinois Press, 1997) and Roger G. Kennedy, *American Churches* (New York: Crossroad, 1982).

58. J. A. Clapham, "Gothic Congregational Churches," *Congregationalist* 7 (April 1878): 206–7; Phoebe B. Stanton, *The Gothic Revival and American Church Architecture: An Episode in Taste, 1840–1860* (Baltimore, Johns Hopkins University Press, 1968), xviii, 240. One mid-century observer wrote, "We have been stopped in front of the largest classical Congregational churches, and been asked the questions, 'What is it?' 'Is it a town-hall?' 'Is it a railway-station?' A Gothic church speaks for itself" (*Congregationalist* 7 [April 1878]: 207).

59. See William Wallace Martin, *Manual of Ecclesiastical Architecture* (Cincinnati: Jennings and Pye, 1897).

60. Stamp, "The Victorian Kirk" in Brooks and Saint, eds., *The Victorian Church*, 108. In its survey of London Congregational churches, Booth's *Life and Labour of the People in London* found the "most typical" arrangement was "octagonal, with galleries on all sides, and roof rising to a low dome" (7:113). Drummond, *Church Architecture of Protestantism*, argues that Henry Hobson Richardson's Trinity Church, built 1872–77 to accommodate the great Episcopal preacher Phillips Brooks, marked a turning point in church design because of its "noble attempt to start with the requirements of an auditorium, in which all could see and hear" (93–95). On Richardson's significance, see also Clyde Binfield, "The Building of a Town Centre Church: St. James's Congregational Church, Newcastle upon Tyne," *Northern History*, 18 (1982): 172, 176.

61. See Clyde Binfield, " 'We Claim our Part in the Great Inheritance': The Message of Four Congregational Buildings," in Keith Robbins, ed., *Protestant Evangelicalism: Britain, Ireland, Germany and America, c. 1750–c. 1950* (Oxford: Basil Blackwell, 1990), 201–44; Clyde Binfield, "A Chapel and its Architect: James Cubitt and Union Chapel, Islington, 1874–1889," in Diana Wood, ed., *The Church and the Arts* (Oxford: Basil Blackwell, 1992), 417–48; Drummond, *Church Architecture of Protestantism*, 75–76.

62. Drummond, *Church Architecture of Protestantism*, 95.

63. The building committee that approved the plans in 1882 argued that there was a double benefit: the auditorium was protected from street noise and the visibility of the Sunday School and parlors gave the church a "life-like & utilized appearance through the week" (First Cong. Ch., Cleveland, *Society Records*, 15 March 1882). Also, A. B. Cristy, ed., *Cleveland Congregationalists, 1895: Historical Sketches of Our Twenty-Five Churches and Missions* (Cleveland: Williams, 1896), 40.

64. Booth, *Life and Labour of the People in London*, 3:65.

65. Quoted by Stamp, "The Victorian Kirk," in Brooks and Saint, *The Victorian Church*, 103.

66. Old South Cong. Ch., Boston, *Society Records*, 13 April 1880.

67. Old South Cong. Ch., Boston, *Church Records*, 4 February 1852, 30 April 1866; *Society Records*, 14 December 1872, 20 December 1872, 10 April 1877.

68. Fifth Avenue Pres. Ch., New York, *Manual 1862*, 5; *Manual 1877*, 7, 10; Second Pres, Ch., Philadelphia, *Session Minutes*, 14 October 1868, 25 May 1872; Fourth U. P. Ch., Pittsburgh, *Trustees' Minutes*, 26 January 1887, 9 March 1896. Fourth Church sold its old building to St. Patrick's Roman Catholic congregation, a sale that was delayed six years while Fourth struggled in court to establish clear title to the property (22 July 1887, 22 August 1887, 24 September 1888, 13 February 1893).

69. Regent Square Pres. Ch., London, *Spring Visitation Magazine* (June 1912): 1; James McCullough Farr, *A Short History of the Brick Presbyterian Church in the City of New York, 1768–1943* (New York: Brick Presbyterian Church, 1943), 7. Earlier, in 1856, Brick's leaders had come to a different decision, choosing to follow the membership north to 37th Street. "If the Church was to serve the people it should be located in the midst of the people," they reasoned. But in the 1880s though its membership had moved still farther up Manhattan, the congregation chose deliberately to remain on 37th Street and to remodel its building; later, at the end of the 1930s, the congregation did move to 91st Street. Ibid., 4–5, 22–23. Kenneth Slack, *The City Temple: A Hundred Years* (London, 1974), 7–9, 12, 18–19.

70. Based on Kaye, *King's Weigh House,* passim; King's Weigh House Cong. Ch., London, *Church Minutes,* 1891–1915; *Deacons' Minutes,* 1891–1915.

## Epilogue

1. Paddock Cong. Ch, Huddersfield, *Year Book 1903,* 37. According to most accounts, the P.S.A. movement had its origins in the mid-1870s when a Congregational deacon named John Blackham brightened up a struggling Bible class with entertainment features borrowed from the 1875 Moody-Sankey revival services in Birmingham. By 1885 a society had been formed to promote the scheme. Strongest first in the Midlands, P.S.A. meetings spread elsewhere in England and across the border to Scotland; Americans, even if they did not adopt the name, organized their own Sunday afternoon diversions for men. See Jones, *Congregationalism in England,* 317–18, and Inglis, *Churches and the Working Classes,* 79; Grant, *Free Churchmanship,* 176, traces the P.S.A. to Liverpool Baptist clergyman H. S. Brown in 1854. Women caught the spirit, too, and at Carr's Lane in Birmingham, there was a "P.M.E. Sisterhood" that met on Monday evenings for lantern slides and singing; there were as well classes in swimming and sewing, a savings bank, and temperance pledges (*Manual 1903,* 16–17).

2. Handsworth Cong. Ch., Birmingham, *Manual 1900,* 8–9.

3. Lyndhurst Road Cong. Ch., London, *Manual 1891,* 16.

4. Quoted by Inglis, *Churches and the Working Classes,* 80–81; see also D. R. Pugh, "The Strength of English Religion in the Nineties: Some Evidence from the North West," *Journal of Religious History* 12 (June 1983): 262–65; Moseley Road Cong. Ch., Birmingham, *Manual 1896–97,* 17.

5. Booth, *Life and Labour of the People in London,* 1:130. Booth thus distinguished "congregationalist" from "congregational," the latter word connoting a system of church government and "the breakdown of the parochial system."

6. Booth, *Life and Labour of the People in London,* 7:113.

7. Quoted by Inglis, *Churches and the Working Classes,* 72.

8. Booth, *Life and Labour of the People in London,* 7:167.

9. *Boston Review* 4 (November 1864): 537, 544–45; also Bebbington, *Evangelicalism in Modern Britain,* 131.

10. Holifield, "Toward a History of American Congregations," in Wind and Lewis, eds., *American Congregations,* 2:33–43.

11. William Leach, *Land of Desire,* xv.

12. Ibid., chap. 7.

13. King's Weigh House Cong. Ch., London, *Church Minutes,* 22 January 1903.

14. Booth, *Life and Labour of the People in London,* 7:118.

15. Ibid., 1:121.

# Bibliography

Part I: Sources Generated by Congregations—Official Records and Reports, Handbooks and Manuals, Anniversary Booklets, Local Histories, and Miscellaneous Papers (arranged by denomination and location)

Unless otherwise noted, English Congregational manuals and other locally printed materials are deposited in the Congregational Library and Dr. Williams's Library, London; the English Presbyterian in the United Reformed Church History Society, London; the Scottish in the New College Library, Edinburgh; the American Congregational in the Congregational Library, Boston; and the American Presbyterian in the Presbyterian History Society, Philadelphia. Locations of manuscript materials are provided below with each listing. Published histories and celebratory volumes generated by congregations are indicated by the particulars of publication.

## A. English Congregational

Bingley
> Kuhne, Alison. *Three Hundred Years of History, 1695–1995, of Bingley United Reformed Church.* Bingley, 1995.

Birmingham: Acocks Green
> *Manual.* 1896.

Birmingham: Carr's Lane
> *Manual for the Members.* 1835, 1839.
> *Manual.* 1871, 1903.
> *Carr's Lane Church, Birmingham: Bicentenary Celebrations, 1748–1948.* Birmingham, 1948.
> *Carr's Lane Meeting House, A Retrospect: 1898.* Birmingham: Hudson, 1898.
> Rumsby, Dorothy, ed. *Carr's Lane Church.* Birmingham, 1990.

Birmingham: Edgbaston
> *Manual.* 1894.

Birmingham: Handsworth
> *Manual.* 1900.

Birmingham: Lozells
> *Manual.* 1899.

Birmingham: Moseley Road
> *Manual.* 1890–91, 1892–93, 1893–94, 1894–95, 1895–96, 1896–97, 1897–98, 1898–99.

Bristol: Redland Park
> *Church Manual.* 1890.
> *One Hundred Years, 1861–1961.* Bristol, 1961.

Huddersfield: Paddock
    *Yearbook.* 1903.
Liverpool: Berkley Street
    *Hand-Book.* 1870.
Liverpool: Crescent (Everton)
    *Annual Report.* 1873.
Liverpool: Norwood
    *Manual.* 1870–71, 1871–72, 1872–73.
Liverpool: Great George Street
    *Manual.* 1870, 1872.
    *Regulations.* 1869.
Liverpool: Walton Park
    *Report and Statement of Accounts.* 1872–73, 1874, 1875.
London: Bedford New Town
    *Manual.* 1854.
London: City Temple
    Slack, Kenneth. *The City Temple: A Hundred Years.* London, 1974.
London: Falcon Square
    *Church Manual.* 1872.
    *Rules and Regulations of the Silver Street Sunday School Society.* 1865.
London: Haverstock
    *Year Book.* 1862.
London: Holloway
    *Year Book.* 1851.
London: King's Weigh House
    *Deacons' Minutes.* 1852–1915. Dr. Williams's Library, London.
    *Minutes of Church Meetings.* 1830–1915. Dr. Williams's Library, London.
    Kaye, Elaine. *The History of the King's Weigh House Church: A Chapter in the History of London.* London: Allen and Unwin, 1968.
London: Lyndhurst Road
    *Deacons' Minutes.* 1881–1914. Dr. Williams's Library, London.
    *Young People's Guild Minutes.* 1890–1898. Dr. Williams's Library, London.
    *News Sheet.* 1893–1913. Dr. Williams's Library, London.
    *Manual.* 1883–1914.
London: New Broad Street
    *Year Book.* 1857.
London: St. Paul's Chapel (Hawley Road), Kentish Town
    *List of Names and Residences.* 1869.
London: Somers Town Mission
    *Annual Report.* 1849–50.
Manchester: Cavendish Street
    *Grand Bazaar.* 1909.
Manchester: Withington
    *Manual.* 1886, 1887, 1890.

## B. English Presbyterian

Hull: Prospect Street
 *Report.* 1880.
 *Thirty Years Work, 1868–1898.* Hull, 1898.
 *"Where Our Fathers Praised Thee": History of the Prospect Street Church.* Hull: Presbyterian
  Church of England, 1923.
Leeds: Cavendish Road
 *Semi-Jubilee Souvenir.* Leeds, 1904.
 *Centenary.* Leeds, 1964.
Liverpool: Canning Street
 *Jubilee Memorial, 1846–1896.* Liverpool: George Reed, 1896.
London: Highgate
 *Jubilee, 1887–1937.* London, 1937.
London: Regent Square
 *Regent Square Miscellaneous Papers.* United Reformed Church History Society, London.
 *Annual Reports.* 1847–56, 1869, 1881, 1884.
 *Hand Book.* 1911.
 *Manual.* 1909.
 *Regent Square Magazine.* "Centenary Number," June 1918.
 *Spring Visitation Magazine.* May 1910, June 1912.
 *A Centenary of Regent Square, 1827–1927.* London, 1927.
London: St. John's, Kensington
 Fingland, E. D. *St. John's Presbyterian Church, Kensington.* London, 1912.
London: St. John's Wood
 *One Hundred Years, 1870–1970.* London, 1970.


## C. Church of Scotland

Dumfries: Greyfriars'
 Reid, James. *The Book of Greyfriars' Church Dumfries: A Bicentenary Sketch, 1727–1927.*
  Dumfries: Standard Press, 1927.
Edinburgh: Greenside
 *Session Minutes.* 1868–1884. Scottish Record Office, Edinburgh.
 Traverner, Neil. *"The Church on the Hill": Greenside Parish Church, Edinburgh, 1839–1989.*
  Edinburgh, 1989.
Edinburgh: Greyfriars
 *Session Minutes.* 1837–1900. Scottish Record Office, Edinburgh.
Edinburgh: St. Andrew's
 *Notes on the History of St. Andrew's Church, Edinburgh.* Edinburgh: Lorimer and Gillies,
  1884.
 Christie, George. *The Story of St. Andrew's, Edinburgh.* Edinburgh, 1934.
Edinburgh: St. George's
 *Session Minutes.* 1847–1915. Scottish Record Office, Edinburgh.

Edinburgh: St. Stephen's
> Johnston, Christopher Nicholson [Lord Sands]. *The Story of St. Stephen's, Edinburgh, 1828–1928.* Edinburgh: William Blackwood, 1927.

Glasgow: Govan
> *Leaflets Relating to Christmas, Holy Week, Easter, Ascension, and Pentecost Services.* 1884–1913. Strathclyde Regional Archives, Glasgow.
> *Liturgy for Use in Children's Service.* 1889–1890. Strathclyde Regional Archives, Glasgow.
> *Session Minutes.* 1856–1907. Strathclyde Regional Archives, Glasgow.
> *Sunday School Minute Book.* 1889–1896. Strathclyde Regional Archives, Glasgow.
> *Young Men's Association Minutes.* 1876–1905. Strathclyde Regional Archives, Glasgow.
> *Govan Literary Association Minutes.* 1905–1914. Strathclyde Regional Archives, Glasgow.
> Wallace, Andrew. *The Parish of Govan as It Was and Is.* Glasgow: Cossar, 1877.

Glasgow: Maxwell
> Brown, Alan C. *The Maxwell Story: Maxwell Parish Church, 1865–1965.* Glasgow, 1965.

Glasgow: Park
> *Session Minutes.* 1859–1914. Strathclyde Regional Archives, Glasgow.

Glasgow: St. Andrew's
> Thomson, James. *History of St. Andrew's Parish Church, Glasgow.* Glasgow: Robert Anderson, 1905.

Glasgow: St. George's
> Cuthbertson, T. W. *Historical Sketch of St. George's Parish Church, Glasgow.* Glasgow: Aird and Coghill, 1894.

Kilmarnock: High
> Railton, John J. *The Old High Kirk of Kilmarnock: The Origin and Building of the Chapel of Ease.* Kilmarnock, 1940.

Kirkcaldy: St. Brycedale
> Livingstone, P. K. *St. Brycedale Church, Kirkcaldy: The Origin and History.* Kirkcaldy, 1957.
> ———. *The Boys' Brigade in Kirkcaldy.* Kirkcaldy, 1953.

Paisley: Paisley Abbey
> Howell, A. R. *Paisley Abbey: Its History, Architecture, and Art.* Paisley: Gardner, 1929.

Perth: North
> Carruthers, J. W. D., ed. *The Ter-Jubilee Book of the North Church of Perth, 1747–1897.* Perth: George Miller, 1898.

Turriff Presbytery
> M'William, T. M., ed. *The Kirks of the Turriff Presbytery.* Banff, 1904.

Urr
> Frew, David. *The Parish of Urr, Civil and Ecclesiastical: A History.* Dalbeattie: Thomas Fraser, 1909.

## D. Free Church of Scotland

Aberdeen: Gilcomston
> *Gilcomston Free Church Quarterly Record.* 1898–1914.

Airdrie: High
> Hay, William C. *The High Church, Airdrie: A Short History Commemorating the Centenary of the Church, March, 1938.* Airdrie, 1938.

Edinburgh: Mayfield
  *Mayfield Free Church, 1875–1896.* Edinburgh, 1896.
  *Mayfield United Free Church, 1875–1925.* Edinburgh, 1925.
Edinburgh: Pilrig
  Turner, Ebenezer. *The Story of Pilrig Church.* Edinburgh: Blackwood, 1913.
Edinburgh: St. Columba's
  Grant, Maurice. *Free St. Columba's: A History of Congregation and Church.* Edinburgh: Columba, 1991.
Edinburgh: St George's
  *Deacons' Court Minutes.* 1843–1911. Scottish Record Office, Edinburgh.
  *Session Minutes.* 1843–1908. Scottish Record Office, Edinburgh.
  MacLagan, David. *St. George's Edinburgh: A History of St. George's Church 1814 to 1843 and of St. George's Free Church 1843 to 1873.* London: Nelson, 1876.
  *The Tradition of St. George's West.* Edinburgh, 1931.
Edinburgh: St. Stephen's
  Thompson, Edward A. *Historical Notices of Free St. Stephen's, Edinburgh.* Edinburgh: Turnbull and Spears, 1888.
Glasgow: College
  *Annual Report.* 1877–1892.
Glasgow: Cowcaddens
  *Congregational Minute Book.* 1867–68. Strathclyde Regional Archives, Glasgow.
  *Deacons' Court Minutes.* 1886–1906. Strathclyde Regional Archives, Glasgow.
  *Session Minutes.* 1865–1914. Strathclyde Regional Archives, Glasgow.
Greenock: St. Andrew's
  *Jubilee Memorial of Saint Andrew's Parish and Congregation, Greenock, and of their First Minister, John James Bonar, D. D.* Greenock: MacKelvie, 1889.
Helensburgh: Park
  Logan, George. *Park Church, Helensburgh: The First Hundred Years.* Glasgow, 1964.

## E. Scottish United Presbyterian

Dumfries: Buccleuch Street
  *Buccleuch Street Church: Dumfries, 1807–1907.* Dumfries, 1907.
Edinburgh: Bristo
  [Thin, James]. *Memorials of Bristo United Presbyterian Church.* Edinburgh: Morrison and Gibbs, 1888.
Edinburgh: Broughton Place
  *History of Broughton Place United Presbyterian Church.* Edinburgh: Oliphant, 1872.
  [Irvine, Charles]. *Thirty Years of Broughton United Free Church, Edinburgh.* Edinburgh: Howie and Seath, 1914.
Edinburgh: Newington
  *Newington United Presbyterian Church, Jubilee Memorial, 1848–1898.* Edinburgh: Hunter, 1898.
Glasgow: Lansdowne
  *Managers' Minutes.* 1864–1914. Strathclyde Regional Archives, Glasgow.
  *Annual Report.* 1865–1911.

Glasgow: Wellington
>   *Historical Sketch of Wellington United Presbyterian Congregation, Glasgow, 1792–1892.* Glasgow: Maclure, 1893.

## F. United States Congregational

Billerica, Massachusetts: Orthodox
>   *Manual.* 1855, 1884.

Binghamton, New York: First
>   *Manual.* 1875, 1894.

Boston: Bowdoin Street
>   *Articles of Faith and Covenant of the Bowdoin Street Church, Boston, with a List of the Members.* 1837, 1856.

Boston: Boylston
>   *Manual.* 1879, 1896.

Boston: Old South
>   *Church Records.* 1830–1914. Congregational Library, Boston.
>   *Society Records.* 1845–1915. Congregational Library, Boston.
>   *Standing Committee Records.* 1842–1876. Congregational Library, Boston.
>   *The Form of Covenant.* 1826, 1833, 1841, 1855.
>   *Members.* 1863.
>   *Service of Admission and Catalogue.* 1888, 1892, 1895, 1899.

Boston: Park Street
>   *Articles of Faith and Covenant.* 1841, 1850, 1859, 1867, 1870, 1916.

Brooklyn: Central
>   *Manual.* 1875.

Brooklyn: Church of the Mediator
>   *Manual.* 1868.

Brooklyn: Clinton Avenue
>   *Manual.* 1857, 1875, 1882.

Brooklyn: Park
>   *Manual.* 1870.

Brooklyn: People's
>   *Manual.* 1885.

Brooklyn: Plymouth
>   *Manual.* 1850, 1854, 1867, 1874.
>   Griswold, Stephen M. *Sixty Years with Plymouth Church.* New York: Revell, 1907.

Brooklyn: South
>   *Manual.* 1868.

Brooklyn: Tompkins Avenue
>   *Manual.* 1877.

Brooklyn: Union
>   *Manual.* 1876.

Chicago: First
>   *Manual.* 1859, 1869, 1873, 1875, 1884.

Chicago: Union Park
>    *Manual.* 1887.
Cincinnati: First Orthodox
>    *Manual.* 1874.
Cincinnati: Vine Street
>    *Manual.* 1878.
Claysville, New York: Pilgrim
>    *Manual,* 1890.
Cleveland
>    Cristy, A. B. ed. *Cleveland Congregationalists, 1895: Historical Sketches of Our Twenty-Five Churches and Missions.* Cleveland: Williams, 1896.
Cleveland: First
>    *Dedicatory Program for New Auditorium.* December 17, 1893. Congregational Library, Boston.
>    *Society Records.* 1857–1893. Congregational Library, Boston.
>    *Trustees' Records.* 1897–1914. Congregational Library, Boston.
>    *Manual.* 1869, 1881.
>    *Yearbook.* 1894, 1896, 1903.
East Hardwick, Vermont
>    *Manual.* 1891.
Hartford, Connecticut: First
>    *Manual.* 1835, 1843, 1858, 1867, 1880, 1885, 1888, 1890, 1893, 1896, 1897.
Hartford, Connecticut: Second
>    *Confession of Faith and Covenant.* 1838.
>    *Manual.* 1860, 1902, 1917.
Hartford, Connecticut: North
>    *Catalogue.* 1839, 1845, 1852.
Huron, South Dakota
>    *Manual.* 1908.
Hyde Park, Massachusetts: First
>    *Manual.* 1870, 1875, 1885, 1895, 1905, 1913, 1915.
Indianapolis: Plymouth
>    *Manual.* 1860.
Iowa City, Iowa
>    *Manual.* 1895.
Ithaca, New York
>    *Manual.* 1882, 1887, 1895.
Jamaica Plain, Massachusetts: Central
>    *Manual.* 1870, 1878, 1898.
New York City: Harlem
>    *Manual.* 1866.
Ridgefield, Connecticut: First
>    *A Concise History of First Congregational Church.* 1843.
>    *A Concise History and Manual of First Congregational Church.* 1868.
>    *Manual.* 1904.

Ridgeway, Pennsylvania: First
  *Manual,* 1895.
Rochester, Massachusetts: First
  *Articles of Faith and Covenant.* 1844.
  *Manual.* 1909.
Rochester, New Hampshire: First
  *Articles of Faith and Form of Covenant.* 1859.
  *Manual.* 1876, 1891.
Rochester, New York: Plymouth
  *Manual.* 1856, 1877.

## G. Presbyterian Church, U.S.A.

Baltimore: Fifth
  *Church Manual.* 1845.
Baltimore: Boundary Avenue
  *Manual.* 1885.
Binghamton, New York
  *Manual.* 1833.
Chicago: First
  *Orders of Service and Miscellaneous Papers.* 1890–1914. Presbyterian Historical Society,
    Philadelphia.
  *Manual.* 1870.
Chicago: Second
  *Manual.* 1856.
  *Year Book.* 1906.
Chicago: Third
  *Manual.* 1876, 1885–86, 1886–87, 1888–89, 1889–90, 1890–91, 1892, 1893, 1894, 1899.
Chicago: Fifth
  *Manual.* 1876.
Chicago: Sixth
  *Manual.* 1877, 1883.
Chicago: Church of the Covenant
  *Manual.* 1885–86, 1886–87.
Chicago: Forty-first Street
  *The Church News.* Vol. 13, no. 8 (February 1906).
  *Manual, Young Men's Bible Class.* 1903.
Chicago: Fifty-second Avenue
  *Year Book and Directory.* 1903–4.
Hyde Park, Illinois: First
  *Manual.* 1886.
Indiana, Pennsylvania: First [now Calvary]
  *Session Minutes.* 1844–1914. Presbyterian Historical Society, Philadelphia.
  Cashdollar, Charles D. *The Heritage of Calvary Church.* Indiana, Pa., 1976.
Indianapolis: First
  *Manual.* 1878.

Indianapolis: Third
    *Hand Book.* 1874.
New York City
    Savage, Theodore F. *The Presbyterian Church in New York City.* New York: Presbytery of
        New York, 1949.
New York City: First
    Fowler, Dorothy Ganfield. *A City Church: The First Presbyterian Church in the City of
        New York, 1716–1976.* New York: First Presbyterian Church, 1981.
New York City: Brick
    *Annual Report.* 1899, 1900, 1902–6, 1910–14.
    *Manual.* 1869
    *Yearbook of Work and Worship.* 1890–91.
    Farr, James McCullough. *A Short History of the Brick Presbyterian Church in the City of
        New York, 1768–1943.* New York: Brick Presbyterian Church, 1943.
New York City: Fifth Avenue
    *History and Manual.* 1877.
    *Manual.* 1862.
    *The Fifth Avenue Presbyterian Church.* New York, 1952.
Philadelphia: First
    *Church Manual for the Use of the First Presbyterian Church in the City of Philadelphia.*
        1841.
    *Manual of the First Presbyterian Church.* 1905.
    Kocher, Donald Roth. *The Mother of Us All: First Presbyterian Church in Philadelphia,
        1698–1998.* Philadelphia: First Presbyterian Church, 1998.
Philadelphia: Second
    *Music Committee Minutes.* 1892–93, 1895–1903. Presbyterian Historical Society, Philadel-
        phia.
    *Session Minutes.* 1830–1914. Presbyterian Historical Society, Philadelphia.
Philadelphia: Third (Pine Street)
    Gibbons, Hughes Oliphant. *A History of Old Pine Street.* Philadelphia: Winston, 1905.
Philadelphia: Bethany
    *Annual Report.* 1894, 1896, 1897, 1899.
    "The Christmas Sabbath at Bethany Sabbath School, December 25, 1887." Presbyterian
        Historical Society, Philadelphia.
    Wasson, Samuel A., compiler. *History of Bethany Presbyterian Church and Sunday School,
        1858–1958.* Philadelphia, 1958.
Pittsburgh: First
    *Communicants' Manual.* 1912.
Rochester, New York: Central
    *Session Minutes.* 1858–1914. Presbyterian Historical Society, Philadelphia.
    *Trustees' Minutes.* 1858–1914. Presbyterian Historical Society, Philadelphia.
St. Louis: First
    *Manual.* 1857, 1861.
St. Louis: Second
    *Church Manual.* 1844, 1857.

Saltsburg, Pennsylvania
> Hadden, Rebecca; Margaret Jackson; and Dorothy Pless. *History of the Saltsburg United Presbyterian Church of Saltsburg, Pennsylvania*. Saltsburg, Pa., 1974.

## H. United Presbyterian Church of North America

Indiana, Pennsylvania: First [now Graystone]
> Rife, Merle. *A History of Graystone United Presbyterian Church, 1808–1978*. Indiana, Pa.: Park Press, 1978.

Mars, Pennsylvania: Old Union
> *Session Minutes*. 1858–1914. [in possession of congregation]
> Cashdollar, Charles D. *A History of Old Union Church*. Mars, Pa., 1973.

Pittsburgh: Fourth
> *Session Minutes*. 1850–1913. Presbyterian Historical Society, Philadelphia.
> *Trustees' Minutes*. 1865–1914. Presbyterian Historical Society, Philadelphia.

## Part II: Memoirs, Administrative Guides, Psalters and Hymnals, Worship Aids, and Other Primary Sources

*Anthem Book of the United Free Church of Scotland*. London: Novello, 1905

Aveling, T. W. "Church Administration." *Congregationalist* 6 (March–July 1877): 168–73, 226–32, 271–77, 345–49, 433–39.

*Bible Songs: A Collection of Psalms Set to Music for Use in Church and Evangelistic Services, Prayer Meetings, Sabbath Schools, Young People's Societies, and Family Worship*. Pittsburgh: United Presbyterian Board of Publication, 1901.

"Biographical Memoir of William M. Goodrich, Organ Builder." *New-England Magazine* 6 (January 1834): 25–44.

Bittinger, Benjamin F. *Manual of Law and Usage*. Philadelphia: Presbyterian Board of Publication, 1888.

Booth, Charles. *Life and Labour of the People in London. Third Series: Religious Influences*. 7 vols. 1902–4. Reprint, New York: AMS Press, 1970.

Boyd, A. K. H. "The Organ." *Frasers Magazine* 53 (March 1856): 355–69.

———. "The Organ in Scotland." *Frasers Magazine* 72 (October 1865): 520–24.

Boynton, George. *The Pilgrim Pastor's Manual: A Handbook of Services and Forms*. 10th ed. Boston: Pilgrim Press, 1916.

Candlish, Robert S. *The Organ Question: Statements by Dr. Ritchie and Dr. Porteous for and against the Use of the Organ in Public Worship in Proceedings of the Presbytery of Glasgow, 1807–8*. Edinburgh: Johnstone, 1856.

*Church of Scotland Psalm and Hymn Tune Book*. Edinburgh: Thomas Nelson, 1869.

Clapham, J. A. "Gothic Congregational Churches." *Congregationalist* 7 (April 1878): 202–7.

Clark, Francis E. *Memoirs of Many Men in Many Lands: An Autobiography*. Boston: United Society of Christian Endeavor, 1922.

Church Service Society (Church of Scotland). *Book of Common Order*. 1st, 4th, and 7th eds. Edinburgh: William Blackwood, 1868, 1877, 1896.

———. *Home Prayers*. Edinburgh: William Blackwood, 1879.

Cochrane, Thomas. *Fifty-One Years in the Home Mission Field and Reminiscences, 1826–1898*. Edinburgh: James Thin, 1898.

Condor, Eustace. "Talks With Children." *Congregationalist* 8 (January–December 1879): 66ff., 152ff., 246ff., 318ff., 426ff., 509ff., 593ff., 681ff., 768ff., 854ff., 950ff., 1032ff.

"Culture of Social Life in the Churches." *Boston Review* 4 (November 1864): 537–46.

Curwen, J. S. "Hymn-Singing." *Congregationalist* 3 (April 1874): 209–17.

Davis, Emerson. *Biographical Sketches of the Congregational Pastors of New England.* 5 vols. Manuscript, pre-1869; typescript, 1930. Congregational Library, Boston.

Dexter, Henry Martyn. *A Hand-Book of Congregationalism.* Boston: Congregational Publishing Society, 1880.

Duncan, Andrew. *The Scottish Sanctuary As It Was and As It Is.* Edinburgh: Andrew Elliot, 1880.

Firth, John. *Reminiscences of an Orkney Parish.* 2d ed. Stromness: John Rae, 1922.

Hastings, Thomas. "Church Music." *New Englander* 6 (July 1848): 424–31.

Hodge, J. Aspinwall. *What is Presbyterian Law?* 1st and 8th eds. Philadelphia: Presbyterian Board of Publication, 1882, 1905.

*The Hymnal.* Philadelphia: Presbyterian Board of Publication, 1895.

"Individual Communion Service." Clipping File. Presbyterian Historical Society, Philadelphia.

"Introduction of Organs in Congregational Churches." *New-England Magazine* 9 (August 1835): 123–28.

Johnston, Christopher Nicholson [Lord Sands]. *Dr. Archibald Scott, of St. George's, Edinburgh, and His Times.* Edinburgh: William Blackwood, 1919.

Kerr, John. *The Renascence* [sic] *of Worship: The Origin, Aims, and Achievements of the Church Service Society.* Edinburgh: Hitt, 1909.

*The Late Rev. William Barras: Memorial Volume.* Glasgow: Aird and Coghill, 1893.

Macleod, Donald. *The Sunday Home Service.* London: Isbister, 1885.

MacNichol, D. *Chapter from the Religious Life of a Highland Parish.* Paisley: Parlane, 1903.

MacRae, Alexander. *Revivals in the Highlands and Islands in the Nineteenth Century.* Stirling: Eneas Mackay, 1905.

Martin, William Wallace. *Manual of Ecclesiastical Architecture.* Cincinnati: Jennings and Pye, 1897.

Martine, John. *Reminiscences and Notices of Ten Parishes of the County of Haddington.* Haddington: Sinclair, 1894.

McFalls, Thaddeus, and Byron Sunderland. *Manual of Presbyterian Law and Usage.* Washington, D.C.: Morrison, 1873.

McGill, Alexander. *Church Government.* Philadelphia: Presbyterian Board of Publication, 1888.

Merrill, James D. "Children." *New Englander* 40 (March 1881): 247–56.

Minshall, Ebenezer. *Fifty Years' Reminiscences of a Free Church Musician.* London: James Clarke, 1910.

Mitchell, John. *The Practical Church Member, Being a Guide to the Principles and Practice of the Congregational Churches of New England.* New Haven: Nathan Whiting, 1835.

M'Laren, Kenneth D. *Memoir of the Very Reverend Professor Charteris.* London: A. and C. Black, 1914.

"Organ-Building in New England." *New-England Magazine* 6 (March 1834): 205–15.

Parker, Joel, and T. Ralston Smith. *The Presbyterian's Hand-Book of the Church for the Use of Members, Deacons, Elders, and Ministers.* New York: Harper, 1861.

Parker, Joseph. *A Preacher's Life: An Autobiography and an Album.* Boston: Crowell, 1899.

Punchard, George. *A View of Congregationalism.* Salem: John Jewett, 1840.

"Relation of Children to the Church." *Congregationalist* 2 (September–December 1873): 513–21, 577–87, 641–47, 705–10.

"Religious Life of Young Children." *Congregationalist* 3 (June 1874): 341–45.

Roberts, William Henry. *Manual for Ruling Elders and Church Sessions.* Philadelphia: Presbyterian Board of Publication, 1897, 1907.

Sage, Donald. *Memorabilia Domestica: Or, Parish Life in the North of Scotland.* 2d ed. Wick: William Rae, 1899.

*Scottish Prose Psalter.* Edinburgh: Thomas Nelson, 1897.

*Scottish Psalter and Free Church Hymn Book.* Edinburgh: Thomas Nelson, 1882, 1892.

Sprott, George W. *The Worship and Offices of the Church of Scotland.* Edinburgh: William Blackwood, 1882.

Talmadge, T. DeWitt. "How to Destroy Congregational Singing." Reprint from *New York Independent* in *Congregationalist* 2 (January 1873): 37–40.

Weber, Herman Carl. *Presbyterian Statistics Through One Hundred Years, 1826–1926.* Philadelphia: General Council, Presbyterian Church, U.S.A., 1927.

Wells, James. *Bible Echoes: Addresses to the Young.* 3d ed. London: Nisbet, 1878.

———. *Bible Children: Studies for the Young.* London: Nisbet, 1885.

Wilson, J. H. *The Gospel and its Fruits: A Book for the Young.* London: Nisbet, 1874.

———. *The King's Message and Other Addresses: A Book for the Young.* London: Nisbet, 1887.

Wotherspoon, H. J. *James Cooper: A Memoir.* London: Longmans, 1926.

## Part III: Secondary Sources

### A. Articles

Abbott, Elizabeth Lee, and Kenneth A. Abbott. "Chinese Pilgrims and Presbyterians in the United States, 1851–1977." *Journal of Presbyterian History* 55 (summer 1977): 125–77.

Baker, Wesley C. "Mission Funding Policies: An Historical Overview." *Journal of Presbyterian History* 57 (fall 1979): 404–23.

Bederman, Gail. "Women Have Had Charge of the Church Work Long Enough: The Men and Religion Forward Movement of 1911–12 and the Masculinization of American Protestantism." *American Quarterly* 41 (September 1989): 432–65.

Bendroth, Margaret. "Women and Missions: Conflict and Changing Roles in the Presbyterian Church in the United States of America, 1870–1935." *American Presbyterians* 65 (spring 1987): 49–59.

Binfield, Clyde. "The Building of a Town Centre Church: St. James's Congregational Church, Newcastle Upon Tyne." *Northern History* 18 (1982): 153–81.

Boyd, Lois A. "Presbyterian Ministers' Wives: A Nineteenth-Century Portrait." *Journal of Presbyterian History* 59 (spring 1981): 3–17.

———. "Shall Women Speak? Confrontation in the Church, 1876." *Journal of Presbyterian History* 56 (winter 1978): 281–95.

Boylan, Anne M. "Timid Girls, Venerable Widows and Dignified Matrons: Life Cycle Patterns among Organized Women in New York and Boston, 1797–1840." *American Quarterly* 38 (winter 1986): 779–97.

Brackenridge, R. Douglas, and Lois A. Boyd. "United Presbyterian Policy on Women and the Church: An Historical Overview." *Journal of Presbyterian History* 59 (fall 1981): 383–407.

Brown, Callum G. "The Costs of Pew-Renting: Church Management, Church-going and Social Class in Nineteenth-Century Glasgow." *Journal of Ecclesiastical History* 38 (July 1987): 347–61.

Carson, Mary Faith, and James J. H. Price. "The Ordination of Women and the Function of the Bible." *Journal of Presbyterian History* 59 (summer 1981): 245–66.

Cashdollar, Charles D. "The Pursuit of Piety: Charles Hodge's Diary, 1819–1820." *Journal of Presbyterian History* 55 (fall 1977): 267–83.

———. "The Recent Turn to Congregational Studies Among Church Historians." *Journal of Presbyterian History* 77 (summer 1999): 107–18.

———. "Ruin and Revival: The Attitude of the Presbyterian Churches toward the Panic of 1873." *Journal of Presbyterian History* 50 (fall 1972): 229–44.

———. "The Social Implications of the Doctrine of Divine Providence." *Harvard Theological Review* 71 (July—October 1978): 265–84.

Crouch, Archie. "Racial-Ethnic Ministry Policies: An Historical Overview." *Journal of Presbyterian History* 57 (fall 1979): 272–312.

Cunningham, Raymond J. "From Preacher of the Word to Physician of the Soul: The Protestant Pastor in Nineteenth-Century America." *Journal of Religious History* 3 (December 1965): 327–46.

Daniel, W. Harrison. "English Presbyterians, Slavery, and the American Crisis of 1860." *Journal of Presbyterian History* 58 (spring 1980): 50–63.

Daniels, Harold M. "Service Books Among American Presbyterians." *American Presbyterians* 71 (fall 1993): 185–96.

Dawson, David G. "Mission Philanthropy, Selected Giving and Presbyterians." Parts 1 and 2. *American Presbyterians* 68 (summer 1990): 121–32; 69 (fall 1991): 203–25.

Dickey, Brian. "Marginalising Evangelicals: Thomas Binney in South Australia, 1858–1859." *Journal of the United Reformed Church History Society* 4 (December 1991): 540–65.

Dickson, Tony, and Tony Clarke. "Social Concern and Social Control in Nineteenth-Century Scotland: Paisley, 1841–1843." *Scottish Historical Review* 65 (April 1986): 48–60.

Field, Clive. "Adam and Eve: Gender in the English Free Church Constituency, 1650–1980." *Journal of Ecclesiastical History* 44 (January 1993): 63–79.

Fisk, William L. "The Seceders: The Scottish High Church Tradition in America." *Journal of Presbyterian History* 62 (winter 1984): 291–305.

Forbes, Bruce David. "William Henry Roberts: Resistance to Change and Bureaucratic Adaptation." *Journal of Presbyterian History* 54 (winter 1976): 405–21.

Fox-Genovese, Elizabeth. "Female Experience in American Religion." *Religion and American Culture* 5 (winter 1995): 16–21.

Gillespie, Franklin B. "Youth Programs of the United Presbyterian Church: An Historical Overview." *Journal of Presbyterian History* 59 (fall 1981): 309–82.

Glass, William R. "Liberal Means to Conservative Ends: Bethany Presbyterian Church, John Wanamaker, and the Institutional Church Movement." *American Presbyterians* 68 (fall 1980): 181–92.

Hall, Stanley R. "American Presbyterians and the Directory of Worship, 1645–1989." *American Presbyterians* 72 (summer 1994): 71–86.

Heidebrecht, Paul H. "Chicago Presbyterians and the Businessman's Religion, 1900–1920." *American Presbyterians* 64 (spring 1986): 38–48.

Hillis, Peter. "Education and Evangelisation: Presbyterian Missions in Mid-Nineteenth-Century Glasgow." *Scottish Historical Review* 66 (April 1987): 46–62.

———. "Presbyterianism and Social Class in Mid-Nineteenth-Century Glasgow: A Study of Nine Churches." *Journal of Ecclesiastical History* 32 (January 1981): 47–67.

Hogeland, Ronald W. "Charles Hodge, the Association of Gentlemen and Ornamental Womanhood: A Study of Male Conventional Wisdom, 1825–55." *Journal of Presbyterian History* 53 (fall 1975): 239–55.

Hudson, Mary Lin. " 'Shall Woman Preach?': Louisa Woosley and the Cumberland Presbyterian Church." *American Presbyterians* 68 (winter 1990): 221–30.

Hunt, James B. "Jane Addams: The Presbyterian Connection." *American Presbyterians* 68 (winter 1990): 231–44.

Irvin, Dale T. "Social Witness Policies: An Historical Overview." *Journal of Presbyterian History* 57 (fall 1979): 353–403.

Johnson, Dale A. "Fissures in Late-Nineteenth-Century English Nonconformity: A Case Study in One Congregation." *Church History* 66 (December 1997): 735–49.

Jordan, Philip D. "Cooperation Without Incorporation: America and the Presbyterian Alliance, 1870–1880." *Journal of Presbyterian History* 55 (spring 1977): 13–35.

Kihlstrom, Mary F. "The Morristown Female Charitable Society." *Journal of Presbyterian History* 58 (fall 1980): 255–73.

Kohl, Lawrence F. "The Concept of Social Control and Jacksonian America." *Journal of the Early Republic* 5 (1985): 21–34.

Koper, Paul W. "The United Presbyterian Church and Christian Education: An Historical Overview." *Journal of Presbyterian History* 59 (fall 1981): 288–308.

Lane, Beldon C. "Presbyterian Republicanism: Miller and the Eldership as an Answer to Lay-Clerical Tensions." *Journal of Presbyterian History* 56 (winter 1978): 311–25.

Macnab, John B. "Bethlehem Chapel: Presbyterians and Italian Americans in New York City." *Journal of Presbyterian History* 55 (summer 1977): 145–60.

Maddex, Jack. "Presbyterians in the South, Centralization, and the *Book of Church Order,* 1861–1879." *American Presbyterians* 68 (spring 1990): 24–45.

Marsh, John L. "The Country Church: A Study in Nineteenth-Century Taste and Twentieth-Century Commitment." *Journal of Presbyterian History* 58 (spring 1980): 3–16.

Martin, Daniel W. "The United Presbyterian Church Policy on the Men's Movement: An Historical Overview." *Journal of Presbyterian History* 59 (fall 1981): 408–39.

McCaffrey, John F. "Thomas Chalmers and Social Change." *Scottish Historical Review* 60 (April 1981): 32–60.

McCoy, Clinton A., Jr. "How This Mustard Seed Grew: The Origin and Impact of the Per Capita Apportionment as a Means of Financing the General Assembly." *American Presbyterians* 66 (spring 1988): 37–49.

McDonald, Kenneth. "The Presbyterian Church and the Social Gospel in California, 1890–1910." *American Presbyterians* 72 (winter 1994): 241–52.

Melton, Julius. "A View from the Pew: Nineteenth-Century Elders and Presbyterian Worship." *American Presbyterians* 71 (fall 1993): 161–74.

Miller, Page Putnam. "Women in the Vanguard of the Sunday School Movement." *Journal of Presbyterian History* 58 (winter 1980): 311–25.

Mohl, Raymond A. "The Urban Missionary Movement in New York City, 1800–1825." *Journal of Religious History* 7 (December 1972): 110–28.

Moorhead, James H. "Charles Finney and the Modernization of America." *Journal of Presbyterian History* 62 (summer 1984): 95–110.

Morris, R. J., and Graeme Morton. "Where Was Nineteenth-Century Scotland?" *Scottish Historical Review* 73 (April 1994): 89–99.

Morton, Richard Allen. " 'Means of Grace': Directions in Presbyterian Home Mission Work, 1870–1885." *American Presbyterians* 72 (summer 1994): 123–34.

Murray, Douglas. "High Church Presbyterianism in Scotland and England." *Journal of the United Reformed Church History Society* 3 (May 1985): 225–34.

Noll, Mark A. "A Precarious Balance: Two Hundred Years of Presbyterian Devotional Literature." *American Presbyterians* 68 (fall 1990): 207–19.

Penfield, Janet Harbison. "Women in the Presbyterian Church: An Historical Overview." *Journal of Presbyterian History* 55 (summer 1977): 107–24.

Perry, Everett L., and Margaret T. Perry. "New Church Development Policies: An Historical Overview." *Journal of Presbyterian History* 57 (fall 1979): 229–71.

Poethig, Richard. "Urban/Metropolitan Mission Policies: An Historical Overview." *Journal of Presbyterian History* 57 (fall 1979): 313–52.

Pugh, D. R. "Christian Opinion in the Nineties: Some Issues and Concerns in the North West of England." *Journal of Religious History* 11 (June 1980): 121–35.

———. "The Strength of English Religion in the Nineties: Some Evidence from the North West." *Journal of Religious History* 12 (June 1983): 250–65.

Reifsynder, Richard. "Presbyterian Reunion, Reorganization, and Expansion in the Late Nineteenth Century." *American Presbyterians* 64 (spring 1986): 27–38.

Robb, George. "Popular Religion and the Christianization of the Scottish Highlands in the Eighteenth and Nineteenth Centuries." *Journal of Religious History* 16 (June 1990): 18–34.

Roy, Andrew. "Overseas Missions Policies: An Historical Overview." *Journal of Presbyterian History* 57 (fall 1979): 186–228.

Shiels, Richard D. "The Feminization of American Congregationalism, 1730–1835." *American Quarterly* 33 (spring 1981): 46–62.

Smith, Gary Scott. "When Stead Came to Chicago: The 'Social Gospel Novel' and the Chicago Civic Federation." *American Presbyterians* 68 (fall 1990): 193–205.

———. "The Spirit of Capitalism Revisited: Calvinists in the Industrial Revolution." *Journal of Presbyterian History* 59 (winter 1981): 481–97.

Smylie, James H. " 'Of Secret and Family Worship': Historical Meditations, 1875–1975." *Journal of Presbyterian History* 58 (summer 1980): 95–115.

Soden, Dale E. "Anatomy of a Presbyterian Urban Revival: J. W. Chapman in the Pacific Northwest." *American Presbyterians* 64 (spring 1986): 49–57.

Sydnor, James Rawlings. "Sing a New Song to the Lord: An Historical Survey of American Presbyterian Hymnals." *American Presbyterians* 68 (spring 1990): 1–13.

Szasz, Ferenc M. "T. DeWitt Talmadge: Spiritual Tycoon of the Gilded Age." *Journal of Presbyterian History* 59 (spring 1981): 18–32.

Taylor, John H., ed. "Letters to a Pastor (1869)." *Journal of the United Reformed Church History Society* 1 (April 1976): 204–7.

Walker, J. Michael. "Louis FitzGerald Benson: The Union of Praise and Prayer." *American*

*Presbyterians* 71 (fall 1993): 175–84.

Wilson, Frank T., ed. "Living Witnesses: Black Presbyterians in Ministry, III." *Journal of Presbyterian History* 55 (summer 1977): 180–238.

Winter, Robert Milton. "American Presbyterians, the Directory for Worship, and Changing Patterns of Sacramental Practice." *American Presbyterians* 71 (fall 1993): 141–60.

———. "Presbyterians and Prayers for the Sick: Changing Patterns of Pastoral Ministry." *American Presbyterians* 64 (fall 1986): 141–55.


## B. Books

Adamson, William. *The Life of Joseph Parker, Pastor of City Temple, London.* New York: Revell, 1902.

Ames, Kenneth L. *Death in the Dining Room and Other Tales of Victorian Culture.* Philadelphia: Temple University Press, 1992.

Andrews, William, ed. *Bygone Church Life in Scotland.* London: William Andrews, 1899.

Baker, Derek, ed. *The Church in Town and Countryside.* Oxford: Basil Blackwell, 1979.

———. *Religious Motivation: Biographical and Sociological Problems for the Church Historian.* Oxford: Basil Blackwell, 1978.

Balmer, Randall, and John R. Fitzmier. *The Presbyterians.* Westport, Conn.: Greenwood, 1993.

Barnes, William Harrison. *The Contemporary American Organ: Its Evolution, Design, and Construction.* Glen Rock, N.J.: Fischer, 1959.

Barr, James. *The United Free Church of Scotland.* London: Allenson, 1934.

Bebbington, D. W. *Evangelicalism in Modern Britain: A History from the 1730s to the 1980s.* London: Unwin Hyman, 1989.

Bell, Marion L. *Crusade in the City: Revivalism in Nineteenth-Century Philadelphia.* Lewisburg, Pa.: Bucknell University Press, 1977.

Benson, Louis F. *The English Hymn: Its Development and Use in Worship.* London: Hodder and Stoughton, 1915.

Best, Geoffrey. *Mid-Victorian Britain, 1851–1875.* New York: Schocken, 1972.

Binfield, Clyde. *So Down to Prayers: Studies in English Nonconformity, 1780–1920.* Totowa, N.J.: Rowman and Littlefield, 1977.

Bledstein, Burton J. *The Culture of Professionalism: The Middle Class and the Development of Higher Education in America.* New York: Norton, 1977.

Bordin, Ruth. *Women and Temperance: The Quest for Power and Liberty, 1873–1900.* Philadelphia: Temple University Press, 1981.

Boyd, Lois A., and R. Douglas Brackenridge. *Presbyterian Women in America: Two Centuries of a Quest for Status.* Westport, Conn.: Greenwood, 1983.

Boyer, Paul. *Urban Masses and Moral Order in America, 1820–1920.* Cambridge: Harvard University Press, 1978.

Boylan, Anne M. *Sunday School: The Formation of an American Institution, 1790–1880.* New Haven: Yale University Press, 1988.

Brooks, Chris, and Andrew Saint, eds. *The Victorian Church: Architecture and Society.* Manchester: Manchester University Press, 1995.

Brown, Callum G. *Religion and Society in Scotland since 1707.* Edinburgh: Edinburgh University Press, 1997.

Burleigh, J. H. S. *A Church History of Scotland.* London: Oxford University Press, 1960.

Cameron, Nigel, ed. *Dictionary of Scottish Church History and Theology.* Edinburgh: T. and T. Clark; Downer's Grove, Ill.: Intervarsity Press, 1993.

Carnes, Mark C. *Secret Ritual and Manhood in Victorian America.* New Haven: Yale University Press, 1989.

Carwardine, Richard. *Transatlantic Revivalism: Popular Evangelicalism in Britain and America, 1790–1865.* Westport, Conn.: Greenwood Press, 1978.

Chadwick, Owen. *The Victorian Church.* 2 vols. London: Adam and Charles Black, 1971–1972.

Chandler, Alfred. *The Visible Hand: The Managerial Revolution in American Business.* Cambridge, Mass.: Belknap Press, 1977.

Chase, Gilbert. *America's Music.* 2d ed. New York: McGraw-Hill, 1966.

Checkland, Olive, and Sydney Checkland. *Industry and Ethos: Scotland, 1832–1914.* 2d ed. Edinburgh: University of Edinburgh Press, 1989.

Cheyne, A. C. *The Transformation of the Kirk: Victorian Scotland's Religious Revolution.* Edinburgh: St. Andrew Press, 1983.

Christiano, Kevin. *Religious Diversity and Social Change: American Cities, 1890–1906.* Cambridge: Cambridge University Press, 1987.

Clark, Clifford E., Jr. *Henry Ward Beecher: Spokesman for a Middle-Class America.* Urbana: University of Illinois Press, 1978.

Coalter, Milton J.; John M. Mulder; and Louis B. Weeks, eds., *The Presbyterian Predicament: Six Perspectives.* Louisville: Westminster/John Knox Press, 1990.

Conkin, Paul. *The Uneasy Center: Reformed Christianity in Antebellum America.* Chapel Hill: University of North Carolina Press, 1995.

Cotkin, George. *Reluctant Modernism: American Thought and Culture, 1880–1900.* New York: Twayne, 1992.

Cox, Jeffrey. *The English Churches in a Secular Society: Lambeth, 1870–1930.* New York: Oxford University Press, 1982.

Crossick, Geoffrey, ed. *The Lower Middle Class in Britain, 1870–1914.* New York: St. Martin's Press, 1977.

Currie, Robert; Alan Gilbert; and Lee Horsley. *Churches and Churchgoers: Patterns of Church Growth in the British Isles Since 1700.* Oxford: Clarendon, 1977.

Curtis, Susan. *A Consuming Faith: The Social Gospel and Modern American Culture.* Baltimore: Johns Hopkins University Press, 1991.

Davies, Horton. *The English Free Churches.* 2d ed. 1963. Reprint, Westport, Conn.: Greenwood, 1985.

———. *Worship and Theology in England, Volume 3: From Watts and Wesley to Maurice, 1690–1850.* Princeton: Princeton University Press, 1961.

———. *Worship and Theology in England, Volume 4: From Newman to Martineau, 1850–1900.* Princeton: Princeton University Press, 1962.

Demos, John. *A Little Commonwealth: Family Life in Plymouth Colony.* New York: Oxford University Press, 1970.

Dillenberger, John T. *The Visual Arts and Christianity in America: The Colonial Period through the Nineteenth Century.* Chico, Calif.: Scholars Press, 1984.

Douglas, Ann. *The Feminization of American Culture.* New York: Knopf, 1978.

Drummond, Andrew L., and James Bulloch. *The Church in Late Victorian Scotland, 1874–1900.* Edinburgh: St. Andrew Press, 1978.

———. *The Church in Victorian Scotland.* Edinburgh: St. Andrew Press, 1975.

Drummond, Andrew Landale. *The Church Architecture of Protestantism: An Historical and Constructive Study.* Edinburgh: T. and T. Clark, 1934.

Drury, Clifford Merril. *Presbyterian Panorama: One Hundred and Fifty Years of National Missions History.* Philadelphia: Board of Christian Education, Presbyterian Church, U.S.A., 1952.

Drysdale, A. H. *The English Presbyterians: A Historical Handbook of Their Rise, Decline, and Revival.* London: Publishing Office of the Presbyterian Church of England, 1891.

Dudley, Carl, ed. *Building Effective Ministry: Theory and Practice in the Local Church.* San Francisco: Harper and Row, 1983.

Dudley, Carl; Jackson Carroll; and James P. Wind, eds. *Carriers of Faith: Lessons of Congregational Studies.* Louisville: Westminster/John Knox Press, 1991.

Epstein, Barbara Leslie. *The Politics of Domesticity: Women, Evangelicalism, and Temperance in Nineteenth-Century America.* Middletown, Conn.: Wesleyan University Press, 1981.

Erickson, Charlotte. *Invisible Immigrants: The Adaptation of English and Scottish Immigrants in Nineteenth-Century America.* Ithaca, N.Y.: Cornell University Press, 1972.

Erikson, Kai. *Wayward Puritans: A Study in the Sociology of Deviance.* New York: Wiley, 1966.

Fladeland, Betty. *Men and Brothers: Anglo-American Antislavery Cooperation.* Urbana: University of Illinois Press, 1972.

Fones-Wolf, Ken. *Trade Union Gospel: Christianity and Labor in Industrial Philadelphia, 1865–1915.* Philadelphia: Temple University Press, 1989.

Ford, Boris, ed. *The Cambridge Cultural History, Volume 7: Victorian Britain.* Cambridge: Cambridge University Press, 1992.

Forrester, Duncan, and Douglas Murray, eds. *Studies in the History of Worship in Scotland.* 2d ed. Edinburgh: T. and T. Clark, 1996.

Fox, Richard Wrightman, and T. J. Lears, eds. *The Culture of Consumption.* New York: Pantheon, 1983.

Gilbert, Alan. *Religion and Society in Industrial England: Church, Chapel, and Social Change, 1740–1914.* London: Longman, 1976.

Gill, Robin. *The Myth of the Empty Church.* London: SPCK, 1993.

Ginzberg, Lori D. *Women and the Work of Benevolence: Morality, Politics, and Class in the Nineteenth-Century United States.* New Haven: Yale University Press, 1990.

Grant, John W. *Free Churchmanship in England, 1870–1940.* London: Independent Press, 1955.

Grier, Katherine C. *Culture and Comfort: Parlor Making and Middle-Class Identity, 1850–1930.* Washington, D.C.: Smithsonian Institution Press, 1988.

Griffin, Clifford S. *Their Brothers' Keepers: Moral Stewardship in the United States, 1800–1860.* New Brunswick, N.J.: Rutgers University Press, 1960.

Haig, Alan. *The Victorian Clergy: An Ancient Profession Under Strain.* London: Croom Helm, 1984.

Hall, Donald E., ed. *Muscular Christianity: Embodying the Victorian Age.* Cambridge: Cambridge University Press, 1994.

Handy, Robert T. *A History of Union Theological Seminary in New York.* New York: Columbia University Press, 1987

Harris, Jose. *Private Lives, Public Spirit: Britain, 1870–1914.* London: Penguin, 1993.

Harrison, Brian. *Drink and the Victorians: The Temperance Question in England, 1815–1872.* Pittsburgh: University of Pittsburgh Press, 1971.

Hayes, Florence. *Daughters of Dorcas: The Story of the Work of Women for Home Missions since 1802*. New York: Board of National Missions, Presbyterian Church, U.S.A., 1952.

Hays, George P. *Presbyterians*. New York: J. A. Hill, 1892.

Henderson, G. D. *The Scottish Ruling Elder*. London: James Clarke, 1935.

Hilton, Boyd. *The Age of Atonement: The Influence of Evangelicalism on Social and Economic Thought, 1795–1865*. Oxford: Oxford University Press, 1988.

Holifield, E. Brooks. *A History of Pastoral Care in America*. Nashville: Abingdon, 1983.

Hopewell, James F. *Congregation: Stories and Structures*. Philadelphia: Fortress, 1987.

Horowitz, Daniel. *The Morality of Spending: Attitudes Toward the Consumer Society in America, 1875–1940*. Baltimore: Johns Hopkins University Press, 1985.

Howe, Daniel Walker, ed. *Victorian America*. Philadelphia: University of Pennsylvania Press, 1976.

Hurlburt, Stephen A., ed., *The Liturgy of the Church of Scotland since the Reformation*. Charleston: St. Albans Press, 1950–52.

Hutchison, William R. *Errand to the World: American Protestant Thought and Foreign Missions*. Chicago: University of Chicago Press, 1987.

Inglis, K. S. *Churches and the Working Classes in Victorian England*. London: Routledge and Kegan Paul, 1963.

Jamison, Wallace N. *The United Presbyterian Story: A Centennial Study, 1858–1958*. Pittsburgh: Geneva Press, 1958.

Johnson, Curtis D. *Islands of Holiness: Rural Religion in Upstate New York, 1790–1860*. Ithaca, N.Y.: Cornell University Press, 1989.

Johnson, Paul E. *A Shopkeepers' Millennium: Society and Revivals in Rochester, New York, 1815–1837*. New York: Hill and Wang, 1978

Jones, R. Tudur. *Congregationalism in England, 1662–1962*. London: Independent Press, 1962.

Kennedy, Roger G. *American Churches*. New York: Crossroad, 1982.

Kernohan, R. D. *Scotland's Life and Work: A Scottish View of God's World through Life and Work, 1879–1979*. Edinburgh: St. Andrew Press, 1979.

Kett, Joseph. *Rites of Passage: Adolescence in America, 1790 to the Present*. New York: Basic Books, 1977.

Kimmel, Michael. *Manhood in America: A Cultural History*. New York: Free Press, 1996.

Kitson Clark, George. *The Making of Victorian England*. Cambridge: Harvard University Press, 1962.

Klein, Maury. *The Flowering of the Third America: The Making of an Organizational Society, 1850–1920*. Chicago: Ivan Dee, 1993.

Knight, Frances. *The Nineteenth-Century Church and English Society*. Cambridge: Cambridge University Press, 1995.

Kunzel, Regina. *Fallen Women, Problem Girls: Unwed Mothers and the Professionalization of Social Work, 1890–1945*. New Haven: Yale University Press, 1993.

Laqueur, Thomas. *Religion and Respectability: Sunday Schools and Working Class Culture, 1780–1850*. New Haven: Yale University Press, 1976.

Leach, William. *Land of Desire: Merchants, Power, and the Rise of a New American Culture, 1880–1920*. New York: Vintage, 1993.

Lester, V. Markham. *Victorian Insolvency: Bankruptcy, Imprisonment for Debt, and Company Winding-Up in Nineteenth-Century England*. Oxford: Clarendon Press, 1995.

Leyburn, James G. *The Scotch-Irish: A Social History*. Chapel Hill: University of North Carolina Press, 1962.

Licht, Walter. *Industrializing America*. Baltimore: Johns Hopkins University Press, 1995.

Loetscher, Lefferts A. *A Brief History of the Presbyterians*. 4th ed. Philadelphia: Westminster, 1983.

M'Crie, Charles Greig. *The Public Worship of Presbyterian Scotland*. Edinburgh: Blackwood, 1892.

MacLaren, A. Allan. *Religion and Social Class: The Disruption Years in Aberdeen*. London: Routledge and Kegan Paul, 1974.

Magnuson, Norris. *Salvation in the Slums: Evangelical Social Work, 1865–1920*. Metuchen, N.J.: Scarecrow, 1977.

Magnusson, Mamie. *Out of Silence: The Woman's Guild, 1887–1987*. Edinburgh: St. Andrew Press, 1987.

Malmgreen, Gail, ed. *Religion in the Lives of English Women*. Bloomington: Indiana University Press, 1986.

Marsden, George. *Fundamentalism and American Culture: The Shaping of Twentieth-Century Evangelicalism, 1870–1925*. New York: Oxford University Press, 1980.

Marty, Martin E. *A Nation of Behavers*. Chicago: University of Chicago Press, 1976.

Mason, Michael. *The Making of Victorian Sexual Attitudes*. Oxford: Oxford University Press, 1994.

———. *The Making of Victorian Sexuality*. Oxford: Oxford University Press, 1995.

Matthews, Jean V. *Toward a New Society: American Thought and Culture, 1800–1830*. New York: Twayne, 1991.

Maxwell, William D. *A History of Worship in the Church of Scotland*. London: Oxford University Press, 1955.

McDannell, Colleen. *The Christian Home in Victorian America, 1840–1900*. Bloomington: Indiana University Press, 1986.

———. *Material Christianity: Religion and Popular Culture in America*. New Haven: Yale University Press, 1995.

McLeod, Hugh. *Class and Religion in the Late Victorian City*. Hamden, Conn.: Archon Books, 1974.

———. *Religion and Society in England, 1850–1914*. New York: St. Martin's Press, 1996.

McLoughlin, William. *The Meaning of Henry Ward Beecher: An Essay on the Shifting Values of Mid-Victorian America, 1840–1870*. New York: Knopf, 1970.

Meller, Helen Elizabeth. *Leisure and the Changing City, 1870–1914*. London: Routledge and Kegan Paul, 1976.

Melton, Julius. *Presbyterian Worship in America: Changing Patterns since 1787*. Richmond, Va.: John Knox Press, 1967.

Moore, R. Lawrence. *Selling God: American Religion in the Marketplace of Culture*. New York: Oxford University Press, 1994.

Morgan, Edmund S. *The Puritan Family: Religion and Domestic Relations in Seventeenth-Century New England*. New York: Harper and Row, 1966.

Nichols, James Hastings. *Corporate Worship in the Reformed Tradition*. Philadelphia: Westminster Press, 1968.

Nissenbaum, Stephen. *The Battle for Christmas*. New York: Knopf, 1996.

Parson, Gerald, ed. *Religion in Victorian Britain.* 4 vols. Manchester: Manchester University Press, 1988.

Patrick, Millar. *Four Centuries of Scottish Psalmody.* London: Oxford University Press, 1949.

Peel, Albert. *These Hundred Years: A History of the Congregational Union of England and Wales, 1831–1931.* London: Congregational Union, 1931.

Phillips, Paul T. *A Kingdom on Earth: Anglo-American Social Christianity, 1880–1940.* University Park: The Pennsylvania State University Press, 1996.

Pollard, Sidney. *The Genesis of Modern Management: A Study of the Industrial Revolution in Great Britain.* Cambridge: Harvard University Press, 1965.

Primer, Ben. *Protestants and American Business Methods.* Ann Arbor, Mich.: UMI Research Press, 1979.

Prochaska, F. K. *Women and Philanthropy in Nineteenth-Century England.* Oxford: Clarendon Press, 1980.

Robbins, Keith, ed. *Protestant Evangelicalism: Britain, Ireland, Germany, and America, c. 1750– c. 1950.* Oxford: Basil Blackwell, 1990.

Robertson, Darrel M. *The Chicago Revival, 1876: Society and Revivalism in a Nineteenth-Century City.* Metuchen, N.J.: Scarecrow, 1989.

Roozen, David; William McKinney; and Jackson Carroll. *Varieties of Religious Presence: Mission in Public Life.* New York: Pilgrim Press, 1984.

Rose, Anne C. *Victorian America and the Civil War.* New York: Cambridge University Press, 1992.

———. *Voices of the Marketplace: American Thought and Culture, 1830–1860.* New York: Twayne, 1995.

Rosenberg, Charles E. *The Cholera Years: The United States in 1832, 1849, and 1866.* Chicago: University of Chicago Press, 1962.

Rosenzweig, Roy. *Eight Hours for What We Will: Workers and Leisure in an Industrial City, 1870–1920.* Cambridge: Cambridge University Press, 1983.

Routley, Erik. *The Music of Christian Hymns.* Chicago: G.I.A. Publications, 1981.

Ryan, Mary. *Cradle of the Middle Class: The Family in Oneida County, New York, 1790–1865.* New York: Cambridge University Press, 1981.

Schlereth, Thomas J. *Victorian America: Transformations of Everyday Life, 1876–1915.* New York: Harper, 1991.

Schmidt, Leigh Eric. *Consumer Rites: The Buying and Selling of American Holidays.* Princeton: Princeton University Press, 1995.

———. *Holy Fairs: Scottish Communions and American Revivals in the Early Modern Period.* Princeton: Princeton University Press, 1989.

Sheils, W. J., ed. *The Church and Healing.* Oxford: Basil Blackwell, 1982.

Sheils, W. J., and Diana Wood, eds. *Women in the Church.* Oxford: Basil Blackwell, 1990.

Sholes, Percy. *Oxford Companion to Music.* 10th ed. London: Oxford University Press, 1970.

Sizer, Sandra. *Gospel Hymns and Social Religion: The Rhetoric of Nineteenth-Century Revivalism.* Philadelphia: Temple University Press, 1978.

Small, Robert. *History of the Congregations of the United Presbyterian Church, from 1733 to 1900.* 2 vols. Edinburgh: David Small, 1904.

Smith, Donald C. *Passive Obedience and Prophetic Protest: Social Criticism in the Scottish Church, 1830–1945.* New York: Peter Lang, 1987.

Smith, Elwyn A. *The Presbyterian Ministry in American Culture: A Study in Changing Concepts, 1700–1900.* Philadelphia: Westminster, 1962.

Smith, Mark. *Religion in Industrial Society: Oldham and Saddleworth, 1740–1865.* Oxford: Clarendon Press, 1994.

Smith, Timothy L. *Revivalism and Social Reform: American Protestantism on the Eve of the Civil War.* Baltimore: Johns Hopkins University Press, 1965.

Smith-Rosenberg, Carroll. *Religion and the Rise of the American City: The New York City Mission Movement, 1812–1870.* Ithaca, N.Y.: Cornell University Press, 1971.

———. *Disorderly Conduct: Visions of Gender in Victorian America.* New York: Oxford University Press, 1985.

Smylie, James H. *A Brief History of the Presbyterians.* Louisville: Geneva Press, 1996.

Stanton, Phoebe B. *The Gothic Revival and American Church Architecture: An Episode in Taste, 1840–1860.* Baltimore: Johns Hopkins University Press, 1968.

Stevenson, Louise L. *The Victorian Homefront: American Thought and Culture, 1860–1880.* New York: Twayne, 1991.

Sweet, Leonard I. *The Minister's Wife: Her Role in Nineteenth-Century American Evangelicalism.* Philadelphia: Temple University Press, 1983.

Thistlethwaite, Frank. *The Anglo-American Connection in the Early Nineteenth Century.* Philadelphia: University of Pennsylvania Press, 1959.

Thomas, George M. *Revivalism and Cultural Change: Christianity, Nation Building, and the Market in Nineteenth-Century United States.* Chicago: University of Chicago Press, 1989.

Thompson, F. M. L. *The Rise of Respectable Society: A Social History of Victorian Britain, 1830–1900.* Cambridge: Harvard University Press, 1988.

Thompson, Paul. *The Edwardians: The Remaking of British Society.* Bloomington: Indiana University Press, 1975.

Trachtenberg, Alan. *The Incorporation of America: Culture and Society in the Gilded Age.* New York: Hill and Wang, 1982.

Valenze, Deborah M. *Prophetic Sons and Daughters: Female Preaching and Popular Religion in Industrial England.* Princeton: Princeton University Press, 1985.

Von Rohr, John. *The Shaping of American Congregationalism, 1620–1957.* Cleveland: Pilgrim Press, 1992.

Warner, Sam Bass, Jr. *Streetcar Suburbs: The Process of Growth in Boston, 1870–1900.* Cambridge: Harvard University Press, 1962.

Watts, Michael. *The Dissenters, Volume 2: The Expansion of Evangelical Nonconformity.* Oxford: Clarendon Press, 1995.

Westerkamp, Marilyn J. *Triumph of the Laity: Scots-Irish Piety and the Great Awakening, 1625–1760.* New York: Oxford University Press, 1988.

Wheeler, Barbara, and Edward Farley, eds. *Shifting Boundaries: Contextual Approaches to the Structure of Theological Education.* Louisville: Westminster/John Knox Press, 1991.

Wienandt, Elwyn A., and Robert H. Young. *The Anthem in England and America.* New York: Free Press, 1970.

Wigley, John. *The Rise and Fall of the Victorian Sunday.* Manchester: Manchester University Press, 1980.

Williams, Peter W. *Houses of God: Region, Religion, and Architecture in the United States.* Urbana: University of Illinois Press, 1997.

Wind, James P. *Places of Worship: Exploring Their History.* Nashville: American Association for State and Local History, 1990.

Wind, James P., and James W. Lewis, eds. *American Congregations.* 2 vols. Chicago: University of Chicago Press, 1994.

Wishy, Bernard. *The Child and the Republic: The Dawn of Modern American Child Nurture.* Philadelphia: University of Pennsylvania Press, 1968.

Wood, Diana, ed. *The Church and Childhood.* Oxford: Blackwell, 1994.

———. *The Church and the Arts.* Oxford: Basil Blackwell, 1992.

Yeo, Stephen. *Religion and Voluntary Organisations in Crisis.* London: Croom Helm, 1976.

# Index

# Index

Deacons' Court, function of, 22
debt, handling of by congregations, 164–65,
   174–76
decision-making, consensus style of, 13–14, 24,
   251 n. 46
Dickinson, Clarence, 96
disciplinary cases, 138–50
   as disincentive to membership, 119
   decline of, 148–50
Disruption of 1843 (Scotland), 4
   impact on pew prices, 285 n. 70, 286 n. 83
Douglass, Frederick, 293 n. 120
Drummond, Henry, 120
Dumfries, Scotland, Greyfriars' parish, 88–89

Eadie, Dr. (Glasgow minister), 237
Easter Day, observance of, 42, 45, 96
Ebsworth, Joseph, 78–79
Ecclesiastical Commissions, 21–22, 167–68
economic depressions, impact of, 174, 286–87 n.
   103
Edinburgh, Scotland
   Arcade Mission, 120
   Barclay Free Church, 66, 235
   Blackfriars' Mission, 205
   Bristo United Presbyterian Church, 19, 42, 90,
      266 n. 57
   Broughton Place United Presbyterian Church,
      49, 77, 90, 193, 207, 228
   Buccleuch Street Free Church, 187
   Buccleuch Street Mission, 194
   Duncan Street Mission, 186
   Fountainbridge Mission, 181, 184–85, 188,
      198–99, 205
   Greenside parish, 17, 21, 35, 81, 84–85, 105,
      115, 148, 155, 175, 228–29, 231, 250 n. 40,
      251 n. 46, 297 n. 61; adoption of business
      methods, 151–52, 160
   Greyfriars parish, 17, 31, 48, 105, 143; finances,
      155, 168, 176; music, 78, 87, 91, 266 n. 44,
      268 n. 86
   Mayfield Free Church, 120, 165, 184, 187
   Newington United Presbyterian Church, 53,
      69, 186, 197
   Nicholson Street Church, 77
   Pilrig Free Church, 30–31, 202–3, 220, 252 n.
      59, 258 n. 78; model housing project, 180,
      203
   Pleasance Free Church, 184, 187
   Port Dundas Mission, 200

Rose Street Mission, 181, 191, 290 n. 53
Roseburn Mission, 185
Springbank Mission, 205–6, 290 n. 46, 292 n.
   104, 293 n. 111
St. Andrew's parish, 50, 78, 227, 255 n. 25, 267
   n. 68
St. George's Free Church, 7, 9, 17, 25, 106,
   123, 137, 153, 157–58, 248 n. 5, 266
   n. 57, 271 n. 21, 282 n. 22, 288 n. 9;
   building, 225, 231–33, 298 n. 19, 299 n. 43;
   children and youth, 128–31, 214–15, 295
   n. 38; disciplinary cases, 141, 145, 147–48;
   finances, 165, 175, 178; home visitation,
   133, 135; mission work, 181, 185, 191,
   198; music, 76–78, 81–82, 90, 266 n. 57;
   worship, 48–50, 52–53, 61, 63, 255 n. 25,
   258 n. 78, 259 n. 95, 263 n. 77
St. George's parish, 115, 132, 160, 225, 228,
   231, 233, 251 n. 46, 270 n. 18; benevolences,
   154–55; elders, 17, 19; finances, 168, 176,
   178, 297–98 n. 15; music, 79–80, 89–90, 96,
   98, 264 n. 6, 267 n. 68, 269 n. 94; worship,
   48, 50
St. John's Free Church, 183–84
St. Mary's parish, 77
St. Stephen's parish, 127, 155, 177, 191; music,
   78–79, 84, 89, 91, 266 n. 44, 267 n. 68;
   worship, 44, 70, 71, 255 n. 25
Tolbooth Mission, 198
education, as mission work, 185, 195–96
efficiency
   admiration of, 11, 151–52
   and baptism, 70
   and church administration, 162–63
   and church manuals, 152
   and church rolls, 122
   and communion tokens, 52–53
   and distribution of communion, 49–51
   and elections, 18
   and home visitation, 133–35
   and single board governance, 22
elders, 15–16, 248 n. 5
   and disciplinary cases, 138–50
   duties of, 15, 26, 135–36, 251–52 n. 52, 261 n.
      35
   election, 16–19, 248 n. 8, 249 n. 15
   ideal characteristics of, 13–14, 19–20
   ordination, 19
elections, of church officers, 16–19
endowment funds, 165, 175, 177–78

# Index